Developing Reading Versatility

ELEVENTH EDITION

W. ROYCE ADAMS

Emeritus, Santa Barbara City College

WADSWORTH
CENGAGE Learning

Australia • Brazil • Japan • Korea • Mexico • Singapore • Spain • United Kingdom • United States

WADSWORTH
CENGAGE Learning™

**Developing Reading Versatility,
Eleventh Edition**
W. Royce Adams

Senior Publisher: Lyn Uhl

Director of Developmental English: Annie Todd

Development Editor: Cathlynn Dodson

Associate Editor: Janine Tangney

Editorial Assistant: Melanie Opacki

Senior Marketing Manager: Kirsten Stoller

Marketing Coordinator: Ryan Ahern

Marketing Communications Manager:
 Martha Pfeiffer

Content Project Manager: Aimee Chevrette
 Bear

Art Director: Jill Ort

Print Buyer: Denise Powers

Permissions Editor: Katie Huha

Photo Manager: John Hill

Production Service: Elm Street Publishing
 Services

Compositor: Integra

For product information and technology assistance, contact us at
Cengage Learning Customer & Sales Support, 1-800-354-9706

For permission to use material from this text or product,
submit all requests online at **www.cengage.com/permissions**
Further permissions questions can be emailed to
permissionrequest@cengage.com

Library of Congress Control Number: 2009936

Sudent Edition:
ISBN-13: 978-0-495-80251-8
ISBN-10: 0-495-80251-4

Wadsworth
20 Channel Center Street
Boston, MA 02210
USA

Cengage Learning is a leading provider of customized learning solutions with office locations around the globe, including Singapore, the United Kingdom, Australia, Mexico, Brazil, and Japan. Locate your local office at **international.cengage.com/region**

Cengage Learning products are represented in Canada by Nelson Education, Ltd.

For your course and learning solutions, visit **www.cengage.com**.

Purchase any of our products at your local college store or at our preferred online store **www.CengageBrain.com**.

Printed in the United States of America
1 2 3 4 5 6 7 13 12 11 10

Contents

Preface

During the revision of this eleventh edition of *Developing Reading Versatility*, various media sources kept pointing out how quickly major city newspapers and magazines were going out of business or suffering losses in readership. Books sales were reported down and independent bookstores were closing their doors. Libraries were cutting back on their hours and lacked sufficient funds to build their inventories. Readers were diminishing, we were told. Worse, student scores and interest in reading weren't improving. Reading of a different sort was now taking place on the computer, iPhones, and Blackberries. These were not encouraging reports for someone trying to develop textbook materials and exercises that would show students the need and benefits of better reading skills.

Teaching college students to develop and improve their reading skills has never been easy. The reasons that hold many students back from their ability to read at a level necessary for successful college studies—let alone develop their appreciation for reading—are numerous and diverse. Attempting to overcome these varied causes in every student can be enormously frustrating and challenging. Why do we reading instructors even try, especially when it seems readers are disappearing?

About this time of economic depression, I read an essay by Juanita Havill entitled "Journey of a Lifetime" in a collection of writings called *The Most Wonderful Books*. Her last paragraph reads:

> A college professor once told me that he had always believed as a child that books on the library shelves came to life when everyone left. The characters and the authors slipped from their volumes and spent the midnight hours discussing, dancing, partying, and doing all the things that real, live people do. It's a joyful image and it comes to my mind whenever I read another futurist describing the demise of the book. Yes, I know, in our new technological world we are told that books will not be needed. The book as we know it will be dead. Then I see Beowulf and the Welsh miner's son, Viola and Mrs. Tiggy-Winkle, Mark Twain telling Ramona to sit still, and Curious George hanging from the ceiling with a few of the Wild Things, and I imagine their reaction. "Dead!" they exclaim. "People are saying we are dead!" And they burst out laughing.

And I laughed. That paragraph reminded me of why we want to teach reading to those who don't read well enough to understand the empowerment of reading beyond the words. We need to bring reading to life. I hope this book can help in that effort.

Practices in literal, critical, and affective comprehension provide students the opportunity to gradually build their reading and analytical skills. The assorted literal practices help students acquire essential skills as they learn to develop their vocabulary, recall main ideas, understand how paragraph patterns can aid comprehension, identify facts, recognize the difference between an author's subject and thesis, and develop reading rate flexibility. The readings range from sentences to short paragraphs to longer essays with some timed reading exercises spaced throughout the text.

In the critical comprehension section, students learn to distinguish between fact and opinion; recognize an author's intent, attitude, and tone; detect bias and propaganda techniques; and discern inferences and form conclusions using inductive and deductive reasoning. Practices continue to reinforce learned literal skills.

Affective comprehension practices help students define and develop aesthetic reactions to language used in imaginative literature. Students are shown strategic ways necessary to recognize and appreciate the power of affective language. Approaches to reading short stories, poems, and imaginative prose provide students with the pleasure and power of creative writings. Yes, we want students to comprehend their textbook assignments; but more than that, we want them to develop a desire to read long after their college courses are over. That can only happen if we develop their affective sensibilities.

The mix of literal, critical, and affective exercises helps students to understand that reading is a complex process; that a student's reading background, purpose, and motivation determine the quality of comprehension; and that some questions do not always have right or wrong answers. Thus, many of the comprehension questions go beyond multiple-choice and true-and-false formats, requiring students to write written responses that show thought has been given to an answer. It is hoped that instructors will elaborate on and challenge such responses through group and classroom discussions.

We recommend that you have students read and that you discuss in class the section "For the Student: Your No-Money-Back Guarantee" as a way to set the tone and challenges of your course. Students need to understand their responsibilities in your classroom.

Some of the more noticeable changes to this edition include the following:

- Eighteen new readings replace outdated materials.

- Study skills approaches providing information and practice to help students enhance their overall academic achievement—now Chapter Three—have been placed in the Literal Comprehension section, which presents exercises using actual textbook readings from various content areas, such as psychology, communication, history, art, and business.

- More pro and con essays in the critical comprehension section help students develop the skills necessary to recognize the strengths and weaknesses of different arguments, analytical styles, and propaganda.

- A few more timed readings are provided for instructors who wish to aid students in their reading speed. Instructors less interested in rate training can tell their students to ignore the timing directions.

- Updated information on the Internet and the use of search engines, now Chapter Seven, provide instructor and student opportunities to research more information on subjects contained in the reading selections. With students using the Internet more than ever, it seems appropriate to offer skills for reading on the Internet.

- Some reading selections were moved to locations that better fit their contexts.

- An optional "On Your Own" section requires students to pick words they didn't know before doing the exercises and write sentences using them in context.

- An annotated instructor's edition providing answers and marginal notes not only can be useful to the instructor but also to graduate teaching assistants and adjunct faculty working in learning centers.

Free for those interested, a DVD with a dramatization of Langston Hughes' "Salvation" (reprinted in Chapter 8) is available when packaged with the text. The DVD also contains interviews with Alice Walker and Arnold Rampersad, the foremost authority on Hughes. This is a useful tool in helping students better understand affective comprehension and the comparison of the printed word with visual media.

An interactive Web site provides teaching and learning resources you can use to get the most from your course. Supplemental student exercises and ancillary tests for use with both this and the last edition of our text can be found online by entering the title of the text in the search box found at: http://www.academic.cengage.com/devenglish/adams

I wish to thank the staff at Wadsworth who shared their knowledge and skills for this revision. Special thanks go to Cathy Richard Dodson, who never failed to return my queries and concerns with prompt answers and aid; Director Annie Todd and her assistant Dan DeBonis, who took on my book with such enthusiasm; Director Elise Kaiser and her Project Managers Lianne Ames and Sarah Sherman; as well as the rest of the talented production staff. I would also like to thank Amanda Hellenthal and the team at Elm Street Publishing Services for their work on this edition.

I also appreciated the contributions of the following instructors, whose reviewer comments helped guide the decisions about the selections and content changes made in this edition:

Margaret J. Terrell, *Columbus Technical College*
Mary Anne Quick, *Bristol Community College, Massachusetts*
J. Altman, *University of Washington*
Charles Duquette, *University of Maryland*
Gene Voss, *Houston Community College, Central*
Carolyn McOmber, *Sacramento City College*
Dr. Sharon M. Ganslen, *University of Mary Hardin-Baylor*

W. Royce Adams
Santa Barbara, California

To the Student

Your "No-Money-Back Guarantee"

This book offers no money-back guarantee if you fail to read any better after completing it than you do now. It is quite possible that you could do well on every exercise in this book and still continue to read the way you do now. Why? Because you might fail to *use* the information gained from this book when you read material outside the book. In other words, unless you practice in *all* your reading what you do and learn in this book, there will be no transfer of skills. You will just be kidding yourself that you are reading better. Thus, while we can guarantee that the book may be helpful, we can't be sure of how you may use it .

However, to get the most for your money, here are some points and suggestions for you to consider.

1. *Turn to the Contents.* Notice that this book is divided into three units. Each unit provides you with a variety of exercises in one level of comprehension. Together, these three different levels of understanding will bring you closer to a total comprehension of what you read. Actually, no Great Reading God in the Sky said, "Let there be three levels of comprehension. Zap!" These divisions are made only to help you see the many facets of comprehension.

2. *Don't feel obligated to do every practice in each unit.* How much practice you need depends on how much more competent you want to be in each area.

3. *Increase your speed.* In each chapter, some of the practices in this book are timed for speed. The pressure of speed is used to prod you from your normal reading habits and get you used to faster rates. But don't make speed your entire goal. Your speed will automatically increase as a by-product of the good reading habits you will learn here. Reading speeds vary depending on purpose, material, and vocabulary levels.

4. *Keep records.* A Student Record Chart is provided in the Appendix so you can keep a record of your various practice work. Don't be worried about ups and downs in rate and comprehension scores. It's normal to fluctuate. Also, don't be fooled into thinking that because your scores go up on the chart, you are reading better in materials outside the text. Only you can actually determine how much success you are achieving.

5. *Learn from your mistakes.* You'll find that your speed increases as your comprehension and vocabulary improve. As you begin this course, you will no doubt make some mistakes in answering some of the comprehension and vocabulary

exercises. That's to be expected. The trick is to learn by understanding *why* you erred. Pay attention to your mistakes; they are the path to developing better reading comprehension.

6. *Don't expect overnight miracles.* Lifetime results can be obtained from the practices you do here if you learn from your mistakes as well as your successes. It takes time, effort, and patience to change reading habits you have developed over many years.

7. *Develop your discussion skills.* Some of the answers to the practice questions can't be found in an answer key, and in these cases the class should discuss them. Discussion is necessary for developing comprehension skills. Engage in class discussion; don't just sit back and listen to others, especially when you are working in Unit Three, Affective Comprehension.

8. *Approach the exercises in this book as opportunities to excel not just in this course, but also in life.* The U.S. National Assessment of Adult Literacy released a 2005 study showing that there has been little change in adult literacy rates since 1992, revealing widespread dismay at the reading difficulty of working-age Americans. The new report shows that "the percentage of college graduates with proficient literacy decreased from 40 percent in 1992 to 31 percent in 2003" (National Center for Education Statistics, *A First Look at the Literacy of America's Adults in the 21st Century*, p. 15). In other words, only 31 percent of college graduates can read a complex book and draw useful information or inferences from it. Today's adults need much more sophisticated literacy skills than did past generations. Use this course to improve the literacy skills that you will need beyond college.

With these things said, you are ready to get down to work. Just remember: The responsibility for learning and transfer of learning is yours. Are you willing to place a money-back guarantee on yourself?

CHAPTER ONE

Developing Vocabulary Skills

Introduction to Vocabulary Development

One of the first places to begin developing reading versatility is with vocabulary. Without good vocabulary, reading is slow and comprehension is poor. In order to understand what you read, you need to recognize not only the definitions of the words being read but also, more important, the way words are used in context.

Think of strategies for increasing vocabulary that you have tried in the past. What do you do when you run across unfamiliar words? In the selection that follows, "How I Discovered Words: A Homemade Education," one famous figure, Malcolm X, tells about his strategy for increasing his vocabulary and learning new words. Throughout this book, we have placed brief biographies and quotes from authors or public figures to inspire you by their examples as well as their words. Start by reading about Malcolm X.

Introducing Malcolm X

Malcolm X was a controversial Black Muslim leader who became one of the most powerful and articulate black leaders to focus on the plight of the urban black poor in the 1960s. Born Malcolm Little, he drifted into the world of drugs, prostitution, and crime as a very young man. While imprisoned for robbery, he converted to the Nation of Islam as a Black Muslim, a rigid sect that brought discipline into the lives of its members. During this period, Little took the name Malcolm X, the letter *X* standing for what he felt was his lost African name. Also while in prison, Malcolm X pursued his "homemade education."

After prison, he was assigned a Muslim temple in Harlem, where he preached black pride and the rejection of integration and called for a separate black nation.

He soon became one of the most powerful and articulate black leaders of the 1960s, causing jealousy among the members of the Nation of Islam and fear among many white people. Expelled from the Nation of Islam in 1963, Malcolm X formed his own group, the Organization of Afro-American Unity.

Eventually, he softened his stance, rejecting racism of all kinds and lecturing on the need for the common bond linking humanity. In 1965, he was shot to death by three Nation of Islam loyalists while giving a speech in Harlem.

Malcolm X was a self-educated man who felt the need and desire for an academic education. In *The Autobiography of Malcolm X*, he states:

My greatest lack has been, I believe, that I don't have the kind of academic education I wish I had been able to get. . . . I have always loved verbal battle, and challenge. You can believe me that if I had the time right now, I would not be one bit ashamed to go back into any New York City public school and start where I left off at the ninth grade, and go on through a degree. Because I don't begin to be academically equipped for so many of the interests that I have. For instance, I love languages. I wish I were an accomplished linguist. I don't know anything more frustrating than to be around people talking something you can't understand. . . .

I would just like to *study*. I mean ranging study, because I have a wide-open mind. I'm interested in almost any subject you can mention.

If you are interested in learning more about Malcolm X, you may want to use the World Wide Web. The official Malcolm X web site is at http://www.cmgww.com/historic/malcolm/index.htm. You can find other information about him by using a search engine such as Google or Yahoo and simply typing in "Malcolm X" in the "Search" box.

Now read the following selection to learn how Malcolm X increased his vocabulary.

HOW I DISCOVERED WORDS: A HOMEMADE EDUCATION

MALCOLM X

1   It was because of my letters that I happened to stumble upon starting to acquire some kind of a homemade education.

2   I became increasingly frustrated at not being able to express what I wanted to convey in letters that I wrote, especially those to Mr. Elijah Muhammad. In the street, I had been the most articulate hustler out there—I had commanded attention when I said something. But now, trying to write simple English, I not only wasn't articulate, I wasn't even functional. How would I sound writing in slang, the way I would say it, something such as, "Look, daddy, let me pull your coat about a cat, Elijah Muhammad . . ."

From *The Autobiography of Malcolm X* by Malcolm X and Alex Haley, copyright 1964 by Alex Haley and Malcolm X. Copyright © 1965 by Alex Haley and Betty Shabazz. Used by permission of Random House, Inc.

3   Many who today hear me somewhere in person, or on television, or those who read something I've said, will think I went to school far beyond the eighth grade. This impression is due entirely to my prison studies.

4   I had really begun in the Charleston Prison, when Bimbi first made me feel envy of his stock of knowledge. Bimbi had always taken charge of any conversation he was in, and I had tried to emulate him. But every book I picked up had few sentences which didn't contain anywhere from one to nearly all of the words that might as well have been in Chinese. When I just skipped those words, of course, I really ended up with little idea of what the book said. So I had come to the Norfolk Prison Colony still going through only book-reading motions. Pretty soon, I would have quit even these motions, unless I had received the motivation that I did.

5   I saw that the best thing I could do was get hold of a dictionary—to study, to learn some words. I was lucky enough to reason also that I should try to improve my penmanship. I was sad. I couldn't even write in a straight line. It was both ideas together that moved me to request a dictionary along with some tablets and pencils from the Norfolk Prison Colony school.

6   I spent two days just riffling uncertainly through the dictionary's pages. I'd never realized so many words existed! I didn't know *which* words I needed to learn. Finally, just to start some kind of action, I began copying.

7   In my slow, painstaking, ragged handwriting, I copied into my tablet everything printed on that first page, down to the punctuation marks.

8   I believe it took me a day. Then, aloud, I read back, to myself, everything I'd written on that tablet. Over and over, aloud, to myself, I read my own handwriting.

9   I woke up the next morning, thinking about those words—immensely proud to realize that not only had I written so much at one time, but I'd written words that I never knew were in the world. Moreover, with a little effort, I also could remember what many of these words meant. I reviewed the words whose meanings I didn't remember. Funny thing, from the dictionary first page right now, that "aardvark" springs to my mind. The dictionary had a picture of it, a long-tailed, long-eared, burrowing African mammal, which lives off termites caught by sticking out its tongue as an anteater does for ants.

10   I was so fascinated that I went on—I copied the dictionary's next page. And the same experience came when I studied that. With every succeeding page, I also learned of people and places and events from history. Actually the dictionary is like a miniature encyclopedia. Finally the dictionary's A section had filled a whole tablet—and I went on into the B's. That was the way I started copying what eventually became the entire dictionary. I went a lot faster after so much practice helped me to pick up handwriting speed. Between what I wrote in my tablet, and writing letters, during the rest of my time in prison I would guess I wrote a million words.

11   I suppose it was inevitable that as my word-base broadened, I could for the first time pick up a book and read and now begin to understand what the book was saying. Anyone who has read a great deal can imagine the new world that opened. Let me tell you something: From then until I left that prison, in every free moment I had, if I was not reading in the library, I was reading on my bunk. You couldn't have gotten me out of books with a wedge. Between Mr. Muhammad's teachings, my correspondence, my visitors—usually Ella and Reginald—and my reading of books, months passed without my even thinking about being imprisoned. In fact, up to then, I never had been so truly free in my life.

Here is a man whose life was changed for the better by discovering the power of words. "I saw that the best thing I could do was get hold of a dictionary—to study, to learn some words," Malcolm X tells us. And because he took the time to do so, he "could for the first time pick up a book and read and now begin to understand what the book was saying."

How well you can read and understand begins at the same place it did for Malcolm X—with words. As a first step in developing reading versatility, this chapter will provide you with some methods and practice in vocabulary building, understanding words in context, and learning word parts and roots.

Vocabulary development means more than just adding new words to those you already know. It also means learning how to change words to different parts of speech, add or delete prefixes and suffixes, and recognize the root elements of a word and its relationship to other words with that root; how synonyms and antonyms form families of words; and how to use words correctly in your own speech and writing.

While this book is not a vocabulary textbook, it places a strong emphasis on vocabulary building because no real reading improvement happens without it. Several approaches for building your vocabulary are described; some may seem more helpful to you than others, but give them all a try until you discover what works best for you. Many words will be presented not only in this chapter but also throughout the book as part of the reading comprehension and vocabulary practices; be selective and learn words that you feel you need to learn. You might want to start with those words you "sort of" know but can't really use well. Devote some part of your day to working on your vocabulary. There is no getting around the work part. Building up your vocabulary is like staying in physical shape; it requires concentrated effort and regular workouts. No one can do it for you.

The first part of this chapter presents three methods for learning words you really want to make your own. Try all three methods before deciding which one you will use during this course.

The second part deals with words in context. For instance, the word *run* can have many different meanings, depending on how it is used in context. Notice these samples:

John plans to run for president.
There was a run on the bank.
She had a run in her stocking.
Run to the store for me.
Pete scored a run in the fifth inning.

In each usage—and there are many others for the word *run*—the meaning is different, depending on the contextual use of the word. Learning to use contextual clues can also save you many trips to the dictionary.

The third section of this chapter deals with word structure, that is, prefixes, roots, and suffixes. Learning how words are structured and what certain commonly used prefixes, roots, and suffixes mean can help bring many unfamiliar words into focus. Useful Greek and Latin word roots are presented in practices to help you develop this aspect of vocabulary building.

Vocabulary development is a lifelong process. This chapter is meant only to get you started; it will be up to you to continue to use the information provided in this chapter. Select a method that aids you in the continuing development of your vocabulary, and use it regularly.

A.   Learning New Words: Three Methods

Method 1: A Vocabulary Notebook or Computer Compilation

One way to develop your vocabulary is to keep a notebook of the words you want to learn. If you intend to write the words down on paper, a spiral-notebook is recommended. Write the words you want to learn, their definitions, and examples of their use in sentences. For instance, a typical entry might look like this:

> *perspicacious* = having keen insight, judgment, or understanding; shrewd.
> If he had been more perspicacious, he might not have lost so much money
> on the stock market.

What type of entries you make is up to you. Some students prefer to include the sentence where the word is first encountered and then write an example sentence of their own. In addition, some students also write in the dictionary entry for the pronunciation of the word, especially if it is one they have never heard before. You may prefer to use your own method for remembering the pronunciation. If you use a computer to compile your list, find a program that allows you to manipulate your new vocabulary words. You may want to alphabetize them, show only the words so you can supply the definition, or scramble the order.

The advantages to the compilation method are that it is a convenient way to keep all new words together and a good source for constant review of older entries as new ones are made. The disadvantage is that the notebook or computer file can, if you let it, become nothing more than a list of words unless you take the effort to review your entries regularly.

Method 2: The Column Folds

With this method, you take a regular piece of notebook paper and fold it into three or four columns (three if you do not need to refer to the phonetic spelling of the word you want to learn). In the first column, you write the words you wish to learn. In the second column, you write the phonetic spelling. In the third column, you write the definition of the word. In the fourth column, you write an example sentence using the word, but instead of writing in the word, you place a blank. You can usually get about ten or twelve words on one sheet of paper.

You can then practice learning the words in several ways. Fold the paper so only the words show; you then see if you can remember the definitions, unfolding the paper to check the answer. Fold the paper so only the definitions show and see if you can identify the word that belongs to that definition. Fold the paper so only the sentences show and try to remember the word that goes in the blank. Fold the paper so that the phonetic spelling shows and try to pronounce the word and give its definition.

The advantage to this method is that it provides you with a means of studying with immediate feedback to the answers. The disadvantage is that the paper can become rather tattered after a while if you require much time to learn the words.

Method 3: Vocabulary Cards

You have probably seen boxed sets of vocabulary cards for foreign languages as well as for English. In such sets, each card has a word on one side and its definition on the other. These ready-made cards can be helpful, but chances are you will already know many of the words on the cards.

You can easily personalize the vocabulary card method by making up your own index file cards. Here's all you need to do:

1. On the front of a card, print the word you want to learn. Use ink, so that after much use it will still be legible. Underneath the word print the phonetic spelling unless you already know how to pronounce the word.

2. On the back of the card, put as much information as needed to help you learn the word. It is recommended that besides the definition you include a synonym (a word that has a similar meaning) and an antonym (a word that has the opposite meaning) if possible. A sentence using the word is also advised, either the sentence in which you found the word or an example of your own.

3. Be selective and make vocabulary cards only for the words you want to overlearn (continued study after you have mastered something). It is important to over-learn new words, not just memorize them, because you will gradually forget their meanings if you do not use them. All the words you presently know you have already overlearned and use without thinking; the only way to have a truly larger vocabulary is to overlearn new words the way you have the ones you now use regularly.

4. Try to learn at least five words a week, more if you can. Practice daily by quickly flashing only the front of the vocabulary card, pronouncing the word mentally or aloud, and providing the word's meaning. Try not to refer to the back of the card unless you can't recall the definition.

5. Carry a small stack of cards around in your handbag or pocket so you can refer to them often. At odd times during the day—between classes, while waiting for a friend, on a bus—practice flashing your cards. If you have a friend who is also using this method, practice flashing each other's cards. The more you practice, the sooner you will begin to overlearn the words and recognize them by sight.

6. As the weeks go by and you accumulate fifty to a hundred or so cards, put aside the cards for words you feel you know very well and probably will never forget. At a later date, review the cards you put aside and see if you still remember them. If there are some you don't remember, put them back in your active stack of cards.

The advantage to the vocabulary card method is that it is a convenient way to learn words: If you have your cards with you, you can practice anywhere, anytime. Once you have all the information you need on a card, you never have to look up the word again. Another advantage of the cards is that rather than learning words from a list where you associate them with other words on the list, you can shuffle and mix up flash cards. The disadvantage is that making up cards does take time, but the advantages far outweigh this.

All this may seem like too much work. Perhaps it's not the method for you, but it has worked very well for many students. Of the three methods mentioned, the personalized vocabulary card method is the one most recommended.

CHECK TEST

How many of the following words that have appeared in what you have read so far do you know? Circle the letter of the definition that best fits the numbered words that follow.

Words used by Malcolm X:

1. *articulate*
   a. seen clearly
   b. forced into
   c. express clearly

2. *emulate*
   a. try to be like
   b. suppress, lock up
   c. plan ahead

3. *riffling*
   a. ridiculing
   b. flicking through
   c. aiming at a target

4. *inevitable*
   a. to be expected
   b. to be imprisoned
   c. to envy

5. *burrowing*
   a. taking what doesn't belong to you
   b. asking permission
   c. digging in

Words used in the textbook:

6. *versatility*
   a. flexibility
   b. quick, rapid
   c. verbal

7. *stance*
   a. distance
   b. method
   c. position, attitude

8. *strategies*
   a. theories
   b. possibilities
   c. plans

9. *mnemonic*
   a. an evil, secret society

       b. aiding the memory

       c. small, close-knit group

10. *perspicacious*

       a. hidden meanings

       b. having keen, shrewd insight

       c. not paying attention

Application I: Learning New Words

Select one of the three vocabulary development methods and use it on new vocabulary for another class. Have another student test you on your words. Turn in the results and a brief summary of how your vocabulary development method worked for you. By the way, if you are unsure of a word's pronunciation, go to http://www.dictionary.com and type in the word you want to learn. The Web site will provide its definition and sound out the word.

B. Learning Words in Context

This section provides practice in figuring out a word's meaning by its use in a particular context. A close look at the context in which a word is used can often, though not always, eliminate the need to use a dictionary.

Contextual Hints

Several different types of context clues will be covered in this section. The first is **contextual hints**. For instance, in the following sentence notice how the meaning of the word *lucid* is hinted at:

> His lucid lectures, along with his clearly presented explanations, made it easy to take notes.

The phrases "clearly presented explanations" and "easy to take notes" give clues to the meaning of the word *lucid*—easy to understand, clear. Thus it's generally a good idea not to stop on words you don't know but rather to read on a bit and see if hints or other clues to the word's meaning might be given.

Here's another sentence written with a contextual hint to a key word's meaning:

> It was imprudent for Lisa to skate on the ice without checking to see how thick it was.

Because we know that skating on ice without making sure it is thick enough to hold our weight is dangerous, we can guess that Lisa was not very wise, perhaps foolish for doing so. Therefore, *imprudent* must mean unwise, rash, or foolish.

PRACTICE B-1: Contextual Hints

Directions: Define the italicized words in the following sentences, and identify the contextual hints.

1. Their *vociferous* chatter made me wish I had earplugs.

    a. *vociferous* means _____

    b. The clue is: _____

2. He was so *impudent* to his mother that I would have spanked him if he had talked to me that way.

    a. *impudent* means _____

    b. The clue is: _____

3. When asked if she liked her aunt's new hat, she *candidly* gave her frank view that it was ugly.

    a. *candidly* means _____

    b. The clue is: _____

4. My dad is so *punctilious* that he always corrects my sloppy speech or points out my incorrect use of certain words.

    a. *punctilious* means _____

    b. The clue is: _____

5. The toy is a *lethal* weapon; the kid almost killed me with it!

    a. *lethal* means _____

    b. The clue is: _____

6. They think of themselves as the *elite* group on campus, looking down their noses at others.

    a. *elite* means _____

    b. The clue is: _____

Make vocabulary cards for any words that gave you trouble, or use whatever method you have decided to use to develop your word power.

Signal Words

Sometimes contextual **signal words** in a sentence indirectly help define an unknown word. Signal words are just that: words that signal that a change is about to occur. Just as stoplights and road signs signal that you should slow down, look for curves, and watch out for cross streets while you're driving, writers use signal words to help you follow their thoughts. For instance, consider the following sentence:

> While his subjects were grieving over their dead, the king was filled with exultation over his military victory.

Notice how the signal word *while* contrasts the way the subjects feel with the way the king feels. The subjects are grieving (sad) while the king is exulting (happy). So if we didn't know what *exultation* meant, the signal word *while* alerts us that it means the opposite of grieving.

Here's another example:

> Despite his fear of the snake, Paul managed to subdue his true feelings as it coiled around his arm.

The signal word here is *despite*, meaning in spite of, or although. Here we have someone who has a fear of snakes, but despite that fear we can guess from the context that he endures having a snake on his arm by managing to control his true feelings.

Here are some signal words that you probably already know but may never have thought about using in this way. In the future, let them help you unlock the meanings to words you may not know.

Signal Words

but	while	in spite of	in contrast
however	despite	rather	although
nevertheless	even though	yet	instead

PRACTICE B-2: Signal Words

Directions: Using the signal words, figure out the meanings of the italicized words in the following sentences and identify the signal words.

1. He is usually *loquacious*, but tonight he's rather silent.

   a. *loquacious* means _____

   b. The signal word(s): _____

2. The boxer *feigned* a punch with his left rather than actually jabbing.

   a. *feigned* means _____

   b. The signal word(s): _____

3. Although the patient is usually *morose*, she seems happy today.

   a. *morose* means _____

   b. The signal word(s): _____

4. Even though our camp spot was rather *remote*, I was afraid other people might discover it.

   a. *remote* means _____

   b. The signal word(s): _____

5. Although his parents were *indigent*, they somehow managed to provide Tommy with proper food and clothing.

   a. *indigent* means _____

   b. The signal word(s): _____

6. She usually is a *laggard*; however, today she was energetic and did her share.

   a. *laggard* means _____

   b. The signal word(s): _____

Make vocabulary cards or use some other method to learn any words that gave you trouble.

Contextual Examples

Another way you can frequently determine an unknown word's meaning is through **contextual examples**. Writers often provide examples of things or ideas that help define a word. For instance, look at these sentences:

> Luis must be very affluent. He wears expensive clothes and jewelry, drives a Rolls-Royce convertible, and owns a $1,750,000 house in Beverly Hills.

Notice all the examples that help define the word *affluent*: expensive clothes, jewelry, and car, and a house in Beverly Hills. All of these are items that require considerable money or wealth. So it doesn't take much work to figure out that *affluent* means wealthy or well-to-do.

Let's look at another instance of the use of contextual examples:

> The navy recruiting officer offered him several inducements to join up, such as the promise of a college education, the opportunity to fly jets, and the chance to be stationed in Hawaii.

© Steve Kelley. Reprinted with permission.

If the word *inducements* is unclear to begin with, a look at the examples of what the recruitment officer promised gives us a hint that the word must mean reasons or motives for joining the navy.

Now try using this technique on the sentences in Practice B-3 on the next page.

PRACTICE B-3: Contextual Examples

Directions: Define the italicized words in the following sentences and give the example clues.

1. Burning the village to the ground, shooting all the villagers, and plundering the area for valuables, the rebels committed one of the most *heinous* acts of the war.

    a. *heinous* means _____

    b. The example clues: _____

2. Sara is very *astute*; she borrowed money at a very low interest rate and built it into a small fortune through wise investments.

    a. *astute* means _____

    b. The example clues: _____

3. In order to show *clemency*, the judge reduced the fine to one dollar and merely gave the man a warning.

    a. *clemency* means _____

    b. The example clues: _____

4. Jerry is so *indolent*! He sleeps late, never does chores unless yelled at, and would rather lounge around the house than look for a job.

    a. *indolent* means _____

    b. The example clues: _____

5. Carnegie was very *frugal*. Even though he did not earn a lot, he saved most of his money and lived on very little until he saved $10,000 for the investment that was to make him rich.

    a. *frugal* means _____

    b. The example clues: _____

6. They *enhanced* the property by pulling weeds, mowing the lawn, and planting trees around the house.

    a. *enhanced* means _____

    b. The example clues: _____

Make vocabulary cards or use some other method to learn the words that gave you trouble.

Definition Clues

The easiest of context clues to recognize is the **definition clue**. Some sentences actually define the unknown word right in the sentence itself. Notice how this is done in the following example:

Sue, serving as the chairperson, presided at the meeting.

The phrase "serving as the chairperson" actually defines the word *preside*, which means to hold the position of authority, to be in charge.

Here's another example of a definition clue in a sentence:

Luke's pretentious manner, standing up and shouting at Sue that he should be running the meeting just to give her a bad time, didn't win him any friends.

Based on Luke's bad manners, we can guess that *pretentious* has something to do with claiming or demanding something when it's unjustified.

While context clues are not always there to help you with unfamiliar words, they do appear with frequency. Take the time in your future readings to look for the various types of clues covered in this section.

PRACTICE B-4: Definition Clues

Directions: Define the italicized words in the following sentences.

1. I always felt the *rapport* between us was good, based on a relationship of trust.

   rapport means _____

2. The most *salient* feature on his face is his chin; it's quite prominent.

   salient means _____

3. I *presumed* or guessed that something was wrong when I smelled the smoke.

   presumed means_____

4. Sherry's ill will or, more accurately, *malevolence* toward her brother became obvious when she tried to push him down the stairs.

   malevolence means_____

5. Hans Zinsser said, "The rat, like men, has become practically *omnivorous*—it eats anything that lets it."

   omnivorous means _____

6. Bret's *jocose* manner soon had all of us laughing and joking.

   jocose means_____

Make vocabulary cards or use some other method to learn the words that gave you trouble.

PRACTICE B-5: Contextual Clues in Paragraphs

Directions: Read the following paragraphs and define each of the boldface words as they are used in context. Read each paragraph in its entirety before attempting to define the boldface words or phrases.

Paragraph 1

Who makes the better boss: men or women? The debate has been **simmering** for some time both in scientific journals as well as in employees' intraoffice e-mails. In order to come to a final **verdict**, researchers at Northwestern University examined 45 studies on the subject that were conducted between 1985 and 2002. Though the difference found in each study was small, the conclusion reported in the *Psychological Bulletin* is that women make better bosses. Females are more likely to serve as role models and **mentors** for employees and to encourage creativity than are males.

    a. simmering _____

    b. verdict _____

    c. mentors _____

Paragraph 2

The findings of the study **beg the question**: If women make better bosses than men, why aren't more women in the higher levels of **corporate America**? The evidence suggests that women should be rising up the **corporate ladder** at least as fast as men, if not faster. But it's not happening. Of the *Fortune 500*'s top jobs—senior vice president and above—only 6 percent are held by women.

    a. beg the question _____

    b. corporate America _____

    c. corporate ladder _____

Paragraph 3

In our **media-intensive** culture, it is not difficult to find differing opinions. Thousands of newspapers and magazines and dozens of radio and television talk shows **resound** with differing points of view. The difficulty lies in deciding which opinion to agree with and which "experts" seem the most credible. The more inundated we become with differing opinions and claims, the more essential it is to **hone** critical reading and thinking skills to evaluate these ideas. (From David L. Bender and Bruno Leone, series editors, *Opposing Viewpoints* series, Greenhaven, 2000)

    a. media-intensive _____

    b. resound _____

    c. hone _____

Paragraph 4

More and more, we Americans like to watch (and not do). In fact, watching is our ultimate addiction. My students were the progeny of two hundred available cable channels and omnipresent Blockbuster outlets. They grew up with their noses pressed against the window of that second spectral world that spins parallel to our own, the World Wide Web. There they met life at second or third hand, peering eagerly, taking in the passing show, or staying remote, apparently untouched by it. So conditioned, they found it almost natural to come at the rest of life with a sense of aristocratic expectation: "What have you to show me that I haven't already seen?" (From Mark Edmunson, *Why Read?*, Bloomsbury, 2004, p. 10.)

a. progeny_____

b. omnipresent _____

c. spectral _____

d. aristocratic _____

Paragraph 5

I became increasingly frustrated at not being able to express what I wanted to **convey** in letters that I wrote. . . . In the street, I had been the most **articulate** hustler out there—I had **commanded** attention when I said something. But now, trying to write simple English, I not only wasn't articulate, I wasn't even **functional**. How would I sound writing slang the way I would say it, something such as, "Look, daddy, let me pull your coat about a cat." (From Malcolm X with Alex Haley, *Autobiography of Malcolm X*, Ballantine, 1965, p. 197.)

For each numbered word, circle the letter of the word closest to its meaning.

1. convey
  a. transport
  b. communicate
  c. believe

2. articulate
  a. funny
  b. mean, tough
  c. clear

3. commanded
  a. ordered
  b. overlooked
  c. exercised authority

4. functional
  a. workable
  b. not usable
  c. worthy

Paragraph 6

An anti-literature attitude exists among some people who feel that reading literature is **impractical** and holds little value. It's frowned upon as being little more than a pleasure-centered, leisure-time activity. Such literary interests are looked upon as **pretentious**, something an "upper-class" or **elite** person pursues. That may be because some people have tried to use literary knowledge in a snobbish way as a status symbol, which is unfortunate.

For each numbered word, circle the letter of the word closest to its meaning.

1. impractical
  a. unknown
  b. unrealistic
  c. important

2. pretentious
  a. false
  b. showy
  c. smart

3. elite
  a. intelligent
  b. superior status
  c. enlightened

PRACTICE B-6: Quick Quiz

Directions: The following words are from the practices you've been doing on context clues. Define each word, and then write a sentence using it correctly in context.

1. *vociferous* (Practice B-1, question 1)

  a. Definition: _____

  b. Sentence:_____

  _____

2. *laggard* (Practice B-2, question 6)

   a. Definition: _____

   b. Sentence:_____

   _____

3. *loquacious* (Practice B-2, question 1)

   a. Definition: _____

   b. Sentence:_____

   _____

4. *frugal* (Practice B-3, question 5)

   a. Definition: _____

   b. Sentence:_____

   _____

5. *astute* (Practice B-3, question 2)

   a. Definition: _____

   b. Sentence: _____

   _____

6. *indolent* (Practice B-3, question 4)

   a. Definition: _____

   b. Sentence:_____

   _____

7. *rapport* (Practice B-4, question 1)

   a. Definition: _____

   b. Sentence:_____

   _____

8. *jocose* (Practice B-4, question 6)

   a. Definition: _____

   b. Sentence:_____

   _____

9. *articulate* (Practice B-5, paragraph 5, question 2)

   a. Definition: _____

   b. Sentence:_____

   _____

10. *pretentious* (Practice B-5, paragraph 6, question 2)

   a. definition _____

   b. sentence _____

   _____

11. *impractical* (Practice B-5, paragraph 6, question1)

   a. Definition: _____

   b. Sentence:_____

   _____

12. *emulate* (Check Test, question 2)

   a. Definition: _____

   b. Sentence:_____

   _____

13. *riffling* (Check Test, question 3)

   a. Definition: _____

   b. Sentence:_____

   _____

14. *inevitable* (Check Test, question 4)

   a. Definition: _____

   b. Sentence:_____

   _____

15. *burrowing* (Check Test, question 5)

   a. Definition: _____

   b. Sentence:_____

   _____

Tear out this quiz and turn it in to your instructor.

Name_____ Section_____ Date _____

> ### *Made-up Words*
>
> *The Washington Post* frequently runs a Mensa Invitational which asks readers to take any word from the dictionary and alter it by adding, subtracting or changing one letter, and supply a new definition. Here are some examples:
>
> intaxication: happiness at getting a tax refund, which lasts until you realize it was your money to begin with
>
> giraffitti: vandalism spray-painted very high
>
> inoculatte: To take coffee intravenously when running late
>
> caterpallor: the color you turn after finding half a worm in the fruit you're eating
>
> esplanade: to attempt an explanation while drunk
>
> flabbergasted: appalled by discovering how much weight one has gained
>
> coffee: the person upon whom one coughs
>
> lymph: to walk with a lisp
>
> Try making up a new word and/or definition.

C.   Learning Word Parts and Structure

Another good way to develop your vocabulary is to learn some of the basic word parts that make up the English language. Many of our words are derived from other languages, and many prefixes, suffixes, and root word parts come from Latin and Greek. You probably already know many of them but have never taken the time to see how frequently they appear in our language or why certain words mean what they do. In this section, you will review and learn some of the commonly used word parts in English.

No doubt you know the word *phonograph*. This common word in English is actually made up of two Greek word roots—*phon*, meaning sound, and *graph*, meaning write or record. Technically, the grooves in a recording are a record of sound, or, if you will, sound written on a record. The advantage of knowing the meaning of word parts is that you can often figure out what an unknown word means by its parts. Look at some of the words that contain the word part *phon*:

phone: informal verb meaning to telephone someone, as well as the informal word for a telephone

phonate: to utter speech sounds

phoneme: one of the set of the smallest units of speech that distinguishes one utterance or word from another; the *b* in *bat* and the *m* in *mat* are phonemes

phonemics: the study of phonemes

phonetic: representing the sounds of speech with distinct symbols

phonetician: an expert in phonetics

phonic: having sound

phonics: the study or science of sound

phonogram: a character or symbol representing a word or phoneme

phonology: the science of speech sounds
phonotype: text printed in phonetic symbols
symphony: a long sonata for orchestra (*sym* means together or in harmony)
euphony: good, pleasant sounds (*eu* means good)
cacophony: harsh, unpleasant sound (*caco* means bad)

Even though some of these words are specialty words, you are one step ahead when you know that all the words have something to do with sound.

Many words in English are made up of *prefixes* (small but meaningful letter groups added before a base word or root that change the root's meaning) and *suffixes* (letter groups that are added to the end of a base word or root). Learning the meaning of these word parts, together with the meaning of common base words and Greek and Latin roots, will give you the key for unlocking the meanings of hundreds of words.

Following are several practices dealing with word parts and structure. Some you will know, and some will be new to you. Make vocabulary cards for those you want to overlearn, or use whatever method you have decided upon for enlarging your vocabulary.

PRACTICE C-1: Prefixes That Express Negativity and Reversal

Directions: Several prefixes (letter groups added before a root word that change the root's meaning) have to do with negation or reversal. For instance, placing the prefix *dis* in front of the root word *approve* creates the word *disapprove*, changing the word to a negative one. Placing the prefix *dis* on the root word *arm* creates the word *disarm*, reversing the root's meaning.

Below are three columns. Column 1 contains some prefixes that express negative or reverse meanings. Column 2 contains words you should know. In column 3, you should write in the words from column 2, adding to each what you think is the correct prefix from column 1 to reverse the root word's meaning. The first one has been done for you. Here are clues for using *il, im,* and *ir*:

use *il* with words beginning with *l*
use *im* with words beginning with *b, m,* and *p*
use *ir* with words beginning with *r*

Column 1 Prefix	Column 2 Root	Column 3 New Word
a	active	1. *inactive* _____
counter	comfortable	2. _____
de	expensive	3. _____
dis	logical	4. _____
non	violent	5. _____
il	fair	6. _____
im	regulate	7. _____

in	typical	8. _____
ir	pleasant	9. _____
un	settle	10. _____
	proper	11. _____
	legal	12. _____
	regular	13. _____
	polite	14. _____
	decisive	15. _____
	easy	16. _____
	movable	17. _____
	possible	18. _____
	rational	19. _____
	legitimate	20. _____

PRACTICE C-2: Prefixes That Express Time and Place

Directions: Below are some commonly used prefixes that express time and place. Study them carefully. Then fill in the blanks in the numbered exercises. The first one has been done for you.

Prefix	Meaning	Prefix	Meaning
intro, intra	inside, within	re	back, again
inter	between, among	super	above
pre	before	trans	across
de	away, undo	sub	under
ex	out, not any longer	retro	back, backward
post	after	circum	around

1. What is the opposite of *inflate* (to fill)? *deflate* _____

2. If a patriot is a loyal countryman, what is an *expatriate*? _____

    _____

3. What is the opposite of *activate*? _____

4. If import means to bring in, *export* means _____

5. If urban refers to the city, what is an *intraurban* truck line? _____

6. Is *postgraduate* work done before or after you graduate from college? _____

7. A *prefix* is called what it is because it is fixed_____ the root word.

8. If the root word *vive* refers to life, what does revive mean?_____

9. A *transatlantic* voyage would take you _____

10. If you *intercede* during an argument, what will you do? _____

11. *Intercollegiate* sports are activities that take place _____ different colleges.

12. *Intracollegiate* sports are activities that take place _____

13. Is the *pre*-Victorian period before or after the Victorian period? _____

14. *Mortem* refers to death; what is a postmortem? an analysis done _____

15. Who is higher in rank, a *subprincipal* or a principal? _____

16. What is meant by a *superhuman* effort?_____

17. What would it mean if your boss said you had some *retroactive* pay coming to you? _____

18. What's the difference between *circumference* and diagonal measurements?

_____

19. Why are *subways* called what they are? _____

20. What is the difference between *interisland* ships and those that *circumnavigate*?

_____

PRACTICE C-3: Miscellaneous Prefixes

Directions: Study the following miscellaneous prefixes and their meanings, then answer the questions that follow. The first one has been done for you.

Prefix	Meaning	Prefix	Meaning
anti	against	hetero	different
auto	self	mis, miso	wrong; hatred
bene	good, well	mal	bad, wrong
bi	two	poly	many
eu	good, nice		

1. If a newspaper is printed *bimonthly*, it is printed *twice a month* .

2. If *phon* means sound, what does *euphonious* mean? _____

_____

3. If *toxin* means poison, what does *antitoxin* mean? _____

_____

4. If *gen* refers to types or kinds, what does *heterogeneous* mean?_____

_____

5. If *homogeneous* is the opposite of *heterogeneous*, what does it mean?_____

_____

6. If *sect* means to cut or divide, what does *bisect* mean?_____

_____

7. If *caco* means bad, or unpleasant, how would you form a word that means the opposite of *euphony*? _____

8. Because *gam* refers to marriage, *misogamy* means _____

_____

9. Because *gyn* refers to women, a *misogynist* is_____

_____

10. What is a *polygamist?*_____

_____

11. Why is an *automatic* transmission called what it is? _____

_____

12. Which is better: a tumor that is *malignant* or *benign?*_____

_____

13. What is *malpractice?* _____

_____

14. Why are fund-raisers often called *benefits?* _____

_____

15. Why are people who donate money called *benefactors?* _____

_____

PRACTICE C-4: Quick Quiz

Directions: Define the following prefixes and write a word that contains each prefix.

Prefix	Definition	Word Using Prefix
1. auto	_____	_____
2. il	_____	_____
3. intra	_____	_____
4. in	_____	_____
5. un	_____	_____
6. ir	_____	_____
7. anti	_____	_____
8. a/an	_____	_____
9. bi	_____	_____
10. de	_____	_____
11. dis	_____	_____
12. hetero	_____	_____
13. bene	_____	_____
14. eu	_____	_____
15. sub	_____	_____

16. im   _____   _____

17. mis   _____   _____

18. post   _____   _____

19. trans   _____   _____

20. re   _____   _____

Show these pages to your instructor.

PRACTICE C-5: Noun Suffixes

Directions: A noun, as you may remember, is frequently defined as a person, place, or thing: *woman, John, city, farm, hammer,* and *car* are all nouns. Some suffixes (letters at the end of a word) change root words into nouns. For instance, *er* on the end of the word *teach* (a verb) forms the word *teacher*, a noun. The suffix *dom* on the end of the adjective *free* creates the noun *freedom*.

Study the following list of suffixes. They all mean "a person who is or does something." Then answer the questions that follow. The first one has been done for you.

ent	ant	ist
er	ar	ee
or	ess	ard

1. Someone who acts is an _actor, actress_____

2. A person who is paid to serve in a household is a _____

3. Someone who gets drunk much of the time is a _____

4. A person who practices science is a _____

5. A woman who waits on tables in a restaurant is a _____

6. One who begs is a_____ _____

7. A person who resides in an apartment is called a _____

8. One who is elected to preside over an organization is called the_____

9. A payer _____ while a payee _____

10. Someone who commits anarchy is an _____

11. A friend who keeps your confidence is called a _____

12. One who sails is a_____

13. Someone who practices biology is a_____ _____

14. A person who narrates is a_____

15. One who studies is a_____

PRACTICE C-6: More Noun Suffixes

Directions: Column 1 contains a list of suffixes that mean "a state or quality of being." For instance, *violence* is the state of being *violent*; *loyalty* is the state of being *loyal*. Column 2 contains some words that can be changed to nouns by adding the suffixes from column 1. Using the suffixes in column 1, write in the correct noun form in column 3. The first one has been done for you.

Column 1	Column 2	Column 3
Suffix	**Root**	**New Word**
ance	fail	1. *failure*
ation	hero	2.
dom	amuse	3.
hood	friend	4.
ion	free	5.
ism	tense	6.
ly	absurd	7.
ment	repent	8.
ness	starve	9.
ty	royal	10.
ship	happy	11.
ure	seize	12.
	lively	13.
	content	14.
	moderate	15.

PRACTICE C-7: Miscellaneous Suffixes

Directions: Study the following list of suffixes and their definitions. Then, using the list, add suffixes to the words that follow. Some words may take more than one suffix. The first one has been done for you.

Suffix	Definition	Suffix	Definition
able, ible	able to	less	without
cy	state or condition	ize	to make
full, ous	full of	ly	a characteristic or in
ic, al	related to		a certain manner
ish, ive	inclined to, similar		

1. care   *careful, careless, carefully, carelessly*

2. depend _____

3. instruct _____

4. infant _____

5. vocal _____

6. expend _____

7. form _____

8. permanent _____

9. live _____

10. tropic _____

11. active _____

12. popular _____

13. combat _____

14. compete _____

15. caution _____

16. word _____

17. history _____

18. wonder _____

19. nature _____

20. defense _____

PRACTICE C-8: Roots

Directions: Using the following list of word roots and their definitions, answer the questions that follow.

Root	Definition	Root	Definition
aud	hear	graph	write, record
chron	time	man, manu	hand
cred	belief	mort	death
dent	tooth	phil	love
dict	tell, say	phon	sound

1. If *meter* means measure, a chronometer _____

   _____

2. If something is audible, you can _____ it.

3. *Incredulous* means _____

   _____ .

4. The suffix *ist* refers to a person; that's why someone who works on your teeth is called a _____ .

5. If *contra* means against or opposite, contradict means _____

   _____ .

6. A chronograph is _____ .

7. The opposite of *automatic* is _____

_____ .

8. Does a *postmortem* occur before or after death? _____

9. If *anthrop* refers to man or mankind, what is a *philanthropist?* _____

_____

10. If you talk into a *Dictaphone*™, you are recording the _____ of your voice.

Practice C-9: More Roots

Directions: Define the following words. Don't look back at any previous exercises. You should be able to define all of these words if you learned from the previous drills.

Root	Definition	Root	Definition
biblio	book	phobia	fear
bio	life	poly	many
gam	marriage	port	carry
gen	kinds, types	tele	far, distance
log(y)	study of	theo	gods, religion
mono	one	vis	see

1. bibliography _____

2. biology _____

3. biography _____

4. monogamy _____

5. polyphonous _____

6. heterogeneous _____

7. bibliophobia _____

8. portable _____

9. televise _____

10. theology _____

Application 2: Finding Word Parts in Other Readings

In your textbooks or other reading material, find at least ten words that use the roots you have learned. Impress your instructor and write out the words and their definitions and turn in the list.

PRACTICE C-10: Quick Quiz

Directions: Define the following words. You should be able to define all of these words if you have learned from previous drills.

1. dictation (Practice C-8): _____

2. credible (Practice C-8): _____

3. bibliography (Practice C-9): _____

4. philanthropist (Practice C-8): _____

5. bibliophile (Practice C-9): _____

6. incredulous (Practices C-1, C-8): _____

7. audiometer (Practice C-8): _____

8. submariner (Practice C-2): _____

9. monogamy (Practice C-9): _____

10. autograph (Practice C-3): _____

11. misanthropist (Practice C-3): _____

12. intraoffice (Practice C-2): _____

13. deflate (Practice C-2): _____

14. heterogeneous (Practices C-3, C-9): _____

15. antitheological (Practice C-3): _____

16. euphonious (Practice C-3): _____

17. bimotored (Practice C-3): _____

18. atypical (Practice C-1): _____

19. irrational (Practice C-1): _____

20. illogical (Practice C-1): _____

Show this page to your instructor. Make vocabulary cards for any words you missed or need to learn better.

Name_____ Section_____ Date _____

D.   Learning Dictionary Skills

There comes a time when context clues and knowledge of word parts are not enough to help you understand an unknown word's meaning. That usually means a trip to the dictionary. The dictionary is more than a recorder of a word's meaning. It gives information on the word's origin; its various meanings, pronunciation, parts of speech, spellings, synonyms, and antonyms; and its formal and informal usage. If you don't have a good, up-to-date dictionary, you should get one. (In a later practice, you will read an essay by Robert M. Pierson titled "What You Should Look For in a Dictionary," which will help you select one appropriate for you.)

Here is a typical dictionary word entry:

¹com•pound \käm-ˈpau̇nd, ˈkäm-ˌ\ *vb* [ME *compounen,* fr. MF *compondre,* fr. L *componere,* fr. *com-* together + *ponere* to put] **1** : COMBINE **2** : to form by combining parts ⟨~ a medicine⟩ **3** : SETTLE ⟨~ a dispute⟩; *also* : to refrain from prosecuting (an offense) in return for a consideration **4** : to increase (as interest) by an amount that can itself vary; *also* : to add to
²com•pound \ˈkäm-ˌpau̇nd\ *adj* **1** : made up of individual parts **2** : composed of united similar parts esp. of a kind usu. independent ⟨a ~ plant ovary⟩ **3** : formed by the combination of two or more otherwise independent elements ⟨~ sentence⟩
³com•pound \ˈkäm-ˌpau̇nd\ *n* **1** : a word consisting of parts that are words **2** : something formed from a union of elements or parts; *esp* : a distinct substance formed by the union of two or more chemical elements **syn** mixture, composite, blend, admixture, alloy
⁴com•pound \ˈkäm-ˌpau̇nd\ *n* [by folk etymology fr. Malay *kampung* group of buildings, village] : an enclosure containing buildings

By permission. From *The Merriam-Webster Dictionary* © 2005 by Merriam-Webster, Incorporated (www.Merriam-Webster.com), p. 236 All rights reserved. Reproduced by permission.

In almost all dictionaries, the main word appears in bold type and is divided into syllables by dots. In the *Merriam-Webster Dictionary* used in these exercises, different definitions of the same word are given separate entries and are distinguished by superscript numerals preceding each word. The word *compound* has four main entries further broken down into ten quite different meanings: The first *compound* has four meanings; the second has three meanings; the third has two meanings; the last entry has only one meaning.

Following the boldface entry word are the pronunciation symbols. If you are unfamiliar with the symbols, a pronunciation key usually appears on the inside front or rear cover of the dictionary. The first exercise in this section will help you learn how to use pronunciation keys. Notice that the first entry of *compound* has a different pronunciation than the other three entries.

Next, abbreviated, is the word's part of speech. The abbreviation *vb* means verb, *adj* means adjective, and *n* means noun; the word *compound* can thus be a verb, adjective, or noun. It's important to understand the part of speech of a word so that you can use it correctly.

The bracketed section that appears near the beginning of an entry provides the word's etymology or its historical origin in English or another language. In this case, the first entry originally came from the Middle English and Middle French. The fourth entry shows that it came from a Malay word, *kampung*: group of buildings, village.

Notice that there are four definitions given for *compound* as a verb, three definitions as an adjective, and three definitions as a noun. In this dictionary, the word meanings are arranged from the oldest to the most recent, so the most common present-day definition of *compound* as a verb is "to increase (as interest) by an amount that can itself vary; also: to add to."

Sometimes the definitions given for words in some dictionaries are not easy to understand. Frequently, a word that is being used in a definition must also be looked up in the dictionary! All dictionaries are not the same, so be selective in your choice.

The following practices should help you become more familiar with how to get the most from whatever dictionary you buy.

PRACTICE D-1: Pronunciation Keys

Directions: Using the pronunciation key on page 35, answer the following questions. Answers with explanations follow each question.

1. The first *o* in the word *loquacious* (lō-kwā´-shəs)—meaning talkative—is pronounced like the *o* in key words such as _____ and _____
   The key words are *bone* and *hollow*. Because the first *o* in loquacious is marked ō, it is necessary to scan the dictionary symbol column and find an ō listed. Such a symbol appears in the first column, seven up from the bottom. This sound is called the "long o" sound. The symbols appearing over the vowel letters are called diacritical marks.

2. The *a* in the word loquacious (lō-kwā´-shəs) is pronounced like the *a* in key words such as _____ and _____.
   The key words are *day* and *fate*. The answer is found in the first column, sixth listing. This sound is called the "long a" sound.

3. The ə symbol used in the pronunciation clues (lō-kwā´-shəs) symbolizes the sound of the letter_____ _____as in the word *circus*.

4. The *a* in the word *chartreuse* (shär-trüz´)—meaning yellowish green—is pronounced like the *a* in the word _____. The two small dots give the *a* a completely different sound, which is sometimes called the "short vowel" sound. The words *bother*, *father*, and *cot* are possible answers listed in the first column.

5. The *u* sound in *chartreuse* (shär-trüz´) is pronounced like the *u* in the words _____. The words *boot* and *few* contain the ü sound. See the second column.

6. The first *e* in the word *egocentric* (ē-gō-sen´-trik)—meaning self-centered—is pronounced like the *e* in the word_____. The ē is the "long e" sound, and the correct answer is *beat* or *easy*.

7. The *dg* in the word *edge* appears as the letter_____ as a pronunciation clue. Unless you already knew the answer, you needed to scan the key words column and look for the word *edge*. It is in the first column, in the twenty-first listing. To the left is the letter *j*, meaning that *dg* is sounded as a *j* sound.

8. Sometimes the letter *s* may be pronounced like the letter *z*. What is one word that has an *s* that sounds like *z*?_____
   In the pronunciation key, go to the letter *z*. Notice that the last key word is *raise*, which is the answer you should have written.

9. What letters besides *sh* are sometimes pronounced as *sh*? _____ .
   Your answer should be *ss*, as in *mission*. Look for the letter *sh* in the second column and find which key words have that sound.

10. The *s* in *pleasure* is pronounced like the letters _____ .
    Find the key word *pleasure* in the second column. Your answer should be *zh*.

PRONUNCIATION SYMBOLS

ə . . . . about, collect, suppose
ˈə, ˌə humdrum
ə . . . . (in ᵊl, ᵊn) battle, cotton; (in lᵊ, mᵊ, rᵊ) French table, prisme, titre
ər . . . operation, further
a . . . . map, patch
ā . . . . day, fate
ä . . . . bother, cot, father
à . . . . a sound between \a\ and \ä\, as in an Eastern New England pronunciation of aunt, ask
aů . . . now, out
b . . . . baby, rib
ch . . . chin, catch
d . . . . did, adder
e . . . . set, red
ē . . . . beat, easy
f . . . . fifty, cuff
g . . . . go, big
h . . . . hat, ahead
hw . . . whale
i . . . . tip, banish
ī . . . . site, buy
j . . . . job, edge
k . . . . kin, cook
ḵ . . . . German Bach, Scots loch
l . . . . lily, cool
m . . . murmur, dim
n . . . . nine, own
ⁿ . . . . indicates that a preceding vowel is pronounced through both nose and mouth, as in French bon \bōⁿ\
ŋ . . . . sing, singer, finger, ink
ō . . . . bone, hollow
ȯ . . . . saw
œ . . . French bœuf, German Hölle
œ̄ . . . French feu, German Höhle
ȯi . . . toy
p . . . . pepper, lip
r . . . . rarity

s . . . . source, less
sh . . . shy, mission
t . . . . tie, attack
th . . . thin, ether
th . . . then, either
ü . . . . boot, few \ˈfyü\
ů . . . . put, pure \ˈpyůr\
ue . . . German füllen
ūe . . . French rue, German fühlen
v . . . . vivid, give
w . . . we, away
y . . . . yard, cue \ˈkyü\
ʸ . . . . indicates that a preceding \l\, \n\, or \w\ is modified by having the tongue approximate the position for \y\, as in French digne \dēnʸ\
z . . . . zone, raise
zh . . . vision, pleasure
\ . . . . slant line used in pairs to mark the beginning and end of a transcription: \ˈpen\
ˈ . . . . mark at the beginning of a syllable that has primary (strongest) stress: \ˈshə-fəl-ˌbōrd\
ˌ . . . . mark at the beginning of a syllable that has secondary (next-strongest) stress: \ˈshə-fəl-ˌbōrd\
- . . . . mark of a syllable division in pronunciations (the mark of end-of-line division in boldface entries is a centered dot •)
( ) . . . indicate that what is symbolized between sometimes occurs and sometimes does not occur in the pronunciation of the word: **bakery** \ˈbā-k(ə-)rē\ = \ˈbā-kə-rē, ˈbā-krē\

PRACTICE D-2: Word Entry Knowledge

Directions: Using the following dictionary word entry, answer the questions that follow.

> ¹**out•side** \aút-'sīd, 'aút-ˌsīd\ *n* **1** : a
> place or region beyond an enclosure
> or boundary **2** : EXTERIOR **3** : the ut-
> most limit or extent
> ²**outside** *adj* **1** : OUTER **2** : coming from
> without ⟨∼ influences⟩ **3** : being apart
> from one's regular duties ⟨∼ activi-
> ties⟩ **4** : REMOTE ⟨an ∼ chance⟩
> ³**outside** *adv* : on or to the outside
> ⁴**outside** *prep* **1** : on or to the outside of
> **2** : beyond the limits of **3** : EXCEPT

By permission. From *The Merriam-Webster Dictionary* © 2005 by Merriam-Webster, Incorporated
(http://www.Merriam-Webster.com), p. 826. All rights reserved. Reproduced by permission.

1. In total, how many definitions are given for the word *outside?* _____

2. For how many parts of speech can outside be used? _____

    _____

3. Two ways to pronounce *outside* are given. What is the difference between the two?

    _____

    _____

4. What does it mean to say there is an "outside chance" you might win?

    _____

    _____

5. A phrase using *outside* in context is provided after the second definition of the
    word as an adjective. Explain in your own words what the phrase means. _____

    _____

    _____

6. What is one meaning of saying you're working at the *outside* of your ability? Hint:
    Outside is used as a noun in this phrase, so look under the noun definitions.

    _____

    _____

7. Use *outside* as a noun in a sentence. _____

    _____

8. Use *outside* as an adjective in a sentence. _____

    _____

9. Use *outside* as an adverb in a sentence. _____

    _____

10. Use *outside* as a preposition in a sentence. _____

    _____

    _____

babble • back out

1 : to talk enthusiastically or excessively **2** : to utter meaningless sounds — **babble** *n* — **bab·bler** \-b(ə-)lər\ *n*

babe \'bāb\ *n* **1** : BABY **2** *slang* : GIRL, WOMAN

ba·bel \'bā-bəl, 'ba-\ *n, often cap* [fr. the Tower of *Babel*, Gen 11:4–9] : a place or scene of noise and confusion; *also* : a confused sound **syn** hubbub, racket, din, uproar, clamor

ba·boon \ba-'bün\ *n* [ME *babewin*, fr. MF *babouin*, fr. *baboue* grimace] : any of several large apes of Asia and Africa with doglike muzzles

ba·bush·ka \bə-'büsh-kə, -'bush-\ *n* [Russ. grandmother, dim. of *baba* old woman] : a kerchief for the head

¹ba·by \'bā-bē\ *n, pl* **babies 1** : a very young child : INFANT **2** : the youngest or smallest of a group **3** : a childish person — **baby** *adj* — **ba·by·hood** *n* — **ba·by·ish** *adj*

²baby *vb* **ba·bied; ba·by·ing** : to tend or treat often with excessive care

baby boom *n* : a marked rise in birthrate — **baby boom·er** \-'bü-mər\ *n*

baby's breath *n* : any of a genus of herbs that are related to the pinks and have small delicate flowers

ba·by–sit \'bā-bē-ˌsit\ *vb* -**sat** \-ˌsat\; -**sit·ting** : to care for children usu. during a short absence of the parents — **ba·by–sit·ter** *n*

bac·ca·lau·re·ate \ˌba-kə-'lòr-ē-ət\ *n* **1** : the degree of bachelor conferred by colleges and universities **2** : a sermon delivered to a graduating class

bac·ca·rat \ˌbä-kə-'rä, ˌba-\ *n* : a card game played esp. in European casinos

bac·cha·nal \'ba-kən-ᵊl, ˌba-kə-'nal, ˌbä-kə-'näl\ *n* **1** : ORGY **2** : REVELER

bac·cha·na·lia \ˌba-kə-'näl-yə\ *n, pl* **bacchanalia** : a drunken orgy — **bac·cha·na·lian** \-'näl-yən\ *adj or n*

bach·e·lor \'ba-chə-lər\ *n* **1** : a person who has received the usu. lowest degree conferred by a 4-year college **2** : an unmarried man — **bach·e·lor·hood** *n*

bach·e·lor·ette \ˌba-chə-lə-'ret\ *n* : a young unmarried woman

bachelor's button *n* : a European plant related to the daisies and having blue, pink, or white flower heads

ba·cil·lus \bə-'si-ləs\ *n, pl* -**li** \-ˌlī\ [NL. fr. ML, small staff, dim. of L *baculus* staff] : any of numerous rod-shaped bacteria; *also* : a disease-producing bacterium — **bac·il·lary** \'ba-sə-ˌler-ē\ *adj*

¹back \'bak\ *n* **1** : the rear or dorsal part of the human body; *also* : the corresponding part of a lower animal **2** : the part or surface opposite the front **3** : a player in the backfield in football — **back·less** \-ləs\ *adj*

²back *adv* **1** : to, toward, or at the rear **2** : AGO **3** : so as to be restrained or retarded **4** : to, toward, or in a former place or state **5** : in return or reply

³back *adj* **1** : located at or in the back; *also* : REMOTE **2** : OVERDUE **3** : moving or operating backward **4** : not current

⁴back *vb* **1** : SUPPORT, UPHOLD **2** : to go or cause to go backward or in reverse **3** : to furnish with a back : form the back of

back·ache \'ba-ˌkāk\ *n* : a pain in the lower back

back–bench·er \-'ben-chər\ *n* : a rank- and-file member of a British legislature

back·bite \-ˌbīt\ *vb* -**bit** \-ˌbit\; -**bit·ten** \-ˌbit-ᵊn\; -**bit·ing** \-ˌbī-tiŋ\ : to say mean or spiteful things about someone who is absent — **back·bit·er** *n*

back·board \-ˌbòrd\ *n* : a board placed at or serving as the back of something

back·bone \-ˌbōn\ *n* **1** : the bony column in the back of a vertebrate that is the chief support of the trunk and consists of a jointed series of vertebrae enclosing and protecting the spinal cord **2** : firm resolute character

back·drop \'bak-ˌdräp\ *n* : a painted cloth hung across the rear of a stage

back·er \'ba-kər\ *n* : one that supports

back·field \-ˌfēld\ *n* : the football players whose positions are behind the line

¹back·fire \-ˌfīr\ *n* : a loud noise caused by the improperly timed explosion of fuel in the cylinder of an internal combustion engine

²backfire *vb* **1** : to make or undergo a backfire **2** : to have a result opposite to what was intended

back·gam·mon \'bak-ˌga-mən\ *n* : a game played with pieces on a double board in which the moves are determined by throwing dice

back·ground \'bak-ˌgraund\ *n* **1** : the scenery behind something **2** : the setting within which something takes place; *also* : the sum of a person's experience, training, and understanding

back·hand \'bak-ˌhand\ *n* : a stroke (as in tennis) made with the back of the hand turned in the direction of movement; *also* : the side on which such a stroke is made — **back·hand** *vb*

back·hand·ed \'bak-'han-dəd\ *adj* **1** : INDIRECT, DEVIOUS; *esp* : SARCASTIC **2** : using or made with a backhand

back·hoe \'bak-ˌhō\ *n* : an excavating machine having a bucket that is drawn toward the machine

back·ing \'ba-kiŋ\ *n* **1** : something forming a back **2** : SUPPORT, AID; *also* : a body of supporters

back·lash \'bak-ˌlash\ *n* **1** : a sudden violent backward movement or reaction **2** : a strong adverse reaction

¹back·log \-ˌlòg, -ˌläg\ *n* **1** : a large log at the back of a hearth fire **2** : an accumulation of tasks unperformed or materials not processed

²backlog *vb* : to accumulate in reserve

back of *prep* : BEHIND

back out *vb* : to withdraw esp. from a commitment or contest

PRACTICE D-3: Finding Information

Directions: Using the dictionary excerpt of "b" entries on page 37, look for the answers to the following questions. Write your answers in the blanks.

1. What is one slang meaning of *babe?* _____

    _____

2. *Babel* is the name of a city, but it also refers to a place of what? _____

    _____

3. Which definition of *baby* is used in this example: "A woman in my book club *babies*

    her husband." _____

4. Where is *baccarat* usually played? _____

5. What is the definition of *bachelor* that has to do with college? _____

    _____

6. What part of speech is *back* in the following sentence: "He wrote back to me within

    a day." _____

7. Explain in your own words what *backbiting* means. _____

    _____

8. Use *backfire* in a sentence, being clear about which definition you are using. _____

    _____

9. What are some synonyms for *backhanded?* _____

10. If you have a *backlog* of class assignments to do, what is the likely outcome? _____

    _____

Application 3: On the Web: How to Use Dictionaries (optional)

Using a computer's search engine, type in: http://www.yourdictionary.com/library/article003.html. Read the on-line article about dictionaries and explore the web links. Write a brief evaluation of what you learned and turn it in to your instructor.

PRACTICE D-4: Quick Quiz

Directions: The dictionary excerpt of "s" entries reproduced on page 40 has some items marked for your identification. Look at the circled material and fill in the blanks with the letter from the following list of items that best describes it. One has been done for you. When finished, tear out the page and turn it in to your instructor.

   a. etymology or word history

   b. parts of speech

   c. contextual examples of word usage

   d. word used as several different parts of speech (*n, vb, adj, adv,* or *prep*)

   e. definition based on history of word

   f. synonyms

   g. the preferred pronunciation of the word

   h. word meaning in its original language

   i. most current definition of the word

   j. guide words that show the first and last word on each page

²**shame** *vb* **shamed; sham·ing 1** : DISGRACE **2** : to make ashamed

shame·faced \ˈshām-ˌfāst\ *adj* : ASHAMED, ABASHED — **shame·faced·ly** \-ˌfā-səd-lē, -ˌfāst-lē\ *adv*

¹**sham·poo** \sham-ˈpü\ *vb* [Hindi *cāpo*, imper. of *cāpnā* to press, shampoo] : to wash (as the hair) with soap and water or with a special preparation; *also* : to clean (as a rug) similarly

²**shampoo** *n, pl* **shampoos 1** : the act or an instance of shampooing **2** : a preparation for use in shampooing

sham·rock \ˈsham-ˌräk\ *n* [Ir *seamróg*, dim. of *seamar* clover] : a plant of folk legend with leaves composed of three leaflets that is associated with St. Patrick and Ireland

shang·hai \shaŋ-ˈhī\ *vb* **shang·haied; shang·hai·ing** [*Shanghai*, China] : to force aboard a ship for service as a sailor; *also* : to trick or force into an undesirable position

Shan·gri-la \ˌshaŋ-gri-ˈlä\ *n* [*Shangri-La*, imaginary land depicted in the novel *Lost Horizon* (1933) by James Hilton] : a remote idyllic hideaway

shank \ˈshaŋk\ *n* **1** : the part of the leg between the knee and the human ankle or a corresponding part of a quadruped **2** : a cut of meat from the leg **3** : the narrow part of the sole of a shoe beneath the instep **4** : the part of a tool or instrument (as a key or anchor) connecting the functioning part with a part by which it is held or moved

shan·tung \ˌshan-ˈtəŋ\ *n* : a fabric in plain weave having a slightly irregular surface

shan·ty \ˈshan-tē\ *n, pl* **shanties** [prob. fr. CanF *chantier* lumber camp, hut, fr. F, gantry, fr. L *cantherius* rafter, trellis] : a small roughly built shelter or dwelling

¹**shape** \ˈshāp\ *vb* **shaped; shap·ing 1** : to form esp. in a particular shape **2** : DESIGN **3** : ADAPT, ADJUST **4** : REGULATE syn make, fashion, fabricate, manufacture, frame, mold

²**shape** *n* **1** : APPEARANCE **2** : surface configuration : FORM **3** : bodily contour apart from the head and face : FIGURE **4** : PHANTOM **5** : CONDITION — **shaped** \ˈshāpt\ *adj*

shape·less \ˈshā-pləs\ *adj* **1** : having no definite shape **2** : not shapely — **shape·less·ly** *adv* — **shape·less·ness** *n*

shape·ly \ˈshā-plē\ *adj* **shape·li·er; -est** : having a pleasing shape — **shape·li·ness** *n*

shard \ˈshärd\ *also* **sherd** \ˈshərd\ *n* : a broken piece : FRAGMENT

¹**share** \ˈsher\ *n* : PLOWSHARE

²**share** *n* **1** : a portion belonging to one person or group **2** : any of the equal interests into which the capital stock of a corporation is divided

³**share** *vb* **shared; shar·ing 1** : APPORTION **2** : to use or enjoy with others **3** : PARTICIPATE — **shar·er** *n*

share·crop·per \-ˌkrä-pər\ *n* : a farmer who works another's land in return for a share of the crop — **share·crop** *vb*

share·hold·er \-ˌhōl-dər\ *n* : STOCKHOLDER

¹**shark** \ˈshärk\ *n* : any of various active, usu. predaceous, and mostly large marine cartilaginous fishes

²**shark** *n* : a greedy crafty person

shark·skin \-ˌskin\ *n* **1** : the hide of a shark or leather made from it **2** : a fabric (as of cotton or rayon) woven from strands of many fine threads and having a sleek appearance and silky feel

¹**sharp** \ˈshärp\ *adj* **1** : having a thin cutting edge or fine point : not dull or blunt **2** : COLD, NIPPING ⟨a ~ wind⟩ **3** : keen in intellect, perception, or attention **4** : BRISK, ENERGETIC **5** : IRRITABLE ⟨a ~ temper⟩ **6** : causing intense distress ⟨a ~ pain⟩ **7** : HARSH, CUTTING ⟨a ~ rebuke⟩ **8** : affecting the senses as if cutting or piercing ⟨a ~ sound⟩ ⟨a ~ smell⟩ **9** : not smooth or rounded ⟨~ features⟩ **10** : involving an abrupt or extreme change ⟨a ~ turn⟩ **11** : CLEAR, DISTINCT ⟨mountains in ~ relief⟩; *also* : easy to perceive ⟨a ~ contrast⟩ **12** : higher than the true pitch; *also* : raised by a half step **13** : STYLISH ⟨a ~ dresser⟩ syn keen, acute, quick-witted, penetrative — **sharp·ly** *adv* — **sharp·ness** *n*

²**sharp** *adv* **1** : in a sharp manner **2** : EXACTLY, PRECISELY ⟨left at 8 ~⟩

³**sharp** *n* **1** : a sharp edge or point **2** : a character # which indicates that a specified note is to be raised by a half step; *also* : the resulting note **3** : SHARPER

⁴**sharp** *vb* : to raise in pitch by a half step

sharp·en \ˈshär-pən\ *vb* : to make or become sharp — **sharp·en·er** *n*

sharp·er \ˈshär-pər\ *n* : SWINDLER; *esp* : a cheating gambler

sharp·ie *or* **sharpy** \ˈshär-pē\ *n, pl* **sharp·ies 1** : SHARPER **2** : a person who is exceptionally keen or alert

sharp·shoot·er \ˈshärp-ˌshü-tər\ *n* : a good marksman — **sharp·shoot·ing** *n*

shat·ter \ˈsha-tər\ *vb* : to dash or burst into fragments — **shat·ter·proof** \ˈsha-tər-ˌprüf\ *adj*

¹**shave** \ˈshāv\ *vb* **shaved; shaved** *or* **shav·en** \ˈshā-vən\; **shav·ing 1** : to slice in thin pieces **2** : to make bare or smooth by cutting the hair from **3** : to cut or pare off by the sliding movement of a razor **4** : to skim along or near the surface of

²**shave** *n* **1** : any of various tools for cutting thin slices **2** : an act or process of shaving

shav·er \ˈshā-vər\ *n* **1** : an electric razor **2** : BOY, YOUNGSTER

shaves *pl of* SHAFT

shav·ing *n* **1** : the act of one that shaves **2** : something shaved off

Name_____ Section_____ Date _____

PRACTICE D-5: "What You Should Look For in a Dictionary" by Robert M. Pierson

Directions: Answer the following questions.

1. What is your method or criteria for selecting a new dictionary?_____

    _____

2. What do you think is an important characteristic of a good dictionary? _____

    _____

3. For what purpose do you most often use a dictionary? _____

    _____

The English language is continually changing, especially American English. Some words become archaic, meaning seldom or no longer used. At some point they are dropped from the dictionary. Other words are added as new technology and other languages make their way into American usage. A dictionary tries to reflect words as used by most people. Because a word appears in the dictionary does not necessarily mean the word is correctly used, only that it is used that way by enough people that it gets reported in the dictionary. The word *ain't* can be found in most dictionaries, but along with the definition, comes an explanation that it is substandard usage.

The following selection provides much information about dictionaries that you should know. Dictionaries are an important tool for increasing your vocabulary and should be chosen carefully. In the following article, the author not only gives you interesting information about what dictionaries do and don't do, but he also helps you evaluate dictionaries by looking at twelve different parts a good dictionary should contain.

Before you begin to read, take a moment to survey or skim over the article. It may seem long, but notice that the twelve parts of a good dictionary are numbered and in bold print as an aid in reading. The point of this practice is to read and understand how these twelve parts can help you select a good dictionary.

WHAT YOU SHOULD LOOK FOR IN A DICTIONARY

ROBERT M. PIERSON

1   First, does it describe or prescribe? Does it tell you how words *are* used or does it tell you how its compiler thinks words *should* be used? Most modern dictionaries do the former—most of the time. They are—or strive to be—objective reports of the state of the language. (The big exceptions are usage manuals and stylebooks—on which more below.) Editors of today's dictionaries may privately shudder at *presently* for *now*, at *hose* for *stockings*, at *cremains* for *ashes of people who have been cremated*, at *home* for *house*. But if Americans choose to use words so, editors are honor-bound to record that fact. The day is therefore past when you can defend the artistic effect of your use of a word by saying, "But I found it in the dictionary."

Excerpted from "A Writer's Guide to Dictionaries" by Robert M. Pierson. Originally published in *Writer's Digest*, November 1993, pp. 34–38. Reprinted by permission.

2   It was not always so. In centuries past, dictionaries existed primarily to establish and maintain good French—or whatever. Sometimes the motive was to replace Latin (a nearly frozen language) with something just as stable and "classic"; sometimes, to make one dialect (that of the capital?) supreme; sometimes, to encourage the use of a national language (as opposed to that of a foreign oppressor). Times have indeed changed.

3   Not that today's dictionaries are completely value-free. They identify some uses as slang, some as obsolete, some as dialectal, some as illiterate—and some words as taboo, even offensive. But even here they strive to explain how society in general views words, not how *the dictionaries* view them. They are not saying that it is "bad" to use *smashed* for *drunk*—only that most people will regard *smashed* as an informal way of putting it. Only you and your editor can decide whether, in a particular situation, you should write *smashed* or *drunk*—or *blotto* or *feeling no pain* or *intoxicated* or *inebriated* or *under the influence* (without, perhaps, saying of what!).

4   Some other points to note in dictionaries:

1. **Their scope.** Are they *general* or are they in some way *specialized*? Do they cover the language as a whole or are they in some way limited? Do they, for example, cover new words only? or slang only? or only the special vocabulary of science—or of one particular science? As a writer, you will surely want a general dictionary—plus one or more specialized ones, depending on your interests.

2. **Their scale** (a result of their *degree of selectivity*). Are they more or less complete—*unabridged*—or are they selective—*abridged*? If the latter, is abridgement a matter of less information about the same number of words or a matter of the same amount of information about fewer words—or, as is usually the case, mostly the latter but with some of the former? As a writer you may, deep in your heart, want an unabridged dictionary, plus a revolving stand to mount it on. You will probably find that an abridged dictionary designated, in its title, as "college" or "collegiate" will meet your needs well enough—and with less pain to your wallet and your arm muscles. If you can afford to do so, get two such dictionaries and, when a problem arises, compare what they have to say.

3. **Their intended readership.** Are they for children or for adults? If for adults, for adults of what level of sophistication? Again, the "collegiate" dictionaries will probably best suit you as a writer: They will give you not only *the* meaning of each word they list but also other meanings, with labels to alert you to how words are likely to be received. They will also tell you a little about the origins and histories of the words they list.

4. **Their overall arrangement.** Basically, are they in one alphabetical sequence or in several? Opinions differ as to which way is best. Should place-names be in a separate list? What about personal names? foreign words widely used in English? abbreviations? How about new words and new uses of old words? Some dictionaries merge all categories into (as information scientists say) one file. Others lift out one or more categories and file them separately. The best solution, so far as users of dictionaries are concerned, is to look, first of all, at each dictionary's table of contents. And once you are within an alphabetical sequence, remember what I said before about word-by-word, letter-by-letter, and keyword-by-keyword alphabetizing. Remember, too, that *Mc* and *Mac* names may be filed as spelled, filed separately, or all filed as if spelled *Mac* (which is how most library catalogs do it, by the way). Again, don't struggle to remember which system is used: just be ready to shift gears.

5. **The order in which they list multiple definitions.** Here are two main sequences: "historical" sequence, with oldest extant uses defined first, newest last; and "frequence" sequence, with most common first, least common last. Historical sequence tends to be featured in Merriam-Webster titles; frequency, in most others. As a writer, you must be aware of all the ways in which the words you use *may* be understood, so always read the whole entry. Just bear in mind that the first meaning listed may or may not be the only most likely to come to mind.

6. **The readability of their definitions.** One of the attractive features of the *American Heritage* titles is their sheer readability. Occasionally, if the editors of dictionaries are not watchful, circular definitions, which leave you where you were, creep in—e.g., [calling] a *prosthesis* a *prosthetic appliance.* Sometimes definitions will seem duskier than the words they are said to illumine. On the other hand, dictionaries tend to be brief—and who said brevity always leads to clarity? If dictionary editors spun out their definitions to make them more readable, their products would weigh and cost much more. Still and all, try looking up some words in fields you know a *little* about and see how they read: if you look up words you already know a lot about, you may "read in" meaning not provided by their definitions; and if you look up totally unfamiliar words, you will be in no position to judge. Either way, try not to mistake oversimplification for genuine clarity: sure, it's "readable" to call an apricot "a delicious fruit of a pale creamy pinky yellow," but would not that definition apply equally well to nectarines and some grapefruits?

7. **Their labeling of meanings and uses.** As suggested earlier, it is helpful to know that *braces* in the sense of *suspenders* is British, as is *suspender* in the sense of *garter*—that in botanical usage, the Irish potato is a *stem*, strawberry not essentially a *fruit*, and a tomato only a *berry!* The constant reminder as to what is *standard* (unlabeled) and what is not really keep us on our toes—as writers. Not that labeling is always perfect: one dictionary I reviewed several years ago carefully labeled racial and religious slurs as offensive, e.g., *nigger* and *kike*, but did not so label *broad* ("woman") and *queer* ("homosexual")—surely just as offensive to those to whom the words are applied—although just possibly, I grant, those particular words are not always *intended* to be offensive. But surely that is just the point. As writers, we need to express ourselves, yes, choosing the words that most exactly say—to us—what we mean; but if we are to communicate successfully, we must also think of how our words are likely to be received, regardless of our intentions. Hence the usefulness of labels. By the way, the American Heritage titles are particularly strong in respect to usage, with more concerning the "social status" of words than you find in other general dictionaries.

8. **What they may tell words besides their meanings.** Pronunciation, syllabification, grammatical inflections (plurals, past tense forms, etc.), origins and histories—and, of course, spelling! [A]ll these are likely to be indicated in "collegiate" dictionaries. Often the presentation of this material is extremely condensed and literally hard to read: I know one dictionary whose print is so small and so dull that it is hard to tell whether the little marks between syllables are only raised periods (meaning, in that dictionary, syllabic division) or actual hyphens (meaning to spell with hyphens). In an age when we are encouraged to read faster and faster, you may need to slow down, as if reading the thorniest Rossetti or Hopkins sonnet! And to be sure to study the system of symbols used—e.g., > for "derived from" and the "schwa" (ə) for the "uh" sound—and abbreviations too, like O.F. for "Old French." There may well be a key at the bottom of the page. Just don't assume that every new dictionary—or dictionary new to you—is, in this respect, like one you are used to.

9. **Their references to related words.** Often defining a word precisely is very difficult. One solution to that problem is to refer to words of more or less similar meaning (from *awkward* to *clumsy*, from *rude* to *boorish*, from *immaculate* to *clean*) or to words of opposite meaning (from *calm* to *agitated*, from *mellifluous* to *harsh*). The more a dictionary does this—and the more it explains subtle differences—the better for you as a writer. Sensitivity to such matters will give your writing precision.

10. **Their use of examples—including quotations—to clarify meaning.** These may be "made-up" illustrations of their usage or they may be quotations from published material. If the latter, observe their age. As a reader of old and new material, you may be helped by a quotation from the Bible or from Shakespeare. As a writer, you may be more helped by a quotation from *TIME* or *Natural History* or *Organic Gardening*. In any case, quotations—giving words in context—may hint at shades of meaning exceedingly difficult to convey otherwise.

11. **Their use of graphics, especially line drawings.** Again, the more the better—to label the parts of a Greek column, for instance, or the components of a threshing machine. I do not share the view that a picture is always worth a thousand words, but sometimes a picture can do what dozens of words fail to do—at least as you and I use them.

12. **The presence of encyclopedic information.** In theory, a dictionary is a word book; an encyclopedia, a subject-matter book. When you define *grizzly bear* so as to make it clear how grizzlies differ, basically, from American black bears, you are doing only what dictionaries traditionally do; when you tell what they feed on (cow parsnips, I am told) and how many are left—and go on to mention a good book on the subject—you are doing, in addition, what encyclopedias do. Some dictionaries go very far along this line, even to the point of giving lists of chemical elements, evolutionary trees for animals and plants and languages, maps of continents, rules of grammar and punctuation, even the text of the Constitution—you name it; some dictionary—some "word book"—will provide it. And when you get into specialized subject dictionaries, the tendency is even more marked—with *dictionary* used to designate just about any book featuring alphabetical sequence. When it comes to selecting a general English-language dictionary of "desk size," my advice is this: don't buy a book on the basis of bonus features unless you really need the bonus features. How much space do you have for other books? Do you already own an encyclopedia? How far do you live from the public library?

5   My advice, then, is this: Get to know your dictionaries. Look at *all* their parts—including those little appendices and supplements at the back. Imagine how you might use what you find. Keep your dictionaries at hand, and form the habit of consulting them often. And read them for pleasure. Though not set up for consecutive reading, as are novels and treatises, they can be read in much the same way. Read in them again and again—and note your findings, whether in your "writer's journal," on note cards for orderly filing, or in that secret file at the back of your mind. Save all these bits and pieces. You never know when they will rise to the surface for you to hook them. They will be there "for you," like old friends, to enrich your creative output; to help you say what you mean, not just something close; to help you convey a sense of truth-telling, not of weary echoing of the thoughts and feelings of others; to help give your writing the sheen, the glow, the magic that we, all of us, strive for but so seldom achieve, let alone sustain.

Comprehension Check

Directions: Answer the following questions without looking back.

1. Some of the examples Pierson uses are words that have changed common meanings since he wrote this article. He says *stockings* would be preferred over *hose,* yet *hose* sounds more current to us. What is one other current term for this piece of clothing? _____

    The following are some of the points the author says to note when looking for a good dictionary. Explain briefly what he means by each:

2. scope _____

    _____

3. scale _____

    _____

4. intended readership _____

    _____

5. overall arrangement _____

    _____

6. What is one of the two ways some dictionaries list multiple definitions? _____

    _____

7. Explain what the author means by circular definitions. _____

    _____

8. According to Pierson, if a Merriam-Webster dictionary lists several definitions of a word, the first definition is the

    a. oldest

    b. most common

    c. slang definition

9. T/F Good dictionaries have more graphics or pictures.

10. T/F The author believes all dictionaries are basically the same.

Vocabulary Check

Directions: Define the following underlined words from the selection.

1. First, does it describe or <u>prescribe</u>? Does it tell you how words *are* used or does it tell you how its compiler thinks words *should* be used? (paragraph 1)_____

    _____

2. Not that today's dictionaries are completely value-free. They identify some uses as slang, some as <u>obsolete</u> . . . (paragraph 3) _____

    _____

3. Only you and your editor can decide whether, in a particular situation, you should write *smashed* for *drunk*—or *blotto or feeling no pain* or . . . <u>inebriated</u> (paragraph 3)

_____

4. Are they more or less complete <u>unabridged</u> or are they selective—*abridged*? (point #2) _____

5. Try not to mistake oversimplification for genuine <u>clarity</u>. (point #6) _____

6. One dictionary I reviewed several years ago carefully labeled racial and religious slurs as <u>offensive</u> . . . (point #7) _____

7. Pronunciation, syllabication, <u>grammatical inflections</u> (plurals, past tense forms, etc.) are all likely to be indicated in collegiate dictionaries. (point #8) _____

_____

8. Often the presentation of this material is extremely <u>condensed</u> and literally hard to read. (point #8) _____

9. One solution to that problem is to refer to words of more or less similar meaning (from *awkward* to *clumsy*, from *rude* to <u>boorish</u>). (point #9)_____

10. Look at *all* their parts—including those little <u>appendices</u> and supplements at the back. (final paragraph) _____

Record the results of the comprehension and vocabulary checks on the Student Record Chart in the Appendix. Each correct answer for both checks is worth 10 points for a total of 100 points possible for comprehension and 100 points for vocabulary.

Remember to make vocabulary cards for any words that gave you trouble.

Application 4: Evaluating Your Own Dictionary

Evaluate the dictionary you currently use according to any six of the twelve criteria for evaluating dictionaries in Robert Pierson's article. Briefly explain what this shows you about your personal dictionary that you didn't know before. Turn in your evaluation and explanation.

Other "Word Banks"

While a good dictionary is most often used to look up new or unfamiliar words, other "word banks" can be useful under certain circumstances.

A Thesaurus

While the dictionary contains definitions and the meanings for words, a thesaurus contains synonyms and antonyms for certain words. These may not be exact definitions of a word, but words that are closely related. For instance, if you look up the word *abnormal*, a definition for the adjective might read "unusual or unexpected, especially in a way that causes alarm or anxiety." However, looking up the same word in a thesaurus might offer the synonyms *unnatural, atypical, unusual, irregular, aberrant, deviant, uncommon, odd, eccentric,* and many more. Not all words would fit the context in which the word *abnormal* is being used. If someone's pulse is abnormal, it would be incorrect to use *deviant, aberrant,* or *irregular* as the meaning.

A thesaurus also offers antonyms for words. In the case of *abnormal*, words such as *normal, natural, typical, regular, familiar,* and *unexceptional* might be cited.

Most computer word-processing systems have a built-in thesaurus and spell-checker. Check your toolbar for the various offerings provided. Use your cursor to highlight the word you want defined and click "Thesaurus." With most word-processing systems a pop-up sidebar appears on the screen and provides you with a definition or synonym.

If your computer word-processing program is not helpful, explore the following sites on the World Wide Web:

http://www.dictionary.com
http://www.yourdictionary.com
http://www.bartleby.com/reference

Glossaries

Most textbooks, on academic subjects, such as psychology, biology, sociology, and history, have glossaries in the back of the book. These can be helpful because the words listed are usually a vocabulary of the subject and provide definitions that fit the way the words are used in the textbook. A dictionary is not likely to provide a definition for *Structural-functional paradigm*. But a sociology textbook's glossary would explain it as used by the sociologist.

E.   Putting It All Together

Following are two reading selections. Both are followed by comprehension and vocabulary checks; the second one is a timed reading. Increasing your ability to read well involves these three components: vocabulary, comprehension, and rate. In this chapter, you have worked primarily on the first component—vocabulary. If you don't recognize the words when you are reading, you will have a hard time understanding what you read.

You will now be asked to answer comprehension questions, too, showing that you understand the selections you are reading. Much of this book will be devoted to increasing your comprehension of what you read. The final reading is a timed reading because if you read too slowly (under 180 words per minute [wpm]), your mind may wander and comprehension may fall. The comprehension questions and timed reading in this section are primarily to help you see what your understanding and reading rate are at the beginning of the book. Your scores at this point are less important than understanding why you may have missed a question. Always make certain you understand why you may have missed any questions. Learn from your mistakes.

PRACTICE E-1: Reading Comprehension Survey

Directions: The following article by Martha Brockenbrough originally appeared as a three-part column online on MSN Encarta. Apply the skills you have learned about word prefixes and suffixes, word roots, and words in context. Mark the words that cause you comprehension difficulties so that you can look them up later.

IS *AIN'T* A WORD?

MARTHA BROCKENBROUGH

1   What makes something a word?

2   I started pondering this after pawing through the mountains of e-mails I've received since writing a Grumpy Martha column that said *irregardless* isn't a word.

3   "It is!" my detractors cry. "It's in the *dictionary!*"

4   And you know what? They're right. It is in many a dictionary, prefaced by the qualifier "nonstandard."

5   So does that make it a word, or not?

6   On my grumpier days, I'd say no. You might as well hollow out two loaves of bread and put them on your feet, because what you'd have then would be a pair of nonstandard loafers. If you like the looks you get when you walk down the street in them, then great! It's your loaf to live.

7   On giddier days, though, I take delight in the flexibility of our language and the creativity of nonstandard word usage.

8   I liked it, for example, when my daughter called cinnamon buns *bottoms*. And when *bling bling* made it Into the dictionary, I said, "Awww yeaahhhhh!" I am personally lobbying for the inclusion of *frathlete*, a noun that refers to that class of good-looking jock who can sometimes be irritatingly popular.

9   So word nerds fall into two basic camps: prescriptive and descriptive. The prescriptives are the grumpy ones, who insist on proper usage. The descriptive camp, on the other hand, observes how people actually use words, because actual usage drives meaning.

10   So which am I? And more importantly, which are you?

11   **Personality quiz: Are you prescriptive *or* descriptive?**

   1. True or false: *Irregardless* is a word, irregardless of how many people say otherwise.
   2. True or false: Homer Simpson's catch phrase—d'oh—belongs in the dictionary.
   3. True or false: Don't bother me. I'm putting bread on my feet.

12   If you answered true to two or more of these, you're a descriptive. If you answered false, you're a prescriptive. And I have some bad news for you: *D'oh* has been in the prestigious *Oxford English Dictionary* for about five years now. (It's not in Encarta's dictionary—d'oh!)

13   Either way, there would be room for you in the exclusive club of worldwide lexicographers. As Encarta's own Richard Bready puts it, "Descriptive lexicographers don't judge words, they only report them, using standards of frequency and importance."

http://encarta.msn.com/encnet/Features/Columns/?article=aint

14   On the other hand, "Prescriptive lexicographers seem, in my personal view, to enjoy being grumpy. They spend a lot of time denouncing words and explaining what the rules used to be."

15   This could be why French, with its persnickety language police, has a declining number of users, Bready says. If language doesn't evolve with the people who use it, people find other ways of saying things.

16   Suddenly I find myself ready to ditch the grumpy attitude. When you look at it his way, being descriptive sounds like a whole lot more fun—especially when you learn how words get into the dictionary. Believe it or not, this can be a good excuse to watch TV.

17   OK, so it's not an excuse to watch TV all the time.

18   Despite Homer Simpson's success with *d'oh*, neologisms don't come only from the television set. (And, giving credit where credit is due, many credit Homer's *d'oh* to a longer *dohhhhh* sound uttered by a character in Laurel and Hardy movies.)

19   In addition to perusing TV and movie scripts, lexicographers listen to the radio and scour books, newspapers, and magazines for new words, or for old words used in fresh ways.

20   At the *Oxford English Dictionary*, a team puts words into a database of dictionary candidates. They look at how many times a word appears, where it appears, and how long it has been in use. A word can't be a bling in the pan and be immortalized in the dictionary. Unless, of course, that word is *bling bling*, which joined the *OED* in 2003. It can take five years (with five mentions in five publications) for a word to make the grade.

21   To compile the *Oxford American Dictionary*, the staff considers the more-than-200-million entries in the *OED*. Then they add in the American National Corpus, a growing database that will someday contain more than 100 million American words. And to that huge pile of words, they add the gems unearthed by its team of lexicographers, says their leader Erin McKean, a witty and bespectacled thirtysomething who is a combination of queen and rock star in the world of lexicographers.

22   McKean also wants to draft word-loving civilians into the hunt. An online submission form for neologisms is in the works, and in the meantime, you can send your favorite new words (and old ones used in new ways) to dictionaries@oup.com.

23   Even if the new usages you've discovered are nonstandard, descriptive lexicographers such as McKean are interested in them.

24   "We put nonstandard words in the dictionary, and label them as such, because people are curious about these words, and because they're part of the English language," McKean says. "I like to say that the dictionary is like a map of the language. You would not use a map that put a fuzzy gray area where the red-light district was, would you?"

25   McKean also contends that including offbeat or misused words is useful. People get a fuller picture of our language, along with the warning to enter that region with caution.

26   This doesn't mean that the funny word you invent has a shot at being the next *bling bling*. McKean was pretty lukewarm, for example, about *frathlete*, dismissing it gently as "a bit ephemeral."

27   I say it's only as short-lived as the feelings of rampant insecurity the rest of us feel) when in the presence of handsome and popular jocks. But maybe she's right. Maybe I should just get over high school already. (And I will, I promise, but not before trying my best to get *frathlete* onto an episode of *The OC*, since these lexicographers now admit to watching TV just like the rest of us.)

28   There's even a way of predicting how likely I am to succeed in sneaking a new word into the lexicon.

29   In a book called *Predicting New Words: The Secrets of Their Success*, Allan Metcalf identifies five factors that separate words with staying power from those that curl up and die from disuse, like *Y2K*.

30   Metcalf, a professor of English at MacMurray College in Jacksonville, Illinois, says a new word must appear frequently. It has to be unobtrusive, it has to be used widely, it has to generate new forms and meanings, and it has to endure.

31   Where *frathlete* is most likely to fail is that it's not exactly unobtrusive. In fact, it's as conspicuous as gleaming white teeth, thick hair, and a letterman's jacket. But it can generate new forms, such as *frathletic*. And, as the lingering popularity of *Grease* will tell you, the phenomenon will endure.

Who has contributed the most words? Shakespeare? Or screwups?

32   It would be hard to imagine any one person contributing more words to the English language than Shakespeare. He gave us about 2,000 words, and many phrases that were fresh when he penned them but have since become trite.

33   On the whole, language numskulls have created many more words out of the thin air of their ignorance. Oops. There goes my natural grumpiness. Looks like I'll have to work on that some more. Ahem.

34   It used to be that we had a word for someone who made us want to puke. That word was *nauseous*, which used to mean sickening to think about. But then, people started saying that when they meant that they felt sick to their stomachs. They meant to say they were nauseated. But now, we've lost that fine distinction. The whole thing would nauseate me if I hadn't sworn off grumpiness just a few sentences back.

35   And in all fairness, it's not just plain Joes who sometimes screw up their words. The dictionary can be wrong, too. Take the case of the mysterious word *dord*.

36   A word that supposedly meant *density*, *dord* appeared in *The Webster's Dictionary* in 1934. No one noticed for five years, when a hurried correction had to be made. What happened, it turns out, was that a chemistry consultant had written a small note that read "D or d." Those letters stood for abbreviations of the word *density*. But it got mixed in with the words, instead of with the abbreviations, and was typed up that way instead.

37   I'm sure that person felt plagued by their own dord for making such a slip, even though it was a pretty good word. But, sadly, it never caught on, and by 1940 it was no longer included in *Webster's*, which is kind of a pity. Perhaps it could gain new life with the definition: a word for something that was never meant to be.

38   As I see it, that ain't a half bad idea. And neither is using the word *ain't* in the correct, informal context, McKean told me. So before you go firing off e-mail telling me I ain't right in doing that, send McKean your favorite neologisms. Who knows? You might just make it into the dictionary.

Comprehension Check

Directions: Answer the following questions without looking back.

1. Which of the following best states the main idea of the article?

   a. to show that words in a dictionary are either prescriptive or descriptive.

   b. to discuss how words are considered and selected for listing in a dictionary.

   c. to determine whether or not *ain't* is a word that should be in a dictionary.

d. to show how the author wants to get *frathlete* in the dictionary.

e. none of the above

2. Which of the following sources do lexicographers use to find new words or words used in new ways?

   a. television and movie scripts

   b. radio

   c. books

   d. newspapers and magazines

   e. all of the above

3. T/F Descriptive lexicographers don't judge words, they only report them, using standards of frequency and importance.

4. T/F There are over 200 million word entries in the Oxford English Dictionary.

5. Some day, the Oxford American Dictionary will contain _____

   _____

6. Who is Erin McKean? _____

7. T/F Shakespeare gave the English language about 2,000 new words and phrases.

8. T/F It is possible for you to submit new words or old words using new meanings to lexicographers for consideration as dictionary entries.

   _____

9. For a new word to appear in a dictionary it must contain five factors: appear frequently, be unobtrusive, used widely, generate new forms and meanings, and

   _____

10. What word appeared in a dictionary by mistake? _____

   For every question you missed, find the place in the article that contains the correct answer. Try to determine why you missed the questions you did.

Vocabulary Check

Directions: Select from the right-hand column the best definition for each word from the article in the left-hand column. Write the letter of the best definition next to the word.

_____	1. ponder	a. make famous, celebrate
_____	2. lobby	b. important, impressive
_____	3. prestigious	c. think about
_____	4. evolve	d. reading carefully
_____	5. perusing	e. wearing glasses
_____	6. immortalize	f. unhappy
_____	7. bespectacled	g. recently made up words
_____	8. ephemeral	h. try to influence
_____	9. rampant	i. short-lived, fleeting
_____	10. neologisms	j. out of control, widespread
		k. change, grow, advance

Record the results of the comprehension and vocabulary checks on the Student Record Chart in the Appendix. Each correct answer is worth 10 points, for a total of 100 points possible for comprehension and 100 points for vocabulary.

PRACTICE E-2: Timed Reading

Directions: This is your first chance to see what your current reading rate is. Remember that your current rate is not as important as understanding why you are reading at that rate and how it helps or hinders you. If you read too slowly (approximately below 180 wpm), keeping your concentration on the reading will be difficult. If you read too quickly and can't answer the questions, you are reading fast but with no comprehension. You want to read this first timed reading at a rate that is fast enough to feel slightly forced but slow enough to understand what you read.

Begin timing:_____

IN PRAISE OF THE F WORD

MARY SHERRY

1   Tens of thousands of 18-year-olds will graduate this year and be handed meaningless diplomas. These diplomas won't look any different from those awarded their luckier classmates. Their validity will be questioned only when their employers discover that these graduates are semiliterate.

2   Eventually a fortunate few will find their way into educational-repair shops— adult-literacy programs, such as the one where I teach basic grammar and writing. There, high-school graduates and high-school dropouts pursuing graduate-equivalency certificates will learn the skills they should have learned in school. They will also discover they have been cheated by our educational system.

3   As I teach, I learn a lot about our schools. Early in each session I ask my students to write about an unpleasant experience they had in school. No writers' block here! "I wish someone would have had made me stop doing drugs and made me study." "I liked to party and no one seemed to care." "I was a good kid and didn't cause any trouble, so they just passed me along even though I didn't read well and couldn't write." And so on.

4   I am your basic do-gooder, and prior to teaching this class I blamed the poor academic skills our kids have today on drugs, divorce, and other impediments to concentration necessary for doing well in school. But, as I rediscover each time I walk into the classroom, before a teacher can expect students to concentrate, he or she has to get their attention, no matter what distractions may be at hand. There are many ways to do this, and they have much to do with teaching style. However, if style alone won't do it, there is another way to show who holds the winning hand in the classroom. That is to reveal the trump card of failure.

Reprinted by permission of Mary Sherry, as published in *Newsweek*, May 6, 1991.

5   I will never forget a teacher who played that card to get the attention of one of my children. Our youngest, a world-class charmer, did little to develop his intellectual talents but always got by. Until Mrs. Stifter.

6   Our son was a high-school senior when he had her for English. "He sits in the back of the room talking to his friends," she told me. "Why don't you move him to the front row?" I urged, believing the embarrassment would get him to settle down. Mrs. Stifter looked at me steely-eyed over her glasses. "I don't move seniors," she said. "I flunk them." I was flustered. Our son's academic life flashed before my eyes. No teacher had ever threatened him with that before. I regained my composure and managed to say that I thought she was right. By the time I got home I was feeling pretty good about this. It was a radical approach for these times, but, well, why not? "She's going to flunk you," I told my son. I did not discuss it any further. Suddenly English became a priority in his life. He finished out the semester with an A.

7   I know one example doesn't make a case, but at night I see a parade of students who are angry and resentful for having been passed along until they could no longer even pretend to keep up. Of average intelligence or better, they eventually quit school, concluding they were too dumb to finish. "I should have been held back" is a comment I hear frequently. Even sadder are those students who are high-school graduates who say to me after a few weeks of class, "I don't know how I ever got a high-school diploma."

8   Passing students who have not mastered the work cheats them and the employers who expect graduates to have basic skills. We excuse this dishonest behavior by saying kids can't learn if they come from terrible environments. No one seems to stop to think that—no matter what environments they come from—most kids don't put school first on their list unless they perceive something is at stake. They'd rather be sailing.

9   Many students I see at night could give expert testimony on unemployment, chemical dependency, abusive relationships. In spite of these difficulties, they have decided to make education a priority. They are motivated by the desire for a better job or the need to hang on to the one they've got. They have a healthy fear of failure.

10   People of all ages can rise above their problems, but they need to have a reason to do so. Young people generally don't have the maturity to value education in the same way my adult students value it. But fear of failure, whether economic or academic, can motivate both.

11   Flunking as a regular policy has just as much merit today as it did two generations ago. We must review the threat of flunking and see it as it really is—a positive teaching tool. It is an expression of confidence by both teachers and parents that the students have the ability to learn the material presented to them. However, making it work again would take a dedicated, caring conspiracy between teachers and parents. It would mean facing the tough reality that passing kids who haven't learned the material—while it might save them grief for the short term—dooms them to long-term illiteracy. It would mean that teachers would have to follow through on their threats, and parents would have to stand behind them, knowing their children's best interests are indeed at stake. This means no more doing Scott's assignments for him because he might fail. No more passing Jodi because she's such a nice kid.

12   This is a policy that worked in the past and can work today. A wise teacher, with the support of his parents, gave our son the opportunity to succeed—or fail. It's time we return this choice to all students.

Finish Timing: Record time here: _____ and use the Timed Reading Conversion Chart in the Appendix to figure your rate: _____ wpm.

Comprehension Check

Directions: Answer the following questions without looking back.

1.   What is the author's main point? _____
     _____
     _____

2.   What does the author mean by the term *educational-repair shops?* _____
     _____
     _____

3.   T/F   The author is a high school English teacher.

4.   Before teaching her present classes, on what things did she blame the poor academic skills of students? _____
     _____

5.   What does she now feel is a major cause of poor academic performance by students?
     _____
     _____
     _____

6.   What, according to the author, is wrong with passing students who have not mastered the course work? _____
     _____
     _____

7.   Most of the author's students have what she calls a "healthy fear of failure." What does she mean? _____
     _____
     _____
     _____

8.   T/F   The author feels that most young people generally don't have the maturity to value education the way adults do.

9.   Why does the author believe flunking students as a regular policy has merit? _____
     _____
     _____
     _____

10.   What does she feel it would take to make her policy work? _____
     _____
     _____
     _____

For every question you missed, find the place in the article that contains the correct answer. Try to determine why you missed the questions you did. If you read faster than you normally do, a score of 60 percent correct is considered good. As you get used to faster speeds, your comprehension scores will improve.

Vocabulary Check

Part A

Directions: Define the following underlined words or phrases from the selection.

1. their <u>validity</u> will be questioned (paragraph 1)

    _____

2. drugs, divorce, and other <u>impediments</u> to concentration (paragraph 4)

    _____

3. don't put school first on their list unless they perceive something is at <u>stake</u> (paragraph 8)

    _____

4. a dedicated, caring <u>conspiracy</u> between teachers and parents (paragraph 11)

    _____

5. testimony on unemployment, <u>chemical dependency</u>, abusive relationships (paragraph 9)

    _____

Part B

Directions: Select from the right-hand column the best definition for each word in the left-hand column. Write the letter of the best definition next to the word.

_____	6. radical (paragraph 6)	**a.**	calmness, tranquility
_____	7. priority (paragraph 9)	**b.**	favoring extreme change
_____	8. flustered (paragraph 6)	**c.**	confused, befuddled
_____	9. steely-eyed (paragraph 6)	**d.**	something given attention over competing alternatives
_____	10. composure (paragraph 6)	**e.**	a hard or severe look

Record the results of the rate, comprehension, and vocabulary checks on the Student Record Chart in the Appendix. Each correct answer is worth 10 points, for a total of 100 points possible for comprehension and 100 points for vocabulary. An average score is around 250 wpm with 70 percent comprehension. Discuss any problems, concerns, or questions you have with your instructor.

Questions for Group Discussion

1. As mentioned on page 23, every year the *Washington* Post offers a Mensa Invitational contest which asks readers to take any word in the dictionary, alter it by adding, subtracting, or changing one letter and supplying a new definition, neologisms of a sort. As a group, discuss the following and determine what original word or words were changed. Try making up some of your own.

    intaxication: happy to get a tax refund until you realize it was your money to start with

    giraffiti: vandalism spray-painted very, very high

    inoculatte: to take coffee intravenously when running late

    caterpallor: the color you turn when you find a worm in the fruit you're eating

    reintarnation: coming back to life as a hillbilly

    Bozone: the substance surrounding stupid people that stops bright ideas from penetrating

2. As a group, discuss the differences in the ways that Malcolm X and you developed your vocabularies.

3. Discuss your reading habits. Who in the group reads the most? Who has experienced reading difficulties? Is reading a pleasure or a chore? Why?

4. As a group, decide which method of vocabulary development helps the most for class terminology you are learning right now.

5. Discuss why, as a group, you agree with Mary Sherry's view that passing students who have not mastered the course work should receive a failing grade.

6. As a group, see how many of you can use the following words in a sentence. Make certain you learn the ones you still may not be able to use or recognize by writing the definition in the blank space.

    a. compound _____

    _____

    b. emulate _____

    c. articulate _____

    d. riffling _____

    e. versatility _____

    f. composure _____

    g. inevitable _____

    h. stance _____

    i. sect _____

    _____

    j. perspicacious _____

On Your Own

Pick ten new words you learned in this chapter, not necessarily those listed in question 6, and on a separate sheet of paper write a sentence for each word, using it correctly in context. Turn in the paper to your instructor.

One last suggestion about vocabulary building: You will find an alphabetical listing of some of the most frequently used words and their definitions at http://www.nytimes.com/learning/students/wordoftheday/archive.html. It's a good reference list for you as you build your vocabulary bank of useful words.

CHAPTER TWO

Developing Literal Recall

Introducing Sherman Alexie
"Superman and Me" by Sherman Alexie

A. Finding the Topic, Main Idea, and Supporting Details

B. Reading For Main Ideas: Paragraph Patterns

C. Finding an Author's Thesis

D. Summarizing as a Way to Test Your Understanding

E. Flexible Reading Rates

F. Putting It All Together

This chapter deals with the development of literal recall, stressing reading for main ideas and supporting details, understanding paragraph patterns, and recognizing an author's thesis. Practices begin with reading and understanding paragraphs and move into longer reading passages, some from actual textbooks you might encounter in your other classes.

Chapter One stressed developing your vocabulary skills to better comprehend what you read and hear. You learned how Malcolm X developed his ability to read and speak effectively. Another way to increase vocabulary is to read widely and well. Sherman Alexie has a lot to say about books, reading, and writing in his essay that follows his introduction.

Introducing Sherman Alexie

Sherman Alexie is a Spokane/Coeur d'Alene Native American from Wellpinit, Washington, on the Spokane Indian Reservation. Alexie has published more than 200 poems, stories, and translations in many magazines and journals. He is the winner of numerous prizes and awards, including a poetry fellowship from the National Endowment of the Arts in 1992. His publications include a best-selling collection of interlinked stories, *The Lone Ranger and Tonto Fistfight in Heaven* (1993), and a novel, *Reservation Blues*, about a Native American rock band called Coyote Springs. He wrote the script for the movie *Smoke Signals*.

Simon Ortiz, a Native American writer, says this of Alexie: "His vision is an amazing celebration of endurance, intimacy, love, and creative insight. Alexie speaks for the spirit of Native American resistance, determination, and sovereignty." Prominent among the issues Alexie raises in his writing is the reconciliation of modern life with existence under the reservation system. Much of Alexie's work reflects the need and power of the imagination just to survive Indian circumstances on the reservation.

In an "On Tour" interview for *Hungry Mind Review* in which he was asked to respond to a question on the theme "Heroes and Villains," Alexie wrote:

> I've always been picky about heroes. Like most American males, I've always admired athletes, particularly basketball players....Unlike many American males, I always admired writers as much as I admired athletes. I loved books and the people who wrote books. John Steinbeck was one of my earliest heroes because he wrote about the poor. Stephen King became a hero because he wrote so well of misfit kids, the nerds and geeks. Growing up on my reservation, I was a poor geek, so I had obvious reasons to love Steinbeck and King. I still love their novels, but I have no idea if they were/are spiritual, compassionate, and gracious men. There is so much spirit, compassion, and grace in their work, I want to assume that Steinbeck and King were/are good people. I would be terribly disappointed to find out otherwise. ...
>
> Most of my heroes are just decent people. Decency is rare and underrated. I think my writing is somehow just about decency. Still, if I was keeping score, and I like to keep score, I would say the villains in the world are way ahead of the heroes. I hope my writing can help even the score.

SUPERMAN AND ME

SHERMAN ALEXIE

1   I learned to read with a *Superman* comic book. Simple enough, I suppose. I cannot recall which particular *Superman* comic book I read, nor can I remember which villain he fought in that issue. I cannot remember the plot, nor the means by which I obtained the comic book. What I can remember is this: I was three years old, a Spokane Indian boy living with his family on the Spokane Indian Reservation in eastern Washington state. We were poor by most standards, but one of my parents usually managed to find some minimum-wage job or another, which made us middle class by reservation standards. I had a brother and three sisters. We lived on a combination of irregular pay-checks, hope, fear, and government-surplus food.

2   My father, who is one of the few Indians who went to Catholic school on purpose, was an avid reader of westerns, spy thrillers, murder mysteries, gangster epics, basketball-player biographies, and anything else he could find. He bought his books by the pound at Dutch's Pawn Shop, Goodwill, Salvation Army, and Value Village. When he had extra money, he bought new novels at supermarkets, convenience stores, and hospital gift shops. Our house was filled with books. They were stacked in crazy piles in the bathroom, bedrooms, and living room. In a fit of unemployment-inspired creative energy, my father built a set of bookshelves and soon filled them with a random assortment of books about the Kennedy assassination, Watergate, the Vietnam War, and the entire twenty-three-book series of the Apache westerns. My father loved books, and since I loved my father with an aching devotion, I decided to love books as well.

3   I can remember picking up my father's books before I could read. The words themselves were mostly foreign, but I still remember the exact moment when I first understood, with a sudden clarity, the purpose of a paragraph. I didn't have the vocabulary to say "paragraph," but I realized that a paragraph was a fence that held words. The words inside a paragraph worked together for a common purpose. They had some specific reason for being inside the same fence. This knowledge delighted me. I began to think of everything in terms of paragraphs. Our reservation was a small paragraph within the United States. My family's house was a paragraph, distinct from the other paragraphs of the LeBrets to the north, the Fords to our south, and the Tribal School to the west. Inside our house, each family member existed as a separate paragraph, but still had genetics and common experiences to link us. Now, using this logic, I can see my changed family as an essay of seven paragraphs: mother, father, older brother, the deceased sister, my younger twin sisters, and our adopted little brother.

4   At the same time I was seeing the world in paragraphs, I also picked up that *Superman* comic book. Each panel, complete with picture, dialogue, and narrative, was a three-dimensional paragraph. In one panel, Superman breaks through a door. His suit is red, blue, and yellow. The brown door shatters into many pieces. I look at the narrative above the picture. I cannot read the words, but I assume it tells me that Superman is breaking down the door. Aloud, I pretend to read the words and say, "Superman is breaking down the door." Words, dialogue, also float out of Superman's mouth. Because he is breaking down the door, I assume he says, "I am breaking down

the door." Once again, I pretend to read the words and say aloud, "I am breaking down the door." In this way, I learned to read.

5   This might be an interesting story all by itself. A little Indian boy teaches himself to read at an early age and advances quickly. He reads *Grapes of Wrath* in kindergarten when other children are struggling through Dick and Jane. If he'd been anything but an Indian boy living on the reservation, he might have been called a prodigy. But he is an Indian boy living on the reservation, and is simply an oddity. He grows into a man who often speaks of his childhood in the third person, as if it will somehow dull the pain and make him sound more modest about his talents.

6   A smart Indian is a dangerous person, widely feared and ridiculed by Indians and non-Indians alike. I fought with my classmates on a daily basis. They wanted me to stay quiet when the non-Indian teacher asked for answers, for volunteers, for help. We were Indian children who were expected to be stupid. Most lived up to those expectations inside the classroom, but subverted them on the outside. They struggled with basic reading in school, but could remember how to sing a few dozen powwow songs. They were monosyllabic in front of their non-Indian teachers, but could tell complicated stories and jokes at the dinner table. They submissively ducked their heads when confronted by a non-Indian adult, but would slug it out with the Indian bully who was ten years older. As Indian children, we were expected to fail in the non-Indian world. Those who failed were ceremonially accepted by other Indians and appropriately pitied by non-Indians.

7   I refused to fail. I was smart. I was arrogant. I was lucky. I read books late into the night, until I could barely keep my eyes open. I read books at recess, then during lunch, and in the few minutes left after I had finished my classroom assignments. I read books in the car when my family traveled to powwows or basketball games. In shopping malls, I ran to the bookstores and read bits and pieces of as many books as I could. I read the books my father brought home from the pawnshops and secondhand stores. I read the books I borrowed from the library. I read the backs of cereal boxes. I read the newspaper. I read the bulletins posted on the walls of the school, the clinic, the tribal offices, the post office. I read junk mail. I read auto-repair manuals. I read magazines. I read anything that had words and paragraphs. I read with equal parts joy and desperation. I loved those books, but I also knew that love had only one purpose. I was trying to save my life.

8   Despite all the books I read, I am still surprised I became a writer. I was going to be a pediatrician. These days, I write novels, short stories, and poems. I visit schools and teach creative writing to Indian kids. In all my years in the reservation school system, I was never taught how to write poetry, short stories, or novels. I was certainly never taught that Indians wrote poetry, short stories, and novels. Writing was something beyond Indians. I cannot recall a single time that a guest teacher visited the reservation. There must have been visiting teachers. Who were they? Where are they now? Do they exist? I visit the schools as often as possible. The Indian kids crowd the classroom. Many are writing their own poems, short stories, and novels. They have read my books. They have read many other books. They look at me with bright eyes and arrogant wonder. They are trying to save their lives. Then there are the sullen and already defeated Indian kids who sit in the back rows and ignore me with theatrical precision. The pages of their notebooks are empty. They carry neither pencil nor pen. They stare out the window. They refuse and resist. "Books," I say to them. "Books," I say. I throw my weight against their locked doors. The door holds. I am smart. I am arrogant. I am lucky. I am trying to save our lives.

COMPREHENSION CHECK

Directions: Answer the following questions without looking back.

1. What is unusual about the author's reading of the *Superman* comic book? _____

    _____

2. The author of this story was raised

    a. in a variety of homes as the family moved.

    b. on a Spokane Indian reservation in Washington state.

    c. in a suburb of Washington, D.C.

    d. in a wealthy family.

3. T / F His father's favorite books were westerns.

4. How was the author's love of books related to his love of his father? _____

    _____

5. When the author first understood the purpose of a paragraph, what did he compare it to? _____ _____ _____

    _____

6. His memory of reading in kindergarten involves reading

    a. *Dick and Jane* books.

    b. *Superman* comic books.

    c. a wide variety of books.

    d. *Grapes of Wrath*.

7. How did being an early and good reader affect his relationship with other Indian students? _____ _____

8. So many of the Indian children failed at school. Why does Alexie feel he didn't fail? _____ _____ _____

9. Why does the author teach creative writing to Indian kids? _____

    _____

    _____

10. In your opinion, how is the author's love of books related to his love of writing?

    _____

    _____

VOCABULARY CHECK

Directions: Define the following underlined words from the selection.

1. My father was an <u>avid</u> reader of westerns, spy thrillers, murder mysteries, gangster epics, . . . and anything else he could find. _____

2. I cannot recall which particular *Superman* comic book I read, nor can I remember which <u>villain</u> he fought in that issue. _____

3. My father loved books, and since I loved my father with an <u>aching</u> devotion, I decided to love books as well. _____

4. Each family member existed as a separate paragraph, but still had <u>genetics</u> and common experiences to link us. _____

5. Each panel of the *Superman* comic book, complete with picture, dialogue, and <u>narrative</u>, was a three-dimensional paragraph. _____

6. If he'd been anything but an Indian boy living on the reservation, he might have been called a <u>prodigy</u>. _____

7. Most Indian children lived up to these expectations inside the classroom, but <u>subverted</u> them on the outside. _____

8. They <u>submissively</u> ducked their heads when confronted by a non-Indian adult, but would slug it out with the Indian bully who was ten years older. _____

9. I refused to fail. I was smart. I was <u>arrogant</u>. _____

10. Then there are the <u>sullen</u> and already defeated Indian kids who sit in the back rows and ignore me with theatrical precision. _____

Record the results of the comprehension and vocabulary checks on the Student Record Chart in the Appendix. Each correct answer for both checks is worth 10 points for a total of 100 points possible for comprehension and 100 points for vocabulary.

Remember to make vocabulary cards for any words that gave you trouble.

A.   Finding the Topic, Main Idea, and Supporting Details

One of the keys to good reading comprehension is the ability to distinguish between the **topic**, the **main idea**, and the details used to **support** the main idea.

Finding the Paragraph's Topic

All well-written paragraphs are made up of sentences dealing with a particular subject or idea called a **topic**. The topic is simply what the paragraph is about. Read the following paragraph looking for the topic.

> We believe that there are three good reasons for you to learn to argue about literature. First, the term **argument** refers to a kind of talk as well as a kind of writing; thus, focusing on this term can help you relate your own written work to discussions in class. Second, you will read a work of literature with greater direction and purpose if you are working toward the goal of constructing arguments about it. Finally, when you argue, you learn a lot, because you have to ponder things you may have taken for granted as well as things unfamiliar to you. (From John Schilb and John Clifford, *Ways of Making Literature Matter*, Bedford/St. Martin's, 2001, p.14.)

With phrases such as "learn to argue," "the term **argument**," and "constructing arguments," it is fairly clear that the paragraph's topic has to do with argument, more specifically learning to argue about literature. But what's the point? Why learn to argue about literature?

Finding the Main Idea

The main idea is the point the author is trying to make about the topic—in this case, learning to argue about literature. The first sentence best expresses the main idea of the paragraph: "We believe that there are three good reasons for you to learn to argue about literature." The sentences that follow support the main idea by stating the "three good reasons."

Recognizing a Topic Sentence

When an author states the main idea of a paragraph, as above, it is called a **topic sentence**. A topic sentence can appear anywhere in a paragraph depending on the writer's method of paragraph development. You'll learn more about paragraph patterns later on. For now, read the following paragraph, identify the topic, and see if the main idea appears in any one sentence.

> Irresponsible drinking on the part of college students is not new. But it has gotten even more serious among today's college students. A recent study at 113 colleges and universities reports that alcohol abuse is responsible for 64 percent of campus incidents of violent behavior, 42 percent of physical injuries, two-thirds of all property damage, and close to 40 percent of both emotional and academic difficulties.

What is the topic of the paragraph? _____

_____

What is the main idea of the paragraph? _____

_____

In what sentence is the main idea stated? _____

_____

If you said the topic of the paragraph is college students, you're partly correct. More specifically, the topic is alcohol abuse among college students. The main idea is that alcohol abuse among college students has gotten worse. The topic sentence is the second sentence. The first sentence helps establish the topic, but it's the second sentence that best states the main idea regarding the growing seriousness of alcohol abuse among today's college students.

Here's another example. Read the following paragraph looking for the topic, the main idea, and the placement of the topic sentence.

> "The first time I applied to college," said Jeff Dinlay of Raleigh, North Carolina, "I figured that one place was as good as another. So I applied to three state universities because the applications were easy to fill out. I was accepted at only one of them, so that didn't give me much of a choice. Still, I went off with the unrealistic expectation that by just being in college, I'd become an educated person. I got an education, all right, but not the kind I was interested in. What I learned from experience was that I had

to value myself, and I had to learn to value learning. When I transferred the following year, I chose my college with great care. I learned there are smart and dumb ways to choose a college." (From Bryna J. Fireside, *Choices: A Student Survival Guide*, Ferguson, 1997)

What is the topic of the paragraph? _____

_____

What is the main idea of the paragraph? _____

_____

In what sentence is the main idea stated? _____

_____

The topic is choosing a college—more specifically, Jeff Dinlay's way of choosing a college. The main idea is that there are smart ways and dumb ways to choose a college. In this case, the topic sentence is the last sentence. It summarizes Dinlay's experience in choosing a college. The rest of the paragraph supports that point by telling what was smart and what was not about the way the student applied for college.

Here's one more example. Carefully read the paragraph looking for the topic, main idea, and topic sentence.

Computers have a place in our schools. They have the potential to accomplish great things. With the right software, they could help make science tangible or teach neglected topics like art and music. In practice, however, computers make our worst educational nightmares come true. Computers dismiss linear argument and promote fast, shallow romps across the information landscape. While we weep over the decline of literacy, computers discount words in favor of pictures and pictures in favor of video. While we worry about basic skills, we allow into the classroom software that will do a student's arithmetic and correct his spelling. (From David Gelernter, "Computers Cannot Teach Children Basic Skills," *Computers and Society*, Greenhaven, 1997)

What is the topic of the paragraph? _____

_____

What is the main idea of the paragraph? _____

_____

In what sentence is the main idea stated? _____

_____

This paragraph requires careful reading. The topic has to do with computers in the schools. But what is the main idea? The author says computers should be in the schools and gives reasons why. But then he says, "Computers make our worst educational nightmares come true," showing their negative effects. In this case, the author does not state his main idea in any one sentence. Instead, it is **implied**. A careful reading shows that the author says computers in schools have potential with the use of the right software, but feels that the way computers are being used is contributing to the decline in literacy. We can determine that the implied main idea is that computers are not being used correctly in our schools.

As you can see from these examples, a paragraph's main idea might be expressed in a topic sentence anywhere in a paragraph: in the beginning, at the end, in the middle, or not at all. When the main idea does not appear in a paragraph at all, it is called an implied main idea.

PRACTICE A-1: More on Main Ideas

Directions: Read the following article. At the end of each paragraph, write a one-sentence statement in the blank, stating what you think is the main idea of the paragraph.

Interviewing for a Job

1. One of the most important components of successful job hunting is the job interview. Thousands of people are entering new careers and searching for job placement. In order to give yourself an edge over others applying for the job you want, it is important to create a solid impression during the job interview.

    Main idea: _____

    _____

2. Because what you say during an interview is so important, there are two rules to remember. One is to present yourself in a favorable way and stress your areas of competence. However, don't exaggerate; tell the truth. Second, listen carefully and get involved in what the interviewer is saying. Notice the interviewer's interests and relate your comments to them.

    Main idea: _____

    _____

3. The job interview is the time to "sell" yourself by giving examples of experiences you've had related to the job and by revealing your good points. It's a good idea to have handy your job résumé or a list of school courses that prepared you for the job. Don't exaggerate the truth. Be honest, but show confidence in yourself and your ability to do the job.

    Main idea: _____

    _____

4. If you are not certain what the job will require of you, ask questions to see whether you do feel qualified. Do more listening than talking. Don't be afraid to ask for a second interview if you need time to gather information that will be more useful in the second interview. Most interviewers will appreciate your questions and your ability to listen and respond.

    Main idea: _____

    _____

5. Some people talk themselves out of a job by saying too much or by digressing. Although it's important to talk about your successful experiences, don't come on too strong and sound like a braggart.

    Main idea: _____

    _____

6. Each of us has sensitive areas, and you might anticipate your responses in the event that you are asked about your own. Such questions could refer to your lack of an academic degree, a long period of unemployment, or your lack of work experience if you are entering a new field. Answer sensitive questions briefly and positively, because even one negative example can create doubt in the interviewer's mind. If you believe that this area presents a real obstacle to a job offer, you could be communicating this doubt to the interviewer. Many times, however, an interviewer will override these sensitive areas if you have a confident, positive attitude.

   Main idea: _____

   _____

7. Making a favorable impression is especially important in light of recent estimates, which show that most hiring is done on an emotional rather than a factual basis. An interviewer who accepts you as a person and is emotionally on your side may consider you favorably for the job—even if you don't fit the preestablished qualifications.

   Main idea: _____

   _____

8. The job interview is an important part of the job search because the attitude and impression you project can make the interviewer feel "with you" or "against you." Remember that you have the power to create a favorable impression. Interviewers have the intelligence to recognize genuine enthusiasm and interest.

   Main idea: _____

   _____

Recognizing Supporting Details

As you have noticed in the examples, the main idea in a paragraph or passage is the most general statement about the topic. The main idea stated in the topic sentence is then developed by **supporting details**. Being able to separate supporting details from the main idea is necessary for good comprehension.

Read the following paragraph looking for the topic, the main idea, and the details or statements that support the main idea.

> Some words are loaded with pleasant associations. Words such as *home*, *happiness*, *tenderness*, *contentment*, *baby*, and *mother* usually bring about favorable feelings or memories, provided the type of home life we've had. The word *mother*, for instance, makes many people think of home, safety, love, care, food, and security.

What is the topic of the paragraph? _____

_____

What is the main idea of the paragraph? _____

_____

In what sentence is the main idea stated? _____

_____

What are some supporting details used to make the main idea clear?_____

_____

The topic of this paragraph is words because every sentence in the paragraph is about words or examples of words. The main idea is the first sentence in the paragraph because it is the most general statement about the topic: Some words bring about favorable memories. Supporting details provided are examples of words that bring about favorable memories: *home, happiness, tenderness, mother, care, love,* and so on.

An outline of the paragraph might look something like this:

Topic:	words
Main idea:	Some words are loaded with pleasant associations.
Supporting details:	1. general word examples: *home, happiness, tenderness, contentment, baby, mother*
	2. specific word example: mother (home, safety, love, care, food, security)

Here's another paragraph example. See if you can find the topic, main idea, and supporting details.

A major part of our self-image is shaped by the work we do. Consider how we describe ourselves: "I'm just a janitor." "I'm only a housewife." "I'm senior vice president of the company." "I'm out of work right now." "I'm the boss here." Even our friends and fellow workers refer to us by our work or status (teacher, student, lawyer, doctor, pilot) and by what we do.

What is the topic of the paragraph? _____

_____

What is the main idea?_____

_____

What are the supporting details the author provides to give specifics about the main idea? _____

_____

The topic of this brief paragraph is work and our self-image. Notice how the topic is a phrase rather than just one word. The most general statement about work and our self-image (the main idea) is the first sentence. What two details are used to show how our work shapes our self-image? The writer talks first about self-descriptions or what we say about ourselves and, second, about how others refer to us by our status or work. All the rest of the paragraph consists of minor details or specifics about our own words or others' descriptions.

Once you have identified the main idea and supporting details, you can outline the paragraph or passage. In an outline, the main ideas are the first points written at the left margin and usually have roman numerals I, II, III, and so on. Supporting details are indented about five spaces and numbered 1, 2, 3, and so on. The specifics or minor details are indented ten spaces and labeled with small letters a, b, c, d, and so on. An outline of a paragraph (or passage) looks like this:

I. (main idea)
  1. (first supporting detail)
      a. (specific example about the detail or minor detail)
      b. (another specific example)

  2. (second supporting detail)
      a. (specific example about the detail or minor detail)
      b. (another specific example)

When you can pick out the main idea and differentiate between supporting and specific details, an outline is one logical way of showing those relationships.

An outline of the preceding paragraph on work and self-image looks like this:

I. The work we do shapes a major part of our self-image.
  1. consider our self-description
      a. just a janitor
      b. only a housewife
      c. senior vice president
      d. out of work
      e. boss

  2. Friends and fellow workers refer to us by our work or status.
      a. teacher
      b. student
      c. lawyer
      d. doctor
      e. pilot

Again, the main idea is more general, with specific details supporting this main idea.

Find the topic, main idea, and supporting details in the following paragraph.

A young college student is constantly discouraged, irritable, and unable to sleep. Frequent crying spells have ended, but she's still very unhappy. A middle-aged man has become increasingly indecisive in business affairs. He has strong feelings of worthlessness and guilt, and has lost interest in sex. An elderly woman complains of fatigue and lack of appetite. Her weight has been dropping steadily. Three different problems? Not really. These people—and millions like them—suffer from the most common mental ailment in the book: depression. (From Maxine Abram, "Rx for Depression," *TWA Ambassador*, January 1987.)

Topic: _____

Main idea: _____

_____

Three supporting details: _____

_____

The topic is depression, and the main idea comes in the last sentence. Everything up to that point is an example of the main idea.

Here's a blank outline of the paragraph for you to practice your outlining skills. Cover up the answer as you try your hand at outlining.

I.

   1.

      a.

      b.

      c.

      d.

      e.

   2.

      a.

      b.

      c.

   3.

      a.

      b.

      c.

Does your outline look like the following? If not, analyze your mistakes and figure out how to do it right the next time. If it does look like this, congratulate yourself on your outlining skills.

I. These people—and millions like them—suffer from the most common mental ailment in the book: depression.

   1. young college student's problems

      a. discouraged

      b. irritable

      c. unable to sleep

      d. frequent crying spells

      e. unhappy

   2. middle-aged man's problems

      a. indecisive

      b. feelings of worthlessness and guilt

      c. lost interest in sex

   3. elderly woman's problems

     a. fatigue

     b. lack of appetite

     c. loss of weight

Now analyze the following paragraph.

Distractibility is one symptom of attention deficit disorder (ADHD) in college students. ADHD students become easily sidetracked and jump from topic to topic in conversation. Time management problems are another symptom. Both procrastination and being unrealistic about how long a task will take are ADHD issues. Lack of organization is yet another symptom of ADHD. ADHD students tend to be messy, have trouble keeping up with several simultaneous projects, and have a difficult time prioritizing. Knowing these and other symptoms of ADHD may help a college student gain better self-awareness.

Fill in the outline, stating the main idea and each of the major and minor details.

Main Idea:

   1.

     a.

     b.

   2.

     a.

     b.

   3.

     a.

     b.

     c.

The topic is ADHD and the main idea is the last sentence of the paragraph. The three symptoms are specifics about ADHD and include distractibility, time management problems, and lack of organization. Notice that this paragraph also contains quite a few specifics (or minor details) about the three symptoms.

Your outline should look something like this:

I. Knowing these and other symptoms of ADHD may help a college student gain better self-awareness. (topic sentence stating main idea)

   1. distractibility (major detail: one of the symptoms)

     a. sidetracked (minor detail)

     b. jump from topic to topic (minor detail)

   2. time-management problems (major detail: a second symptom)

     a. procrastination (minor detail)

     b. being unrealistic about time (minor detail)

3. lack of organization (major detail: a third symptom)
   a. tend to be messy (minor detail)
   b. trouble keeping up (minor detail)
   c. trouble prioritizing (minor detail)

The next two paragraphs are more complex and have implied main ideas. See if you can apply the skills you've learned so far to these paragraphs from actual articles and texts.

> This is the story of a sturdy American symbol which has now spread throughout most of the world. The symbol is not the dollar. It is not even Coca-Cola. It is a simple pair of pants called blue jeans. ...Blue jeans are favored equally by bureaucrats and cowboys; bankers and deadbeats; fashion designers and beer drinkers. They draw no distinctions and recognize no classes; they are merely American. Yet they are sought after almost everywhere in the world—including Russia, where authorities recently broke up a teenaged gang that was selling them on the black market for two hundred dollars a pair. They have been around for a long time, and it seems likely that they will outlive even the necktie. (From Carin Quinn, "The Jeaning of America—and the World," *American Heritage*, April/May 1978.)

Topic: _____

Main idea (in your own words): _____

_____

Three supporting details: _____

_____

The topic is blue jeans, even though the introductory statements about American symbols may have distracted you. The main idea is not stated in any one sentence. You must combine part of the first sentence and the fourth sentence to come up with the main idea. The main idea is: Blue jeans, an American symbol, are popular all around the world. The first supporting detail is that jeans are popular across socioeconomic classes and in a variety of groups. The second detail is that they are sought everywhere in the world. The third detail is that they've been around for a long time and will stay around for a long time. All the other details are specifics or minor details about these major details.

Here's one last paragraph example, taken from a history textbook. Don't try to remember all the facts and figures for this reading; just look for the main idea in it:

> In 1840, only one-twelfth of the American population lived in cities of 8,000 or more. By 1860, the proportion of city-dwellers had grown to one-sixth, and by 1900 to one-third of the population. In 1900, more than 25 million Americans were living in cities, most of them in the metropolises that had grown so lustily in the preceding 50 years. In 1850, New York City and independent Brooklyn together had a population of 1,200,000. By 1900 (after official consolidation in 1898),

their population had soared to over 3 million. In that same period, Philadelphia rose from 560,000 to 1,300,000. Most spectacular of all was Chicago. Starting out in 1831 as a muddy trading post on the prairie with 12 families and a meager garrison as its only inhabitants, Chicago had grown to 30,000 by 1850; 500,000 by 1880. In the next 20 years, its population soared to 1,700,000, a figure that placed it far ahead of Philadelphia and second only to New York in size. (From Richard Hofstadter, William Miller, and Daniel Aaron, *The United States: The History of a Republic*, Prentice-Hall, 1957, p. 510.)

Topic: _____

Implied main idea: _____

_____

Three supporting details: _____

_____

The topic is American population in cities. Note once again that a topic may be a phrase rather than a single word. You need to think about all the details and what they are saying in order to come up with a main idea. It isn't stated anywhere in the paragraph. The main idea is: In the second half of the nineteenth century, Americans moved to cities at startling rates. The three main examples the historians use are New York City, Philadelphia, and Chicago.

Because the authors provide us with dates and statistics, we are able to infer the main idea. Notice that all of the dates provided are between 1850 and 1900, the second half of the nineteenth century. All of the cities (New York, Philadelphia, and Chicago) are examples of fast population growth during this time. Because of these details, we see for ourselves, without the authors telling us, that America urbanized very rapidly during the second half of the nineteenth century.

As you can see, sometimes it is easy to figure out an author's main idea and separate it from details, but sometimes we have to be more alert to what is being said. As you work through the following practices, become more conscious of how writers express their main points and provide details to support them.

PRACTICE A-2: Recognizing Topics, Main Ideas, and Supporting Details

Directions: Read the following paragraphs and in the appropriate blanks write the topic, the main idea, and the supporting details. The first one has been done for you.

Paragraph 1

Many of us impose unnecessary limitations on ourselves. We say, or think, we can't do something without checking. We hold ourselves back when we could move ahead. We assume that certain good occupations are closed to us when they're really not closed at all. We think we're not as good as the next person when we really are.

Topic: *limitations*

Main idea: *Many of us limit our potential unnecessarily.*

Supporting details:

1. *We say we can't without really knowing.*

2. *We hold back.*

3. *We think we're not good enough for certain jobs.*

4. *We think we're not as good as others.*

Paragraph 2

Nature has provided natural means to soothe the mind and body. Herbal remedies for sleeplessness have been used successfully for centuries. Valerian root, for example, lessens irritability and excitement in the nervous system by rebuilding frayed nerve endings. Skullcap produces a peacefully drowsy feeling and restful sleep. A cup of chamomile tea is also a sleep producer and is a delicious break from stimulating hot caffeine drinks at night. Other valuable herbs for relaxing include hops, yellow jasmine, and lady slipper. Herbs also offer the advantage of containing important vitamins and minerals, which further increases their benefit to your general mental and physical health. (From Josie Knowles, "The Big Business of Falling Asleep," *Soma*, September/October 1980.)

Topic: _____

Main idea: _____

_____

Supporting details: _____

_____

_____

_____

Paragraph 3

Fundamental changes in human life began to take shape around 11,000 B.C.E., the dawn of the Neolithic or "New Stone" Age. These breakthroughs included the development of managed food production, the beginnings of semipermanent and permanent settlements, and the rapid intensification of trade, both local and long distance. For the first time, it now became possible for individuals and communities to accumulate and store wealth on a large scale. The results were far-reaching. Communities became more stable, and human societies more complex. Specialization developed, along with distinctions of status and rank. This "revolution" was a necessary step before cities in the truest sense could appear toward the end of the fourth millennium B.C.E. (From Judith Coffin and Robert C. Stacy, *Western Civilizations*, brief edition, Norton, 2005, p. 8.)

Topic: _____

Main idea: _____

Supporting details: _____

_____

_____

_____

_____

_____

Paragraph 4

Our studies on people also produced striking results. Because of the 21 minimum drinking age law, we studied people ages 21–29. Alcohol impaired learning much more in 21–24-year-olds than in those just a few years older at 25–29. During young adulthood, alcohol is a very potent drug, and it interferes with memory formation. The effects might be even more striking in teens. (From Scott Swartzwelder, "Alcohol and the Adolescent Brain," Opposing Viewpoints Resource Center.)

Topic: _____

Main idea: _____

Supporting details: _____

_____

_____

_____

Paragraph 5

The meanings of words change as their uses change. "Stout" at one time meant "valiant." Today it is used to characterize people who are portly. "Courtesan" once meant "lady at court" and "wench" meant any young girl. "Get off," according to Harper Barnes, "started as a drug term, became a sexual term and ending up meaning, more or less, to have a good time." "Sophomore" no longer means "person with the wisdom of a moron," and "professor" no longer means "person who has taken religious vows." Some words have no contemporary meaning at all, and if they are listed in the dictionary are labeled "archaic" or "obsolete." We usually find the word "prithee," but most dictionaries no longer include such splendid terms from the past as "snollygoster," "poop-noddy," "snodderclout," "bedswerver," and "mubblefubbles." (From Gerald Runkle, *Good Thinking: An Introduction to Logic*, 3rd edition, Holt, Rinehart and Winston, 1991, p. 14.)

Topic: _____

Main idea: _____

Supporting details: _____

_____

_____

_____

_____

Paragraph 6

Caffeine speeds up the heart, promotes the release of stomach acid, and increases urine production; also, it dilates some blood vessels while narrowing others. In large amounts, caffeine may cause convulsions, but this is highly unlikely. It takes about ten grams of caffeine, the equivalent of 100 cups of coffee, to run a serious risk of death. Caffeine has various effects on the body and mind. Psychologically, caffeine suppresses fatigue or drowsiness and increases feelings of alertness.

Topic: _____

Main idea: _____

Supporting details: _____

_____

_____

_____

Paragraph 7

Most of us are unaware that we use probably only a third of our lung capacity. Our breathing is shallow and occurs about fifteen to seventeen times a minute, taking in about a pint of air each time. Yet our lungs can hold eight times as much air. Therefore, shallow breathing provides only a limited amount of fresh oxygen and doesn't fully expel all the burnt gases, such as carbon dioxide. Despite the central role breathing plays in our lives as organisms, few of us have been taught to breathe. (From Richard Stein, "What Is the Best Form of Exercise?" *Personal Strategies for Living With Stress*, John Gallagher Communications, 1983, p. 1.)

Topic: _____

Main idea: _____

Supporting details: _____

_____

_____

_____

Paragraph 8

Do people really need stress as a motivator? Apparently so, but perhaps many people confuse stress with goals. For example, getting through school is stressful, but the stress is not the reason for finishing school. Graduating and reaping the benefits of education are the motivation. This is an important distinction. The stress encountered while pursuing a goal, however, does seem to be less destructive when the goal is kept in mind. Stress that drives us seems to be more harmful than stress that results from our own interests. We suspect that the statement, "If it weren't for stress, I would be a vegetable," really means, "If I didn't have goals, I would be a vegetable." Even so, stress is not all bad. (From Judith Green and Robert Shellenberger, *The Dynamics of Health and Wellness*, Holt, Rinehart and Winston, 1991, p. 83.)

Topic: _____

Main idea: _____

Supporting details: _____

_____

_____

_____

_____

Paragraph 9

Forecasting is an imprecise art, but here are a few basic strokes to the picture. Even Pentagon planners are concerned that global climate change may reach a "tipping point," after which widespread drought would turn farmland into dust and forests to ash. Even without accelerated weather change, parts of the Great Plains and Midwest will become desert as the Ogallala aquifer further shrinks. In Appalachia, more mine waste will choke more rivers below more decapitated mountaintops. The soil of California's San Joaquin Valley will be too polluted to grow food. There will be fewer wetlands and forests to sustain fewer species of birds, fish and mammals. By 2050, our children will pay dearly for scarce water as well as energy and food. Ditto for national security, because large parts of Africa and Asia will suffer great harm induced by global warming before we do. Cancer incidence will be higher; viruses are likely to be stronger. (From Yvon Chouinard, "Time's Up," Patagonia Catalogue, 2004.)

Topic: _____

Main idea: _____

Supporting details: _____

_____

_____

_____

_____

Paragraph 10

Why do American students remember so little of the history that they are taught? When the National Assessment of Educational Progress tested for knowledge of U.S. history in 1994 and 2001, more than half of high school seniors scored below basic, which is as low as one can score. In no other subject—not in mathematics or science or reading—do American seniors score as low as they do in U.S. history. Maybe it is because their textbooks are so dull; maybe it is because so many of their history teachers never studied history and can't argue with the textbooks' smug certainty. Maybe it is because the students don't know why they are supposed to remember the parade of facts that are so glamorously packaged between two covers. Or maybe it is because, with the teenager's usual ability to spot a scam, they know that much of what is taught to them is phony and isn't worth remembering. (From Diane Ravitch, *The Language Police*, Knopf, 2003.)

Topic: _____

Main idea: _____

Supporting details: _____

_____

_____

_____

_____

Practice A-3: Separating Main Ideas from Supporting Details

Directions: For each of the paragraphs that follow, circle the topic and underline the main-idea sentence. Then, in the space provided, write the major supporting details.

1. An unrealistically poor self-concept can also arise from the inaccurate feedback of others. Perhaps you are in an environment where you receive an excessive number of downer messages, many of which are undeserved, and a minimum of upper messages. We've known many housewives, for example, who have returned to college after many years spent in homemaking, where they received virtually no recognition for their intellectual strengths. It's amazing that these women have the courage to come to college at all, so low are their self-concepts; but come they do, and most are thrilled to find that they are much brighter and more competent intellectually than they suspected. In the same way, workers with overly critical supervisors, children with cruel "friends," and students with unsupportive teachers are all prone to low self-concepts owing to excessively negative feedback. (From Ronald B. Adler and Neil Towne, *Looking Out, Looking In*, 6th edition, Holt, Rinehart and Winston, 1990, p. 69.)

   Supporting details: _____

   _____

   _____

2. Most people believe that the preferred form of marriage through the ages has been between one man and one woman, but the preferred form that has been approved by more societies than any other is polygamy—one man and many women. That family form is the one mentioned most often in the first five books of the Bible. In some cases, one woman could marry several men. In others, two families could bond by marrying off a son or daughter to the "ghost" of the other family's dead child. The main reason for marrying throughout history was not love or sex, but managing property and enlarging the family's holdings. (Information from http://www.nytimes.com/imagepages/2006/02/18/opinion/19coontz.html?scp=6&sq=Feb%2018%202006&st=Search)

   Supporting details: _____

   _____

   _____

3. A reader is not like a miner, recovering the meaning buried in the text, but more like a detective, reconstructing what happened by gathering bits of evidence and putting together a coherent picture, filling in the gaps. Both the reader and writer construct meaning. Similarly, a writer is not like a computer, merely printing out "data"; meaning is not somehow buried in the writer's mind. The writer constructs meaning, starting with some purpose (to get a job through a letter of application, to explain a complex process, to convince readers they should take certain actions). The writer then assembles the "data" he or she has gained through experience, education, and research and uses his or her skills with language to present that

data to readers. (From W. Ross Winterowd and Geoffrey R. Winterowd, *The Critical Reader, Thinker, and Writer*, 2nd edition, Mayfield, 1997, p. 1.)

<u>Supporting details:</u> _____

_____

4. With digital television (DTV), benefits will include spectacular picture quality and better sound. The screen will be wider, so televisions will look quite different than they do today. Better reception is another plus; we'll no longer get poor reception when certain weather patterns hang over our area. Even more impressive will be the wider choices of programs and the interactivity. If the news anchor mentions problems in Malaysia, the viewer can click on Malaysia and find out background information about that country. DTV represents a major revolution in broadcasting technology with the potential to significantly change, for the better, the way televisions are used and viewed.

   Supporting details: _____

   _____

   _____

5. Simply put, evolution is the scientific theory that all life-forms on earth today are descended from a single cell, or at most a very few different cells. The diversity we see among species is the result of biological changes that have taken place over many hundreds of millions of years. During that time, new variations of plants and animals have appeared, through what the National Association of Biology Teachers terms "an unsupervised, impersonal, unpredictable, and natural process of temporal descent. ..." Those new variations best able to adapt—to find food, escape predators, protect living space, or produce offspring—survived to pass along their traits to future generations. This is the process that Charles Darwin termed "natural selection" in his seminal 1859 work, *On the Origin of Species by Means of Natural Selection.* (From Leon Lynn, "The Evolution of Creationism," *Rethinking Schools*, Winter 1997/1998.)

   Supporting details: _____

   _____

   _____

   _____

6. Language and meanings change over time. In the 1950s, *gay* meant "lighthearted and merry"; today it is generally understood to mean men who are sexually oriented toward men. Until the 1980s, the word *apple* was assumed to refer to a fruit, but today it is equally likely to refer to a computer company and its products. College students are particularly creative in making up new language. The first time a student told me my class was "da bomb," I was offended. I thought he meant that the course was really bad! He explained that "da bomb" is a compliment. Students also seem to be the originators of "101" as a generic description of something elementary. Apparently the fact that "101" generally signifies introductory courses (Comm 101, Psych 101) has been generalized to expressions such as "dating 101" and "recycling 101." (From Julia Wood, *Communication in Our Lives*, 4th edition, Thomson Wadsworth, 2006, p. 119.)

   Supporting details: _____

   _____

> ### *Application 1: Finding Main Ideas and Supporting Details*
>
> In a textbook for another class, select five paragraphs throughout the text and mark the main idea for each paragraph or write the implied main idea. List the supporting details for each paragraph. Bring your text to class and be prepared to justify your choice of main ideas with a class study partner.

B.   Reading for Main Ideas: Paragraph Patterns

Another way to distinguish between an author's main ideas and supporting points is to pay attention to the writing patterns used frequently by authors. Authors use a variety of writing patterns to develop their ideas: illustration or example, definition of terms, comparison or contrast, sequence of events, cause and effect, description, or a combination of these. These patterns are called **rhetorical modes**. They are useful for better understanding paragraphs and entire reading passages. If you have taken an English composition course, you may already know the terms. They are frequently used to teach students how to write better. As you read, your awareness of these patterns can help you more readily identify an author's main idea and supporting details. Let's examine each pattern.

Example

An easy writing pattern to spot is the use of an *example* (or examples) to support a main idea. Phrases such as *for example*, *for instance*, and *to illustrate* all signal or alert you that an example or examples are about to be given. It's a good guess that the example given is not the main idea of the paragraph. Instead, it is being used to support a main idea that probably has already been stated or will be stated.

Notice in the following paragraph how in the first sentence, the topic is made clearer with the support of examples:

> It would seem the lesson to be gained from famous love stories is that passionate love and marriage do not mix. For instance, witness the ending to the stories of Antony and Cleopatra, Tristan and Isolde, Lancelot and Guinevere, Dante and Beatrice, and poor Cyrano and Roxanne. Even Romeo and Juliet ran into problems.

All of the names listed in the paragraph are given as examples to illustrate and support the main idea: Marriage and passionate love don't seem to go together. Even if you don't know who all the characters listed are, you can infer that they were all passionate lovers who never got married, or if they did, the marriages didn't last. Otherwise, the author wouldn't use them as examples to support the main idea.

Here is another example showing how this writing pattern works:

> It's hard to believe, but in the ninth decade of the twentieth century, *The Catcher in the Rye*, *Of Mice and Men*, *Huckleberry Finn*, and *The Diary of*

Anne Frank, among other books, are still the objects of censorship in the nation's public schools. And the incidence of book bannings is going up, according to a report by People for the American Way, the liberal watchdog group. In the last year, the study found, there were efforts to ban books in the schools in 46 of the 50 states, including California. Many of them succeeded. ("See the Busy Book-Burners," *Los Angeles Times*, August 20, 1985.)

In this case, no signal words are given. But examples of books that have been and continue to be banned in public schools are used to support the surprise of the author that such censorship is still happening.

You've probably noticed by now how we are using examples here to explain the use of this writing pattern and to illustrate how recognizing it can help you sort out main ideas from supporting details.

Definition

Another frequently used writing pattern is *definition*, or an attempt to explain what is being discussed through elaborate defining of terms. Here is an example:

A word generally has two meanings: a denotative meaning and a connotative meaning. The denotative meaning of a word is its most direct or literal meaning as found in the dictionary. What the word suggests or implies beyond its literal definition is its connotative meaning.

The author's main point here is to define the terms *denotative* and *connotative*.

Frequently, when authors define a word or term, they also use examples. Notice in the following example how a definition of *inference* is provided, then an example of how we make inferences is given:

An inference is a statement about the unknown made on the basis of the known. In other words, an inference is an educated guess. If a woman smiles when we see a man whisper something in her ear, we can infer or assume that she is pleased or amused. Because smiles generally mean pleasure and frowns generally mean displeasure, we can infer that she is pleased.

In this example, the definition of inference is given followed by an example of how we make inferences, thus combining both the definition and illustration/example patterns.

Comparison/Contrast

The *comparison/contrast* writing pattern is also used with some frequency. With this pattern, authors attempt to develop the main point by either comparing or contrasting one thing or idea with another, or by using both. Here's an example of the use of comparison/contrast:

Crime as presented on television is different from what it is in reality. On television, murder, assault, and armed robbery are the most common crimes. However, in reality, quiet burglaries, clever larcenies, unspectacular auto thefts, and drunkenness are the most common. Video detectives solve 90 percent of their cases. But in reality, the figure is much lower. On

TV only 7 percent of violence occurs between relatives. In reality, family violence accounts for 25 to 30 percent of interpersonal violence.

Notice that what is being contrasted is crime as portrayed on television and what it is like in reality. The author's main idea is that television does not portray crime realistically. To prove this, the author contrasts three points: the most common crimes as portrayed on television and in real crime, the difference in the number of cases detectives solve on television and in reality, and the percentage of family violence on television and in reality.

In the following paragraph, only a contrast is being drawn. See if you understand what is being contrasted.

> Sweden offers a unique and independent voice in today's international debates. With a tradition of social democracy, its society is influenced by a *multilateral* approach to international cooperation. In contrast, the United States is an uncontested world power and the September 11 attacks have served to strengthen the already *unilateralist* direction of its foreign policy. A recent survey of public opinion in 44 nations concluded that U.S. citizens' views on fundamental world problems differ greatly from public attitudes in the rest of the world. A serious joint discussion of critical world issues by students from each society could be exciting, timely, and educational. (From Linda York, "Summer in Sweden," *World 2003*, University of California, 2003.)

Notice that the attitudes of Swedish citizens toward the way foreign problems should be handled is termed *multilateral*, or shared by all nations. In contrast—the same words used in the paragraph—the U.S. policy toward handling foreign affairs is *unilateral*, or doing things alone. Another contrast is shown in the results of the poll mentioned, which reveals that public opinion in 44 nations encompasses views different from those of U.S. citizens. The main idea is that a serious joint discussion of these differences among students would be "exciting, timely, and educational."

As this example shows, sometimes signal words are used to alert you to a contrast or comparison, sometimes not. Still, be alert to signal words and phrases that show comparison, such as *in comparison, similar, like, also, too,* and *the same as*. Words and phrases that reveal contrast are *in contrast, on the contrary, however, but, on the other hand,* and *even though*. When you see such a word or phrase being used, you know that you are being provided with supporting details or information, not the main idea. The main idea will be whatever the comparison or contrasting details are supporting.

Sequence of Events

A fourth writing pattern is *sequence of events*. This pattern is used when directions are given, when there is a certain order to events, or when chronology is important. Sometimes certain key words, such as *first, second, third,* or the numbers themselves, are used. Words such as *then, later, finally,* and *thus* also serve as guides to a sequence of events. Notice the sequence of events in the following example:

> An algorithm is a step-by-step procedure for solving a problem in a finite amount of time. When you start your car, you go through a step-by-step procedure. First, you insert the key. Second, you make sure the transmis-

sion is in neutral or park. Third, you depress the gas pedal. Fourth, you turn the key to the start position. If the engine starts within a few seconds, you then release the key to the ignition position. If the engine doesn't start, you wait ten seconds and repeat steps three through six. Finally, if the car doesn't start, you call the garage. (From Nell Dale, *Programming in Pascal*, Heath, 1990, pp. 27–28.)

Notice how the author has related the sequence of events necessary to start a car. Numbers and words such as *first*, *second*, *then*, and *finally* aid the reader. An awareness of this use of words provides a pattern for understanding as you read, as well as a way to remember the information.

Sometimes numbers or signal words are not used to make clear the sequence of events. See if you can recognize and follow the sequence of events in the following paragraph:

When you receive an unexpected physical threat, what happens to your system during the first ten or fifteen seconds? The moment your stress response is triggered by a threat your heartbeat quickens to pump more blood into your vital organs. Part of this additional blood is taken from blood vessels under your skin, leaving you with cold, clammy hands. As your heartbeat quickens, raising your blood pressure, more blood is received by the muscles and brain enabling you to react more quickly. Sugar is poured into the system from the liver, supplying quick energy. The adrenal glands pump adrenaline for strength. The digestive system shuts down so there will be no wasted energy. In all, stress activates the body's entire mental and physical systems causing more than 1400 physiological changes. All this happens in a matter of seconds. (From David Danskin and Mark Crow, *Biofeedback: An Introduction and Guide*, Mayfield, 1981, p. 4.)

The sequence of events described here shows what happens in a matter of seconds to your body when you are physically threatened. The paragraph lists step by step what happens:

- Your heartbeat quickens, pumping more blood into your vital organs.
- Part of this additional blood is taken from blood vessels under your skin, leaving you with cold, clammy hands.
- Your heartbeat quickens, raising your blood pressure.
- The muscles and brain receive more blood, enabling you to react more quickly.
- Sugar is poured into the system from the liver, supplying quick energy.
- The adrenal glands pump adrenaline for strength.
- The digestive system shuts down so there will be no wasted energy.

Each step provides details of what happens when the body is physically threatened. The actual order in which events take place is important in understanding how the body reacts.

Cause and Effect

Still another writing pattern is the use of *cause and effect*. With this pattern, the author attempts to show how one action or a series of actions causes something to happen. For instance, tapping a raw egg on a skillet causes it to crack. In a cause/effect paragraph, the author links what causes an event with the effects it brings. Here is an example of cause/effect relationship in a paragraph:

> The permissive nature of society in the United States is notorious. With Dr. Benjamin Spock's books on child raising, the Bible of the last generation of parents, family life has become very democratic. In recent decades, many schoolteachers have urged children to express themselves, to give their opinions rather than to regurgitate the rote recitations that used to characterize—and still characterize elsewhere—much of what we call education. The point is not that there is no discipline or authoritarianism in the family or school, but that there is considerably less than in the American past or in the present of most other nations. (From John Gillingham, "Then and Now," *The Radical Reader*, The New Press, 2003 .)

Notice that the point of the paragraph is that permissiveness in the United States is greater than ever (the effect). The use of Dr. Spock's books in rearing children (a cause) and the urging of children by teachers to give their opinions rather than to learn by rote (a cause) explain why discipline in the family and school is less than in the past. Thus, the author of the preceding paragraph sees the effect of two causes.

Look for cause and effect in the following paragraph:

> If you're within a few miles of a nuclear detonation, you'll be incinerated on the spot! And if you survive that blast, what does the future promise? The silent but deadly radiation, either directly or from fallout, in a dose of 400 rems could kill you within two weeks. Your hair would fall out, your skin would be covered with large ulcers, you would vomit and experience diarrhea and you would die from infection or massive bleeding as your white blood cells and platelets stopped working. (From Ken Keyes, Jr., *The Hundredth Monkey*, Vision, 1981.)

Here the *cause* is a nuclear detonation. The *effects* of such a detonation include possibly being reduced to ashes on the spot and the effects of radiation from fallout.

Description

Another pattern is the use of *description*. Usually the author is attempting to give you a visual picture or a feeling for something. Generally, but not always, there is no topic sentence. Notice this example:

> The old fire road runs through the pines for several miles, winding its way around the shoulders of the mountain. The footing is good, so I let my horse step up from a trot into a slow gallop. But once the fire in her blood is lit, the wind fans her flame and she stretches her legs and burns the miles. I am riding with only a bareback pad, and the faster she runs the easier it is to find the still point behind her withers where I can sit motionless and become one with her motion, horse and man a single centaur. The road dips and passes through a swampy place. Aspens replace the pines, the underbrush is thick, and the roadway is muddy. I rein my mare

down to a walk. She doesn't like it, but once or twice I have seen bears eating berries in this thicket and I don't want to surprise one in the middle of a meal. (From Sam Keen, *Fire in the Belly*, Bantam, 1991, pp. 181–182.)

As you can see, there is no topic sentence. The whole paragraph is a description of horseback riding on an old fire road in the mountains.

Narration

When authors want to tell a story about something that has happened in their lives, they use *narration*. It is not always easy to spot a topic sentence in narrative paragraphs because a story is being told and events move from one paragraph to another. In the following example, the author uses first-person narration:

> I was saved from sin when I was going on thirteen. But not really saved. It happened like this. There was a big revival at my Auntie Reed's church. Every night for weeks there had been much preaching, singing, praying, and shouting, and some very hardened sinners had been brought to Christ, and the membership of the church had grown by leaps and bounds. Then just before the revival ended, they held a special meeting for children, "to bring the young lambs to the fold."...That night I was escorted to the front row and placed on the mourners' bench with all the other young sinners. (From Langston Hughes, "Salvation," *The Big Sea*, Farrar, 1968.)

The author reflects on an incident in his past, a time when he "was saved from sin. ...But not really saved." The paragraph sets us up for more of the story to come. You will see how this paragraph is developed when you read the entire story in a later reading practice.

Combination of Patterns

Some paragraphs use more than one pattern. What two patterns that you have learned are used in the following paragraph?

> One of the most controversial data collection practices on the Web involves the use of "cookies." A cookie is a file created by a Web server and stored on your host machine. It's a small file that patiently awaits your next visit to the Web. Any Web server can check to see if you have a cookie file and, if so, whether it has any useful information about you. For example, suppose that the last time you visited a particular site, you spent all your time on two particular pages. A cookie can record this information so that the next time you visit the site, the server might greet you with a page display that makes it especially easy to navigate to those pages again. (From Wendy Lehnert, *Light on the Internet and the World Wide Web*, Longman, 1999.)

In this case, the author uses the patterns of definition and example. A definition of a *cookie* is given, and then an example of how a cookie works.

Your ability to understand what you read can be enhanced by an awareness of these writing patterns. The patterns themselves are not important, but an awareness of how an author presents information can aid comprehension. To help you develop this ability, the next practices provide you with opportunities to work on identifying writing patterns.

As you progress through this section, keep in mind the fourth objective listed in the introduction to this unit. You should be able to identify the following writing patterns: illustration/example, definition, cause and effect, comparison/contrast, description, and sequence of events.

PRACTICE B-1: Finding Main Ideas through Paragraph Patterns

Directions: For each of the following paragraphs, look for the main idea and key supporting details. As organizational patterns get more complex, main ideas are often implied. Then identify which of the organizational patterns listed best describes the paragraph. In the space provided, explain how the pattern is used.

a. illustration/example   e. cause/effect

b. definition   f. description

c. comparison/contrast   g. combination (include the letters of the patterns)

d. sequence of events

Write the letter of the correct pattern in the blank before the paragraph.

_____ 1.   College athletes ought to be paid a salary on top of any scholarships and allowances they receive. Major college athletics is a form of entertainment. As with other entertainments, talented people perform for audiences who pay to watch. What universities are doing is using performance for publicity purposes. College athletes should be paid for their part in this. Other people in the collegiate-sport industry—coaches, athletic directors, trainers—are making a good living. Why not the athletes, the actual producers of the event?

_____

_____

_____

_____

_____ 2.   College athletes should not be paid a salary on top of any scholarships and allowances they receive. A student athlete is a part of a university family, along with other students, the faculty, and so on. Only a handful of students—a maximum of 110 in men's football and basketball—play sports that generate revenue. A school's resources, regardless of how they are generated, should be used to benefit the entire college. To pay athletes in football and basketball—most of whom already receive full tuition and room and board—the institution would have to cut some nonrevenue sports or reassign resources from some other academic area. How about other athletes, such as wrestlers, swimmers, and softball players? They must train as rigorously and may receive only a partial grant or none at all.

_____

_____

_____

_____

_____ **3.** Here is a four-step method to prevent your mind from wandering while reading. First, before you attempt to read anything, look over the length of the material to see whether you have time to read it all; if not, mark a spot where you intend to stop. Second, read the title and the first paragraph, looking for the main idea of the article. Next, read the boldface headings, if there are any, and the first sentence of each paragraph. Finally, read the last paragraph, which probably contains a summary of the material. These steps condition your mind to accept the material you want to read and keep it from wandering.

_____

_____

_____

_____

_____ **4.** Irony is a figure of speech whereby the writer or speaker says the opposite of what is meant; for the irony to be successful, however, the audience must understand the writer's true intent. For example, if you have slopped to school in a rainstorm and your drenched teacher enters the classroom saying, "Ah, nothing like this beautiful sunny weather," you know that your teacher is being ironic. Perhaps one of the most famous cases of irony occurred in 1938, when Sigmund Freud, the famous Viennese psychiatrist, was arrested by the Nazis. After being harassed by the Gestapo, he was released on the condition that he sign a statement swearing he had been treated well by the secret police. Freud signed it, but he added a few words after his signature: "I can heartily recommend the Gestapo to anyone." Looking back, we easily recognize Freud's jab at his captors; the Gestapo, however, apparently overlooked the irony and let him go. (From Jean Wyrick, *Steps to Writing Well*, 3rd edition, Holt, Rinehart and Winston, 1987, p. 112.)

_____

_____

_____

_____

_____ **5.** In the United States, the age-old problem of excessive drinking is taking a disturbing new turn and affecting new kinds of victims. On a New York subway train, a school-bound fifteen-year-old holds his books in one hand, a brown paper bag containing a beer bottle in the other. He takes a swig, then passes the bottle to a classmate. In a San Francisco suburb, several high school freshmen show up for class drunk every morning, while others sneak off for a nip or two of whiskey during the lunch recess. On the campuses, the beer bash is fashionable once again, and lowered drinking ages have made liquor the high without the hassle.

_____

_____

_____

_____

_____ **6.** But Walnut Canyon offered the Sinagua more than cozy homesites. A dependable supply of water flowed along the streambed on the floor of the canyon. Fertile volcanic-cinder soil lay within about two miles of the canyon rim. A great variety of trees, for fuel and implements, grew within the canyon and on the mesa. Other wild plants, a source of food and medicines, lined the banks of the stream and blanketed the slope. Game, furred and feathered, abounded in the canyon and on the mesa top. (From *Walnut Canyon*, Superintendent of Documents, U.S. Government Printing Office, 1968.)

_____

_____

_____

_____

_____ **7.** The patients wandered aimlessly about, mumbling incoherently. Violent ones were wrapped in wet sheets with their arms pinned, or they wore straitjackets. Attendants, in danger of assault, peered at their charges through screens. The floor lay bare, because rugs would have quickly been soiled with excrement. The large mental institution of thirty years ago was a madhouse.

_____

_____

_____

_____

_____ **8.** Because of the way prime-time television portrays them, we have a distorted image of America's elderly. Only one out of every fifty fictional television characters is over 65; in real life one out of every ten people has passed that age. Studies show that in 1,365 nighttime programs, older people are portrayed as stubborn, eccentric, ineffectual, sexually unattractive, and sometimes silly. Older women appear on television shows seldom and in roles with few romantic possibilities. Old men are shown as having evil powers. Because the largest group of people watching television is over 55, television could end up alienating its most faithful viewers.

_____

_____

_____

_____

_____ **9.** There are basically two different types of purchasers who respond to advertising. One type rushes out to buy 50 percent of all the products they see advertised. Such buyers help make advertising a highly successful, multibillion-dollar-a-year industry. People of the second type think they are immune to ads; they think most ads are silly, stupid, and "beneath their dignity." This type of purchaser believes ads are aimed at the "suckers" of the first type. Yet 90 percent of the nation's adults who believe themselves immune are responsible for about 90 percent of all purchases of advertised products.

_____

_____

_____

_____

_____ **10.** Television is addictive. For example, when a set breaks, most families rush to have it repaired, often renting one if the repair process takes longer than a day or two. When "nothing's on TV," people experience boredom with their lives, not knowing what to do with themselves. Perhaps the best example of television addiction was an experiment in Germany in which 184 volunteers were paid to go without television for a year. At first, most volunteers did well, reporting that they were spending more time with their children, reading, and visiting friends. Then, within a month, tension, restlessness, and quarreling increased. Not one volunteer lasted more than five months without a television set. Once the sets were on again, people lost their anxieties and returned to normal.

_____

_____

_____

_____

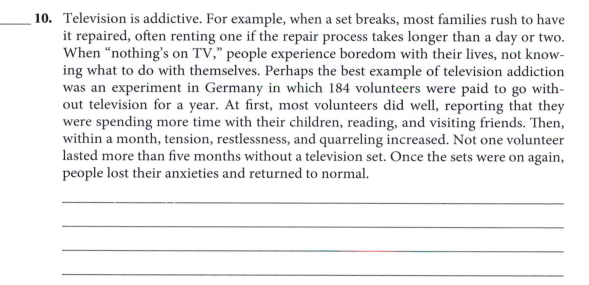

Application 2: Finding Paragraph Patterns

In a textbook for another class, find an example of at least five different paragraph patterns. Label each one, put a line in the margin by the main idea sentence or sentences, and number the supporting details. Bring your paragraphs to class and be prepared to justify your paragraph patterns with a class study partner.

PRACTICE B-2: Main Ideas in Longer Passages

Directions: The following reading passages are longer than the ones in the previous drills. Read them and answer the questions that follow. Use what you have learned about main ideas, supporting details, and paragraph patterns.

Passage A

The two most popular aerobic exercises are jogging and swimming. The latter is more enthusiastically recommended because it avoids the trauma to the legs and spine of jogging and utilizes the arms and chest muscles as well as the legs. It is done with the help, or buoyancy, of water. The gravitational force on your joints is not nearly so great as when standing out of water. Your weight in the water (with only your head and neck exposed) is only one-tenth what it is out of water.

Since the water, and not your body, bears much of your weight, swimming is an excellent exercise for those suffering with arthritis. At the same time the buoyancy also spares your knees, ankles, and lower back from the constant pounding associated with jogging. In fact swimming is often prescribed for those people who have suffered joint injuries from other sports or exercise activities. It strengthens the muscles of your abdomen and has been prescribed as the one exercise program for those with chronic back problems. (From Richard Stein, "What Is the Best Form of Exercise?" *Personal Strategies for Living With Stress*, John Gallagher Communications, 1983.)

1. Which statement best describes the main idea of the passage?
   a. The two most popular aerobic exercises are jogging and swimming.
   b. Jogging is better than swimming.
   c. Swimming is more popular than jogging.
   d. Swimming is recommended over jogging.

2. The writing pattern most used in this passage is
   a. definition.   **c.** cause/effect.
   b. comparison/contrast   **d.** both b and c

3. In the space provided, list some of the details given to support your answer to question 1.

   _____

   _____

   _____

   _____

Passage B

Race is a social concept that varies from one society to another, depending on how the people of that society feel about the importance of certain physical differences among human beings.

In biology, *race* refers to an in-breeding population that develops distinctive physical characteristics that are hereditary. But the choice of which physical characteristics to use in classifying people into races is arbitrary. Skin color, hair form, blood type, and facial features such as nose shape and eyefolds have been used by biologists in such efforts. In fact, however, there is a great deal of overlap among the so-called races in the distribution of these traits.

Of course these races exist. But they are not a set of distinct populations based on biological differences. The definitions of race used in different societies emerged from the interaction of various populations over long periods of human history. The specific physical characteristics that we use to assign people to different races are arbitrary and meaningless—people from the Indian sub-continent tend to have dark skin and straight hair; Africans from Ethiopia have dark skin and narrow facial features; American blacks have skin colors ranging from extremely dark to extremely light. There is no scientifically valid typology of human races; what counts is what people in a society define as meaningful. (From William Kornblum, *Sociology in a Changing World*, Harcourt Brace College Publishers, 1994, Chap. 13.)

1. Which basic pattern is used in the preceding passage?
   a. illustration/example   **c.** cause/effect
   b. definition   **d.** comparison/contrast

2. Explain why you selected the writing pattern you circled.

   _____

   _____

   _____

   _____

3. While the basic pattern is one of the choices in question 1, what other method is also used to a lesser degree?
   a. illustration/example
   b. definition
   c. cause/effect
   d. comparison/contrast

4. Explain your answer to question 3.

   _____

   _____

   _____

5. What is the main idea of this passage?

   _____

   _____

   _____

Passage C

Modern unionism also concentrates power and control in industry and government. A union will attempt to establish uniform wage rates in all plants in which the majority of workers are members of that union. In competition with other unions for members and power, it cannot accept lower rates of pay than those secured by other unions, even in different industries. Union competition of this kind tends to equalize wage rates for comparable work throughout a given industry and ultimately narrows the spread between wages paid for similar skills in different industries. But it is the bigger and longer established companies which are in the best position to absorb added wage costs to production. A particular handicap is presented new companies, with limited capital, once they are caught in such a competitive wage spiral. The established corporation, with a quasi-controlled market, can invariably pass on added labor costs either to distributors or to consumers, which a new company is unable to do. The charge has been made that some big corporations welcome "another round" of wage increases that will eliminate newer companies from "free competition." (From Arnold Green, *Sociology: An Analysis of Life in Modern Society*, McGraw-Hill, 1984, p. 265.)

1. What writing pattern is used in this passage?
   a. definition
   b. sequence of events
   c. comparison/contrast
   d. cause/effect

2. Two results occur when a union attempts to establish uniform wage rates in all plants in which the majority of workers are union members. Name them.

   _____

   _____

3. State in your own words what you think the main idea of this passage is.

   _____

   _____

   _____

   _____

Passage D

An analogy is a figure of speech in which two things are asserted to be alike in many respects that are quite fundamental. Their structure, the relationships of their parts, or the essential purposes they serve are similar, although the two things are also greatly dissimilar. Roses and carnations are not analogous. They both have stems and leaves, and may both be red in color. But they exhibit these qualities in the same way; they are of the same genus. The comparison of the heart to a pump, however, is a genuine analogy. These are disparate things, but they share important qualities: mechanical apparatus, possession of valves, ability to increase and decrease pressures, and capacity to move fluids. And the heart and the pump exhibit these qualities in different ways and in different contexts.

In discussing a crowded city, we do not offer an analogy when we compare it with another city. We are *merely* making a comparison. But if we compare the crowded city to an ant colony, we are setting forth an analogy. The two cities are not analogs; the city and the ant colony are. A ship manned by officers and a crew and crossing a stormy sea is a common analogy for a political state passing through perilous times. This is a popular analogy, for it brings out the striking similarities between two things notably dissimilar.

Like all figures of speech, the analogy serves rhetorical purposes. It enlivens discourse and may be used to stir the emotions. An analogy may, in addition, serve the descriptive function of giving a concrete and vivid simile for a concept that is too abstract or remote from ordinary experience to be clearly grasped. (From Gerald Runkle, *Good Thinking*, 3rd edition, Holt, Rinehart and Winston, 1991, p. 242.)

1. What is an analogy?

   _____

   _____

2. Why can an analogy be made between a heart and a pump?

   _____

   _____

3. Why can't an analogy be made between roses and carnations?

   _____

   _____

4. Why is the comparison of a crowded city with an ant colony considered an analogy?

   _____

   _____

5. What is the purpose of an analogy?

   _____

   _____

Passage E

Perceptual differences make communication challenging enough between members of the same culture. But when communicators come from different backgrounds, the potential for misunderstandings is even greater. Culture provides a perceptual filter that influences the way we interpret even the most simple events. This fact was demonstrated in studies exploring the domination of vision in one eye over the other. Researchers used a binocular-like device that projects different images to each eye. The subjects were 12 Americans and 12 Mexicans. Each was presented with ten pairs of photographs, each pair containing one picture from U.S. culture (e.g., a baseball game) and one from Mexican culture (e.g., a bullfight). After viewing each pair of images, the subjects reported what they saw. The results clearly indicated the power of culture to influence perceptions: Subjects had a strong tendency to see the image from their own background.

2   The same principle causes people from different cultures to interpret the same event in different ways. Blinking while another person talks may be hardly noticeable to North Americans, but the same behavior is considered impolite in Taiwan. A "V" made with fingers means victory in most of the Western world...as long as the palm is facing out. But in some European countries the same sign with the palm facing in roughly means "shove it." The beckoning finger motion that is familiar to Americans is an insulting gesture in most Middle and Far Eastern countries.

3   Even beliefs about the very value of talk differ from one culture to another. North American culture views talk as desirable and uses it for social purposes as well as to perform tasks. Silence has a negative value in this culture. It is likely to be interpreted as lack of interest, unwillingness to communicate, hostility, anxiety, shyness, or a sign of interpersonal incompatibility. Westerners are uncomfortable with silence, which they find embarrassing and awkward. Furthermore, the *kind* of talk Westerners admire is characterized by straightforwardness and honesty. Being indirect or vague—"beating around the bush," it might be labeled—has a negative connotation.

4   On the other hand, most Asian cultures discourage the expression of thoughts and feelings. Silence is valued, as Taoist sayings indicate: "In much talk there is great weariness," or "One who speaks does not know, one who knows does not speak." Unlike Westerners who are uncomfortable with silence, Japanese and Chinese believe that remaining quiet is the proper state when there is nothing to be said. To Easterners a talkative person is often considered a show-off or insincere. And when an Asian does speak up on social matters, the message is likely to be phrased indirectly to "save face" for the recipient.

5   It is easy to see how these different views of speech and silence can lead to communication problems when people from different cultures meet. Both the talkative Westerner and the silent Asian are behaving in ways they believe are proper, yet each views the other with disapproval and mistrust. Only when they recognize the different standards of behavior can they adapt to one another, or at least understand and respect their differences. (From Ronald Adler and George Rodman, *Understanding Human Communication*, fourth edition, copyright © 1991 by Harcourt, Inc. Reprinted by permission of the publisher.)

1. What is the main idea of paragraph 1? _____

_____

_____

2. What paragraph pattern is used in paragraph 2 and for what purpose? _____

_____

_____

3. What is being contrasted in paragraphs 3 and 4 _____

_____

_____

4. The topic of the passage is perception and culture. What main point is being made?

_____

_____

C.   Finding an Author's Thesis

Now is the time to put together all the skills you have learned and practiced in paragraphs. When you are reading essays or articles, you will need to follow many of the same steps used in reading individual paragraphs to increase your comprehension, but note that they often have slightly different terminology.

Every article or essay has a topic or subject. The topic or subject is what the author is writing about, such as computers, good manners, horse racing, war, a country, and the like. The *thesis*, or main idea, is not the same as the topic or subject. A thesis is what the author wants to say about the subject or the author's feelings about the subject. Every well-written essay or article contains a thesis or a main idea about the subject that the author wants the reader to accept or think about.

Instead of finding the main idea in each paragraph, you will now want to look at the entire essay or article and figure out what the thesis of the whole piece is. Let's say you are reading an essay about grades and their value. That would be the subject or topic of the essay. But you need to understand the main point the author is making about grades. Is the author in favor of grades or against them? Is the author presenting a new concept about grading that he or she wants the reader to accept? A thesis, then, is what the author wants to say about that particular subject. Recognizing an author's thesis is basic to developing good literal comprehension.

A thesis of an article or essay is often near the beginning or end of the article. The thesis may not be the first or last paragraph, however, because authors often use introductory and concluding paragraphs to get the interest of the reader. Find the thesis in the same way you look for topics and main ideas in paragraphs. First, read through the article quickly to discover the subject or topic. Then use headings or subheadings to get the big picture about what the author is saying about this subject. Now look through the article for the most general statement about that topic. Don't forget that main ideas may be implied.

Finding the subject and thesis of an article is central to understanding the article. Poor readers often get bogged down in details and then have no idea what the article is about. Make this search for the author's subject and thesis the first priority of your reading.

The next few practices help you recognize an author's thesis.

PRACTICE C-1

Directions: Read carefully, looking for the subject, the thesis, and the supporting details in the essay.

WAR ON PREJUDICE STARTS WITH OURSELVES

MICHAEL YACHNIK

1   All of us have prejudices. We might like to believe that we outgrow most of them. Unfortunately, a large number of prejudices begin early in life and linger until we confront and change them.

2   That is because early life exposure to society's rejection of select groups is profound. Sadly, the attitudes of fear and loathing are often delivered to us by people we love and depend on. The messages of intolerance and mistrust of others are interwoven with messages of nurturing and affection for us.

3   When we were children and our caregivers expressed their affection by telling us about threats and promising to protect us from *them*, that made us feel loved and secure. But if those caregivers didn't differentiate between "real threats" (people who drive recklessly, push drugs or bully others) and "imagined threats" (people who have a different race, religion or sexual orientation), then we developed fears and dislikes of people who are merely different. Those fears, though irrational, were paired with early memories of love and security—and that makes them powerful and enduring.

4   As children, we weren't sophisticated enough to determine which messages were necessary for our survival and which reflected the prejudices of our caregivers. Unwittingly, we went along, reinforcing negative ideas about others because we trusted those who gave us those ideas in the first place. Many of us arrive at adulthood with some harmful baggage.

5   So what can we do about it now?

6   A lot. First, we can examine the many messages we have received and determine which we want to foster and which we want to change. It is possible to value the loving and nurturing messages we received from caregivers while acknowledging that they grew up with prejudices that may have been inadvertently passed along to us.

7   Next, we can educate ourselves and confront any false ideas we have about people who are different. The many cultural events in Los Angeles, including festivals, fairs, films and art exhibits, offer a great way to learn something new while having fun. If nothing new is allowed in, we're stuck with the information that created the prejudices in the first place.

8   Finally, we can put our learning into action. Do we let derogatory remarks about others pass without comment because we can remember hearing someone from our past say them? Or do we remind ourselves and others that we need to shed some of our old ideas and develop new ones? Do we structure our lives to avoid people who are different from us because "that's the way it's always been"? Or do we evaluate our behavior rationally and try to change it?

9   Examining old attitudes, seeking out information to form new ones and changing behavior—those are the key elements to winning the war on prejudice.

10   What is the most effective way to do these things on a regular basis? If, in our personal and professional lives, we reach out to meet and interact with people who are different from us, we will be able to confront old attitudes regularly. New friends can help educate us by sharing their life experiences and listening to ours. As the friendships grow, our motivation to change will also grow. And as the number of friendships and acquaintances increases, we will have more examples of people in our lives who reinforce new ideas about others who may be different.

Los Angeles Times, March 28, 1994, B5. Reprinted by permission of Michael Yachnik, Ph.D.

Directions: Now answer the following questions. You may need to reread portions of the essay, especially when certain paragraphs are referred to.

1. Which of the following best states the main idea of the essay?
   a. All of us have prejudices, but they change as we grow older.
   b. We are exposed to prejudices as children but can change them by examining our messages, educating ourselves, and changing our actions.
   c. The way to win the war on prejudice is to meet and interact with a diverse group of people.
   d. None of the above.

2. In paragraph 3, what does the author say about caregivers and threats that may then develop into prejudices? _____

   _____

3. T/F We can infer from this essay that it is each person's responsibility to overcome prejudices that caregivers pass on. Explain why you think this inference is true or false. _____

   _____

4. List details that show how people in Los Angeles can educate themselves and perhaps change their prejudices._____

   _____

5. List the three ways this essay gives us to overcome our prejudices._____

   _____

6. Give an example of how you have used one of the three elements to overcome a prejudice in your own life. _____

   _____

   Finding the thesis in a reading selection such as the one you just read is similar to finding the main idea in a paragraph. The difference is that in a longer selection, paragraphs are used to support the thesis whereas sentences are used to support the topic sentence in a paragraph. Of course, the longer the selection, the more difficult it can be to separate supporting details from the thesis.
   See how well you did on the questions you just answered.

1. b

2. need to differentiate between real threats and imagined threats

3. True. The author says we can't help the messages we received as children, but as adults we can do a lot about them.

4. cultural events, including festivals, fairs, films, and art exhibits

5. examine our messages, educate ourselves, put our learning into action.

6. Answers will vary. But keep what the author says in mind the next time you catch yourself being prejudiced about someone or something.

   Before going on to the next practice, make certain you understand any mistakes or misinterpretations you may have made in answering the preceding questions.

PRACTICE C-2

Directions: Follow the same directions as the last practice. Read carefully, looking for the subject, the thesis, and the supporting details in the essay.

WHY RACE ISN'T AS "BLACK" AND "WHITE" AS WE THINK

BRENT STAPLES

1   People have occasionally asked me how a black person came by a "white" name like Brent Staples. One letter writer ridiculed it as "an anchorman's name" and accused me of making it up. For the record, it's a British name—and the one my parents gave me. "Staples" probably arrived in my family's ancestral home in Virginia four centuries ago with the British settlers.

2   The earliest person with that name we've found—Richard Staples—was hacked to death by Powhatan Indians not far from Jamestown in 1622. The name moved into the 18th century with Virginians like John Staples, a white surveyor who worked in Thomas Jefferson's home country, Albemarle, not far from the area where my family was enslaved.

3   The black John Staples who married my paternal great-great-grandmother just after Emancipation—and became the stepfather of her children—could easily have been a Staples family slave. The transplanted Britons who had owned both sides of my family had given us more than a preference for British names. They had also given us their DNA. In what was an almost everyday occurrence at the time, my great-great-grandmothers on both sides gave birth to children fathered by white slave masters.

4   I've known all this for a long time, and was not surprised by the results of a genetic screening performed by DNAPrint Genomics, a company that traces ancestral origins to far-flung parts of the globe. A little more than half of my genetic material came from sub-Saharan Africa—common for people who regard themselves as black—with slightly more than a quarter from Europe.

5   The result that knocked me off my chair showed that one-fifth of my ancestry is Asian. Poring over the charts and statistics, I said out loud, "This has got to be a mistake."

6   That's a common response among people who are tested. Ostensibly white people who always thought of themselves as 100 percent European find they have substantial African ancestry. People who regard themselves as black sometimes discover that the African ancestry is a minority portion of their DNA.

7   These results are forcing people to re-examine the arbitrary calculations our culture uses to decide who is "white" and who is "black."

8   As with many things racial, this story begins in the slave-era South, where sex among slaves, masters and mistresses got started as soon as the first slave ship sailed into Jamestown Harbor in 1619. By the time of the American Revolution, there was a visible class of light-skinned black people who no longer looked or sounded African. Free mulattos, emancipated by guilt-ridden fathers, may have accounted for up to three-quarters of the tiny free-black population before the Revolution.

9   By the eve of the Civil War, the swarming numbers of mixed-race slaves on Southern plantations had become a source of constant anguish to planters' wives, who knew quite well where those racially ambiguous children were coming from.

10   Faced with widespread fear that racial distinctions were losing significance, the South decided to define the problem away. People with any ascertainable black ancestry at all were defined as black under the law and stripped of basic rights. The "one drop" laws defined as black even people who were blond and blue-eyed and appeared white.

11   Black people snickered among themselves and worked to subvert segregation at every turn. Thanks to white ancestry spread throughout the black community, nearly every family knew of someone born black who successfully passed as white to get access to jobs, housing and public accommodations that were reserved for white people only. Black people who were not quite light enough to slip undetected into white society billed themselves as Greek, Spanish, Portuguese, Italian, South Asian, Native American—you name it. These defectors often married into ostensibly white families at a time when interracial marriage was either illegal or socially stigmatized.

12   Those of us who grew up in the 1950's and 60's read black-owned magazines and newspapers that praised the racial defectors as pioneers while mocking white society for failing to detect them. A comic newspaper column by the poet Langston Hughes—titled "Why Not Fool Our White Folks?"—typified the black community's sense of smugness about knowing the real racial score. In keeping with this history, many black people I know find it funny when supposedly white Americans profess shock at the emergence of blackness in the family tree. But genetic testing holds plenty of surprises for black folks, too.

13   Which brings me back to my Asian ancestry. It comes as a surprise, given that my family's oral histories contain not a single person who is described as Asian. More testing on other family members should clarify the issue, but for now, I can only guess. This ancestry could well have come through a 19th-century ancestor who was incorrectly described as Indian, often a catchall category at the time.

14   The test results underscore what anthropologists have said for eons: racial distinctions as applied in this country are social categories and not scientific concepts. In addition, those categories draw hard, sharp distinctions among groups of people who are more alike than they are different. The ultimate point is that none of us really know who we are, ancestrally speaking. All we ever really know is what our parents and grandparents have told us.

Directions: Answer the following questions. You may need to reread portions of the essay to answer all the questions.

1. What is the topic or subject of the essay?

2. What is the thesis or point the author makes about the topic?

3. In what paragraph, if any, is the thesis best stated?

4. What reasons does the author give to support his thesis?

_____

_____

_____

5. What did the author find out about his heritage that surprised him?

_____

6. If you had your DNA tested by DNAPrint Genomics, do you think you might be surprised at your ancestral heritage? Explain.

_____

D.   Summarizing as a Way to Test Your Understanding

Now that you have practiced identifying main ideas and supporting details, recognizing basic patterns, and finding the thesis of longer articles, you have the skills to put all these together by learning how to summarize. You will need to use all the skills you've learned in this chapter in order to write a summary.

Frequently, instructors in your college classes will ask you to write summaries of reading assignments. In addition, many essay exams you will be required to take are really nothing more than a test of your ability to write summaries in answer to questions based on sections from your textbooks. What, then, *is* a summary, and how do you write one?

A summary is a brief statement in your own words of the main ideas and support used in a reading selection. Writing summaries requires that you include only the most vital information presented in a piece of writing. The practices you have been doing that require you to separate the main ideas from details provide the basis for writing summaries.

There are three basic things to keep in mind when you write a summary: Be brief, be complete, and be objective. This can sound easier than it is. If you are too brief, you may not be complete; if you try to be too complete, you may write too much; if you're not careful, you may slip into subjectivity, allowing your own feelings and opinions to creep in. A summary has no place for your views. As a guideline, a good rule of thumb in writing summaries is to make them no longer than one-quarter of the length of the passage you are summarizing. But this may vary depending on the instructor's summary assignment.

Let's say you are asked to summarize the essay you just read in Practice C-1, "War on Prejudice Starts with Ourselves." The best way to get started is to begin with the author's thesis, which is reflected in his title. Yachnik believes that doing away with prejudice starts with each person. Why? What does he want us to do about these prejudices?

As we look over the essay paragraph by paragraph, we see that the first two paragraphs set up the idea that we all have prejudices and they start early in life.

The third and fourth paragraphs show how caregivers pass on prejudices, often unwittingly by failing to differentiate between real and imagined threats.

Paragraph 6 uses the signal word *first* so we clearly recognize it as a first major point, that we need to examine the messages we received as children.

Paragraph 7 uses the signal word *next* to signal the next major point, that we can educate ourselves about people who are different from us.

Paragraph 8 uses the signal word *finally* to show the third major point, that we need to change our actions.

Paragraph 9 summarizes these three points as an extra assurance that we will recognize their importance.

The last paragraph ends with specific ideas each of us can use on a daily basis to overcome prejudices, emphasizing the need to make friends with people who are different from us.

As we move through the paragraphs, we can list what the author suggests to recognize and overcome prejudices.

1. All of us have prejudices, which will stay the same unless we take steps to change them.

2. Our prejudices often started in childhood when our caregivers didn't differentiate between real and imagined threats, so we received some negative ideas.

3. The first thing we can do to overcome prejudice is examine the messages we have received.

4. The second thing we can do to overcome prejudice is educate ourselves and confront prejudices.

5. The third thing we can do to overcome prejudice is to put our plan into action, not allowing prejudice in others around us.

6. We can do this on a regular basis by developing friendships with people who are different from us.

Now, if we put all this together, we might have a summary that says something like this:

> In his essay "War on Prejudice Starts with Ourselves," Michael Yachnik states that each of us has prejudices and that doing away with them takes work. These prejudices, he feels, start in childhood when caregivers don't differentiate between real and imagined threats, so we receive some negative ideas. He says we can do three things to overcome these prejudices. The first step is to examine the messages we have received. The second step is to educate ourselves about people who are different. The third step is to change our actions, refusing to participate in prejudice or encourage it in others. Yachnik concludes that we can do this on a daily basis by seeking out friendships with people who are different from us.

Obviously things have to be left out of a summary, but this example is brief, complete in presenting the thesis and support used by Yachnik, and objective.

In order to write this summary, it was necessary to go over Yachnik's essay very carefully. Summary writing requires using the skills necessary for separating main ideas from details and identifying the author's thesis, both skills that were taught in this unit. The practice of writing summaries of what you read can be of great benefit to your literal comprehension development.

PRACTICE D-1: Practice in Summarizing

Directions: Read the following article by Brian Clark, a writer, producer, new media entrepreneur, founding editor of Copyblogger (www.copyblogger.com) and co-founder of DIY

Themes, a blog development tool, and Lateral Action, a web publication dedicated to creativity. Read for his main idea and his supporting details. You will be asked to summarize the article.

10 MENTAL BLOCKS TO CREATIVE THINKING

BRIAN CLARK

1   Whether you're trying to solve a tough problem, start a business, get attention for that business, or write an interesting article, creative thinking is crucial. The process boils down to changing your perspective and seeing things differently than you currently do.

2   People like to call this "thinking outside of the box," which is the wrong way to look at it. Just like Neo needed to understand that "there is no spoon" in the film *The Matrix*, you need to realize "there is no box" to step outside of.

3   You create your own imaginary boxes simply by living life and accepting certain things as "real" when they are just as illusory as the beliefs of a paranoid delusional. The difference is, enough people agree that certain man-made concepts are "real," so you're viewed as "normal." This is good for society overall, but it's that sort of unquestioning consensus that inhibits your natural creative abilities.

4   So, rather than looking for ways to inspire creativity, you should just realize the truth. You're already capable of creative thinking at all times, but you have to strip away the imaginary mental blocks (or boxes) that you've picked up along the way to wherever you are today.

5   I like to keep this list of 10 common ways we suppress our natural creative abilities nearby when I get stuck. It helps me realize that the barriers to a good idea are truly all in my head.

10 *Things that Suppress Creativity*

6   1. Trying to Find the "Right" Answer

One of the worst aspects of formal education is the focus on finding the correct answer to a particular question or problem. While this approach helps us function in society, it hurts creative thinking because real-life issues are ambiguous. There's often more than one "correct" answer, and the second one you come up with might be better than the first.

7   Many of the following mental blocks can be turned around to reveal ways to find more than one answer to any given problem. Try reframing the issue in several different ways in order to prompt different answers, and embrace answering inherently ambiguous questions in several different ways.

8   2. Logical Thinking

Not only is real life ambiguous, it's often illogical to the point of madness. While critical thinking skills based on logic are one of our main strengths in evaluating the feasibility of a creative idea, it's often the first enemy of truly innovative thoughts.

9   One of the best ways to escape the constraints of your own logical mind is to think metaphorically. One of the reasons why metaphors work so well in communications is that we accept them as true without thinking about it. When you realize that "truth" is often symbolic, you'll often find that you are actually free to come up with alternatives. (Tip: Compare or contrast two things or ideas that seem unlike but actually share something important. One famous example, "My heart is a lonely hunter that hunts on a lonely hill," by William Sharp, "The Lonely Hunter.")

10 3. Following Rules

One way to view creative thinking is to look at it as a destructive force. You're tearing away the often arbitrary rules that others have set for you, and asking either "why" or "why not" whenever confronted with the way "everyone" does things.

11 This is easier said than done, since people will often defend the rules they follow even in the face of evidence that the rule doesn't work. People love to celebrate rebels like Richard Branson, but few seem brave enough to emulate him. Quit worshipping rule breakers and start breaking some rules.

12 4. Being Practical

Like logic, practicality is hugely important when it comes to execution, but often stifles innovative ideas before they can properly blossom. Don't allow the editor into the same room with your inner artist.

13 Try not to evaluate the actual feasibility of an approach until you've allowed it to exist on its own for a bit. Spend time asking, "What if?" as often as possible, and simply allow your imagination to go where it wants. You might just find yourself discovering a crazy idea that's so insanely practical that no one's thought of it before.

14 5. Play is Not Work

Allowing your mind to be at play is perhaps the most effective way to stimulate creative thinking, and yet many people disassociate play from work. These days, the people who come up with great ideas and solutions are the most economically rewarded, while worker bees are often employed for the benefit of the creative thinkers.

15 You've heard the expression "work hard and play hard." All you have to realize is that they're the same thing to a creative thinker.

16 6. That's Not My Job

In an era of hyper-specialization, it's those who happily explore completely unrelated areas of life and knowledge who best see that everything is related. This goes back to what ad man Carl Ally said about creative persons—they want to be know-it-alls.

17 Sure, you've got to know the specialized stuff in your field, but if you view yourself as an explorer rather than a highly specialized cog in the machine, you'll run circles around the technical master in the success department.

18 7. Being a "Serious" Person

Most of what keeps us civilized boils down to conformity, consistency, shared values, and yes, thinking about things the same way everyone else does. There's nothing wrong with that necessarily, but if you can mentally accept that it's actually nothing more than groupthink that helps a society function, you can then give yourself permission to turn everything that's accepted upside down and shake out the illusions.

19 Leaders from Egyptian pharaohs to Chinese emperors and European royalty have consulted with fools, or court jesters, when faced with tough problems. The persona of the fool allowed the truth to be told, without the usual ramifications that might come with speaking blasphemy or challenging ingrained social conventions. Give yourself permission to be a fool and see things for what they really are.

20 8. Avoiding Ambiguity

We rationally realize that most every situation is ambiguous to some degree. And although dividing complex situations into black and white boxes can lead to disaster, we still do it. It's an innate characteristic of human psychology to desire certainty, but it's the creative thinker who rejects the false comfort of clarity when it's not really appropriate.

21 Ambiguity is your friend if you're looking to innovate. The fact that most people are uncomfortable exploring uncertainty gives you an advantage, as long as you can embrace ambiguity rather than run from it.

22 9. Being Wrong Is Bad

We hate being wrong, and yet mistakes often teach us the most. Thomas Edison was wrong 1,800 times before getting the light bulb right. Edison's greatest strength was that he was not afraid to be wrong.

23   The best thing we do is learn from our mistakes, but we have to free ourselves to make mistakes in the first place. Just try out your ideas and see what happens, take what you learn, and try something else. Ask yourself, what's the worst that can happen if I'm wrong? You'll often find the benefits of being wrong greatly outweigh the potential penalties.

24   10. I'm Not Creative

Denying your own creativity is like denying you're a human being. We're all limitlessly creative, but only to the extent that we realize that we create our own limits with the way we think. If you tell yourself you're not creative, it becomes true. Stop that.

25   In that sense, awakening your own creativity is similar to the path reported by those who seek spiritual enlightenment. You're already enlightened, just like you're already creative, but you have to strip away all of your delusions before you can see it. Acknowledge that you're inherently creative, and then start tearing down the other barriers you've allowed to be created in your mind.

Directions: On a separate sheet of paper, write a summary of the article you just read. Remember, be brief, be complete, and be objective. Turn the summary in to your instructor.

PRACTICE D-2: Practice in Summarizing

Directions: On a separate sheet of paper, write a summary of passage B on page 90, which you have already read. You may want to use the answers to your questions as a guide.

PRACTICE D-3: More Summarizing

Directions: On a separate sheet of paper, write a summary of passage E on pages 92–93, which you have already read. You may want to use your answers as a guide.

> ### Application 3: Summarizing Materials of Your Own Choice
>
> Find a 750–1000-word article in a current magazine or a textbook and summarize it. Turn in a copy of the article and the summary.

E.   Flexible Reading Rates

Another skill you will find essential is developing reading-rate versatility. How fast a person reads is irrelevant if good comprehension doesn't match the speed. Yet with a little training, most people can easily increase their reading rate without a loss in comprehension. Most people have never been trained in reading rate, yet college students are often hard pressed to keep up with assignments, and their concentration may wander when a textbook is open.

There are several factors to consider when discussing reading speed. First, not everything can be—or should be—read at the fastest rate. Your reading rate should depend on your *purpose* for reading. Surveying to get an idea of what you will be reading, looking for specific items, and reviewing for tests are purposes that allow fast reading rates. Some textbooks may be easy enough that faster rates are appropriate. But if you have been assigned to write an essay about a poem in your English textbook, you will probably need to read that poem several times before you can even begin to get an idea for your essay. You may need to look up the definitions of many of the words used, considering their connotative meanings. You may need to consider the rhyme schemes used and the form of the poem. With poetry, you will get more out of it if you read aloud. The reading and understanding of that poem may take longer than the reading of fifty pages in a psychology text. Reading rates vary with reading purposes.

A second factor in reading speed has to do with your *concentration* as you read. The most intense concentration in difficult school tasks occurs in about twenty-minute segments. This does *not* mean you can study for only twenty minutes, but it does mean you will concentrate better if you set short, frequent study sessions and change study activities more often. Learn to take advantage of the short concentration span, especially with college assignments that do not automatically grab your interest and keep it. People who set long study periods ("I'll study all day Saturday") are usually deluding themselves. Are you aware when your concentration wanders? Is there a pattern to when you can and cannot concentrate? What is your shortest concentration span? Your longest? The important point is *not* to sit with your book open while your mind drifts. Once you have allowed yourself to drift, just opening that book will often trigger daydreaming. The minute your mind wanders, turn away from that book immediately.

A third factor affecting reading speed is lack of knowledge about how to read faster. Old reading habits are hard to break. Because most people are never trained to read quickly, reading habits learned early in life are never broken. Training in four areas can help you speed up your reading rate with no loss in comprehension:

1. *Reading for ideas and detecting patterns.* Untrained readers read as if every word is equally important in every kind of reading. Instead, you should read for ideas and think about what you're reading.

a. The first exercise to help you read for ideas is *closure*, or the mind's ability to fill in blanks without seeing every detail. If I say, "Tom went to the _____ and bought a loaf of _____," your mind closes on the blank spaces, and you know he went to the store or bakery and bought a loaf of bread.

Here is an exercise to help you understand how closure works. In the following paragraph, twenty-five of the sixty-one words are crossed out, yet the meaning is still clear.

> Another study skill ~~you will find~~ essential ~~is developing~~ reading-rate versatility. How fast ~~a person reads is~~ irrelevant if good comprehension doesn't match ~~the~~ speed. ~~Yet~~ with ~~a little~~ training, ~~most~~ people ~~can easily~~ increase ~~their~~ reading rate without ~~a~~ loss in comprehension. ~~Most~~ people read ~~as~~ slowly ~~as they do~~ because ~~they've~~ never ~~been~~ shown how to read faster.

With twenty-five words crossed out, the paragraph now reads:

> Another study skill essential reading-rate versatility. How fast irrelevant if good comprehension doesn't match speed. With training, people increase reading rate without loss in comprehension. People read slowly because never shown how to read faster.

Do you see how you can get full meaning without stopping at each word? You can practice closure in your textbooks.

b. The second exercise to help you read faster for ideas is to pick out main ideas, select supporting details, and detect paragraph patterns. These skills, which you learned in this chapter, will enable you to read faster with better comprehension.

Practice reading for ideas by seeing how quickly you can pick out main ideas and figure out the pattern of details in the following paragraphs.

> As a technical writer, you need to remember these four ethical principles. First, don't leave out any vital information (such as safety hazards). Next, don't exaggerate (such as claims for absolute success). Third, create a clear understanding of what the information means. Finally, respect copyrighted information. Don't knowingly download or distribute copyrighted information.

Where is the main idea? _____

How many supporting details are there? _____

> When interviewing for a job, don't ask about salary or bonuses during the first interview. Be prepared to ask questions that show your knowledge of the job or the company. Act as if you are determined to get the job. These are some of the tips to help you function most effectively in a job interview.

Where is the main idea? _____

How many supporting details are there? _____

> Low-level concentration is characterized by an inability to settle on one activity or to discipline the mind to follow one track at a time. People who operate at this level are often very busy people who try to do two or three tasks at the same time. Dabblers, another group with low concentration, do a lot of different things but never seem to master any of them. A third group is daydreamers, who may have textbooks open but their minds are not engaged.

Where is the main idea? _____

How many supporting details are there? _____

Here are the answers: In the first paragraph, the main idea is the first sentence and there are four major details (don't omit, don't exaggerate, be clear, respect copyrights). In the second paragraph, the main idea is the last sentence, and there are three major details (no salary questions, ask questions, be determined). In the third paragraph, the main idea is the first sentence, and there are three major details (busy people, dabblers, daydreamers).

2. *Increasing vocabulary.* If a page has three or more unfamiliar words on it, you will not be able to speed-read it. You therefore need to continue the vocabulary strategies you learned in Chapter One. As your vocabulary increases, you will find more materials you can read quickly. If you want to read quickly, you need to learn the terminology first.

3. *Learning pacing strategies.* Untrained readers often find their minds wandering while they read. Training yourself to read at a forced rate with good concentration will take practice. Use an index card to cover each line as you read it, moving it down the page a little faster than you currently read. Another pacing strategy is to use your hand or a pen to keep you reading at a forced rate. Do not use your hand to trace each word or each line. Pull it straight down the page at a rate a little faster than your current rate.

4. *Practicing fast reading rates.* The only way to learn flexible reading rates is to practice for a short time each day with fast rates. Find an easy, interesting book with no new vocabulary. Students have found it helpful to check out young juvenile literature from the library for this exercise. Work up to more difficult books as you feel more comfortable with fast rates.

Start with five- to ten-minute practice sessions and work up to longer periods of time as your concentration and rate increase. If your concentration wanders, stop your practice session and turn away from your book.

Surveying

In order to increase your reading rate, you need to start surveying selections *before* you start reading. Surveying is defined as the ability to identify *main ideas* while very rapidly and selectively skimming over the reading material. Surveying is a technique used to find out how a news story, magazine article, or textbook chapter is organized and what it is generally about in a short time. You will learn more about the SQ3R study method (Survey, Question, Read, Recite, Review) in the next chapter.

Contrary to what most readers think, surveying is not a sloppy, hit-or-miss technique. To survey a news story, you need to understand the organizational pattern of writing news stories. Usually each sentence or two is a paragraph in itself. This style prevents paragraphs from looking too long in the narrow columns that newspapers often use. The opening sentence to a news story often covers *who*, *what*, *where*, *when*, and sometimes *why*. At the very least, most stories tell *who* and *what* in the opening line. Thus, when surveying a newspaper story, it is always advisable to concentrate on the opening sentence.

A magazine article or essay has a different organization. Titles are more reliable here than in newspaper stories, which can be misleading. Magazine titles tend to reveal a subject and sometimes a thesis or the author's attitude. This is an aid to surveying. For instance, if the title of a magazine article reads "Lake Havasu: A Fisherman's Paradise," you already have a clue to the article's content and the author's attitude or point of view. As you survey, you would then look for reasons the author feels the lake is a "paradise" for fishermen.

Some magazine articles are set up the same way as most textbook chapters. In addition to helpful titles, most contain headings and subheadings to alert the reader that a new idea related to the subject is being introduced. The word *alert* is the key to being a good surveyer.

Here is what to be alert to when you survey magazine articles:

1. Read the title and scan the opening paragraph or two, looking for the subject of the article and the author's thesis or point of view about the subject.

2. Read the first sentence or parts of the first sentence of each following paragraph, looking for ideas related to or supporting the author's thesis.

3. Read the last paragraph (or last two paragraphs, depending on the article), looking for a summary or conclusion about the subject.

4. If there are questions (as in the following selection), look at the questions during your survey.

This approach or a modification of it will help you preview an article's contents. At least you will know whether you want or need to read the article more closely.

F.   Putting It All Together

The next two practices give you the opportunity to use what you have learned about reading to find an author's thesis and use of main ideas and supporting details. Before you begin, it is recommended that you refer to the Student Record Chart and review your scores for the reading selections in Chapter One. Note your comprehension and vocabulary scores. Try to either match your scores or do better this time. As you progress through this book, use these scores as a motivation and challenge to do better each time. Your only competition is yourself.

PRACTICE F-1

Directions: As you read the following essay, distinguish between the subject and the thesis and note what main ideas and supporting details are used to back up the author's thesis.

THINKING: A NEGLECTED ART

CAROLYN KANE

1   It is generally agreed that the American educational system is in deep trouble. Everyone is aware of the horrible facts: school systems are running out of money, teachers can't spell.

2   Most of us know or think we know who is to blame: liberal courts, spineless school boards, government regulations. It is easy to select a villain.

3   But possibly the problem lies not so much in our institutions as in our attitudes. It is sad that although most of us profess to believe in education, we place no value on intellectual activity.

4   We Americans are a charitable and humane people: we have institutions devoted to every good cause from rescuing homeless cats to preventing World War III. But what have we done to promote the art of thinking? Certainly we make no room for thought in our daily lives. Suppose a man were to say to his friends, "I'm not going to PTA tonight

(or choir practice or the baseball game) because I need some time to myself, some time to think"? Such a man would be shunned by his neighbors; his family would be ashamed of him. What if a teenager were to say, "I'm not going to the dance tonight because I need some time to think"? His parents would immediately start looking in the Yellow Pages for a psychiatrist. We are all too much like Julius Caesar: we fear and distrust people who think too much. We believe that almost anything is more important than thinking.

5   **Guilty:** Several years ago a college administrator told me that if he wanted to do any serious thinking, he had to get up at 5:30 in the morning—I suppose because that was the only time when no one would interrupt him. More recently I heard a professor remark that when his friends catch him in the act of reading a book, they say, "My, it must be nice to have so much free time." And even though I am an English teacher—a person who should know better—I find myself feeling vaguely guilty whenever I sneak off to the library to read. It is a common belief that if people are thinking or reading, they are doing nothing. Through our words and our actions, we express this attitude every day of our lives. Then we wonder why our children refuse to take their studies seriously and why they say to their teachers, "This stuff won't do me any good because I'll never need to use it."

6   It is easy to understand the causes of this prejudice against thinking. One problem is that to most of us, thinking looks suspiciously like loafing. *Homo sapiens* in deep thought is an uninspiring sight. He leans back in his chair, props up his feet, puffs on his pipe and stares into space. He gives every appearance of wasting time; he reminds us more of Dagwood and Beetle Bailey than of Shakespeare and Einstein. We wish he would get up and *do* something; mow the lawn, maybe, or wash the car. Our resentment is natural.

7   But thinking is far different from laziness. Thinking is one of the most productive activities a human being can undertake. Every beautiful and useful thing we have created—including democratic government and freedom of religion—exists because somebody took the time and effort to think of it.

8   And thinking does require time and effort. It is a common misconception that if a person is "gifted" or "bright" or "talented," wonderful ideas will flash spontaneously into his mind. Unfortunately, the intellect does not work in this way. Even Einstein had to study and think for months before he could formulate his theory of relativity. Those of us who are less intelligent find it a struggle to conceive even a moderately good idea, let alone a brilliant one.

9   **Seclusion:** Another reason why we distrust thinking is that it seems unnatural. Human beings are a social species, but thinking is an activity that requires solitude. Consequently, we worry about people who like to think. It disturbs us to meet a person who deliberately chooses to sit alone and think instead of going to a party or a rodeo or a soccer match. We suspect that such a person needs counseling.

10   Our concern is misplaced. Intelligence is just as much a part of human nature as sociability. It would certainly be unnatural for a person to retreat into total seclusion. It would be equally unnatural for a person to allow his mind to die of neglect.

11   If Americans ever became convinced of the importance of thought, we would probably find ways to solve the problems of our schools, problems that now seem insurmountable. But how can we revive interest in the art of thinking? The best place to start would be in the homes and churches of our land. Ministers should admonish their congregations to do some purposeful procrastination every day, to put off one chore in order to have a few minutes to think. Family members should practice saying such things as, "I'll wash the dishes tonight because I know you want to catch up on your thinking."

12   This may sound un-American, possibly sacrilegious. But if we are to survive as a free people, we will have to take some such course of action as soon as possible, because regardless of what some advertisers have led us to believe, this country does not run on oil. It runs on ideas.

Comprehension Check

Directions: Answer the following questions without looking back.

1. What is the *subject* of the essay you just read? _____
    _____

2. What is the *thesis* of this essay? _____
    _____

3. According to the author, if someone is thinking or reading, that person is fre-
    quently thought of as
        a. weird.   **c.** studying.
        b. doing nothing.   **d.** not using his or her time wisely.

4. State two reasons the author gives for prejudice against thinking: _____
    _____
    _____

5. According to the author, thinking requires
        a. time.   **c.** solitude.
        b. effort   **d.** all three.

6. The author uses Einstein as an example to support one of her main ideas. What
    point is she making?_____
    _____

7. If a person chooses to sit alone and think instead of going to a party or sports
    event, we tend to suspect that that person
        a. is a nerd.   **c.** needs counseling.
        b. is another Einstein.   **d.** none of these.

8. How, according to the author, can we revive interest in the art of thinking? _____
    _____
    _____

9. T /F The author claims that while we profess to believe in education, we place no
    value on intellectual activity.

10. The author concludes that this country runs on _____

Vocabulary Check

Directions: Define the following underlined words from the selection.

1. spineless school boards (paragraph 2)
    _____

2. will flash spontaneously into his mind (paragraph 8)
    _____

3. he could formulate his theory (paragraph 8)
    _____

4. problems that now seem <u>insurmountable</u> (paragraph 11)

_____

5. should <u>admonish</u> their congregations (paragraph 11)

_____

6. some purposeful <u>procrastination</u> (paragraph 11)

_____

7. may sound…possibly <u>sacrilegious</u> (paragraph 12)

_____

8. <u>shunned</u> by his neighbors (paragraph 4)

_____

9. What is the suffix in <u>spineless</u> and what does it mean? (Chapter One, Practice C-7)

_____

10. What is the first prefix in <u>insurmountable</u> and what does it mean? (Chapter One, Practice C-1)

_____

Record the results of the comprehension and vocabulary checks on the Student Record Chart in the Appendix. Make certain you understand any mistakes you may have made before going on. Use whatever method you are using to learn any words you missed.

Practice F-2: Timed Reading

Directions: You have a lot of information about vocabulary and literal comprehension strategies now. The third—and most often overlooked—strategy to improve your reading is to increase your reading rate. The purpose is not to make you read faster and lose your comprehension but rather to read faster and increase your comprehension. Very slow readers (under 180 wpm) often lose concentration and focus only on details or isolated words rather than understanding what the article or essay is saying. If you read too slowly, you also can't get through all your college assignments (unless you give up sleep!).

The first step to reading faster is to decide what rate you want to set, based on three factors. The first factor is how familiar you are with the topic in the first place. In this article, you can look at the title, "Putting Reading in Its Proper Place," and realize that it is about reading and what importance we give to it. This topic is familiar to all of us, even if we haven't actually thought about it before. If the topic is particle physics, on the other hand, you probably don't know much about it and would need to set a slower rate.

The second factor to help you set your rate is the difficulty of the material. Glance at any paragraph and see if you understand the vocabulary. If there are more than three unfamiliar words on a page, you will find the material more difficult and will need to set a slower rate. Can you figure out the unfamiliar words from context, or will it affect your comprehension if you don't know the words? If English is not your primary language, you may find that unfamiliar words hamper your comprehension.

If so, practice the rate exercises and learn the skills, but make comprehension your primary goal.

The third factor is your purpose for reading the material. In this text, the purpose is to answer the comprehension questions accurately and well. In order to help you do this, you should look at the questions first—before you even start reading. This will help you decide what you need to get out of the reading. If there are questions at the end of your college textbook chapters, read them first. If the instructor asks questions in class, let those questions guide your reading. Now look at the ten comprehension questions in the Comprehension Check at the end of the selection and read them before you actually start reading the article.

At this point, you should have looked at the title and read the comprehension questions. Now you want to read this 460-word article at a faster rate. Try to read at least 50 wpm faster than you read the timed-reading article in Chapter One. See if it helps your comprehension to push yourself as you read.

Begin timing: _____

PUTTING READING IN ITS PROPER PLACE

DOMINIC F. MARTIA

1   As more and more Americans depend exclusively on television for information and ideas, the nation's reading proficiency suffers—and so does society.

2   It isn't hard to see why TV is so appealing. It offers the immediacy of real life. Yet, TV doesn't merely give us real life. Events in real life occur without commentary. In contrast, televised events are often delivered from prefabricated perspectives. In real life, we are forced to make up our own minds as to the meaning of events. When we see televised news events, the meaning often is supplied through selection, angle, emphasis, and accompanying narrative.

3   But the point isn't that TV may be biased. So may books, magazines or newspapers. The point is that television's seductive and misleading immediacy lulls our critical judgment. Watching TV requires much less effort than reading does. Our preference for TV as a source of information and ideas is a measure of intellectual laziness.

4   TV long ago won the battle for our attention. But the real loser has been our ability to read, which, like other learned abilities, needs regular practice to maintain its strength.

5   As we seek a better balance between our dependence on TV and our use of the print media, we will increase the time we spend reading. This will be a good start. If overreliance on TV has atrophied our reading skill, then reading more should help restore it. But besides reading more, we need to become more selective and more critical readers. Much of what we might read isn't worth reading. It panders to the same laziness that induces us to turn on the TV rather than open a book.

6   In a nation our size, it would be surprising if there weren't a persistent market for serious and high-quality publications. But the demise of many newspapers, the shaky economics of journals of opinion and the unprofitability of serious books indicate that the general level of reading taste has declined sharply since the '50s.

7   Our concern for providing basic literacy to adults seems to recognize the importance of reading. But let's also encourage people who are already literate to aspire to a higher level of reading skill and taste. It will take some thought, study and debate before we can decide exactly what should be done to achieve this goal. Schools, libraries and publishers would be the logical ones to begin the process, the guiding assumption of which is that reading is essential to education and to effective citizenship.

8   The issue is not a simple one of whether one source of information and ideas is better than another. We need them all. But intelligent use of our media requires the critical judgment that is best developed through reading. So let's put reading where it belongs—in first place.

Finish timing: Record time here:_____and use the Timed Reading Conversion Chart in the Appendix to figure your rate:_____wpm.

Comprehension Check

Directions: Answer the following questions without looking back.

1. What is the *subject* of the essay you just read? _____
_____

2. What is the *thesis* of this essay? _____
_____

3. According to the author, TV, as opposed to reading, is appealing because
   a. it forces us to make up our own minds.
   b. the meaning to events is supplied.
   c. we are intellectually lazy.
   d. All of the above.

4. T/F The author believes that TV is biased whereas reading books, newspapers, and magazines are not.

5. Because TV has won the battle for our attention, the author believes that the real loser is
   a. our ability to read.   **c.** our need to read.
   b. our desire to read.   **d.** our children.

6. In order to maintain a proper balance between our dependence on TV and our use of the print media, we need to increase the time we spend _____
_____

7. According to the author, our reading skills require regular _____
_____

8. Besides reading more, we need to become
   a. more selective in our reading.   **c.** Both a and b.
   b. more critical readers.   **b.** None of the above.

9. What support does the author provide for his statement that the general level of reading taste has declined since the 1950s? _____
____ _____ _____ _____

10. The author believes that reading
    a. is essential to education.
    b. is essential to effective citizenship.
    c. is essential to developing critical judgment.
    d. All of the above.

Vocabulary Check

Directions: Define the following underlined words from the selection.

1. the nation's reading <u>proficiency</u> suffers (paragraph 1) _____
   _____

2. often delivered from <u>prefabricated</u> perspectives (paragraph 2)_____
   _____

3. it <u>lulls</u> our critical judgment (paragraph 3) _____
   _____

4. TV has <u>atrophied</u> our reading skill (paragraph 5) _____
   _____

5. it <u>panders</u> to the same laziness (paragraph 5) _____
   _____

6. the same laziness that <u>induces</u> us to turn on the TV (paragraph 5) _____
   _____

7. the <u>demise</u> of many newspapers (paragraph 6) _____
   _____

8. to <u>aspire</u> to a higher level of reading (paragraph 7) _____
   _____

9. the guiding <u>assumption</u> (paragraph 7)_____
   _____

10. intelligent use of our <u>media</u> (paragraph 8)_____
    _____

Record the results of the rate, comprehension, and vocabulary checks on the Student Record Chart in the Appendix.

PRACTICE F-3: Timed Reading

Directions: As you did in Practice F-2, read the title of the following reading selection. Think about what you may know or have read about the subject elsewhere. Briefly look over the comprehension questions as a guide to what to focus on as you read. When finished, begin timing.

Begin timing: _____

TILTING THE LEVEL PLAYING FIELD? IT'S NOTHING NEW

ERIC WEINER

1   Former Senate Majority Leader George Mitchell's report on the "serious drug culture, from top to bottom," within Major League Baseball is just the latest evidence that sports are not always conducted on a level playing field.

2   The scandals may be disturbing, but they're really nothing new. Seeking an edge in sports is as old as the noble Olympiads. During the Greek games, athletes caught cheating paid fines. The money was used to erect statues of Zeus. These statues were placed along the passageway that led to the stadium, with the name of the cheater inscribed on their bases — a public humiliation, the precursor to bad press.

3   Some of the ancient Greek athletes were known to ingest hallucinogenic mushrooms — as well as animals' hearts and testicles — all to enhance performance, according to Charles Yesalis, professor of health and human development at Penn State, quoted in *The Washington Post*.

World's First Dopers

4   In other words, the ancient Greeks, fathers of democracy and Western culture, were also the world's first dopers. The Romans weren't much better. Gladiators used stimulants in the famed Circus Maximus (circa 600 B.C.) to overcome fatigue and injury.

5   In modern times, runners doped themselves with strychnine as early 1904.

6   Today's technology is, of course, more sophisticated. But the underlying problem remains the same: some athletes are willing to cheat to win, by doping or other means.

7   And not just athletes, by the way: NBA referee Tim Donaghy recently admitted that he cooperated with gamblers. New England Patriots coach Bill Belichick was penalized by the NFL for illegally videotaping coaching activities on the opposite sideline.

8   Some analysts say the reason for a seeming spurt in cheating is simple: the stakes are higher. Salaries and prize money are at record levels so, simply put, it pays to cheat. "It's more rational to take risks if the pay-off is very large," says David Callahan, author of *The Cheating Culture*. "And as cheating spreads in a given sport, the non-cheaters feel they are paying a price for remaining honest."

Worse Than Dirty Politics

9   Judging from the media coverage, dirty athletes seem to evoke more public outrage than dirty politicians. That's because cheating in sports is more clear-cut than cheating in politics, says sportswriter Frank Deford, a regular commentator on NPR's *Morning Edition*. "We expect politicians to be dirty, and we realize that rap singers aren't moral paragons, but we want our sports to be clean. What all of these scandals have shown is that sports is no different from anything else."

10   Deford has a theory: Athletes taking part in individual sports, such as cycling or track, are more vulnerable to allegations of cheating than athletes taking part in team sports. In a team sport, the blame for any transgression can be spread around. Plus, "the team loyalty keeps you going year after year. That gives you a base, a foundation," he says. For individual athletes, there is no such redemption. They and they alone are to blame.

11   Sports scandals go to the heart of the American split personality, says Callahan. On the one hand, we value egalitarianism and fair play; on the other hand, we admire those who succeed, even if sharp elbows are employed in the climb to the top. "There

is something very sacred about sports to America, a country infatuated with egalitarian ideals, at least on paper, so when sports are tarnished by cheating we are disillusioned."

12   **The Games Go On**

Perhaps, but none of the cheating scandals has made a dent in attendance figures, at least not in this country. NFL attendance is on the rise. A record number of fans are paying to watch big-league baseball, steroids notwithstanding. (NBA attendance has been flat; the Donaghy scandal broke during the off-season so it's too soon to measure its impact.)

13   But some think American sports fans will not tolerate this trend indefinitely.

14   "Most people still have great faith in the integrity of the game. If that is lost, it will eventually affect attendance," says Robert Simon, author of a book on cheating and sports. That has already happened in Europe, where professional cycling has suffered a major setback from the recent doping scandals at the Tour de France.

15   On the other end of the spectrum is golf: one sport that remains untainted by even a whiff of scandal. Golf retains a code of honor that seems almost quaint in this day of steroids and surreptitious videotaping. Golfers will call a penalty on themselves — if, for instance, they accidentally jostle their ball on the green — even if no one else witnessed the infraction.

16   Smith says we shouldn't make too much of the recent spike in cheating scandals. "We forget the thousands and thousands of games are played where people do the right thing," he says.

17   Deford agrees. "To suggest that we have descended to the depths of Hades all of a sudden, I wouldn't buy into that. These cheating scandals, though, do show that athletes are susceptible to the same kind of venality as the rest of us."

Finish timing: Record time here:_____and use the Timed Reading Conversion Chart in the Appendix to figure your rate:_____wpm.

Comprehension Check

Directions: Answer the following questions without looking back.

1.   What is the *subject* of the essay you just read?_____

_____

2.   What is the *thesis* of this essay? _____

_____

3.   What happened to athletes caught cheating in ancient Greek Games? _____

_____

4.   For what was the money paid in fines used? _____

_____

5.   T/F   Some of the ancient Greek athletes were know to eat hallucinogenic mushrooms, animal hearts, and testicles to enhance performance.

6. The author believes that the present spurt in cheating in sports is due to _____

_____ _____ _____ _____

7. Why, according to the author, does the public get more outraged at dirty athletes than dirty politicians?
   a. It's unfair to clean athletes.
   b. Americans value fair play in sports but accept that politicians are crooked.
   c. Cheating in sports is more clear-cut and obvious than cheating in politics.
   d. The media gives dirty sports more coverage than dirty politicians.

8. T/F Cheating scandals in sports has caused a drop in attendance at sports games in the United States.

9. The one game that has not been tainted by scandal is _____

10. T/F We should remember that thousands of games are played where people do the right thing.

Vocabulary Check

Directions: Define the following underlined words from the selection.

1. level playing field _____

_____

2. inscribed on their bases _____

_____ _____

3. the precursor to bad press _____

_____

4. known to ingest hallucinogenic mushrooms _____

_____

5. hallucinogenic mushrooms _____

_____ _____

6. seem to evoke public outrage_____

_____

7. rap singers aren't moral paragons _____

_____ _____ _____

8. to blame for any transgression_____

_____

9. we value egalitarianism _____

_____ _____ _____

10. surreptitious videotaping_____

_____

Record the results of the rate, comprehension, and vocabulary checks on the Student Record Chart in the Appendix.

Before you go on to the next chapter, make certain you understand any mistakes or problems you may have encountered in this one. It is important that you learn from mistakes, so don't despair when you make them. Accept mistakes as normal. Making mistakes is often the best way to discover what you do and don't know.

Questions for Group Discussion

1. As a group, come up with a summary of what this chapter taught you about how to improve your comprehension.

2. "Thinking: A Neglected Art" and "Putting Reading in Its Proper Place" deal with problems with thinking and reading in our culture today. Compare and contrast what Kane and Martia say.

3. Why do you think the first two chapters in this text deal first with vocabulary and second with comprehension? Can you think of other orders or other topics that should be covered first?

4. Have everyone in the group come up with at least one thing learned in this chapter that he or she didn't know before.

5. As a group, see how many of you can use the following words from this chapter in a sentence. Make certain you learn the ones you still may not be able to use or recognize by writing the definition in the blank space.

   a. genetics: _____

   b. ostensibly: _____

   c. arbitrary: _____

   d. smugness: _____

   e. stigmatized: _____

   f. thesis: _____

   g. profound: _____

   h. perceptual: _____

   i. typology: _____

   J. incoherent: _____

On Your Own

Pick ten new words you learned in this chapter, not necessarily those listed in question 5, and on a separate sheet of paper write a sentence for each word, using it correctly in context. Turn in the paper to your instructor.

CHAPTER THREE

Developing Study Reading Strategies

G. Putting It All Together

A.   Surveying Textbooks

In addition to being able to understand word meanings, recall main ideas and supporting details, and recognize the difference between a subject and a thesis (the content of Chapters One and Two), you need to develop a study-reading strategy. A study-reading strategy is a method or approach to studying that will offer you the best results for the time and effort you put into studying.

As you know, textbooks are expensive, so you want to take advantage of every helpful study aid they offer. Before plunging into your first reading assignment, take time to survey your book and see what you bought. Read the table of contents to see what the book will cover. Check to see how the chapters are structured, how long they are, and what study aids are provided. See if a glossary is available to help with unfamiliar words. Skim over the index and see if you recognize any of the subjects or names listed. Knowing what is in the book will help you better comprehend the subject. Some textbooks offer helpful study aids, such as previews and summaries of each chapter, definitions of words you will encounter in the chapter, and periodic quizzes for you to check your understanding as you read along.

Here is a detailed list of what to look for when you survey your textbooks:

1. *Title page*: This gives you the full title of the book, the edition, the authors and their school affiliation, and the publishing company. The complete title often helps you understand what the book will cover in regard to the subject. For instance, an introductory textbook is going to be more general than one that specifies a particular area. A history text that states "Volume 2" on the title page indicates that an entire volume of history should have been studied before that one.

2. *Copyright page*: This tells you when the book was published and the date of any previous editions, so you will have some idea how dated the information in the book is.

3. *Preface*: This explains the author's purpose for writing the book, describes the readers for whom the book is intended, and usually includes an acknowledgment of people who helped with the book.

4. *Table of contents*: This shows how the book is organized—an outline of sorts. Some tables of contents are very comprehensive, some not; but at least they show you if the book is divided into units, chapters, and sections, and whether there is a glossary, index, or appendix.

5. *Index*: This is an alphabetical listing of the various topics covered in the book. Names, places, events, definitions of terms, and the like are usually listed. Looking over an index can give you an idea of the book's subject matter, plus call to mind anything you may already have studied in the past in another course.

6. *Glossary*: The glossary is a small dictionary of sorts that usually defines the specialized terms covered in the book. It can save you from using the dictionary, and better yet, it defines the words and terms as they are used in the context of the book.

7. *Appendixes*: Textbooks frequently contain an appendix (sometimes more than one) that provides supplemental information related to the topic of the book. It is provided for the reader's use but is often overlooked.

How helpful these components of a textbook are varies from book to book. All too often, students do not examine them very thoroughly. This is unfortunate because, as you progress through a particular course, these aids can sometimes be very beneficial. It is doubtful you would buy a car without driving it, looking it over carefully to see what features it has, and even comparing it with other cars. But when it comes to textbooks, most students buy them because they are required and never bother to get to know what they offer.

PRACTICE A-1: Surveying This Book

Directions: Using the checklist for surveying a textbook, answer the following questions.

1. This book is in what edition? _____
2. In what year was the book published? _____
3. What is the author's purpose for writing this book? _____
   _____
4. How does each chapter relate to the title of the book? _____
   _____
5. Is there an index? _____
6. Is there a glossary? _____
7. Is there an appendix? _____
8. What did you learn about the book or its contents that you didn't know before?
   _____
   _____

PRACTICE A-2: Surveying Another Textbook

Directions: Select one of your other textbooks from an academic subject, such as history, biology, or business, and survey it, looking for the answers to the following questions:

1. The book is in what edition? _____
2. Is the date of publication fairly recent? _____
3. What is the author's purpose for writing this book? _____
   _____
4. How does each chapter relate to the title of the book? _____
   _____
5. Is there an index? _____ If so, do you recognize any names or places in the listings? _____

6. Is there a glossary? _____

7. Is there an appendix? _____ If so, what does it contain?

_____

_____

8. Do the chapters offer any study reading aids? _____

9. Are there any previews, summaries, or quizzes? _____

10. What did you learn about the book or its contents that you didn't know before?

_____

_____

B.   Surveying Textbook Chapters: The SQ3R Study Technique

Another mistake some students make is to begin reading a textbook assignment without preparing to read it. They simply turn to the assigned pages and start reading. Soon they discover that their minds have wandered and they don't even remember what they have read up to that point. One of the most important parts of a good study strategy is to prepare to read an assignment. Just as you need to look over your textbooks to get to know their content, so should you look over any assignment before reading it to see how long it will take, what subject will be covered, and what aids are provided in the chapter to help you comprehend better.

A proven technique for study reading is the SQ3R formula, introduced by Dr. Francis Robinson more than forty years ago. Many versions of this method exist, but we will present Dr. Robinson's original study method. The name of this study technique, SQ3R, is a mnemonic device to help you remember each of the five important steps in learning to study read. Each step will be explained.

Survey

Step 1: Just as you should survey your textbook before beginning your first reading assignment, so should you survey each chapter before you read. If it is a long chapter, you might want to divide it up into different reading segments. Note the headings that divide the chapter. Read the captions under any pictures or graphs. If there is a summary at the end of the chapter, read it. Look at any questions at the end of the chapter. Keep them in mind as you read. All this gives you a sense of purpose for what you are about to read and aids your concentration.

Question

Step 2: If you survey what you are going to read, it should raise some questions that you want answered as you read. Having questions to answer keeps your mind from wandering. Learn to turn headings into questions. For instance, if a history textbook has a heading "Main Causes of the Civil War," turn this into "What were the main causes of the Civil War?" Read to answer the question. Also, read any questions at the end of the chapter. Just because they appear at the end of the chapter doesn't mean you can't read them first.

Read

Step 3: The first of the three Rs in SQ3R is read. Read to answer any questions raised in step 2. But read only from one heading or section to the next. Then stop and take notes or mark the important passages. (More on this in the next step.) Your mind can assimilate only so much information at once. Our minds like to wander. So take control by reading short segments, then stopping to make sure you understand what you just read before going on.

Recite

Step 4: The second R, recite, reminds you to "recite" back what you read. This ties in with step 3, read. Recite by taking notes or marking the passage at the important points being made. It helps reinforce what you read and aids memory if you write notes in a notebook for that particular class. As you continue reading through other assignments in the book, you will remember better what you already read if you have notes to which you can refer in the future. Once you have made sure you understand what you've read, move on, repeating step 3, reading from one heading to the next, then stopping to "recite" through notes and markings for that passage. Repeat steps 3 and 4 until you have completed the assigned reading.

Review

Step 5: After reading the entire chapter, review (the third R) all of your notes. Make sure you have answered all the questions raised by your surveying and any at the end of the chapter. If you still can't answer a question, go back and find it. If you can't find it, make a note to ask your instructor about it. If no questions are supplied at the end of the chapter, pretend you are the instructor and make up some questions for a test and see if you can answer them. An even better way to review is to form a study group or ask another student in the class to get together to study.

Research has shown that using the SQ3R formula or a similar method improves reading comprehension and retention. It may seem at first that it takes too much time, but once you become familiar with applying the steps to your study reading, your time will be better spent because your approach will focus your mind on what you are doing—study reading.

As you know by now, textbooks come in different sizes, shapes, and formats. So do the chapters within the textbooks. That's why surveying a chapter before you settle in to read closely is important. Some chapters contain helpful reading and study aids. Sometimes chapter headings are turned into questions that are answered in the content. Some have boxed information with definitions of terms used in the content. Others may have questions for the reader to answer to make certain the material is understood before reading on. And still others may have no aids.

The next practices use sections of chapters taken from various textbooks used in many colleges. Each selection differs in format and usage of reading aids.

PRACTICE B-1: Surveying and Reading a Psychology Textbook Chapter

Directions: The following pages, taken from a chapter in *Introduction to Psychology* by Dennis Coon, provide several reading aids.

Step 1: On the following page, begin surveying at the heading "The Cardiac Personality" and stop when you get to the last heading. When finished, return to the next steps below.

Step 2: The subject matter has to do with Type A personalities and health. Based on your survey, what do you think you will learn when you read the selection?____

_____

_____

Step 3: What questions do you have that you want answered as you read?_____

_____

_____

Step 4: Carefully read the entire selection and recite by marking the key passages in a manner that will help you remember the content.

The Cardiac Personality

It would be a mistake to assume that stress is the sole cause of psychosomatic diseases. Genetic differences, organ weaknesses, and learned reactions to stress combine to do damage. Personality also enters the picture. As mentioned earlier, a general disease-prone personality type exists. To a degree, there are also "headache personalities," "asthma personalities," and so on. The best documented of such patterns is the "cardiac personality"—a person at high risk for heart disease.

Two cardiologists, Meyer Friedman and Ray Rosenman, offer a glimpse at how some people create stress for themselves. In a landmark study of heart problems, Friedman and Rosenman (1983) classified people as either **Type A personalities** (those who run a high risk of heart attack) or **Type B personalities** (those who are unlikely to have a heart attack). Then they did an 8-year follow-up, finding more than twice the rate of heart disease in Type A's than in Type B's (Rosenman et al., 1975).

Type A

What is the Type A personality like? Type A people are hard driving, ambitious, highly competitive, achievement oriented, and striving. Type A people believe that with enough effort they can overcome any obstacle, and they "push" themselves accordingly.

Perhaps the most telltale signs of a Type A personality are *time urgency* and chronic *anger* or *hostility*. Type A's seem to chafe at the normal pace of events. They hurry from one activity to another, racing the clock in self-imposed urgency. As they do, they feel a constant sense of frustration and anger. Feelings of anger and hostility, in particular, are strongly related to increased risk of heart attack (Niaura et al., 2002). One study found that 15 percent of a group of 25-year-old doctors and lawyers who scored high on a hostility test were dead by age 50. The most damaging pattern may occur in hostile persons who keep their anger "bottled up." Such people seethe with anger, but don't express it outwardly. This increases their pulse rate and blood pressure and puts a tremendous strain on the heart (Bongard, al'Absi, & Lovallo, 1998).

To summarize, there is growing evidence that anger or hostility may be the core lethal factor of Type A behavior (Krantz & McCeney, 2002; Niaura et al., 2002). To date, hundreds of studies have supported the validity of the Type A concept. In view of this, Type A's would be wise to take their increased health risks seriously.

How are Type A people identified? Characteristics of Type A people are summarized in the short self-identification test presented in ■ Table 15.7. If most of the list applies to you, you might be a Type A. However, confirmation of your type would require more

Individuals with Type A personalities feel a continuous sense of anger, irritation, and hostility.

Hisham Ibrahim/Getty Images

TABLE 15.7

Characteristics of the Type A Person

Check the items that apply to you. Do you

_____ Have a habit of explosively accentuating various key words in ordinary speech even when there is no need for such accentuation?

_____ Finish other persons' sentences for them?

_____ *Always* move, walk, and eat rapidly?

_____ Quickly skim reading material and prefer summaries or condensations of books?

_____ Become easily angered by slow-moving lines or traffic?

_____ Feel an impatience with the rate at which most events take place?

_____ Tend to be unaware of the details or beauty of your surroundings?

_____ Frequently strive to think of or do two or more things simultaneously?

_____ Almost always feel vaguely guilty when you relax, vacation, or do absolutely nothing for several days?

_____ Tend to evaluate your worth in quantitative terms (number of A's earned, amount of income, number of games won, and so forth)?

_____ Have nervous gestures or muscle twitches, such as grinding your teeth, clenching your fists, or drumming your fingers?

_____ Attempt to schedule more and more activities into less time and in so doing make fewer allowances for unforeseen problems?

_____ Frequently think about other things while talking to someone?

_____ Repeatedly take on more responsibilities than you can comfortably handle?

Shortened and adapted from Meyer Friedman and Ray H. Rosenman, *Type A Behavior and Your Heart* (New York: Knopf, 1983).

powerful testing methods. Also, remember that the original definition of Type A behavior was probably too broad. The key psychological factors that increase heart disease risk appear to be anger, hostility, and mistrust (Krantz & McCeney, 2002; Smith et al., 2004). Also, although Type A behavior appears to promote heart disease, depression or distress may be what finally triggers a heart attack (Denollet & Van Heck, 2001; Dinan, 2001).

Because our society places a premium on achievement, competition, and mastery, it is not surprising that many people develop Type A personalities. The best way to avoid the self-made stress this causes is to adopt behavior that is the opposite of that listed in ■ Table 15.7 (Karlberg, Krakau, & Unden, 1998). It is entirely possible to succeed in life without sacrificing your health or happiness in the process. People who frequently feel angry and hostile toward others may benefit from the advice of Redford Williams, a physician interested in Type A behavior.

Strategies for Reducing Hostility

According to Redford Williams, reducing hostility involves three goals. First, you must stop mistrusting the motives of others. Second, you must find ways to reduce how often you feel anger, indignation, irritation, and rage. Third, you must learn to be kinder and more considerate. Based on his clinical experience, Williams (1989) recommends 12 strategies for reducing hostility and increasing trust.

1. Become aware of your angry, hostile, and cynical thoughts by logging them in a notebook. Record what happened, what you thought and felt, and what actions you took. Review your hostility log at the end of each week.
2. Admit to yourself and to someone you trust that you have a problem with excessive anger and hostility.
3. Interrupt hostile, cynical thoughts whenever they occur. (The Psychology in Action section of Chapter 17 explains a thought-stopping method you can use for this step.)
4. When you have an angry, hostile, or cynical thought about someone, silently look for the ways in which it is irrational or unreasonable.
5. When you are angry, try to mentally put yourself in the other person's shoes.
6. Learn to laugh at yourself and use humor to defuse your anger.
7. Learn reliable ways to relax. Two methods are described in this chapter's Psychology in Action section. Another can be found in the Psychology in Action discussion of Chapter 17.
8. Practice trusting others more. Begin with situations where no great harm will be done if the person lets you down.
9. Make an effort to listen more to others and to really understand what they are saying.
10. Learn to be assertive, rather than aggressive, in upsetting situations. (See Chapter 18 for information about self-assertion skills.)
11. Rise above small irritations by pretending that today is the last day of your life.
12. Rather than blaming people for mistreating you, and becoming angry over it, try to forgive them. We all have shortcomings.

Hardy Personality

How do Type A people who do not develop heart disease differ from those who do? Psychologists Salvatore Maddi and others have studied people who have a **hardy personality.** Such people seem to be unusually resistant to stress. The first study of hardiness began with two groups of managers at a large utility company. All of the managers held high-stress positions. Yet some tended to get sick after stressful events, whereas others were rarely ill. How did the people who were thriving differ from their "stressed-out" colleagues? Both groups seemed to have traits typical of the Type A personality, so that wasn't the explanation. They were also quite similar in most other respects. The main difference was that the hardy group seemed to hold a worldview that consisted of three traits (Maddi, Kahn, & Maddi, 1998):

1. They had a sense of personal *commitment* to self, work, family, and other stabilizing values.
2. They felt that they had *control* over their lives and their work.
3. They had a tendency to see life as a series of *challenges*, rather than as a series of threats or problems.

How do such traits protect people from the effects of stress? Persons strong in *commitment* find ways of turning whatever they are doing into something that seems interesting and important. They tend to get involved rather than feeling alienated.

Persons strong in *control* believe that they can more often than not influence the course of events around them. This prevents them from passively seeing themselves as victims of circumstance.

Finally, people strong in *challenge* find fulfillment in continual growth. They seek to learn from their experiences, rather than accepting easy comfort, security, and routine (Maddi, Kahn, & Maddi, 1998). Indeed, many "negative" experiences can actually enhance personal growth—if you have support from others and the skills needed to cope with challenge (Armeli, Gunthert, & Cohen, 2001).

Positive Psychology: Hardiness, Optimism, and Happiness

Good and bad events occur in all lives. What separates happy people from those who are unhappy is largely a matter of attitude. Happy people tend to see their lives in more positive terms, even when trouble comes their way. For example, happier people tend to

Type A personality A personality type with an elevated risk of heart disease; characterized by time urgency, anger, and hostility.

Type B personality All personality types other than Type A; a low cardiac-risk personality.

Hardy personality A personality style associated with superior stress resistance.

Now "review" by answering these questions:

1. T/F Type A personalities run an elevated risk of heart attack.

2. Circle the letter of the following characteristics that are found in Type A personalities.

    a. ambitious

    b. highly competitive

    c. achievement oriented

    d. striving

    e. anger and hostility

3. T/F The validity of the Type A personality behavior presented needs to be sub-jected to further study.

4. Why should hostile people keep their anger "bottled up"? ___ _____
   _____

5. The key psychological factors that don't appear to increase heart disease risk are

    a. anger

    b. hostility

    c. mistrust

    d. all of the above

    e. none of the above

6. T/F Because our society places a premium on achievement, competition, and mastery, it is not surprising that many people develop Type A personalities.

7. T/F Reducing hostility involves three goals: stop mistrusting others, find ways to reduce feelings of anger, and be kinder and more considerate.

8. Physician Redford Williams recommends strategies for reducing hostility. How many strategies does he offer? _____
   _____

9. T/F People with a "hardy personality" are those with an unusually high resistance to stress.

10. T/F Personality traits that protect people from the effects of stress include a per-sonal sense of commitment to self, work, and family; a feeling of control over their lives; and a tendency to see life as a series of challenges.

PRACTICE B-2: Surveying and Reading a Communications Textbook Chapter

Directions: The following selection is taken from Chapter 12 of *Communication in Our Lives* by Julia Woods. It is reproduced exactly the way it appears in the textbook. Read only what is stated in Step 1.

Step 1: Begin your survey at the heading "Analyze Mass Communication" and stop at the heading "Be Involved with Issues Surrounding Mass Media." Read only the headings and the first sentence under each heading. What is the selection about?

_____

_____

Step 2: What question or questions do you have about the subject that you want answered?_____

_____

Step 3: Read the selection carefully and answer the questions that follow it.

Communication Highlight

Convergence and Access

Convergence is a key to the future of technology. **Convergence** is the interconnectivity of various devices to each other and to the Internet or web. Bill Joy, Sun Microsystems' chief scientist, says convergence will relieve people of having to deal with many of the current difficulties in making technology work. According to Joy, in the near future, computers will work like small appliances—say, toasters or electric drills. When we buy computerized products, they will truly be "plug and play" (Sandberg, 1999).

But that's just half the story. The other half is abandoning the idea of a single PC in your home or office. Instead of that "old technology," says Bill Gates, we're moving quickly into the "PC-plus era" (Gates, 1999, p. 64). In the PC-plus era, people who can afford the newest technology will have multiple computerized devices, some of which will be connected to each other (for instance, when your computerized alarm clock rings, your computerized coffee maker will start) and all of which will all be linked to the net (for instance, the net will automatically reset your alarm clock and all other timer devices when you go on and off daylight savings time or after a power outage).

But a huge question remains: Who will have access to converging technologies, and who will not? If access is based on wealth, convergence will increase the divide between haves and have nots.

tive politically, you might read a conservative columnist in your daily paper and listen to conservative radio and television programs. The problem with that is that you don't expose yourself to criticisms of conservative policies and stances, and you don't give yourself the opportunity to learn about more liberal policies and positions. The same is true if you are politically liberal—you cannot be fully informed if you read, watch, and listen only to liberal sources. If you listen only to popular music, you'll never learn to understand, much less appreciate, classical music, jazz, or reggae. You cannot be informed about any issue or type of media unless you deliberately expose yourself to multiple, and even conflicting, sources of information and perspectives.

Exposing yourself to multiple media also means attending to more than entertainment. Television focuses primarily on entertainment, trends, and celebrities and officials in popular culture. One study of children ages 9 to 12 found that 98% of respondents knew who Michael Jordan and Michael Jackson were, but only 21% knew who Boris Yeltsin was, and only 20% recognized the name of Nelson Mandela ("Names & Faces," 1997). Tuning into celebrity culture is not sufficient for media literacy. So the access component of media literacy includes both being able to access mass communication and choosing to expose yourself to varied sources of information, opinion, and perspective.

Analyze Mass Communication

When we are able to analyze something, we understand how it works. If you aren't aware of English grammatical structure and rules, you can't write, read, or speak English effectively. If you are unaware of patterns that make up basketball, you will not be able to understand what happens in a game. If you don't understand how church or synagogue services are organized, you won't appreciate the meaning of those services. In the same way, if you don't understand patterns in media, you can't understand fully how music, advertising, programming, and so forth work. Learning to recognize patterns in media empowers you to engage media in critical and sophisticated ways.

Chapter 12 *Mass Communication and Media Literacy* / 323

James Potter (2001) points out that there are a few standard patterns that media use repeatedly. For example, despite the variety in music, media use a few basic chords, melody progressions, and rhythms. Even the content of music tends to follow stock patterns, most often love and sex (Christianson & Roberts, 1998). Most stories, whether in print, film, or television, open with some problem or conflict that progresses until it climaxes in final dramatic scenes. Romance stories typically follow a pattern in which we meet a main character who has suffered a bad relationship or has not had a serious relationship. The romance pattern progresses through meeting Mr. or Ms. Right, encountering complications or problems, resolving the problems, and living happily ever after (Riggs, 1999).

Just as media follow a few standard patterns for entertainment, they rely on basic patterns for presenting news. There are three distinct, but related features by which media construct the news (Potter, 2001).

- Selecting what gets covered: Only a minute portion of human activity is reported in the news. Gatekeepers in the media decide which people and events are newsworthy. By presenting stories on these events and people, the media make them newsworthy.

- Choosing the hook: Reporters and journalists choose how to focus a story, or how to "hook" people into a story. In so doing, they direct people's attention to certain aspects of the story. For example, in a story on a politician accused of sexual misconduct, the focus could be the charges made, the politician's denial, or the increase in sexual misconduct by public figures.

- Choosing how to tell the story: In the above story, media might tell it in a way that fosters sympathy for the person who claims to have been the target of sexual misconduct (interviews with the victim, references to other victims of sexual misconduct) or to tell it in a way that inclines people to be sympathetic toward the politician (shots of the politician with his or her family, interviews with colleagues who proclaim the politician's innocence). Each way of telling the story encourages people to think and feel distinctly about the story.

Critically Evaluate Messages from Mass Communication

Once you can analyze mass communication to understand how it works, you are prepared to take the next step: critically evaluating messages from mass media. When interacting with mass communication, you should use critical thought to assess what is presented. Rather than accepting news accounts unquestioningly, you should be thoughtful and skeptical. It's important to ask questions such as these:

- Why is this story getting so much attention? Whose interests are served, and whose are muted?

- What is the source of the statistics and other forms of evidence? Are the sources current? Do the sources have any interest in taking a specific position? (For example, tobacco companies have a vested interest in denying or minimizing the harms of smoking.)

- What's the hook for the story, and what alternative hooks might have been used?

Communication Highlight

Puffery: The Very Best of Its Kind!

One of the most popular advertising strategies is **puffery**, superlative claims that seem factual but are actually meaningless. For instance, what does it mean to state that a particular juice has "the most natural flavor"? Most natural in comparison to what—other juices, other drink products? Who judged it to have the most natural flavor: the corporation that produces it? A random sample of juice drinkers? What is the meaning of an ad that claims a car is "the new benchmark"? Who decided this was the new benchmark? To what is this car being compared? It's not clear from the ad, which is only puffery. And media literate people don't buy the claim or the product!

- Are stories balanced so that a range of viewpoints are given voice? For example, in a report on environmental bills pending in Congress, do news reports include statements from the Sierra Club, industry leaders, environmental scientists, and so forth?

- How are different people and viewpoints represented by gatekeepers (e.g., reporters, photographers, experts)?

It's equally important to be critical in interpreting other kinds of mass communication, such as music, magazines, billboards, and the web. When listening to popular music, ask what view of society, relationships, and so forth it portrays, who and what it represents as normal, and what views of women and men it fosters. Raise the same questions about the images in magazines and on billboards. When considering an ad, ask whether it offers meaningful evidence or merely puffery. Asking questions such as these allows you to be critical and careful in assessing what mass communication presents to you.

Respond Actively

People may respond actively or passively to mass communication and the worldviews that it portrays, depending on how media literate they are. If we respond passively, we mindlessly consume messages and the implicit values in them. On the other hand, if we respond actively, we recognize that the worldviews presented in mass communication are not unvarnished truth but partial, subjective perspectives that serve the interests of some individuals and groups while disregarding or misrepresenting the interests of others. Responding actively to mass communication includes choosing consciously how and when to use it, questioning what is presented, and involving yourself in controversies about media, particularly the newer technological forms.

Use Mass Communication Consciously

Do you ever just turn on the TV and watch whatever is on? Do you ever get on the web and spend an hour or more surfing with no particular goal in mind? If so, you're not making a deliberate choice that allows you to select media to suit your needs and goals. Sophisticated media users realize that media serve many purposes, and they make deliberate choices that serve their goals and needs at particular times. For example, if you feel depressed and want to watch television, it might be better to watch a comedy or action drama than to watch a television movie about personal trauma and pain. If you have used all the money you budgeted for entertainment, don't check out pop-up ads for new CDs.

You can also use media to respond to media. Since the 1970s, the Guerrilla Girls have used media-savvy techniques to critique sexism and racism, particularly in the art world (Kollwitz & Kahlo, 2003). Some organizations now rely on virual e-mail to get their messages out to large numbers of people. A virual e-mail is not a virus that infects a computer, it is an e-mail that is so provocative or interesting that receivers are eager to send it to others, thus getting the message out. People from all walks of life call in to talk radio shows to express their opinions and to challenge those of others. And letters to the editor remain a way for people to respond to newspaper coverage.

–Manuel–

I was really angry about a story in the local paper. It was about Mexicans who come to the U.S. The story only mentioned Mexican Americans who get in trouble with the law, are on welfare, or are illegal residents. So I wrote a letter to the editor and said the story was biased and inaccurate. The editor invited me to write an article for the opinion page, and I did. In my article, I described many Mexican Americans who are hard-working, honest citizens who are making this country better. There were a lot of responses to my article, so I know I made a difference.

Manuel's experience demonstrates that assuming agency is not just personally empowering; it can also enrich cultural life. Don't succumb to thinking there's nothing you can do to affect mass media. There is a great deal that each of us can do on both the personal and the cultural level (Potter, 2002). People have an ethical responsibility to challenge messages of mass communication that they consider inaccurate or harmful.

To assume an active role in interacting with media, you must recognize that you are an agent who can affect what happens around you. Believing that we are powerless to control how mass communication affects us can become a self-fulfilling prophecy. Therefore, not recognizing your agency could induce you to yield the degree of control you could have.

Be Involved with Issues Surrounding Mass Media Responding actively is not just looking out for ourselves personally. It also requires us to become involved in thinking about how mass media influence social life and how, if at all, mass communication should be regulated. We've already discussed the escalation of violence in media, which can affect how people view violence and its appropriateness. But there are other issues, particularly in

Communication Highlight

Responding Actively

If you want to learn more about gender and media, or if you want to become active in working against media that foster views of violence as normal, girls and women as subordinate, and buying as the route to happiness, visit these websites:

Action Coalition for Media Education:
http://www.acmecoalition.org

Center for Media Literacy: http://www.medialit.org

Children Now: http://www.childrennow.org

Media Watch: http://www.mediawatch.com

National Association for Family and Community Education:
http://www.nafce.org

National Coalition on Television Violence:
http://www.nctvv.org

TV Parental Guidelines Monitoring Board:
http://www.tvguidelines.org

Now "review" by answering the following questions.

1. T/F Learning to recognize patterns in media empowers you to engage media in critical and sophisticated ways.

2. T/F If you don't understand patterns in media, you can't understand fully how music, advertising, programming, and so forth work.

3. T/F According to James Potter, there are many standard patterns that media use repeatedly.

4. Which of the following are patterns by which media construct the news?

    a. Selecting what gets covered

    b. Choosing the "hook"

    c. Choosing how to tell the story

    d. All of the above

    e. None of the above

5. T/F When interacting with mass communication, you should use critical thought to assess what is being presented.

6. Provide at least two of the thoughtful and skeptical questions mentioned that you should ask yourself rather than just accepting news accounts. _____

    _____ __ _____

    _____

7. T/F It is not as important to be critical of popular music, billboards, or the Internet as it is of the news.

8. Responding actively to mass communication includes the following:

    a. _____

    b. _____

    c. _____

9. T/F Viral e-mail is an example of how you can use media to respond to media.

10. T/F Taking an active role in interacting with the media is to recognize that you are an agent who can affect what happens around you and have accepted the responsibility to challenge messages of mass communication that you consider inaccurate or harmful.

C.   Marking and Underlining Textbooks

In Section B, you learned that reciting is one of the three Rs in the SQ3R study method. While oral recitation was described, it was recommended that you take some form of notes during the read-recite cycle. It is strongly suggested that you use one of the methods described here and in the section on note taking.

Basically, there are two ways to take notes as you read: (1) You can mark your book, using the margins for your own observations and underlining and circling important words and phrases; or (2) you can take notes from the text in a notebook. Section D will cover taking reading notes. This section deals with marking and underlining correctly.

Take a look at the following passage and how it is marked:

lithosphere,
outer layer;
asthenosphere,
inner layer

It is now believed that the earth's outer layer of rock, called the lithosphere, is divided into large, rigid plates that fit together like pieces of a huge jigsaw puzzle. There are twelve major plates (and numerous subplates, each about sixty miles thick and some almost as wide as the Pacific Ocean. They float on a layer of dense, viscous rock called the asthenosphere, which, in turn, surrounds the earth's hot core.

How helpful are all those markings going to be when you review for a test? What do they mean? The act of underlining is not in itself a helpful comprehension or recall device.

Notice the same passage marked in a more sensible way:

It is now believed that the earth's outer layer of rock, called the lithosphere, is divided into large, rigid plates that fit together like pieces of a huge jigsaw puzzle. There are twelve major plates (and numerous subplates), each about sixty miles thick and some almost as wide as the Pacific Ocean. They float on a layer of dense, viscous rock called the asthenosphere, which, in turn, surrounds the earth's hot core.

Here, only the key points are highlighted. The student used what was learned about finding main ideas and supporting details. Thought went into what was to be marked for later review as well as what would be helpful for understanding the passage during the read-recite portion of SQ3R.

While there is no particular way to mark or underline, good note takers seem to follow two basic principles: (1) Mark only the main points and (2) be consistent in the way you mark. Here are some suggestions for marking and underlining:

1. Use pen, not pencil. Pencil marks will fade and smear over time.
2. Underline main ideas and circle important words or phrases. Studies show that when students were allowed to underline only one sentence in a paragraph, they took more time and underlined only important sentences, which produced better comprehension and recall.
3. Underline minor, yet important, points with broken lines. Later, during a review, such markings will make it easy for you to distinguish between main ideas and minor but relevant ones.
4. Use numbers in the margins to indicate a series of points or items being discussed.
5. Use the margins to write what you feel is important, questions you have for the instructor, or notes to yourself.
6. Draw rectangles around names or places that might be used in a test or quiz.
7. Use small Post-it notes to jot key words, sticking them on the page and paragraph you want to remember.
8. From these Post-it notes, write notes on your computer. Propping your textbook on a book stand or music stand helps the process.

Remember that these are just suggestions. You may want to use your own type of marking that is consistent and meaningful to you as you read and helps you later during reviews.

Marking and underlining are not as efficient as note taking *unless* you invest the time to discern what is important to underline and later review your notations. Underlining and marking are faster than note taking, but it doesn't do you any good to underline if you don't actually study-read as you do it.

PRACTICE C-1: Surveying, Reading, and Marking a History Textbook Chapter

Directions: Apply the following steps to a passage on the following pages from a history textbook, *American Passages: A History of the United States*, by Edward L. Ayers et al.

Step 1: Beginning at the heading "Terrorism and the Bush Presidency," survey the passage ending at the heading "The Chapter in Review." Notice, but do not read, the extra boxed material provided. Do note and read the captions under the photographs. What is the main subject of the passage? _____

_____

_____

Step 2: What questions about the subject do you have that you want answered as you read thoughtfully? _____

_____

_____

Step 3: Read the passage carefully and "recite" by marking it in a way that will help you understand the content. Then answer the questions that follow the passage.

worldwide celebrations of the calendar change, Americans turned to the onset of the presidential election season.

The 2000 Presidential Campaign: Bush versus Gore

The Republican front-runner was Governor George W. Bush of Texas, the son of the former president. Elected in 1994 and reelected in 1998, the Texan announced for president in mid-1999 and soon amassed a campaign treasury that ultimately reached more than $100 million. Bush promised that he would be "a compassionate conservative" who would "change the tone" in Washington after the partisan discord of the Clinton era. He advocated a $1.6 trillion tax cut and promised to reform the educational system.

Bush lost the New Hampshire primary to Senator John McCain of Arizona, but then won a number of primaries to lock up the delegates needed to control the national convention in Philadelphia. With Richard "Dick" Cheney as his running mate, Bush had a double-digit lead over his Democratic opponent, Vice President Al Gore.

Gore had easily won his party's nomination but had problems separating himself from the scandals of the Clinton years. He also faced a hostile press corps that focused on every lapse to paint Gore as indecisive and opportunistic. Gore emerged from the Democratic convention behind Bush but closed the gap during September 2000. The election hinged on the three presidential debates.

Although neither candidate did well, Bush exceeded the low expectations that media pundits set for him. Gore was better on substance but was labeled arrogant

© Reuters/CORBIS

The three televised debates between George W. Bush and Albert Gore proved unusually important in deciding the outcome of the 2000 presidential election.

and condescending. As a result, the race remained tight down to the election. As the votes were counted, the Republicans retained control of the House of Representatives, and the Senate split evenly with 50 Democrats and 50 Republicans. Gore led in the presidential popular vote, but the electoral vote produced a dead heat. It became clear that the state of Florida would determine the result because its 25 electoral votes would push either of the two candidates past the 271 electoral votes needed. State officials put Florida in the Bush column by fewer than 600 ballots after going over the official returns that came in during the week after the election. Gore's forces noted irregularities and flawed ballots in several Democratic counties and sought a recount in those areas.

The Bush camp insisted that the result favoring its man should be final, and charges of fraud, manipulation, and political pressure flashed back and forth throughout November. Finally, the case of *Bush v. Gore* reached the U.S. Supreme Court in mid-December. On the key issue of whether a recount should occur, the Court ruled 5–4 in favor of Bush in a decision that many commentators dubbed both hasty and partisan. Gore accepted the outcome as final and conceded the election.

Terrorism and the Bush Presidency

In office, Bush governed as a conservative who opposed abortion, rolled back environmental regulations, and pursued foreign policy initiatives that placed less reliance on working with the nation's overseas allies. Congress enacted Bush's large tax cut, but the president saw control of the Senate slip out of Republican hands when Senator James Jeffords of Vermont left the GOP to become an independent. The economy was slowing and the stock market experienced substantial losses. Corporations such as Enron and WorldCom led a wave of corporate failures based on corrupt accounting.

September 11, 2001, and After

One issue, international terrorism, had not been of central concern to most Americans during the 1990s. A bombing of the World Trade Center in New York City in 1993 had not shaken the nation out of its indifference to the threat. Other attacks on American embassies in Africa in 1998 and a similar assault on the destroyer USS *Cole* in Yemen in October 2000 had not brought the issue home. The name of the leader of one terrorist group—Osama bin Laden—was largely unknown to the

DOING HISTORY

Colin Powell and Weapons of Mass Destruction, February 5, 2003

IN THE RUN-UP to the invasion of Iraq in March 2003, one of the decisive moments was the speech that Secretary of State Colin Powell delivered to the Security Council of the United Nations on February 5. Using information supplied to him by George Tenet, director of the Central Intelligence Agency, Powell made the case that Saddam Hussein had weapons of mass destruction and was engaged in the systematic violation of the sanctions of the United Nations. Powell put his personal prestige behind the speech and it had a significant impact on press opinion in the United States and around the world. One of the key points of the address was the charge that Iraq possessed the capability to use biological weapons from mobile laboratories. As the secretary said in his remarks:

"One of the most worrisome things that emerges from the thick intelligence file we have on Iraqi weapons is the existence of mobile production facilities used to make biological agents. Let me take you inside the intelligence file and share with you what we know from eye witness accounts. We have first hand descriptions of biological weapons factories on wheels and on rails.

The trucks and train cars are easily moved and are designed to evade detection by inspectors. In a matter of months they can produce a quantity of biological poison equal to the amount that Iraq claimed to have produced in the years prior to the Gulf War. Although Iraq's mobile production program began in the mid-1990s, U.N. inspectors at that time had only vague hints of such programs. Confirmation came later, in the year 2000.

The source was an eye witness, an Iraqi chemical engineer who supervised one of these factories and actually was present during biological agent production runs. He was also at the site when an accident occurred in 1998. Twelve technicians died from exposure to biological agents."

Powell then added that the defector was "currently hiding in another country with the certain knowledge that Saddam Hussein will kill him if he finds him."

Source: "U.S. Secretary of State Colin Powell Addresses the U.N. Security Council," February 5, 2003, at www.whitehouse.gov/news/releases/2003/02/20030205-1.html.

In August 2005, CNN did an analysis about the Powell speech and the assertion that "Saddam had bioweapons mounted on trucks that would be almost impossible to find." The program then went on to say:

"In fact, Secretary Powell was not told that one of the sources he was given as a source of this information had indeed been flagged by the Defense Intelligence Agency as 'a liar, a fabricator,' according to David Kay, the chief weapons inspector for the CIA in Iraq. That source, an Iraqi defector who had never been debriefed by the CIA, was known in the intelligence community as 'Curveball.'"

The program then quoted Powell's chief of staff, Colonel Lawrence Wilkerson, about the secretary's reaction to this news when he learned it from CIA director George Tenet:

"George actually did call the Secretary, and said 'I'm really sorry to have to tell you. We don't believe there were any mobile labs for making biological weapons.' This was the third or fourth telephone call. And I think it's fair to say the Secretary and Mr. Tenet at that point, ceased being close. I mean, you can be sincere and you can be honest and you can believe what you're telling the Secretary, but three or four times on substantive issues like that? It's difficult to maintain any warm feelings."

Source: "Former aide: Powell WMD speech 'lowest point in my life.'" CNN.com, August 19, 2005.

Questions for Reflection

1. How important were the allegations about the existence of weapons of mass destruction in Iraq in shaping American public opinion behind the war against the regime of Saddam Hussein?

2. What pressures existed on the Central Intelligence Agency to find evidence of weapons of mass destruction?

3. How did the revelations about the absence of these weapons in Iraq influence attitudes toward the war in 2004–2005?

Explore additional primary sources related to this chapter on the Wadsworth American History Resource Center or HistoryNOW websites:

http://history.wadsworth.com
http://now.ilrn.com/ayers_etal3e

Flashpoints   Cindy Sheehan and the Iraq War, 2005

By the summer of 2005, the war in Iraq had become a polarizing, contentious issue in the United States. More than 2 years after the invasion that toppled the regime of Saddam Hussein, the American military was fighting a persistent, effective insurgency in Iraq that had killed more than 1,800 U.S. troops and wounded thousands of others. As the war dragged on without a clear end in sight, protests at home intensified. The poll numbers for President George W. Bush sank and support for the war eroded as well. Republicans and Democrats continued to endorse the American presence in Iraq and to resist calls for a withdrawal timetable to reduce the nation's presence in that Middle Eastern country.

As President Bush vacationed during August 2005 at his residence in Crawford, Texas, a single antiwar protester became the focus of media attention. Cindy Sheehan of Vacaville, California, came to Crawford to see President Bush. Her son, Casey Sheehan, had been killed in combat in Iraq in 2004. She had had a brief visit with Bush after her son's death that left her unsatisfied with the president's reaction to her family's sacrifice. Now she wanted to ask what was "the noble cause" in Iraq for which her son had lost his life. The president would not see her, and so Sheehan camped out on a road near the president's place throughout the month of August. The mass media found her lonely vigil compelling television, especially during the relatively quiet month of August when other news was scarce.

Seeing Sheehan as a political enemy, the White House and its conservative allies mounted an attack on her credibility and antiwar political views that verged

Cindy Sheehan, whose son Casey died in combat in the Iraq war, became an antiwar critic of President Bush and took her protest to the president's ranch in Crawford, Texas, in August 2005.

© Jeff Mitchell/Reuters/CORBIS

into personal invective. One pundit argued that the dead Casey Sheehan would have opposed what his mother was doing on his behalf. Sheehan attracted followers herself and "Camp Casey" swelled in size. Counterprotesters came to harass Sheehan herself and demonstrate on behalf of the president and his policies. After first ignoring Sheehan, President Bush began arguing that the sacrifice of the soldiers in Iraq required carrying the war on to a successful conclusion. By the end of August 2005, Sheehan was preparing for a nationwide bus tour to keep the pressure on the president. The hurricane disasters took attention away from Sheehan as August ended, but she intended to persist in her campaign. The rights and wrongs of Sheehan's protest or Bush's policies would not be evident for years, but the episode of the grieving mother outside the president's vacation residence symbolized the many ways in which the Iraq war had revealed serious fault lines in American society.

Questions for Reflection

1. What had happened during the first 2 years of the Iraq war to erode support for President Bush and his policies?

2. What strains did the war place on the American military and their families?

3. In what ways did the presence of the mass media shape the actions of those in favor or against Sheehan's protest?

4. How difficult is it for democratic nations to fight unpopular wars?

average citizen, even though bin Laden, a fundamentalist Muslim of Saudi Arabian origin, sought the violent end of American influence in the Middle East from his base in Afghanistan. Even a frightening report from a prestigious commission in February 2001 warning of a likely terrorist attack on American soil did little to disturb the lack of alertness that pervaded the government and the mass media. President Bush received a briefing on August 6, 2001, that bin Laden was planning an attack somewhere inside the United States.

950   *Chapter 32* **FROM PROSPERITY TO TERRORISM, 1992–2005**

Ground Zero After the Attack of September 11, 2001

The terrorist attack of September 11, 2001, left many enduring images of the pain that Americans felt when the World Trade Center towers were hit and then collapsed. The area where the debris from the two buildings came down was quickly named Ground Zero as crews worked tirelessly to remove the rubble and look for the remains of the dead. The devastation of the site itself, within the buildings of Lower Manhattan, confirmed the impact of this calamitous event. Yet plans for reconstruction of the area and work to remove the effects of the terrorist assault began almost at once as society rebounded. This concluding image for the Picturing the Past section thus speaks to the continuity of American history and the resilience of the American people in moments of trial and danger. In time this picture, like all the others that have been discussed in this phase of the textbook, will slip into the past and become an artifact of a vanished era. For the moment, with the pain of September 11 still fresh, it reveals the dangers and hope that the country faces as the twenty-first century begins.

© Pool/Don EMMERT/AFP/Getty Images

On the morning of **September 11, 2001,** two hijacked jetliners slammed into the twin towers of the World Trade Center in New York City. Both buildings collapsed into flames and rubble, and almost 3,000 people died. A third airliner crashed into the Pentagon leaving another 200 people dead. A fourth plane fell to the ground in rural Pennsylvania after the passengers attacked the hijackers. All air traffic was grounded for several days, consumer spending slumped, and the weakened economy slipped into recession.

This devastating attack on American soil, which was quickly linked to bin Laden and his terrorist network, Al Qaeda, rattled the nation's morale as it became clear that the terrorists sought nothing less than the destruction of the United States itself. President Bush promised "**war on terrorism**" and launched air strikes and ground troops into Afghanistan to fight its Taliban regime that harbored bin Laden. Soon the Taliban government had been toppled and Al Qaeda disrupted, but American forces remained in Afghanistan into 2005 as the Taliban resisted the presence of outside troops.

The Bush administration targeted Saddam Hussein and his government in Iraq as the other focus of the antiterrorist effort. The White House argued that Iraq was linked to Al Qaeda, but the evidence for such a connection was thin. Convinced that the invasion of Iraq was necessary, the Bush administration issued warnings that weapons of mass destruction could be used against the United States. This policy led Washington, in the words of a British official, to see that intelligence was "fixed" (or manipulated) around the policy of invading Iraq.

Preparations for war accelerated during 2002 while the White House sought diplomatic support for efforts to curb Hussein and the weapons of mass destruction he possessed. By the autumn of 2002, a United Nations resolution calling on Hussein to admit inspectors had

AP/Wide World Photos

The American invasion of Iraq in 2003 ended the regime of Saddam Hussein, but the interaction between American troops and the average Iraqi contributed to the resentment at an occupation that fueled the insurgency against the presence of the United States.

© Jeff Christensen/Reuters/CORBIS

Colin Powell's speech to the United Nations on February 5, 2003, was national news, and New Yorkers followed what he said on the giant screen in Times Square in Manhattan.

been passed. Hussein said that his government would agree to the resolution, but his previous flouting of the inspections process made the United States suspicious. The administration moved toward war as 2002 ended. The director of the Central Intelligence Agency, George Tenet, responded to a question from President Bush about where weapons of mass destruction existed in Iraq by saying it was "a slam dunk" that they were present.

The terrorist threat validated George W. Bush as a national leader, and his popularity rose. In the congressional elections of 2002 the Republicans, using a strong organization and ample campaign contributions, rode Bush's campaigning and the public confidence in his leadership to victory. Security issues affected the voters more than did the faltering economy and the Democratic emphasis on domestic problems. The GOP regained control of the Senate and widened its majority in the House. As 2003 began, the president and his party seemed poised to enact their conservative agenda.

Meanwhile, preparations for war with Iraq intensified. Secretary of State Colin Powell argued the case for war in a speech to the United Nations in February 2003. Powell's calm, direct presentation convinced many skeptics that Iraq and Saddam Hussein did indeed possess destructive weapons. Only after the war began did it become apparent that Powell's speech was based on faulty, misleading, and fabricated evidence.

Dissatisfied with the work of the United Nations weapons inspectors, the United States had failed to obtain a second United Nations resolution authorizing force. The strong opposition of the international community to an American invasion of Iraq, combined with diplomatic setbacks by the Bush White House, left Washington frustrated. The Bush administration, along with its only major ally, Great Britain, decided that an attack on Saddam Hussein's brutal regime could not be delayed. Expectations were for a swift resolution of the fighting on the order of what had occurred during the ground war in the Gulf in 1991. Vice President Cheney said that "significant elements" of Hussein's military force were "likely to step aside" once war began. In this mood of confidence about victory, President Bush told the military "let's go" on March 19, 2003, and the war commenced.

Once launched, the powerful offensive of the American coalition swept through Iraq in a dramatic 3-week campaign that left the United States in military control of the nation. Saddam Hussein was either dead or in hiding, the major officials of Iraq were captured, and the symbols of Hussein's rule had been destroyed. On May 1, 2003, President Bush declared the major combat phase of the war at an end.

951 *Chapter 32* **FROM PROSPERITY TO TERRORISM, 1992–2005**

George Bush and John Kerry held three presidential debates in the fall of 2004. Kerry won the debates; Bush triumphed in the election.

The devastation of Hurricane Katrina in late August and early September 2005 left many residents of New Orleans, Louisiana, begging for help from potential rescuers.

Convinced that they would win an easy victory, the Bush administration had not made plans for the occupation of Iraq. Soon they faced an insurgent movement that resisted the American presence through car bombs, improvised explosive devices that blew up under the lightly armored U.S. vehicles, and guerrilla attacks. By September 2005, almost 1,900 American troops had been killed and thousands more wounded. No weapons of mass destruction were found and inspectors concluded that Hussein had abandoned these efforts after his 1991 defeat. Political efforts to provide a new government for Iraq continued well into 2005.

Angry Democrats looked for a winning presidential candidate in 2004 without success. The election pitted Senator John F. Kerry of Massachusetts against President Bush in a bitterly contested race. Bush won a majority of the popular vote and secured 286 electoral votes to 252 for Kerry. The Republicans picked up seats in both the House and the Senate, and spoke of a mandate for their conservative philosophy during the 4 years to come.

Bush's second term, however, got off to a rocky start. An intense effort from Bush to change Social Security toward private accounts encountered Democratic resistance and popular discontent. The war in Iraq, with no end in sight and persistent American casualties each month, became a political liability for the president. His poll ratings slipped in the summer of 2005 to their lowest levels for his time in office.

In August 2005, Hurricane Katrina hit the Gulf Coast, devastating large portions of Alabama, Mississippi, and Louisiana. New Orleans became flooded, and estimates of the loss of life reached into the tens of thousands, although those numbers were eventually revised downward. Although there had been ample warnings of the dangers to the city of a Category 4 hurricane and forecasts of where Katrina would hit as landfall approached, the city, state, and federal governments performed badly in the crisis. The actions of the federal government represented the greatest shortfall in actual results. President Bush had named inept cronies to head the Department of Homeland Security and the Federal Emergency Management Agency, and those two arms of the national government were late, slow, and inefficient in meeting the challenges of the crisis. A terrible disaster worsened because of the shoddy reaction of Washington and the Bush administration.

The result called into question whether the United States could respond to a terrorist attack where there would be no warning in advance. Bush's standing as a national leader also sagged when he failed to cut short his vacation to deal with the crisis and seemed out of touch when he visited the stricken area. By September 2005, the people of the United States wondered whether they really were any safer than they had been when terrorism struck on September 11, 2001.

Conclusion

As the twenty-first century began in January 2001, the United States seemed to be an optimistic and confident society with a strong economy, declining crime rates, and a powerful international position. By the end of the year, the future seemed darker. The terrorist threat posed the likelihood of a long, expensive conflict that might change the openness of American society into a more disciplined and less free nation. Whether the people of the United States fully grasped the danger that they faced remained in doubt.

Beyond the immediate menace of terrorism lay other concerns. The issue of race amid an increasingly diverse population was still unresolved, with the potential to disrupt the social fabric. The exploitation of the environment threatened the degradation of the natural world and the resources on which prosperity depended. Within national politics, there were signs that the public's commitment to democratic values could be fraying. The United States had made a significant historical journey from the time when Europeans first appeared on the North American continent down to the age of the Internet. But the future course of the American Passage was an unfolding story in which the optimism of the nation's history would be a precious asset in the dangerous times that lay ahead for the people of the United States.

The Chapter in Review

In the years following Bill Clinton's election as president in 1992:

- Political turmoil culminated in Republican control of Congress after 1994.
- Racial, ethnic, and cultural tensions continued unabated.
- The rise of the Internet and a growing reliance on computers changed the way people do business and communicate.
- Bill Clinton was impeached and acquitted.
- George W. Bush was elected president in 2000.
- The attacks of September 11, 2001, brought the threat of domestic and foreign terrorism to the forefront of Americans' consciousness.
- A prolonged war in Iraq dragged on.

Making Connections Across Chapters

LOOKING BACK

The 1990s and early 2000s have become contested terrain in the polarized politics of the modern United States. The two most recent presidents, Bill Clinton and George W. Bush, aroused intense feelings for and against them. The emphasis on personality and character that dominated politics also diverted attention from the serious problems that the nation faced as the threat of terrorism and environmental disasters arose.

1. Where does Bill Clinton fit within the recent history of the Democratic party?

2. Why did terrorism not receive more attention during the 1990s?

3. How did the conservatism of George W. Bush resemble or differ from previous conservative presidencies?

4. What are the political strengths and weaknesses of American government in the early twentieth century?

LOOKING AHEAD

This is the last chapter of the book and so these questions are not for further reading. Think about these issues as you ponder the sweep of American history and what could occur during your lifetime as the national passage moves on.

1. What will it take to win the war on terrorism? What should the United States do to resolve the conflict while at the same time preserving its democratic heritage?

2. How different will American society be in 25 years because of the developments in the 1990s and early twenty-first century?

3. Should optimism or pessimism be the dominant theme in evaluating the future of the United States in light of the history you have just finished reading?

Now review by answering one of the following questions on a separate sheet of paper. You may use your markings or notes. Turn in your paper to your instructor.

1. Discuss terrorism and the Bush presidency as reflected in the selection.

   _____   _____

2. Based on what you read, what inferences can be drawn about the authors' opinion of the Bush presidency up to 2005? Give specific examples from the text.

   _____   _____

PRACTICE C-2: Reading and Marking an Art History Textbook Chapter

Directions: Read the following passage from an art history textbook, *Living with Art*, by Rita Gilbert and William McCarter. Apply the SQ3R technique, by surveying, questioning, and then reading and reciting by marking the passage in a way that will help you understand the content.

THE ROLE OF THE ARTIST

1   Nobody questions the role farmers play in society. They produce the food necessary to sustain life. Much the same is true of furniture makers, car and clothing manufacturers, and nowadays computer programmers and bankers. But what of artists? What role do they fill? What do they contribute to society, and do we really need them? Would our world be seriously diminished if there weren't any artists? To answer these questions, let us focus briefly on those people who live actively with art every day of their lives—the artists themselves.

2   We should first consider who the artist is. Thanks to Hollywood movies and popular fiction, many people have a stereotype in mind. (The two artists whose biographies appear in this chapter were both subjects of sensationalized Hollywood films, thus contributing to the stereotype.) According to this idea, the artist is a free spirit, unbridled by any moral code; poorly dressed and not very well washed; high nearly all the time on drugs or drink or both; housed in a drafty but picturesque studio, surrounded by paint cans, nude models, and bohemian friends; apt to dash off at any moment to Majorca or the South Pacific to live primarily on peeled grapes, pausing every now and again to splash onto canvas the tortured outpourings of an Intense Inner Turmoil. The artist's death comes tragically early, usually by suicide or overindulgence in strong drink. Is this image romantic? Absolutely. Is it accurate? Almost never. The fact is that most great artists become great by channeling their personal vision into hard work and discipline.

3   This picture of the artist—a charming one, to be sure—really applies only to a few artists, influenced by Romantic ideals of the late 19th century. Throughout history artists have filled many different kinds of social roles. In ancient Egypt, Greece, and Rome, artists usually had very low social status, and some were actually slaves whose task was to carry out the artistic requirements of their masters. During the Middle Ages the artist moved into the realm of the craftsman, occupying a social level roughly equivalent to that of today's fine cabinetmaker. Only by the time of the Renaissance, the 15th century, were artists accepted in "good" society, and still their creations were

under the rigorous control of wealthy patrons. Today's artists in most countries enjoy a social status like that of Renaissance artists—a special elite apart from class—but their freedom of expression is greater than that of artists even a few generations ago.

4   The social role of artists has changed over time, but their function remains basically the same. Like their counterparts in earlier times, contemporary artists fulfill a practical function, designing virtually every structure and object in the environment. Today this practical role is carried out by artists with specialized, often technical, training—industrial and graphic designers, architects, craft artists, and fashion designers, among others. But what about the painters and sculptors, the photographers and cinematographers? What needs do they meet in our computer age? We can identify at least four basic functions for the artist—all of them age-old, all expanding in complexity.

5   First, artists *record*. They give us visual images that can be preserved for historical reference. This idea is so obvious that we take it for granted, forgetting how overwhelming our ignorance otherwise would be. Were it not for artists, we would have no idea what people from the past looked like. Thomas Jefferson was one of the founders of our country, principal author of the Declaration of Independence, and third president of the United States. He is well known to us from his extensive writings. His splendid architecture stands today and is still admired. But Jefferson died more than a decade before the invention of photography, and were it not for artists' portraits, including the sensitive one by Rembrandt Peale, we would have no visual image of the man to match the achievement. Nor could we form any visual image of historical places and events. Before the invention of the camera in the early 19th century, artists recorded images mainly through painting and sculpture. Today we rely more heavily on photography, cinema, and television to keep our history, but of course the people behind these media are also artists. Even with the prevalence of mechanical recording, there is a renewed interest in the painted portrait, and a great many well-known artists are thriving on portrait commissions.

6   Second, artists *give tangible form to the unknown*. In other words, they attempt to record what cannot be seen with the eyes or what has not yet occurred. This role has been important throughout the history of art, and it is no less vital today. Ancient artists had a somewhat different list of unknowns to contend with. They puzzled over and feared such things as tornadoes, floods, eclipses, and the wrath of spirits. Even in an age when satellites predict the weather and spirits have been tamed, there still are certain unknowns, and artists still are struggling to give them tangible form. What would a nuclear holocaust be like? We do not know and dare not find out. What exists at the edge of our universe? Scientists will know eventually, but not soon. What do our dreams and nightmares really mean? None of us can analyze them definitely. These unknowns are frightening to us, just as the Thunder God must have been to our ancestors. If artists can present them to us in some concrete form, we can tame them and go about our business.

7   Third, artists *give tangible form to feelings*. These may be the artist's own feelings that are expressed in paint or marble or whatever the medium. But surely they are feelings shared by many people—love, hate, despair, fear, exhilaration, anger, admiration, the terror of nightmares. When we respond to a work of art, when we pay attention to the emotions it evokes, we are communicating in a way with the artist and with other people who share these responses.

8   Fourth, artists *offer an innovative way of seeing*, a unique visual perspective. When we experience a work of art, we confront the artist's perspective, compare it to our own, and take note of both the similarities and the differences. Art encourages us to think, to question, to imagine, to explore, to dream. It stretches our own horizons by confronting us with someone else's.

9   To sum up, then, artists perform at least four important functions in society: they record, they visualize the unknown, they portray feelings, and they stretch one's ability to see. All of these functions have to do with communication. Artists are able to fill these roles because they *create* new visual images. The words *creative* and *creativity* will come up often in this book, so it might be well to pause a bit and consider what they really mean.

Now review by answering **one** of the following questions on a separate sheet of paper. You may use your markings or notes. Turn in your paper to your instructor.

1. Compare and contrast the mistaken lifestyles of the stereotyped picture of an artist with reality.

   _____

2. Discuss in some detail the four basic functions of an artist.

   _____

D.   Taking Reading Notes

Some students don't want to mark or underline their textbooks because they want to sell them when the course is over. This is understandable considering the cost of textbooks these days. Still, marking and underlining, if done correctly, are preferable to taking notes for the reasons described in the previous section. But there are times when you use books that are not yours, so a method for taking notes is needed.

The main thing to remember about taking reading notes is not to copy word for word from the book. Rephrase what the author says in your own words as much as possible. Many students make the mistake of copying right from the book, thinking that they are doing a good job of studying. Such action usually produces no results. The purpose of taking notes is to make certain that you understand what you are reading at the time and to record it for later review.

As with marking and underlining, there is no one way to take notes. But here are some guidelines for you to follow:

1. At the top of the notebook page, always write down the title of the book, the chapter title, and the pages your notes cover. There may be a time in the future when your notes aren't as helpful as you thought and you need to refer back to the book. This information will help you find the material in the book quickly.

2. Write the main ideas of the passage as your own heading, then list the supporting details under this heading. In effect, you are summarizing main ideas and supporting details just as you did in Chapter Two with paragraphs and essays.

3. Don't write anything down until you have studied a short passage and understand it. Let the writing patterns discussed in the last chapter help you sort out the key points. If an author is defining a term or concept, make certain your notes contain the definition. If the author is comparing or contrasting two items, make certain your notes reflect the comparison, contrast, and so on.

4. Remember, don't use the same words as the author unless they are necessary. If you do use the author's own words, make certain you know their meanings.

5. Keep track of words you need to look up. If the vocabulary is difficult, you may need to look up words in the glossary or in a dictionary before you can take notes.

6. Write down questions that you can't answer or that give you trouble so that you can ask your instructor about them at the next class meeting.

Feel free to modify these suggestions. Just make certain that you are not going through the motions of taking notes without really understanding what you are writing down.

Mapping: Another Type of Note Taking

Mapping is a technique used to place notes for an entire chapter on one or two notebook pages. Mapping forces you to see a chapter as a whole rather than in pieces, and it helps you store what you read in your long-term memory. As with any study device, it is only as good as you make it.

Mapping works well with the SQ3R study method. Rather than taking reading notes as discussed before, some students prefer the mapping technique. Look carefully at the map below of a selection you read from a communications textbook chapter. Notice how the title of the source material appears in a triangle in

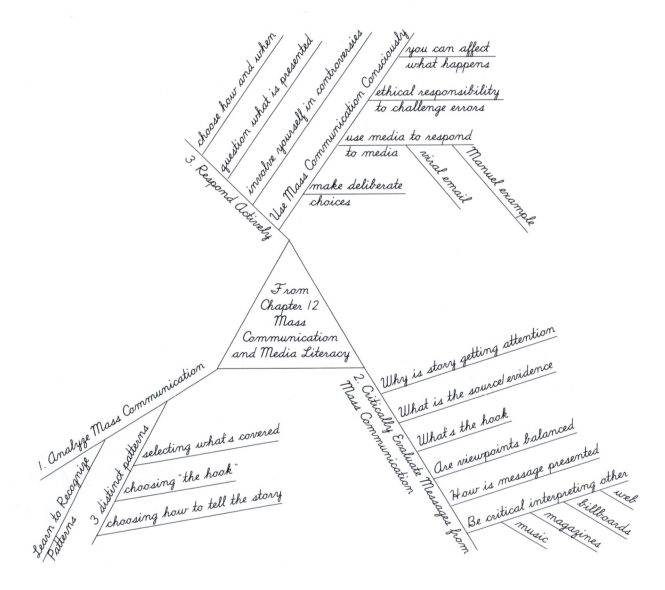

a. Usually, true-false tests will contain more true answers than false ones. (That's *usually*, not always!)

b. Long statements tend to be false, because in order for a question to be true everything in it must be true. The longer the question, the more chance of a false statement. However, in multiple-choice answers, long statements tend to be the correct answer.

c. Don't change an answer unless you are absolutely sure you were wrong the first time you marked it.

d. With multiple-choice questions, "all of the above" tends to be a correct answer.

e. When answers to multiple-choice questions require a number, it's best to disregard the highest and lowest numbers and go for something in between.

f. If you are in doubt about an answer, think of your instructor. What would she or he probably want as an answer based on what has been said in class?

g. If a question uses double negatives, remove the negatives to see how the question reads. For example, take out the negatives in this statement:

It is *not un*advisable to guess when you don't know an answer on a test.

The statement then reads:

It is advisable to guess when you don't know an answer on a test.

This makes the statement true, unless you are penalized for wrong answers.

h. When taking a matching test with two columns, read both columns before marking any answers. Make a mark near the answers you use so that you don't use them twice.

Remember, these suggestions are not always going to work in your favor. But if you have studied carefully, chances are they can help you achieve a better grade.

What to Do with Tests after You Get Them Back

Unless you learn to evaluate what you got right and wrong on a test, you will continue to make the same mistakes again and again. When you get a test back, take some time to figure out your strengths and weaknesses on that exam. The following questions will help you learn from your mistakes:

- Were the questions you missed from the textbook or the lecture notes?
- Did you misread any of the directions?
- Did you generally miss main ideas or details?
- Were the questions you missed from one particular part of the chapter or notes (for example, are the missed questions often from the end of the class lecture)?
- Did you miss questions because you didn't know that information? If you didn't know it, why not?
- Were the test questions what you expected? If these weren't the test questions you predicted, why not?
- Did you miss questions because you didn't leave enough time to do one section of the test or you didn't finish the test?
- Is this the grade you predicted for yourself on this test? Why or why not?

F.   Scanning Graphic Aids

Scanning is what you do when you look for a friend's telephone number in a phone book. It is the technique used when locating a word in a dictionary, when seeking a page number in an index, or when checking to see what television programs are offered at eight o'clock. In all these examples, you know what you are looking for before you begin to read. You have to use guides and aids to find what you want rather than reading everything on the page. Good scanning ability, then, depends on knowing what you want to find and knowing the organization of the material to be read.

Scanning is something you already know how to do, but you may or may not be very proficient at it. In either case, the practices in this chapter will help you increase your scanning speed and become more aware of the organizational patterns in materials where scanning is best utilized.

Scanning graphic aids in textbooks is an important study skill. You need to learn how to scan charts, maps, graphs, indexes, and tables quickly in order to get the most information in the least amount of time. The following practice exercises are designed to help you become proficient at this skill. Try to keep to the time limits suggested.

As you do these practices, try finding a scanning technique that works well for you. Remember that you are not reading in the normal sense of the word; you are learning to develop a skill. Feel free to experiment and don't worry about mistakes. This is the place to make mistakes and to learn from them.

PRACTICE F-1: Charts

Directions: First take a minute to look at the following chart. Then scan the chart for the answers to the questions under the chart. Write your answers in the blanks provided. You should finish in less than three minutes.

CALORIES USED PER HOUR

	Body Size		
	120 Pounds	150 Pounds	175 Pounds
Calisthenics	235–285	270–300	285–335
Running	550–660	625–700	660–775
Walking	235–285	270–330	285–335
Bowling	150–180	170–190	180–210
Swimming	425–510	480–540	510–600
Bicycling	325–395	370–415	395–460
Tennis	335–405	380–425	405–470
Golf	260–315	295–335	315–370

HOURS: MINUTES PER WEEK TO BURN 1,500 CALORIES

	Body Size		
	120 Pounds	150 Pounds	175 Pounds
Calisthenics	5:16–6:23	5:00–5:33	4:29–5:16
Running	2:16–2:44	2:09–2:25	1:56–2:16
Walking	5:16–6:23	5:00–5:33	4:29–5:16
Bowling	8:20–10:00	7:54–8:49	7:09–8:20
Swimming	2:56–3:32	2:47–3:08	2:30–2:56
Bicycling	3:48–4:37	3:37–4:03	3:16–3:48
Tennis	3:42–4:29	3:32–3:57	3:11–3:42
Golf	4:46–5:46	4:29–5:05	4:03–4:46

Begin timing : _____

1. If you weigh about 120 pounds, what form of exercise burns the most calories?

   _____

2. If you weigh about 150 pounds, will you burn more calories if you swim or if you *run*? _____

   _____

3. If you weigh about 175 pounds, how long will it take you to burn 1,500 calories per week by walking? _____

   _____

4. What activity on the chart is the slowest way to burn calories at any weight?

   _____

   _____

5. If you want to burn as many calories as you can in order to lose weight, what activity should you do? _____

   _____

6. If you don't like the activity in the answer to question 5, what's the next best activity to do to burn calories? _____

   _____

7. If you weigh about 120 pounds, how many hours/minutes per week would you have to spend bowling in order to burn 1,500 calories? _____

   _____

8. Is bicycling a faster or slower way to burn calories than tennis? _____

   _____

Time : _____   **Number Correct :** _____

WEATHER REPORT—FEBRUARY			
City	Average Temperature	Number of days	
		Cloudy	Clear
Seattle	60	23	5
Los Angeles	70	8	20
Santa Fe	75	14	14
Salt Lake City	65	18	10
Denver	63	10	18
Portland	55	10	8
Phoenix	72	8	20
Pierre	46	20	8

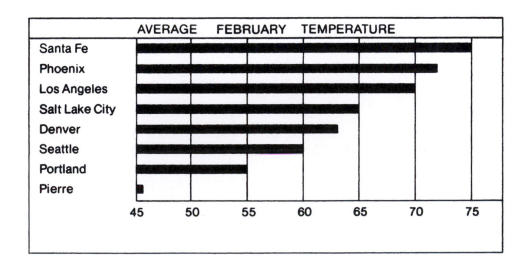

PRACTICE F-2: A Map, Graph, and Chart

Directions: Using the map, graph, and chart on page 152, scan for the answers to the following questions. Circle the letter of the correct response. Answers are provided as a learning tool. Don't read them until after you have scanned.

1. The city with the lowest number of clear days during February is located in
   a. California.
   b. Washington.
   c. Arizona.
   d. South Dakota.

The correct answer can be found by looking under "Number of Days—Clear" on the weather report chart. The city is Seattle, with five clear days. To find the state in which the city is located, look on the map provided. The correct answer is Washington.

2. The city with the same number of cloudy and clear days during February is
   a. Portland.
   b. Denver.
   c. Santa Fe.
   d. Salt Lake City.

To find the correct answer, you would compare the "Cloudy" and "Clear" columns on the weather report chart to find equal numbers of cloudy and clear days. The correct answer is Santa Fe, with fourteen days of each.

3. The city with the lowest average temperature during February is
   a. Seattle.
   b. Pierre.
   c. Los Angeles.
   d. Portland.

The correct answer can be found under "Average Temperature" on the weather report chart, or more quickly on the average temperature graph below it. The correct answer is Pierre, with 46°, a high for that month!

4. The average temperature during February of the city shown in Colorado is
   a. 63°.
   b. 58°.
   c. 55°.
   d. 65°.

The correct answer can be found by first finding the city in Colorado on the map, then looking down the weather report chart or the graph for the average temperature of Denver. The correct answer is 63°.

5. The city with the highest average temperature during February is nearest on the map to

    a. Salt Lake City.

    b. Los Angeles.

    c. Denver.

    d. Portland.

The correct answer can be found by looking at the weather report chart or the graph for the highest average temperature, and then locating that city on the map. Look to the adjacent cities to see which one is nearest to it. The correct answer is Denver, which is nearest to Santa Fe.

6. The number of cloudy days in Los Angeles during February is equal to the number of cloudy days in

    a. Portland.

    b. Santa Fe.

    c. Seattle.

    d. Phoenix.

The correct answer can be found by looking at the cloudy days for Los Angeles on the weather report chart and scanning the list to find which other city has the same number of cloudy days. The correct answer is Phoenix, with eight cloudy days.

7. The city located nearest the Pacific Ocean had how many clear days in February?

    a. 15

    b. 5

    c. 20

    d. 8

The correct answer can be found by first looking at the map and locating the city nearest the Pacific. Then look at the clear days on the weather report chart to find the city. The city is Los Angeles, and the correct answer is twenty clear days.

8. The city with the greatest number of cloudy days during February had what average temperature?

    a. 65°

    b. 60°

    c. 58°

    d. 63°

The correct answer can be found by first looking under "Cloudy" on the weather report chart to locate the city with the greatest number of cloudy days. Then you should look under "Average Temperature" for the correct answer. The correct answer is 60° for Seattle.

9. The city appearing nearest the middle of the map is located in which state?

   a. Arizona

   b. Utah

   c. Colorado

   d. California

The correct answer can be found by simply locating the middle point of the map and looking to see what city is nearest that point. It is Salt Lake City, Utah.

10. The city farthest east on the map had how many cloudy days in February?

   a. 5

   b. 12

   c. 20

   d. 8

The correct answer can be found by locating the city farthest east on the map. The city is Pierre, South Dakota. Then look under the "Cloudy" column of the weather report chart to find the number of cloudy days. The correct answer is twenty cloudy days.

PRACTICE F-3: An Index

Directions: Scan the index listing on page 157 for the answers to the following questions. Circle the letter of the correct answer. You should finish in less than three minutes.

Begin timing: _____

1. On what page would you find information about Mayan Indians?

   a. 6

   b. 44

   c. 243

2. On what pages would you find information about Meriwether Lewis?

   a. 136, 148–149

   b. 138–139

   c. 144–145

3. On what page would you find a definition of Manifest Destiny?

   a. 208

   b. 182

   c. 149

4. How many pages are listed for information on the Missouri Compromise?

   a. One

   b. Two

   c. Three

5. On what page would you find information on the "Log Cabin" Bill?

   a. 206

   b. 207

   c. 208

6. Are Mohawk Indians listed in the index?

   a. No

   b. Yes

   c. Can't tell

7. On what pages will you find information about Lincoln's debates with Douglas?

   a. 237–246

   b. 233, 247

   c. 219, 231

8. How many pages are listed for Bishop Las Casas?

   a. One

   b. Two

   c. Three

9. Under what other listing besides "Massachusetts Bay Colony" could you find more information about the colony?

   a. Founding of Maryland

   b. Puritan colonies

   c. Native Americans

10. How many pages are given to moonshiners?

    a. One

    b. Two

    c. Three

Time : _____   **Number Correct :** _____

From *From Columbus to Aquarius: An Interpretive History*, Vol. 1, by George E. Frakes and W. R. Adams. Reprinted by permission of the authors.

PRACTICE F-4: A Table

Directions: Scan the temperature listings below for the answers to the following questions. Write your answers in the blanks that follow the questions. Try to finish in two minutes or less.

Begin timing : _____

1. What is the high temperature in Honolulu? _____

2. What is the low temperature in Fairbanks? _____

3. In what city is the highest temperature listed? _____

4. In what city is the lowest temperature listed? _____

5. What city received the most rain (Pr.)? _____

6. In how many cities was there rain? _____

7. Who prepared the weather listings? _____

Time : _____   **Number Correct :** _____

TEMPERATURES

Temperature and precipitation table for the 24-hour period ending at 4 A.M. Pacific Time, as prepared by the National Weather Service in San Francisco:

	High	Low	Pr.		High	Low	Pr.
Albany	69	45	...	Memphis	75	61	.16
Albuquerque	81	52	...	Miami	82	78	...
Atlanta	83	61	.16	Milwaukee	60	48	.03
Bakersfield	107	75	...	Minneapolis	63	43	...
Bismark	73	47	...	New Orleans	81	69	.54
Boise	91	51	...	New York	64	58	...
Boston	71	51	...	North Platte	63	34	.05
Brownsville	79	57	2.25	Oakland	86	54	...
Buffalo	67	50	...	Oklahoma City	70	46	...
Charlotte	83	66	...	Omaha	68	53	...
Chicago	64	54	.12	Palm Springs	104	71	...
Cincinnati	86	62	...	Paso Robles	105	52	...
Cleveland	76	64	...	Philadelphia	71	61	...
Dallas	78	52	.01	Phoenix	100	70	...
Denver	74	43	...	Pittsburgh	75	56	...
Des Moines	64	53	.01	Portland, Me.	62	42	...
Detroit	70	59	...	Portland, Ore.	69	43	...
Eureka	56	48	...	Rapid City	71	47	...
Fairbanks	55	37	.02	Red Bluff	100	66	...
Fresno	103	66	...	Reno	91	59	...
Helena	83	52	.01	Richmond, Va.	76	59	...
Honolulu	85	72	.01	Sacramento	104	59	...
Indianapolis	82	62	.37	St. Louis	65	55	.30
Kansas City	67	47	...	Salt Lake City	78	53	...
Las Vegas	96	66	...	San Diego	74	62	...
Los Angeles	88	59	...	San Francisco	80	52	...
Louisville	87	63	.24	Seattle	62	47	...

G.   Putting It All Together

PRACTICE G-1: Surveying a Chapter from a Business Textbook

Directions: Take less than two minutes to survey the following selection from a business textbook, *Moral Issues in Business*. Note the title of the book. What does the title tell you about the subject matter of the material? Apply what you have learned about surveying. Do not read the selection, just survey it.

ETHICS

William H. Shaw and Vincent Barry

1   **Ethics** (or moral philosophy) is a broad field of inquiry that addresses a fundamental query that all of us, at least from time to time, inevitably think about—namely, How should I live my life? That question, of course, leads to others, such as, What sort of person should I strive to be? What values are important? What standards or principles should I live by? Exploring these issues immerses one in the study of right and wrong. Among other things, moral philosophers and others who think seriously about ethics want to understand the nature of morality, the meaning of its basic concepts, the characteristics of good moral reasoning, how moral judgments can be justified, and, of course, the principles or properties that distinguish right actions from wrong actions. Thus, ethics deals with individual character and with the moral rules that govern and limit our conduct. It investigates questions of right and wrong, fairness and unfairness, good and bad, duty and obligation, and justice and injustice, as well as moral responsibility and the values that should guide our actions.

Summary 1.1
Ethics deals with individual character and the moral rules that govern and limit our conduct. It investigates questions of right and wrong, duty and obligation, and moral responsibility.

2   You sometimes hear it said that there's a difference between a person's ethics and his or her morals. This can be confusing because what some people mean by saying that something is a matter of ethics (as opposed to morals) is often what other people mean by saying that it is a matter of morals (and not ethics). In fact, however, most people (and most philosophers) see no real distinction between a person's "morals" and a person's "ethics." And almost everyone uses "ethical" and "moral" interchangeably to describe people we consider good and actions we consider right, and "unethical" and "immoral" to designate bad people and wrong actions. This book follows that common usage.

3   **Business and Organizational Ethics**

The primary focus of this book is ethics as it applies to business. Business ethics is the study of what constitutes right and wrong, or good and bad, human conduct in a business context. For example, would it be right for a store manager to break a promise to a customer and sell some hard-to-find merchandise to someone else, whose need for it is greater? What, if anything, should a moral employee do when his or her superiors refuse to look into apparent wrong-doing in a branch office? If you innocently came across secret information about a competitor, would it be permissible for you to use it for your own advantage?

4   Recent business scandals have renewed the interest of business leaders, academics, and society at large in ethics. For example, the Association to Advance Collegiate Schools of Business, which comprises all the top business schools, has introduced new rules on including ethics in their curricula, and the Business Roundtable recently

unveiled an initiative to train the nation's CEOs in the finer points of ethics. But an appreciation of the importance of ethics for a healthy society and a concern, in particular, for what constitutes ethical conduct in business go back to ancient times. The Roman philosopher Cicero (106–43 B.C.E.), for instance, discussed the contested example of an honest merchant from Alexandria, who brings a large stock of wheat to Rhodes, where there is a food shortage. On his way there, he has seen other traders sailing from Alexandria to Rhodes with substantial cargos of grain. Should he tell the people of Rhodes, or say nothing and sell at the best price he can? Some ancient ethicists argued that although the merchant must declare defects in his wares as required by law, as a vendor he is free—provided he tells no untruths—to sell his goods as profitably as he can. Others, including Cicero, argued to the contrary that all the facts must be revealed and that buyers must be as fully informed as sellers.

5   "Business" and "businessperson" are broad terms. "Business" may denote a corner hot-dog stand or a multinational corporation that operates in several countries. A "businessperson" may be a gardener in business for herself or a company president responsible for thousands of workers and millions of shareholder dollars. Accordingly, the word **business** will be used here simply to mean any organization whose objective is to provide goods or services for profit. **Businesspeople** are those who participate in planning, organizing, or directing the work of business.

Summary 1.2
Business ethics is the study of what constitutes right and wrong (or good and bad) human conduct in a business context. Closely related moral questions arise in other organizational contexts.

6   But this book takes a broader view as well. It is concerned with moral issues that arise anywhere that employers and employees come together. It is as much about organizational ethics as about business ethics. An *organization* is a group of people working together to achieve a common purpose. The purpose may be to offer a product or a service primarily for profit, as in business. But the purpose also could be health care, as in medical organizations; public safety and order, as in law-enforcement organizations; education, as in academic organizations; and so on. The cases and illustrations presented in this book deal with moral issues and dilemmas in both business and nonbusiness organizational settings.

7   People occasionally poke fun at the idea of business ethics, declaring that the term is a contradiction or that business has no ethics. Such people take themselves to be worldly and realistic. They think they have a down-to-earth idea of how things really work. In fact, despite its pretense of sophistication, their attitude is embarrassingly naive. It shows that they have little grasp of the nature of ethics and only a superficial understanding of the real world of business. After you read this book, you will perhaps see the truth of this judgment.

8   **Moral Versus Nonmoral Standards**

Moral questions differ from other kinds of questions. Whether your office computer can download a copyrighted album from the Web is a factual question, not a moral question. Whether you should download the album is a moral question. When we answer a moral question or make a moral judgment, we appeal to moral standards. These standards differ from other kinds of standards.

9   Wearing shorts to a formal dinner party is boorish behavior. Murdering the King's English with double negatives violates the basic conventions of proper language usage. Photographing the finish of a horse race with low-speed film is poor photographic technique. In each case a standard is violated—fashion, grammatical, technical—but the violation does not pose a serious threat to human well-being.

Moral standards concern behavior that seriously affects human well-being.

10   **Moral standards** are different because they concern behavior that is of serious consequence to human welfare, that can profoundly injure or benefit people. The conventional moral norms against lying, stealing, and killing deal with actions that can hurt people. And the moral principle that human beings should be treated with dignity and respect uplifts the human personality. Whether products are healthful or

harmful, work conditions safe or dangerous, personnel procedures biased or fair, privacy respected or invaded are also matters that seriously affect human well-being. The standards that govern our conduct in these matters are moral standards.

Moral standards take priority over other standards.

11   A second characteristic follows from the first. Moral standards take priority over other standards, including self-interest Something that morality condemns—for instance, the burglary of your neighbor's home—cannot be justified on the nonmoral grounds that it would be a thrill to do it or that it would pay off handsomely. We take moral standards to be more important than other considerations in guiding our actions.

The soundness of moral standards depends on the adequacy of the reasons that support them.

12   A third characteristic of moral standards is that their soundness depends on the adequacy of the reasons that support or justify them. For the most part, fashion standards are set by clothing designers, merchandisers, and consumers; grammatical standards by grammarians and students of language; technical standards by practitioners and experts in the field. Legislators make laws, boards of directors make organizational policy, and licensing boards establish standards for professionals. In those cases, some authoritative body is the ultimate validating source of the standards and thus can change the standards if it wishes. By contrast, moral standards are not made by such bodies. Their validity depends not on authoritative fiat but rather on the quality of the arguments or the reasoning that supports them. Exactly what constitutes adequate grounds or justification for a moral standard is a debated question, which, as we shall see in the next chapter, underlies disagreement among philosophers over which specific moral principles are best.

13   Although these three characteristics set moral standards apart from others, it is useful to discuss more specifically how morality differs from three things with which it is sometimes confused: etiquette, law, and professional codes of ethics.

Now answer the following questions.

1. What is the subject of the chapter?

    _____

2. What is the primary focus of the book from which the chapter is taken?

    _____

3. What study aids does the chapter provide?

    _____

4. What is your definition of ethics?

    _____

PRACTICE G-2: Study Reading and Marking a Surveyed Chapter

Directions: Apply all you have learned about study reading to the chapter on ethics in business that you surveyed in Practice G-1. When finished, answer the questions that follow.

1. T/F Ethics, according to the textbook authors, deals with individual character and with the moral rules that govern and limit our conduct.

2. T/F The subject of ethics investigates questions of right and wrong, duty and obligation, and moral responsibility.

3. T/F There is a difference between a person's ethics and his or her morals.

4. Circle all of the following that are examples of business ethics that are the primary focus of the textbook from which this selection was taken.

   a. Should a store manager break his promise to a customer and sell a hard-to-find item to a person with greater need?

   b. What should an employee do when his superiors refuse to look into wrong-doing?

   c. Should you use secret information about a competitor to your own advantage?

   d. none of the above

   e. all of the above

5. Define "business ethics." _____ _____ _____ _____

   _____

6. Define a "business person." ___ _____ ___ _____

7. T/F Moral standards concern behavior that seriously affects human well-being and take priority over other standards.

8. Give an example of the difference between a moral and a nonmoral standard.

   _____ _____

   _____

9. T/F Legislators, boards of directors, and licensing boards are examples of powers that establish moral principles.

10. What will the next chapter in this business textbook cover? _____ _____

   _____ _____ _____

   _____

Each question is worth 10 points. Record the results of the test on the Record Chart in the Appendix.

UNIT TWO

CRITICAL COMPREHENSION

Ariel Skelley/Blend Images/Jupiter Images

U nit Two builds on what you learned in Unit One. A look at the comprehension triangle on the next page shows what you learned about literal comprehension and what you will learn about critical comprehension in this unit. As you work through this unit, you will continue to develop your ability to read at the literal level while learning to develop your ability to read critically.

What Is Critical Comprehension?

Critical comprehension is that level of understanding that entails distinguishing fact from opinion; recognizing an author's intent, attitude, or bias; drawing inferences; and making critical judgments. It's the second branch on the comprehension triangle explained in Unit One. Critical comprehension is a more sophisticated level of understanding than literal comprehension. A well-known reading expert, Dr. Francis Triggs, says, "Critical reading requires a contribution by both the author and the reader and an interplay which usually results in a new understanding." For instance, Jonathan Swift's *Gulliver's Travels* appeals to young people because

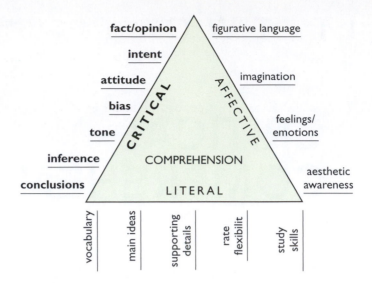

at the literal level it reads like a fairy-tale adventure story about a man who lives with giants and miniature people. However, when the story is read at a more critical level of understanding, it is a very bitter satire on mankind. In other words, an understanding beyond the literal level is necessary for thorough comprehension.

What Does This Unit Cover?

There are four chapters in this unit, each one covering a different facet of critical comprehension. Chapter Four deals with separating fact from opinion. Exercises will call your attention to how we think we are dealing with fact when often we are accepting opinion.

Chapter Five provides exercises for developing the ability to recognize an author's intent or real purpose in writing. Sometimes authors "disguise" their true purpose or thesis by the use of metaphor, satire, irony, or humor. Other times, authors use propaganda or present their evidence in a biased way. Chapter Five should help you analyze an author's actual intention and evaluate bias.

Chapter Six contains practices for discovering how both the author and the reader often draw inferences. Rather than coming right out and saying what they mean, authors sometimes imply or suggest what they want the reader to understand. Likewise, readers often draw inferences about what an author says. When you hear students talking about the "hidden meaning" of a work, or when you hear the statement "Read between the lines," drawing inferences is what is meant. This chapter also provides an opportunity to react to quoted statements, advertisements, and short articles, using what you learned in previous chapters to help you make critical judgments and draw conclusions.

Chapter Seven provides information on developing computer reading skills. Many college classes, as well as a variety of jobs, require not only the ability to read "hard copy," but also the ability to make use of the World Wide Web. More and more information is becoming available on the Internet making it necessary to learn your way around the Web and how to critically evaluate valid information sites. All the reading skills in this unit need to be applied to reading sources found on the Internet.

A comment regarding reading rate is in order here. As you learned in Unit One, speed of reading is not as important as good comprehension. By now you should have realized that although you can increase your overall speed, your reading rate fluctuates with your interest in the topic, the length of the reading selection, your knowledge of the subject, the level of difficulty, and even how you feel on a certain day. That is natural. Some reading selections in this section of the book are timed, mostly for your own concern; most students developing their reading versatility like to have some idea of how fast they are reading. That's fine. Go ahead and practice reading faster. Just remember not to let speed be your goal. As you get to be a better reader, your reading speed also will increase.

What Should You Know after Completing This Unit?

Here are six objectives to work toward in this unit. By the time you complete this unit, you should be able to:

1. Distinguish fact from opinion.
2. Recognize an author's intent, attitude, and tone.
3. Recognize an author's bias and use of propaganda.
4. Recognize inferences being made by an author and make your own inferences from what you read.
5. Make critical judgments and draw conclusions by analyzing the author's diction, style, and use of figurative language.
6. Be familiar with some Internet search engines and how to apply critical reading skills to information found on the World Wide Web.
7. Write a definition of critical comprehension.

If you have any objectives of your own, write them down below and share them with your instructor.

Personal reading objectives for Unit Two:

_____

_____

_____

_____

_____

_____

_____

_____

For now, concentrate on objective 1, distinguishing fact from opinion, which is covered in the next chapter.

CHAPTER FOUR

Distinguishing Fact from Opinion

Distinguishing fact from opinion is not always easy. A fact is usually defined as a truth, something that can be tested by experimentation, observation, or research and shown to be real. But even that is an elusive definition. For example, in 1930 it was generally accepted as fact that the atom was the smallest particle of an element and could not be split. With the advent of atomic power in the 1940s, scientists split the atom, making what was once thought to be a fact a fallacy. Today, physicists are just beginning to understand subatomic particles and refer to many of their findings as theory rather than fact. The point is that facts are sometimes "slippery."

An opinion, on the other hand, is often easier to distinguish. Your belief, feeling, or judgment about something is an opinion. It is a subjective or value judgment, not something that can be objectively verified. Even though you base your opinion on fact, others may not agree; an opinion cannot be proven to everyone's satisfaction. For instance, you may be of the opinion that George Clooney is the greatest actor of our time, but there is no way to make your opinion fact. Others have their own favorite actors, while still others do not know who George Clooney is. The only fact that you can prove is that Clooney is an actor.

Test your skill in recognizing fact from opinion by placing an *F* in the blank next to each of the following statements that you believe to be fact.

_____ **1.** Harry S. Truman was the president of the United States.

_____ **2.** Truman was one of the best presidents the United States has had.

_____ **3.** Generally speaking, movies are more entertaining than books.

_____ **4.** *TIME* is a better magazine than *Newsweek*.

_____ **5.** Columbus, in 1492, was the first person to discover America.

Now see how well you did. You should have marked the first one as a fact. It is a fact that can be verified objectively. The second statement, however, is not a fact. It is a subjective statement claiming "Truman was one of the best." This claim is a value judgment; although we can prove that Truman was a president, historians may never agree that he was one of the best, even though he might have been. Words that give something value, such as *great*, *wonderful*, *beautiful*, *ugly*, *intelligent*, or *stupid*, make statements subjective opinions, not verifiable facts.

The third statement is not fact; it is a value judgment. To say something is "more entertaining" or "better" or "worse" is to place a personal value on something. Value judgments may be based on facts, but they are opinions nonetheless.

The fourth statement is not a fact. You may believe one magazine is better than another, but the use of the word "better" needs clarification. Better in what way? Editorial content? News coverage? Critical reviews? Again, "better" implies a value judgment. *TIME* may have a larger circulation than does *Newsweek*, but that in itself does not make it a better magazine.

The fifth statement is one of those "slippery" facts. According to many sources, Columbus did discover America in 1492. Yet, factually, he never actually landed on the continent; Vikings are said to have explored America long before Columbus, and evidence indicates that Native Americans inhabited America more than 25,000 years before Columbus. Obviously, he wasn't the first person to discover America. It is a European viewpoint that many history books continue to express, yet many textbooks are now changing wording to clarify this historical point. As stated, the fifth statement is not an opinion; it is more an erroneous statement than anything else.

On the other hand, if someone claimed that Columbus sailed to the New World in 1592 rather than 1492, it would be easy enough to consult historical records to show that the correct date was 1492. Knowledge that we share and agree upon as a society is called *shared knowledge*. Agreed-upon facts, then, are generally referred to as objective. If we argue that Columbus was a better sailor than Magellan, we get into the subjective realm of opinion. Unless we can find objective evidence that one was better than the other, we can't speak factually.

Which of the following statements are based on objective evidence?

_____ **1.** Coca-Cola tastes better than Pepsi-Cola.

_____ **2.** The capital of Illinois is Springfield.

_____ **3.** The moon revolves around the earth.

_____ **4.** Italians make great lovers.

Both statements 1 and 4 are based on subjective evidence. You might get fifty people to say Coke tastes better than Pepsi, but you can get another fifty to say the opposite. The same goes for Italians as great lovers. These statements are opinions, not facts. Statements 2 and 3 can be verified by checking agreed-upon information; thus they are facts based on objective evidence until such time as Springfield is no longer the capital and the moon quits revolving around the earth.

Just as our purpose for reading affects our speed and comprehension needs, it also affects the degree to which we must be aware of the differences in objective and subjective statements. When we read the paper for the news of the day, we want facts based on objective reporting. If we want to read someone's interpretation of the facts and what implications that news may have for us, we read editorials and columnists' opinions to see how they subjectively interpret the news. When we read a recipe, we want factual measurements, not opinions on how the finished product will taste. When we read an encyclopedia, we want the facts. But when we read a critic's opinion or interpretation of the importance of those facts, we are looking for a subjective reaction, an opinion.

As a critical reader of all kinds of writing, you need to be able to discern between objective and subjective statements and then draw your own conclusions. The following drills will help you develop your ability to distinguish facts, opinions, and erroneous-sounding statements. If some of the answers seem "picky," just remember that the point is to sharpen your reading versatility.

A.   Fact-Finding

PRACTICE A-1: Fact-Finding

Directions: Read each of the following statements and place an *F* in the blank next to each statement that you feel is *mostly* fact and an *O* in the blank next to each statement that is *mostly* opinion.

_____ **1.** A world auction record for a single piece of furniture—$415,800 for a Louis XVI table—was set today at a sale of the French furniture collection of the late Mrs. Anna Thomson Dodge of the Detroit auto fortune. (From a United Press International release.)

_____ **2.** The junior college is a better place to attend school for the first two years than is a university or four-year school. This is so primarily because classes are smaller at a junior college and more individualized attention can be given to students.

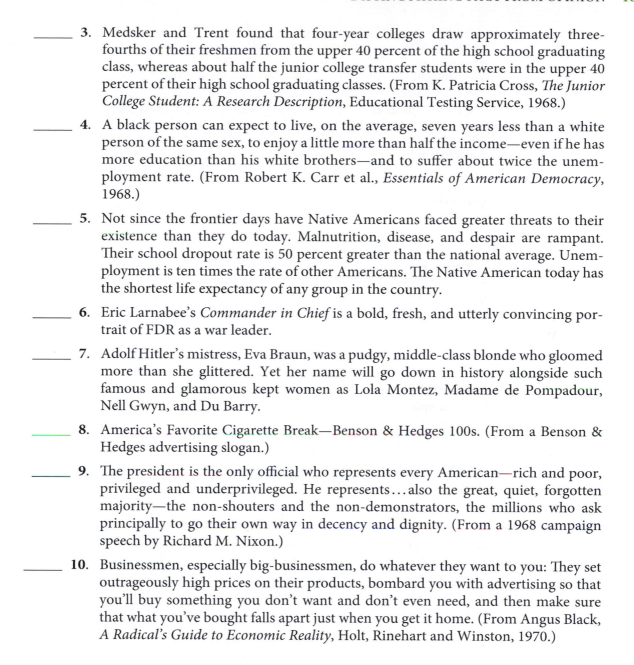

_____ 3. Medsker and Trent found that four-year colleges draw approximately three-fourths of their freshmen from the upper 40 percent of the high school graduating class, whereas about half the junior college transfer students were in the upper 40 percent of their high school graduating classes. (From K. Patricia Cross, _The Junior College Student: A Research Description_, Educational Testing Service, 1968.)

_____ 4. A black person can expect to live, on the average, seven years less than a white person of the same sex, to enjoy a little more than half the income—even if he has more education than his white brothers—and to suffer about twice the unemployment rate. (From Robert K. Carr et al., _Essentials of American Democracy_, 1968.)

_____ 5. Not since the frontier days have Native Americans faced greater threats to their existence than they do today. Malnutrition, disease, and despair are rampant. Their school dropout rate is 50 percent greater than the national average. Unemployment is ten times the rate of other Americans. The Native American today has the shortest life expectancy of any group in the country.

_____ 6. Eric Larnabee's _Commander in Chief_ is a bold, fresh, and utterly convincing portrait of FDR as a war leader.

_____ 7. Adolf Hitler's mistress, Eva Braun, was a pudgy, middle-class blonde who gloomed more than she glittered. Yet her name will go down in history alongside such famous and glamorous kept women as Lola Montez, Madame de Pompadour, Nell Gwyn, and Du Barry.

_____ 8. America's Favorite Cigarette Break—Benson & Hedges 100s. (From a Benson & Hedges advertising slogan.)

_____ 9. The president is the only official who represents every American—rich and poor, privileged and underprivileged. He represents…also the great, quiet, forgotten majority—the non-shouters and the non-demonstrators, the millions who ask principally to go their own way in decency and dignity. (From a 1968 campaign speech by Richard M. Nixon.)

_____ 10. Businessmen, especially big-businessmen, do whatever they want to you: They set outrageously high prices on their products, bombard you with advertising so that you'll buy something you don't want and don't even need, and then make sure that what you've bought falls apart just when you get it home. (From Angus Black, _A Radical's Guide to Economic Reality_, Holt, Rinehart and Winston, 1970.)

Practice A-2: More Fact-Finding

Directions: Read each of the following statements. Circle the number of any that you think are primarily factual or can be objectively proven. Then underline any words in the statements that you feel are too subjective to be verified as factual.

1. In the first seven months of 1988, once-private companies raised $17.4 billion through initial public offerings, or two-thirds more than in the same period of 1987.

2. There are still young people who read for pleasure and who do well in school, but their number dwindles. The middle range of children muddle through high school and some go through college, but the general level of their academic achievement is significantly below what it was thirty years ago.

3. In the presidential election of 1828, Andrew Jackson defeated John Quincy Adams with a popular vote of 647,286 votes over 508,064 for Adams.

4. Take the plunge into the splashiest resort on the most spectacular beach on the most exquisite island in Hawaii—the new Willoughby Maui Hotel. Join in the dreamlike atmosphere of waterfalls, tropical lagoons, and lush tiered gardens—or simply soak up the sun.

5. While grammar usage offers the most immediate clues to a person's educational background, another important clue is vocabulary. The writer or speaker who uses words appropriately and accurately is probably well educated. One who often misuses words or phrases is not soundly educated, because a major purpose of education is to teach people to use their native tongue with accuracy.

6. Since 1957, writes Ben J. Wattenberg in his *The Birth Dearth*, the average American woman's fertility rate has dropped from 3.77 children to 1.8—below the 2.1 size needed to maintain the present population level. Meanwhile, he argues, Communist-bloc countries are producing at a rate of 2.3 children per mother, while the Third World rate is rising so fast that within fifty years its population may be ten times that of the West.

7. But specific challenges to Wattenberg's data have been raised. Some demographers question his projections, because he gathered his information from population trends with little or no regard for such unpredictable factors as wars, epidemics, famines, and baby booms.

8. Scientific data show that, although the Sahara desert moved south between 1980 and 1984, it went north in 1985 and 1986. In 1987 the Sahara's border shifted south, north in 1988, and south again in 1989 and 1990. To find any long-term trends in these annual fluctuations, the researchers say, data would have to be taken for several decades.

PRACTICE A-3: Fact versus Opinion

Directions: Each sentence is lettered in the following statements. On the line below each statement, write the letter of each sentence you think can be accepted as a statement of fact. The first one has been done for you.

1. (a) The last great Greek astronomer of antiquity was Claudius Ptolemy (or Ptolemeus), who flourished about a.d. 140. (b) He compiled a series of thirteen volumes on astronomy known as the *Almagest*. (c) All of the *Almagest* does not deal with Ptolemy's own work, for it includes a compilation of the astronomical achievements of the past, principally of Hipparchus. (d) In fact, it is our main source of information about Greek astronomy. (e) The *Almagest* also contains accounts of the contributions of Ptolemy himself. (From George Abell, *Exploration of the Universe*, Saunders College Publisher, 1982.)

   (a), although the phrase last great may not be fact (b), (c), (d), (e)

2. (a) The July 1987 Almanac states that there are four West Coast species of salmon. This is incorrect. (b) There are five species. (c) The West Coast species belong to the genus *Oncorhynchus*. (d) Their common names are chinook, also called the spring or king salmon; the chum or dog salmon; the coho or silver salmon; the pink salmon; and the sockeye or red salmon.

3. We hold these truths to be self-evident, (a) that all men are created equal; (b) that they are endowed by their Creator with certain unalienable rights; (c) that among these are life, liberty, and the pursuit of happiness; (d) that to secure these rights, governments are instituted among men. (From the Declaration of Independence.)

---

4. (a) If the American political system is to survive without repression, it will be because of positive political leadership that faces up to the problems and convinces both private citizens and public officials that these problems are serious and interrelated; (b) that they must be attacked, attacked immediately, and attacked together by coordinated and probably expensive programs. (c) As we have said so many times... if there is to be positive leadership in American politics, it can only come from the president. (d) Even then the Madisonian system may stalemate. (e) But without presidential leadership there is no hope that the system can move with any speed or controlled direction.

---

5. (a) *The Glass Bead Game* by Hermann Hesse appeared in Switzerland in 1943. (b) It was his last major work of any importance. (c) It is also the best of all his novels, an "act of mental synthesis through which the spiritual values of all ages are perceived as simultaneously present and vitally alive." (d) It was with full artistic consciousness that Hesse created this classic work.

---

6. (a) Although over 500 ruins are recorded within the Grand Canyon National Park, we know only the outline of this area's prehistory. (b) Most ruins are small surface pueblos in and along the north and south rims of the canyon. (c) No large communal centers have been found. (d) Small cliff dwellings and numerous granaries occupy caves and niches in the canyon walls. (e) A few early pit houses, some ruins of late Havasupai houses, and occasional hogans and sweat lodges left by the Navajos complete the roster. (From Joe Ben Wheat, *Prehistoric People*, Grand Canyon Natural History Association, 1959.)

PRACTICE A-4: Interpreting "Facts"

Directions: Read the following two paragraphs. They are accounts of the same historical event written by two different historians. Notice how they both use facts and how they interpret these facts.

When anarchy visited Nicaragua, Coolidge had no choice but to act unilaterally First, in 1925, he withdrew a token force of marines from that nation, which then seemed capable of servicing its foreign debt and preserving its internal stability. But the appearance was deceptive. Almost at once revolution broke out, and Coolidge again landed the marines, in time some five thousand. Regrettably, in its quest for order, the United States chose to support the reactionary faction, whose identification with large landowners and foreign investors had helped provoke the revolution in the first place. (From John Blum et al., *The National Experience*, Harcourt Brace Jovanovich, 1963, p. 617.)

The United States, despite the current anti-war sentiment, was reluctantly forced to adopt warlike measures in Latin America. Disorders in Nicaragua, perilously close to the Panama Canal jugular vein, had jeopardized American lives and property and in 1927 President Coolidge felt compelled to dispatch over 5,000 troops to this troubled banana land. His political foes, decrying mailed-fist tactics, accused him of waging a "private war," while critics south of the Rio Grande loudly assailed *Yanqui* imperialism. (From Thomas A. Bailey, *The American Pageant*, 2nd edition, Heath, 1961, p. 503.)

1. Underline the main idea in each paragraph, and be ready to justify your answer.

2. List two supporting details that support the main idea in *each* of the paragraphs.

   _____

   _____

   _____

3. What facts reported in the first passage are also reported in the second one? Are there any differences in the reporting of facts? _____

   _____

   _____

4. Explain whether the two authors agree on the reason Coolidge sent troops to Nicaragua. _____

   _____

5. Do the two authors agree on the reactions to Coolidge's action? Explain.

   _____

   _____

PRACTICE A-5: Comparing "Facts"

Directions: In 2003, the U.S. Court of Appeals for the Ninth Circuit in California declared unconstitutional the phrase "one nation under God" in the Pledge of Allegiance. At the time of this writing, the ruling has been sent to the Supreme Court on appeal. Two essays on the issue are presented here. One author believes the phrase should not be in the pledge; the other author believes it belongs there.

Before you read the essays, check one of the following statements:

_____ **1.** I believe the phrase "one nation under God" belongs in the pledge.

_____ **2.** I believe the phrase "one nation under God" does not belong in the pledge.

_____ **3.** I don't know.

Now read both of the following essays. As you read them, underline any statements you think are factual.

DO WE NEED GOD IN THE PLEDGE?

JAY SEKULOW

IT'S A STATEMENT OF PATRIOTISM, NOT RELIGION

1   As our nation battles terrorism—at home and abroad—there is a very real threat that millions of students in the western United States will no longer have an opportunity to express their patriotism by voluntarily reciting the Pledge of Allegiance with the phrase "one nation under God."

2   That phrase has been declared unconstitutional by the U.S. Court of Appeals for the 9th Circuit in California. The full appeals court refused to reconsider an earlier ruling by a three-judge panel of the appeals court that determined the phrase "one nation under God" violates the separation of church and state. Now, the only recourse rests with the Supreme Court.

3   The Supreme Court is being asked to take the case and ultimately uphold the constitutionality of a phrase that has become a time-honored tradition—an integral part of the Pledge for nearly 50 years.

4   The Pledge first appeared in print in 1892 as a patriotic exercise expressing loyalty to our nation. Congress added the phrase "under God" in 1954. That phrase first appeared in President Lincoln's Gettysburg Address, which concluded that "this nation, under God, shall have a new birth of freedom—and that the government of the people, by the people, shall not perish from the earth."

5   While the Supreme Court has never ruled directly on the constitutionality of the Pledge, there are numerous cases over the years where justices concluded that the phrase "one nation under God" is not an establishment of religion, but merely a way for the government to acknowledge our religious heritage.

6   In 1962, in *Engel v. Vitale*, Justice Potter Stewart referred to the Pledge of Allegiance as an example of governmental recognition when he quoted a 1952 finding by the court (*Zorach v. Clauson*) that Americans "...are a religious people whose institutions presuppose a Supreme Being."

7   In *Abington v. Schempp*, Justice William Brennan wrote in 1963 that such patriotic exercises like the Pledge do not violate the Establishment Clause of the First Amendment because such a reference, as he put it, "may merely recognize the historical fact that our nation was believed to have been founded 'under God.' Thus reciting the pledge may be no more of a religious exercise than the reading aloud of Lincoln's Gettysburg Address."

8   In 1984, the court in *Lynch v. Donnelly* recognized "there is an unbroken history of official acknowledgement by all three branches of government of the role of religion in American life." Among the many examples of our government's acknowledgement of our religious heritage, according to the court, is the phrase "one nation, under God."

9   And in 1985, Justice Sandra Day O'Connor, quoting herself from *Lynch v. Donnelly*, argued in *Wallace v. Jaffree* that the inclusion of the words "under God" in the Pledge is not unconstitutional because they "serve as an acknowledgement of religion with 'the legitimate secular purpose of solemnizing public occasions, and expressing confidence in the future.'"

10   The California appeals court relied on faulty legal reasoning in reaching a troubling conclusion that can now only be overturned by the Supreme Court. There is no guarantee that the high court will hear the case. But it should. The Pledge is a patriotic expression—not an affirmation of a particular faith.

11   As the Supreme Court considers what to do, it's important to note that the decision will not be made in a vacuum. After all, the court has its own time-honored tradition at stake. Each session begins with the sound of a gavel—and a dramatic call to order that concludes with these words: "God save the United States and this honorable court."

12   The Supreme Court should take the case and keep the Pledge intact.

Now answer the following questions.

1. Is this essay mostly fact or opinion? _____

    _____

2. What is the author's thesis or main idea? _____

    _____

3. Is the thesis or main argument based on facts? Explain. _____

    _____

    _____

4. Did the author convince you of his position? _____

    _____

5. Do you think the Supreme Court should take the case and keep the Pledge intact?

    _____

The following essay offers the opposite opinion regarding the pledge. As you read, underline any statements you feel are factual.

GOVERNMENT SHOULDN'T IMPOSE RELIGION ON CITIZENS

BARRY W. LYNN

1   A federal appeals court decision declaring school-sponsored recitation of the Pledge of Allegiance unconstitutional has generated tremendous confusion, to say nothing of downright hysteria.

2   Contrary to popular belief, the use of the phrase "under God" in the Pledge does not have a long history in America. The Pledge was written in 1892 by a clergyman, and it was originally secular. "Under God" was inserted by Congress in 1954 at the behest of conservative religious pressure groups.

3   To hear some tell it, removing "under God" from the Pledge would all but ensure America's downfall. In fact, the United States won two world wars, survived the Great Depression, and became a world economic and military powerhouse with a non-religious Pledge.

4   Under the Constitution, our laws are supposed to have a secular purpose. What is the secular purpose of having schoolchildren recite a pledge with religious content everyday? It can't be to foster love of country and respect for democracy. Those goals could be—and in the past were—met with a non-religious pledge.

5   No, the politicians who altered the Pledge in 1954 by adding "under God" knew exactly what they were doing. They wanted to make a religious statement. They wanted to send the message that belief in God is an essential part of being a good American. "God and country" was their motto.

6   The problem with this is that not everyone believes in God. Some Americans believe in no God, others believe in many gods.

7   For them, "under God" in the Pledge and "In God We Trust" on our money are a constant slap in the face, a daily reminder that they are different, that they are indeed not full members of the American experiment. That they're out of step—and wrong.

8   But it isn't just atheists and polytheists who are offended by government's use of generic religiosity. Many devoutly religious people are offended by the emptiness of such "God and Country" rhetoric. Real devotion to God, they argue, is not enhanced by the endless repetition of a phrase.

9   Some courts have upheld government's use of generic religious language, calling it "ceremonial deism." It's all right for the government to employ ceremonial deism, the argument goes, because it's not really that religious, and the government's constant use of a phrase like "under God" drains it of religious meaning.

10   As a minister, I find this argument bizarre and offensive. Religious terminology does not lose its sacred meaning just because people use it a lot, no more so than a prayer becomes non-religious through frequent repetition.

11   If that argument were true, it should be all the more alarming to the devout because it suggests that the state may promote religion as long as it first drains it of all meaning and power. In other words, we can have an official, government-supported religion in the United States—as long as it is bland, watered-down, generic, and ultimately meaningless.

12   In fact, the U.S. Constitution allows for no establishment of religion, specific or generic. The U.S. Congress lost sight of that fact in 1954 when it altered the Pledge of Allegiance. It has taken nearly 50 years for a federal court to recognize Congress' mistake. It shouldn't take another 50 for people to realize that "ceremonial deism" is a fraudulent myth that offends both church and state.

Now answer the following questions.

1. Is this essay mostly fact or opinion? _____

_____

2. What is the author's thesis or main idea? _____

_____

_____

3. Is the thesis or main argument based on facts? Explain. _____

_____

_____

4. Did the author convince you of his position? _____

_____

5. Have you changed your opinion after reading these two essays? Explain why or why not? _____

_____

_____

As a point of information, the Supreme Court did hear the case and overturned the 2002 ruling by California's 9th Circuit Court.

B. Reading Opinions of Others

PRACTICE B-1

Directions: Take a few seconds to survey the following selection. Referring to the title, the headings, and your brief survey, write in the space below what you think the article will cover.

Probable coverage _____

Now read the article, underlining factual statements.

HOW GOOD ARE YOUR OPINIONS?

VINCENT RYAN RUGGIERO

1   "Opinion" is a word that is often used carelessly today. It is used to refer to matters of taste, belief, and judgment. This casual use would probably cause little confusion if people didn't attach too much importance to opinion. Unfortunately, most do attach great importance to it. "I have as much right to my opinion as you to yours" and "Everyone's entitled to his opinion" are common expressions. In fact, anyone who would challenge another's opinion is likely to be branded intolerant.

2   Is that label accurate? Is it intolerant to challenge another's opinion? It depends on what definition of opinion you have in mind. For example, you may ask a friend "What do you think of the new Buicks?" And he may reply, "In my opinion, they're ugly." In this case, it would not only be intolerant to challenge his statement, but foolish. For it's obvious that by opinion he means his *personal preference*, a matter of taste. And as the old saying goes, "It's pointless to argue about matters of taste."

3   But consider this very different use of the term. A newspaper reports that the Supreme Court has delivered its opinion in a controversial case. Obviously the justices did not state their personal preferences, their mere likes and dislikes. They stated their *considered judgment*, painstakingly arrived at after thorough inquiry and deliberation.

4   Most of what is referred to as opinion falls somewhere between these two extremes. It is not an expression of taste. Nor is it careful judgment. Yet it may contain elements of both. It is a view or belief more or less casually arrived at, with or without examining the evidence.

5   Is everyone entitled to his opinion? Of course. In a free country this is not only permitted, but guaranteed. In Great Britain, for example, there is still a Flat Earth Society. As the name implies, the members of this organization believe that the earth is not

spherical, but flat. In this country, too, each of us is free to take as creative a position as we please about any matter we choose. When the telephone operator announces "That'll be 95¢ for the first three minutes," you may respond, "No, it won't—it'll be 28¢." When the service station attendant notifies you "Your oil is down a quart," you may reply "Wrong—it's up three."

6   Being free to hold an opinion and express it does not, of course, guarantee you favorable consequences. The operator may hang up on you. The service station attendant may threaten you with violence.

7   Acting on our opinions carries even less assurance. Some time ago in California a couple took their eleven-year-old diabetic son to a faith healer. Secure in their opinion that the man had cured the boy, they threw away his insulin. Three days later the boy died. They remained unshaken in their belief, expressing the opinion that God would raise the boy from the dead. The police arrested them, charging them with manslaughter. The law in such matters is both clear and reasonable. We are free to act on our opinions only so long as, in doing so, we do not harm others.

OPINIONS CAN BE MISTAKEN

8   It is tempting to conclude that, if we are free to believe something, it must have some validity. But that is not so. Free societies are based on the wise observation that since knowledge often comes through mistakes and truth is elusive, every person must be allowed to make his own path to wisdom. So in a way, free societies are based on the realization that opinions can be wrong.

9   In 1972 a British farmer was hoeing his sugar beet field when he uncovered a tiny statue. It looked to him like the figure of a man listening to a transistor radio. In his opinion, it was a piece of junk. Yet it turned out to be a work of art made of gilt bronze in the twelfth century and worth more than $85,000. He was free to have his opinion. But his opinion was wrong.

10   For scores of years millions of people lit up billions of cigarettes, firm in their opinion that their habit was messy and expensive, but harmless. Yet now we know that smoking is a significant factor in numerous diseases and even does harm to nonsmokers who breathe smoke-polluted air and to unborn babies in the wombs of cigarette addicts. Those millions of people were free to believe smoking harmless. But that didn't make them right. Nor did it protect their bodies from harm.

KINDS OF ERROR

11   There are four general kinds of error that can corrupt anyone's beliefs. Francis Bacon classified them as follows: (1) errors or tendencies to error common among all people by virtue of their being human; (2) errors that come from human communication and the limitations of language; (3) errors in the general fashion or attitude of an age; (4) errors posed to an individual by a particular situation.

12   Some people, of course, are more prone to errors than others. John Locke observed that these people fall into three groups. He described them as follows:

- Those who seldom reason at all, but do and think according to the example of others, whether parents, neighbors, ministers, or whoever else they choose or have implicit faith in, to save themselves the pain and trouble of thinking and examining for themselves.
- Those who are determined to let passion rather than reason govern their actions and arguments, and therefore rely on their own or other people's reasoning only so far as it suits them.

- Those who sincerely follow reason, but lack sound, overall good sense, and so do not have a full view of everything that relates to the issue. They talk with only one type of person, read only one type of book, and so are exposed to only one viewpoint.

INFORMED VERSUS UNINFORMED OPINION

13   In forming our opinions it helps to seek out the views of those who know more than we do about the subject. By examining the views of informed people, we broaden our perspective, see details we could not see by ourselves, consider facts we were unaware of. No one can know everything about everything. It is not a mark of inferiority but of good sense to consult those who have given their special attention to the field of knowledge at issue.

14   Each of us knows something about food and food preparation. After all, most of us have eaten three meals a day all our lives. But that experience doesn't make us experts on running a restaurant or on the food packaging industry. Many of us have played varsity sports in high school. But it takes more than that experience to make us authorities on a particular sport.

15   Some years ago the inmates of Attica prison in New York State overpowered their guards and gained control of the prison. They took a number of hostages and threatened to kill them if their demands were not met. Negotiations proceeded for a time. Then they were at an impasse. The situation grew tense. Finally lawmen stormed the prison and, before order was restored, a number of the hostages were killed. In the wake of the tragedy were two difficult questions: Had the prisoners' demands been reasonable? And who was responsible for the breakdown in negotiations?

16   A number of people in public and private life offered their opinions. One newspaper editorial stated that the main fault lay with the prisoners, that they had refused to negotiate reasonably. A letter to the editor explained that the prisoners were unquestionably in the wrong simply because they were prisoners, and thus had forfeited all rights and privileges. A U.S. senator from another state declared that the blame lay with American life in general. "We must ask," he said, "why some men would rather die than live another day in America."

17   The governor of New York State issued this statement: "The tragedy was brought on by the highly-organized, revolutionary tactics of militants who rejected all efforts at a peaceful settlement, forcing a confrontation, and carried out cold-blooded killings they had threatened from the outset."

18   In a much less publicized statement, a professor at a small liberal arts college, an expert in penology (the study of prison systems), expressed sympathy with the prisoners, criticized the terrible conditions in the nation's prisons, agreed fully with many of the prisoners' demands, rejected a few as absurd, and explained some of the underlying causes of prison unrest.

19   Now all those opinions deserved some consideration. But which was most helpful in coming to an understanding of the issue in all its considerable complexity? Certainly the most informed opinion. The opinion of the expert in penology.

20   For all of us, whether experts or amateurs, it is natural to form opinions. We are constantly receiving sensory impressions and responding to them first on the level of simple likes and dislikes, then on the level of thought. Even if we wanted to escape having opinions, we couldn't. Nor should we want to. One of the things that makes human beings vastly more complex and interesting than trees or cows is their ability to form opinions.

21   This ability has two sides, though. If it can lift man to the heights of understanding, it can also topple him to the depths of ludicrousness. Both the wise man and the fool have opinions. The difference is, the wise man forms his with care, and as time increases his understanding, refines them to fit even more precisely the reality they interpret.

Comprehension Check

Part A

Directions: Answer the following questions. Don't look back unless you are referred to a particular paragraph for an answer.

1. Circle the letter of the statement that best expresses the thesis of the article:

   a. We need to form our opinions with care.

   b. It is natural to form opinions.

   c. The word *opinion* is used carelessly today.

   d. Everyone has a right to his or her own opinion.

2. T/F The statement "Being free to hold an opinion and express it does not, of course, guarantee you favorable consequences" is a fact.

3. T/F Paragraph 9 is mostly factual in content.

4. Which of the following are mentioned as the kinds of error that can corrupt anyone's beliefs?

   a. errors posed to an individual by a particular situation

   b. errors or tendencies to error common among all people by virtue of being human

   c. errors in the general fashion or attitude of an age

   d. errors that come from limitations of language

5. T/F In forming our opinions, it helps to seek out the views of those who do not know more than we do about the subject.

6. T/F "No one can know everything about everything" is an opinion.

7. In paragraph 19, the author claims that the expert in penology was the most helpful in coming to an understanding of the prison riot issue. Why would this opinion be better than the others mentioned? _____

   _____

8. What is the difference between personal preference and considered judgment?

   _____

   _____

   _____

9. "One of the things that makes human beings vastly more complex and interesting than trees or cows is their ability to form opinions," says the author. Is this a statement of fact or opinion? _____ Explain. _____ _____

   _____

   _____

10. Is the article mostly fact or opinion? _____ .___ Explain. _____

    _____

    _____

Part B

Directions: The preceding questions can be answered objectively. The following questions require subjective responses. Be ready to explain your answers in class discussion.

1. "We are free to act on our opinions only as long as, in doing so, we do not harm others," says the author. Is this a good rule to follow?_____ Explain.

   _____ _____

   _____

   _____

2. The author refers to a couple who took their diabetic son to a faith healer as an example of how acting on our opinions can be dangerous. Give an example of an opinion you hold or held at one time that could be dangerous in certain circumstances. _____ _____

   _____

   _____

   _____

3. Reread paragraph 12. In your opinion, do you fit any one of the three groups? Explain. _____

   _____

   _____

   _____

4. Give an example of an opinion you once held but no longer do. Explain why you changed your viewpoint. _____ _____

   _____

   _____

   _____

   _____

Vocabulary Check

Part A

Directions: Define the following underlined words from the selection.

1. their <u>considered</u> judgment

   _____ _____ _____

2. it must have some <u>validity</u>

   _____

3. errors <u>posed</u> to an individual

   _____

4. some are more <u>prone</u> to errors

_____

5. they have <u>implicit</u> faith in themselves

_____

Part B

Directions: Write each word from the following list in the appropriate blank.

overpowered   inmates   tense   impasse   proceeded

"Some years ago the **(6)** _____ of Attica prison in New York State **(7)** _____ their guards and gained control of the prison. Negotiations **(8)** _____ for a time. Then they were at an **(9)** _____. The situation grew **(10)** _____."

Record the results of the comprehension (Part A only) and vocabulary checks on the Student Record Chart in the Appendix. Each correct answer is worth 10 points, for a total of 100 points possible for comprehension and 100 points for vocabulary. Discuss any problems or questions with your instructor before you continue.

PRACTICE B-2: Evaluating Differing Opinions

Part A

According to the organization called Law Enforcement Against Prohibition (LEAP), the so-called "War on Drugs" costs the United States an estimated $69 billion a year and does not see law enforcement ever winning the war. They and others call for the legalization of drugs and taxing them as we do alcohol and tobacco. Opponents feel that ending the prohibition of drugs would cause a rise in drug use and create enormous costs in accidents and productivity loss. Still others feel that only marijuana should be legalized. The subject produces many opinions and calls for substantial facts.

Directions: Following are two differing arguments on the subject of legalizing and taxing drugs, especially marijuana. Before you read them, use the space below to write why you would or would not support legalizing drugs presently illegal.

_____

_____

_____

The following selection was written by Brian O'Dea, one of the biggest marijuana smugglers in U.S. history and author of *High: Confessions of an International Drug Smuggler*. He presently produces film and television projects in Toronto, Canada. As you read, use what you have learned to distinguish between facts and opinions.

AN EX-DRUG SMUGGLER'S PERSPECTIVE

BRIAN O'DEA

1   I was one of the "masterminds" behind the importation and sale of approximately 75 tons of pot from Southeast Asia to the U.S. in 1986 and 1987. It was the culmination of a 20-year career as a drug smuggler, a deal that netted in excess of $180 million wholesale. And the only thing the government got out of those drug hauls was the sales tax from the cash my gang spent. There were, of course, some financial forfeitures once my gang was finally rounded up some years later. However, had rational minds prevailed over the past 70-plus years, the U.S. government would have reaped huge benefits from organizations like ours.

2   But no. Rather than accept the fact that some 30 million Americans cannot possibly be criminals, our society has squandered almost a trillion dollars in a futile effort to stop drug use.

3   We're hearing a lot about drug-related violence in Mexico these days. But listening to the news recently, I heard of a police sweep in Toronto—where I live some months out of the year. The operation involved more than 1,000 police officers and netted, among other things, a vast quantity of firearms, including loaded AK-47s, sawed-off shotguns and 34 handguns, none of which were obtained legally. These weapons came from the United States and were smuggled north. Here is how it works (I know firsthand): Canadian gangs grow pot in apartment buildings, putting everyone who lives there in danger. Once harvested, the pot is traded to U.S. gangs for cocaine and guns. America's arcane drug laws provide the currency for these gangs to exist.

4   South of the border, it's even worse. Some analysts say Mexico is on the slipperiest of slopes toward becoming a failed state, and illegal drugs are playing a huge part. Drug traffickers are able to operate only because they have currency. Take away the currency, you take away the drug traffickers.

5   In my days in that business, guns were nowhere to be found. Now, however, I cannot imagine anyone being in the trade without a gun. It has to stop, but how?

6   Steve Lopez, a Los Angeles Times columnist, recently wrote, "I'm sitting in Costa Mesa with a silver-haired gent who once ran for Congress as a Republican and used to lock up drug dealers as a federal prosecutor, a man who served as an Orange County [California] judge for 25 years. And what are we talking about? He's begging me to tell you we need to legalize drugs in America."

7   A judge is saying this. Say it ain't true, baby, but it is. And he's not the only one saying it. Former Seattle Police Chief Norm Stamper (in whose jurisdiction I was sentenced to 10 years in prison) says the same thing. That's why he is involved with Law Enforcement Against Prohibition, a group of former and current police officers, government agents and other law-enforcement agents who oppose the war on drugs.

8   According to LEAP, "After nearly four decades of fueling the U.S. policy of a war on drugs with over a trillion tax dollars and 37 million arrests for non-violent drug offenses, our confined population has quadrupled, making building prisons the fastest growing industry in the United States." More than 2.3 million U.S. citizens are in jail, and every year we arrest 1.9 million more, guaranteeing prisons will be busting at their seams. Every year, the war on drugs will cost U.S. taxpayers another $69 billion.

9   While the U.S. has only 5 percent of the world's population, it has 25 percent of the world's known prison population. This startling number is due to one major factor: our arcane drug laws. It is time we stopped treating a medical condition with law enforcement.

Brian O'Dea, "An Ex-Drug Smuggler's Perspective," *Chicago Tribune*, April 12, 2009. Reproduced with permission.

10   Ultimately, does the fact that people smoke pot make them criminals? Is the struggling heroin addict a criminal? If he is, it is only because we are not treating the root of the problem.

11   It is time to legalize marijuana. The tax revenue generated could then be used to help addicts. I work with these folks every day, in one way or another, and not one of them wants to live the way they do, but they don't know how to stop. They need help, not punishment.

12   Back in the 1920s, America saw one of the most violent organized criminal elements in history. Who can forget the tommy guns, the blood on the street and names like Luciano and Capone? Well, they exist today, it's just that the names have been changed to Escobar and Huerta Rios. As LEAP so succinctly puts it: Alcohol prohibition, drug prohibition, same problem, same solution.

Now answer the following questions:

1. What is the main idea of the essay? _____

_____ _____ _ _____

2. Is the essay mostly fact or opinion? _____

_____

3. What is the author's main argument for legalizing marijuana? _____

_____

_____

4. What factual support does the author use in favor of his opinion? _____

_____

_____

5. Did the author convince you of his argument? _____ Explain._____

_____ _____

_____

Part B

Directions: The next essay offers the opposite view on legalizing marijuana and other illegal drugs. As you read, apply what you have learned about separating facts from opinions.

SHOULD WE TAX POT?

PATT MORRISON

1   Barack Obama is probably getting more letters than Santa Claus this year.

2   The transition office's mailbox must be full of pleas: "Dear President-elect Obama: I realty want a My Little Pony Pinkie Pie – Love. Susie." and "Dear President-elect

Obama: I really want a Mustang hybrid model that will sell half a million units in the first year – Love, Alan Mulally."

3   In Philadelphia this week, the nation's governors did everything but climb into Obama's lap with their wish lists for money to build roads and bridges and schools. Gov. Arnold Schwarzenegger's list alone runs to about $28 billion. Americans want healthcare reform and safe pensions and, truly, world peace.

4   But who's coming up with the money for this? Do we think we can stick our bicuspids under the pillow and the national tooth fairy will leave $800 billion? No? Then what about legalizing and taxing one of our biggest, oldest vices?

5   That notion arose because Friday is the 75th anniversary of the end of a nation-wide ban on a substance that millions of Americans broke the law and bought anyway: liquor. Criminalizing it turned out to have complications so enormous and expensive that in 1933 a new president, faced with a profound economic crisis, wanted it legalized and taxed again.

6   Now, as we're desperately trying to reinvent the economy, should we consider marijuana?

7   We've dipped a toe in those waters already in California. Sales of medical marijuana are taxable – $11.4 million worth for 2005–2006, the most recent (though admittedly murky) figures available.

8   How much more might we raise from the tons of now-illegal marijuana? When we tried to tax it decades ago, it wasn't so much about raising money as about cutting the demand for dope. In 1937, a new federal tax added so much cost and red tape to purveying marijuana that even doctors were priced out of legally prescribing the stuff. Once pot was banned outright, the tax became a double-dipping opportunity for lawmen. They got you for possessing or selling and for not paying the tax too. In 1968, the feds busted a Santa Barbara couple with 600 pounds of marijuana – and gave them a tax bill for $1,622,000.

9   Of course, by paying the tax, you would be confessing to breaking the law. Timothy Leary was busted for not paying a marijuana "transfer" tax, but the Supreme Court said the law amounted to self-incrimination and threw his case out.

10   However, if we keep charging a tax – something above and beyond a sales tax – but take away the criminality, we'd be win-win, right? We don't mind paying "sin" taxes, or levying them, like Schwarzenegger's plan to help beat the deficit with a new 5-cent-a-drink tax.

11   Marijuana is a huge component of the nation's underground economy. A couple of years ago, the legalize-it forces estimated that the U.S. marijuana crop was worth $35 billion a year. California's share of that was $13.8 billion.

12   If the number is even half that, any tax windfall, on top of money saved by not prosecuting marijuana crimes, would mean a bonanza, wouldn't it?

13   Sacramento would be doing the backstroke in black ink. With all the new parks and health clinics, we'd have more ribbon-cuttings than a baby shower. Is this just a pipe dream?

14   Rosalie Pacula says that in all likelihood, yes. She's a senior economist at the Rand Corp. and co-director of its drug policy research center. Here's how she burst my bubble:

15   First, you have to consider that legalizing it would have its own costs. Recent research, Pacula says, shows marijuana to be more addictive than was thought. Because marijuana is illegal, and because its users often smoke tobacco or use other drugs, teasing out marijuana's health effects and associated costs is almost impossible. And more people would smoke it regularly if it were legal – Pacula estimates 60% to 70% of the population as opposed to 20% to 30% now – and the social costs would rise.

16   She takes issue with figures from Harvard's Jeffrey Miron, among others, who says that billions spent on enforcing marijuana laws could all be saved by legalization. Rand's research, Pacula says, finds that many marijuana arrests are collateral – say, part of DUI checks or curfew arrests – and many arrestees already have criminal records, meaning they might wind up behind bars for something else even if marijuana were legal.

17   Legalization also wouldn't do away with pot-related crime entirely. There would likely be a black market, just as there is in other regulated substances, such as cigarettes and liquor. That means police and prosecution, which cost money.

18   As to the tax benefit, that's partly a function of the price point for legalized pot. If everyone could legally grow and consume dope, then the crop probably wouldn't be worth $35 billion and the taxes wouldn't be anything to write home about.

19   "I have a hard time believing the tax revenue would offset the full cost of regulating and enforcing the legal market," Pacula concludes.

20   No golden pot tax in the pot at the end of the rainbow, then? Pacula left me thinking that the unintended consequences of legalizing marijuana in 2009 might match the unintended consequences of outlawing liquor in 1919.

21   I'm sorry to let you down, President-elect Obama.

22   I think I'll go have a drink. Here's your tax nickel, Arnold. Oh heck – I want to do my bit for California. Here's a dime.

Now answer the following questions.

1. What is the main idea of the essay? _____
    _____
    _____

2. Is the essay mostly fact or opinion? Mostly _____

3. What facts does the author give in support of her thesis? _____
    _____
    _____

4. Is the main argument based mostly on facts? _____ Explain _____
    _____
    _____
    _____

5. Did the author convince you of Pacula's argument? _____ Explain._____
    _____
    _____
    _____

6. Reread your stated opinion on the subject (page 181). Then explain why you have or have not changed your mind after reading these two essays. _____
    _____
    _____
    _____

7. What would it take to change your opinion? _____

_____   _____

_____

_____

Optional Exercise

Directions: If you are interested in the pros and cons of legalizing drugs, you may wish to go online and type in *legalizing drugs* in a search engine. Exploring some of the listings, you will find many more pro and con opinions and facts on the subject.

PRACTICE B-3: Quick Quiz on Fact/Opinion

Part A

Directions: Place an *O* in the blank next to each statement of opinion; place an *F* in the blank next to each statement that is fact or can be verified.

_____ 1. Fifty-seven items in the L. L. Bean Women's Outdoor Catalog are offered in various shades of pink.

_____ 2. We can no longer get along in our present society without telephones.

_____ 3. It is important for college students to have good study skills if they are to succeed in the academic world.

_____ 4. The Tobacco Institute donated $70,000 to help underwrite the antidrug booklet *Helping Youth Say No.*

_____ 5. The two most interesting things in the world, for our species, are ideas and the individual human body, two elements that poetry uniquely joins together.

_____ 6. Last year, as a result of the worldwide collapse of oil prices, the Mexican economy shrank 5 percent, and underemployment reached 50 percent. Things are worse in El Salvador.

_____ 7. The United States is a nation of immigrants, and of immigration policies—policies designed to facilitate the orderly entry of people into the country, but also to keep them out.

_____ 8. War against the Plains Indians in the early nineteenth century was a hopeless proposition for Europeans armed with swords, single-shot pistols, and breech-loading rifles. The Indians were infinitely better horsemen and could loose a continuous fusillade of arrows from beneath the neck of a pony going at full tilt.

_____ 9. Mark Hunter's comments on the lack of spirit and spontaneity found in contemporary rock music are accurate. But his attack on MTV is misguided and his assertion that rock music is no longer worth listening to is absurd.

_____ 10. Your jeweler is the expert where diamonds are concerned. His knowledge can help make the acquisition of a quality diamond of a carat or more a beautiful, rewarding experience.

Part B

Directions: In the space provided, explain what kind of evidence you would have to gather to prove each statement as fact.

1. The viewing of violence on television has created a more violent society._____

2. City slums breed crime. _____

3. Solar energy is the most efficient way to heat homes in some parts of the United States. _____

4. A college education provides better job opportunities. _____

5. If you are rich, you probably won't get convicted of a crime as easily as you will if you are poor. _____

Discuss your answers in class.

C.   Detecting Propaganda

Before you begin this section on propaganda, answer the following questions.

1. Define *propaganda*: _____

2. Does the word *propaganda* have a positive or negative connotation for you? Explain. _____ _____

_____

_____

3. Give some examples of the use of propaganda. _____ _____

_____

_____

_____

_____

4. Do you think you are always aware of propaganda when it is being used? Explain.

_____

_____

_____

Now read the following information, comparing your definition and examples of propaganda with those provided here.

Propaganda is the deliberate attempt on the part of a group or an individual to sway our opinions in their favor. Contrary to what some think, propaganda is not merely a tool used by dictatorial governments. We are exposed to various propaganda techniques nearly every day of our lives. Politicians use propaganda, along with other devices, to get us to accept their opinions and vote for them. Newspapers and magazines use propaganda techniques to influence our opinions on political and social issues. Religious leaders use propaganda to influence our opinions on morality. Advertisers, through television, radio, newspapers, magazines, and the Internet, use propaganda techniques to get us to buy things we often don't need or to change the brand of soap we use.

Propaganda techniques usually appeal to our emotions or our desires rather than to our reason. They cause us to believe or do things we might not believe or do if we thought and reasoned more carefully. When we are too lazy to think for ourselves, we often become victims of propaganda. Propagandists are usually not concerned with good or bad, right or wrong. They are more concerned with getting us to believe what they want us to believe. The techniques they use can range from outright lies to subtle truths.

The power of propaganda cannot be overrated. While some propaganda may be socially beneficial, it can also be harmful. Through propaganda techniques, our opinions can be changed to be "for" or "against" certain nations, political rulers, races, moral values, and religions. What we must guard against is having our opinions formed for us by others. We must not let ourselves be used or fooled, even for good causes.

The Institute for Propaganda Analysis identified seven of the most frequently used propaganda techniques:

1. *Name calling*: an attempt to arouse people with emotionally charged words that appeal to our fears or hatred. The technique is used with the hope that we will reject a person or idea on the basis of a negative symbol or word. Labeling someone as a *terrorist, fascist, fag,* or *radical* is done with the intent of creating a negative response to that person. However, sometimes name calling is done in reverse. The government changed the name of the War Department to the Department of

Defense. The MX missile, a weapon of destruction, is called the *Peacekeeper*. The term *shell shock* was changed to *combat fatigue*, then later to *post-traumatic stress disorder* in an attempt to lose its connection to war.

The institute suggests that we ask these questions when we spot name calling being used:

    a. What does the name mean?

    b. Is there a real connection between the name and the person or idea being labeled?

    c. Leaving the name out of it, what are the merits of the idea or person?

2. *Glittering generalities*: using words such as *justice, founding fathers, freedom, love of country, loyalty, the American way, and patriot* that are vague but have positive connotations that appeal to our emotions; propagandists often use them because they know we will be touched by such words. *Defending democracy* has a nice ring to it, but what is being planned or done in the name of *defending democracy* may be wrong when the concept is examined beyond the glittering generality. It is name calling in reverse.

   When you spot this technique being used:

       a. Consider the merits of the idea itself when separated from specific words.

       b. Ask whether you are being manipulated by the use of your feelings toward the words being used.

3. *Transfer*: linking something we like or respect to some person, cause, or product; symbols are frequently used. If we respect the flag or the Christian cross, our respect for the symbol is transferred to whatever use it is being associated with. While at war in Iraq, people transfer their support by wearing pins of the American flag or by placing yellow ribbons on their cars saying "Support Our Troops." Cartoons of Uncle Sam smiling or frowning are used to reflect the government's approval or disapproval on an issue. Those referred to as the enemy, on the other hand, burn the American flag in protest using the symbol to transfer their feelings. Transfer is often used in politics to transfer the blame or bad feelings from one politician to another or from one political party to another. Transfer, then, can be used for or against causes and ideas.

   When you spot this method being used:

       a. Consider whether the symbol being used really applies to the person, product, or cause.

       b. Ask whether you are being manipulated by the use of the symbol.

4. *Testimonial*: using well-known people to testify that a certain person, idea, or product is "the best." Famous or respected people are used to sell us ideas or products, because we transfer our positive feelings for them to the product or idea being sold. Look at advertisements in magazines or on television and you will see how many actors and athletes give testimonials for products, hoping we will transfer that respect to the product. This technique is closely connected to the transfer technique.

   When you spot this method being used:

       a. Ask yourself whether the person giving the testimonial has any knowledge about the subject or product.

       b. Ask yourself whether you are being convinced by the person or by the facts of the testimonial.

       c. Ask how factual the content of the testimonial is.

5. *Plain folks*: an attempt to convince the public that the propagandist's views reflect those of the common person and that he or she is working in their best interests. A politician speaking to a blue-collar audience may roll up his sleeves, undo his tie, and attempt to use the specific idioms of the crowd. He may even use language incorrectly on purpose to give the impression that he is "just one of the folks." This technique usually also employs the use of glittering generalities to give the impression that the politician's views are the same as those of the crowd being addressed. Labor leaders, businesspeople, ministers, educators, and advertisers have used this technique to win our confidence by appearing to be just plain folks like ourselves.

   When you spot this method being used:

   a. Ask what the propagandist's ideas are worth when separated from his or her personality.

   b. Ask what the plain folks approach is covering up.

   c. Check for the facts, not the hype.

6. *Card stacking*: including only the information that is for or positive about a certain person or position and omitting evidence to the contrary. This technique stacks the evidence against the truth by omitting, changing, or evading facts; telling half-truths; or stating things out of context. This technique is very effective in convincing the public because most people don't bother to examine the other side of the issue being exploited, especially if the information is being offered by someone whom we admire or who we feel is serving our best interests. This is often used in advertising, in which a product might claim it "helps stop bad breath," leading us to think it *does* stop bad breath.

   When you see this method at work:

   a. Evaluate what is being presented as fact.

   b. Get more information about the subject before making up your mind.

7. *The bandwagon*: an appeal to join in, come aboard, follow the crowd. This technique appeals to our desire to be on the winning side, to be like or better than everyone else, and to be "one of the gang." It is an attempt to make us believe that we will be in the minority if we don't join or believe what's being offered. The propagandist directs the appeal to groups held together by common ties, such as religion, sex, race, and nationality, and uses the fears, hatreds, prejudices, ideals, and convictions of a group to join in or lose what you hold dear. In 2006, public figures found it difficult to criticize the Bush administration's foreign policies because the bandwagon mentality asserts that everyone must unite in the fight against terrorism, weapons of mass destruction, and those opposed to freedom and democracy. On the other hand, the United States has more weapons of mass destruction, sells more arms to other countries than any other nation in the world, and seems willing to destroy countries in order to bring them democracy.

   When you see this method at work:

   a. Ask yourself what the propagandist's program is.

   b. Ask yourself if there is evidence for or against the program.

   c. Ask whether the program really serves or undermines your own interests.

   Propaganda, for good or bad, tries to manipulate us. As Paul R. Lees-Haley reminds us:

   > Manipulators strive to divorce us from the facts. Rather than encouraging us to examine the evidence and reasoning of people who appear to disagree

with us, they block communications and openly or indirectly try to persuade us that people who disagree with their views are dishonest, not trustworthy, incompetent, biased, racist, only concerned with money, insulting our intelligence, corrupt, betrayers of the American dream, and so on. The subtext is: "Do not consider alternative points of view. Do what we tell you, without realizing that we are controlling you." Like cult leaders, manipulators encourage us to close ranks and form an in-group suspicious of those who question the party line. (From Paul R. Lees-Haley, "Propaganda Techniques Related to Environmental Scares," Quackwatch, http://www.quackwatch.org/01QuackeryRelatedTopics/propa.html.)

Most of these devices work because they appeal to our emotions, our fears, our ignorance, or our desire to do the "right thing." But by sorting facts from opinions, and by recognizing these propaganda techniques when used, we won't become victims, but rather thoughtful readers and thinkers who see these techniques for what they are.

PRACTICE C-1: Detecting Propaganda Techniques

Directions: Read each of the following items and in the space provided write in the propaganda technique or techniques being used and why you think so.

1. "My opponent, Senator Glick, has a record of being soft on crime at a time when we need to be strong." _____

    _____

    _____

2. "Senator Cluck cares what happens to the farmers; he cares for the future of the American tradition of prosperity. He'll put this country back on track!" _____

    _____

    _____

3. "Jerry Seinfeld. Cardmember since 1986" (American Express ad). _____

    _____

    _____

4. "M Lotion helps skin keep its moisture … discourages tired-looking lines under eyes." _____

    _____

5. "Over 8,000,000 sold! Why would anyone want to buy anything else?" _____

    _____

    _____

6. "Buy Banhead. It contains twice as much pain reliever." _____

    _____

    _____

7. "Mayor Naste has shown time and again he's for the little guy. You don't see him driving a big limo or wearing fancy suits. No, sir. You'll find him out talking to us folks to see how he can serve us better." _____

_____

_____

8. "Buy the Sportsman's Shaving System, appointed the exclusive skin care system for the Winter Olympics." _____

_____

_____

9. "Yes, I lied. But I did it for my country. As God is my witness, I felt in my heart—and still do—that what I did was right, and the people of this country who want to preserve its freedom will thank me some day." _____ _ _____

_____

_____

10. "Drive to class reunions in the new Hummer 3 and even Mr. Most-Likely-to- Succeed will be envious." _____ _____

_____

_____

PRACTICE C-2

Directions: Survey the following passage from a textbook titled *Preface to Critical Reading* by reading the opening paragraph, some of the first sentences in selected paragraphs, and the questions that follow the reading. Then use the information from the survey to read the selection, marking key points.

DETECTING PROPAGANDA

RICHARD D. ALTICK and ANDREA A. LUNSFORD

1   All of us, whether we admit it or not, are prejudiced. We dislike certain people, certain activities, certain ideas—in many cases, not because we have reasoned things out and found a logical basis for our dislike, but rather because those people or activities or ideas affect our less generous instincts. Of course we also have positive prejudices, by which we approve of people or things—perhaps because they give us pleasure or perhaps because we have always been taught that they are "good" and never stopped to reason why. In either case, these biases, irrational and unfair though they may be, are aroused by words, principally by name-calling and the use of the glittering generality. Both of these techniques depend on the process of association, by which an idea (the specific person, group, proposal, or situation being discussed) takes on emotional coloration from the language employed.

2   *Name-calling* is the device of arousing an unfavorable response by such an associa-tion. A speaker or writer who wishes to sway an audience against a person, group, or principle will often use this device.

> The bleeding-heart liberals are responsible for the current economic crisis.
> The labor union radicals keep honest people from honest work.
> Environmental extremists can bankrupt hard-pressed companies with their fanatical demands for unnecessary and expensive pollution controls such as chimney-scrubbers.

3   Name-calling is found in many arguments in which emotion plays a major role. It rarely is part of the logic of an argument but instead is directed at personalities. Note how the speakers here depend on verbal rock throwing in their attempt to win the day:

> He's no coach, but a foul-mouthed, cigar-chomping bully who bribes high-school stars to play for him.
> The Bible-thumping bigots who want to censor our books and our television shows represent the worst of the anti-intellectual lunatic fringe.
> Mayor Leech has sold the city out to vested interests and syndicates of rack-eteers. City Hall stinks of graft and payola.

4   The negative emotional associations of the "loaded" words in these sentences have the planned effect of spilling over, onto, and hiding, the real points at issue, which demand—but fail to receive—fair, analytical, objective judgment. Generating a thick emotional haze is, therefore, an affective way for glib writers and speakers to convince many of the unthinking or the credulous among their audience.

5   The *glittering generality* involves the equally illogical use of connotative words. In contrast to name-calling, the glittering generality draws on traditionally positive asso-ciations. Here, as in name-calling, the trouble is that the words used have been applied too freely and thus are easily misapplied. Many writers and speakers take advantage of the glitter of these words to blind readers to real issues at hand. *Patriot, freedom, democ-racy, national honor, Constitution, God-given rights, peace, liberty, property rights, international cooperation, brotherhood, equal opportunity, prosperity, decent standard of living*: words or phrases like these sound pleasant to the listener's ear, but they can also divert attention from the ideas the speaker is discussing, ideas which are usually too complex to be fairly labeled by a single word.

> The progressive, forward-looking liberal party will make certain that we enjoy a stable and healthy economy.
> The practical idealists of the labor movement are united in supporting the right of every person to earn an honest living.
> Dedicated environmentalists perform an indispensable patriotic service for us all by keeping air-polluting industries' feet to the fire.
> He's a coach who is a shining light to our youth. He believes that football helps to build the character, stamina, and discipline needed for the leaders of tomorrow.
> The decent, God-fearing people who want to protect us from the violence and depravity depicted in books and on television represent the best of a moral society.
> Mayor Leech has stood for progress, leadership, and vision at a time when most cities have fallen into the hands of the corrupt political hacks.

6   The effectiveness of name-calling and the glittering generality depends on stock responses. Just as the scientist Pavlov, in a classic experiment, conditioned dogs to

increase their production of saliva every time he rang a bell, so the calculating persuader expects readers to react automatically to language that appeals to their prejudices.

7   The abuse of authority is one of the *transfer devices* which exploit readers' willingness to link one idea or person with another, even though the two may not be logically connected. The familiar *testimonials* of present-day advertising provide an instance of this device. In some cases, the "authority" who testifies has some connection with the product advertised. The problem to settle here is, when we try to decide which brand of sunburn cream is best, how much weight may we reasonably attach to the enthusiastic statements of certain nurses? When we are thinking of buying a tennis racket, should we accept the say-so of a champion who, after all, is well paid for telling us that a certain make is the best? In other cases, the testifying authorities may have no formal, professional connection with the products they recommend. An actor, who may very well be a master of his particular art, praises a whiskey, a coffee, or an airline. He likes it, he says. But, we may ask, does the fact that he is a successful actor make him better qualified than any person who is not an actor to judge a whiskey, a coffee, or an airline? Competence in one field does not necessarily "transfer" to competence in another.

8   Furthermore, advertisers often borrow the prestige of science and medicine to enhance the reputation of their products. Many people have come to feel for the laboratory scientist and the physician an awe once reserved for bishops or statesmen. The alleged approval of such people thus carries great weight in selling something or inducing someone to believe something. Phrases such as "leading medical authorities say ..." or "independent laboratory tests show ..." are designed simply to transfer the prestige of science to a toothpaste or deodorant. Seldom are the precise "medical authorities" or "independent laboratories" named. But the mere phrases carry weight with uncritical listeners or readers. Similarly, the title "Dr." or "Professor" implies that the person quoted speaks with all the authority of which learned people are capable— when, as a matter of fact, doctoral degrees can be bought from mail-order colleges. Therefore, whenever a writer or speaker appeals to the prestige that surrounds the learned, the reader should demand credentials. Just *what* "medical authorities" say this? Can they be trusted? What independent laboratories made the tests—and what did the tests actually reveal? Who are the people who speak as expert educators, psychologists, or economists? Regardless of the fact that they are "doctors," do they know what they are talking about?

9   Another closely related form of transfer is the borrowing of prestige from a highly respected institution (country, religion, education) or individual (world leader, philosopher, scientist) for the sake of enhancing something else. Political speakers sometimes work into their speeches quotations from the Bible or from secular "sacred writings" (such as a national constitution). Such quotations usually arouse favorable emotions in listeners, emotions which are then transferred to the speaker's policy or subject. When analyzing an appeal that uses quotations from men and women who have achieved renown in one field or another, the chief question is whether the quotation is appropriate in context. Does it have real relevance to the point at issue? It is all very well to quote George Washington or Abraham Lincoln in support of one's political stand. But circumstances have changed immensely since those statements were first uttered, and their applicability to a new situation may be dubious indeed. The implication is, "This person, who we agree was great and wise, said certain things which 'prove' the justice of my own stand. Therefore, you should believe I am right." But to have a valid argument, the writer must prove that the word of the authorities is really applicable to the present issue. If that is true, then the speaker is borrowing not so much their prestige as their wisdom—which is perfectly justifiable.

10　　Another version of the transfer device is one which gains prestige not through quotations or testimonials of authorities but from linking one idea to another. Here is an advertisement that illustrates how this device works.

THE TELEPHONE POLE THAT BECAME A MEMORIAL

The cottage on Lincoln Street in Portland, Oregon, is shaded by graceful trees and covered with ivy.

Many years ago, A. H. Feldman and his wife remodeled the house to fit their dreams ... and set out slips of ivy around it. And when their son, Danny, came along, he, too, liked to watch things grow. One day, when he was only nine, he took a handful of ivy slips and planted them at the base of the telephone pole in front of the house.

Time passed ... and the ivy grew, climbing to the top of the pole. Like the ivy, Danny grew too. He finished high school, went to college. The war came along before he finished—and Danny went overseas. And there he gave his life for his country.

Not very long ago the overhead telephone lines were being removed from the poles on Lincoln Street. The ivy-covered telephone pole in front of the Feldman home was about to be taken down. Its work was done.

But, when the telephone crew arrived, Mrs. Feldman came out to meet them. "Couldn't it be left standing?" she asked. And then she told them about her son.

So the pole, although no longer needed, wasn't touched at all. At the request of the telephone company, the Portland City Council passed a special ordinance permitting the company to leave it standing. And there it is today, mantled in ivy, a living memorial to Sergeant Danny Feldman.

11　　What did the telephone company wish to accomplish by this ad? Readers are not urged to install a telephone, equip their homes with extra telephones, or use any of the various new services the company has developed. Nor are they told how inexpensive and efficient the telephone company thinks those services are. Instead, this is what is known as an "institutional" advertisement. Its purpose is to inspire public esteem, even affection, for the company.

12　　How do such advertisements inspire esteem and respect? Simply by telling an anecdote, without a single word to point up the moral. In this ad, every detail is carefully chosen for its emotional appeal: the cottage ("home, sweet home" theme), the ivy (symbol of endurance through the years; often combined, as here, with the idea of the family home), the little boy (evoking all the feelings associated with childhood), the young man dying in the war (evoking patriotic sentiment). Thus at least four symbols are combined—all of them with great power to touch the emotions. Then the climax: Will the company cut down the ivy-covered pole? To many people, *company* has a connotation of hardheartedness, impersonality, coldness, which is the very impression this particular company, one of the biggest in the world, wants to erase. So the company modestly reports that it went to the trouble of getting special permission to leave this one pole standing, "mantled in ivy, a living memorial."

13　　The writer of this advertisement has, in effect, urged readers to transfer to the telephone company the sympathies aroused by the story. The ivy-covered pole aptly symbolizes what the writer wanted to do—"mantle" the pole (symbolizing the company) with the ivy that is associated with home, childhood, and heroic death. If it is possible to make one feel sentimental about a giant corporation, an advertisement like this one—arousing certain feelings by means of one set of objects and then transferring those feelings to another object—will do it. But the story, although true enough, is after all only one incident, and a sound generalization about the character of a vast company cannot be formed from a single anecdote. The company may well be as "human" as the advertisement implies, but readers are led to that belief through an appeal to their sympathies, not their reason.

14   A third kind of fallacy involves *mudslinging*, attacking a person rather than a principle. Mudslingers make personal attacks on an opponent (formally known as *ad hominem* arguments, those "against the man"), not merely by calling names, but often by presenting what they offer as damaging evidence against the opponent's motives, character, and private life. Thus the audience's attention is diverted from the argument itself to a subject which is more likely to stir up prejudices. If, for example, in denouncing an opponent's position on reducing the national debt, a candidate refers to X's connection with certain well-known gamblers, then the candidate ceases to argue the case on its merits and casts doubt on the opponent's personal character. The object is not to hurt X's feelings but to arouse bias against that person in the hearer's mind. Critical readers or listeners must train themselves to detect and reject these irrelevant aspersions. It may be, indeed, that X has shady connections with underworld gamblers. But that may have nothing to do with the abstract right or wrong of his stand on the national debt. Issues should be discussed apart from character and motives. Both character and motives are important, of course, since they bear on any candidate's fitness for public office and on whether we can give him or her our support. But they call for a separate discussion.

15   A somewhat more subtle kind of personal attack is the *innuendo*, which differs from direct accusation roughly as a hint differs from a plain statement. Innuendo is chiefly useful where no facts exist to give even a semblance of support to a direct charge. The writer or speaker therefore slyly plants seeds of doubt or suspicion in the reader's or listener's mind, as the villainous Iago does in the mind of Shakespeare's *Othello*. Innuendo is a trick that is safe, effective—and unfair. "They were in the office with the door locked for four hours after closing time." The statement, in itself, may be entirely true. But what counts is the implication it is meant to convey. The unfairness increases when the doubts that the innuendo raises concern matters that have nothing to do with the issue anyway. An example of the irrelevant innuendo is found in the writings of the historian Charles A. Beard. In assailing the ideas of another historian, Admiral Alfred T. Mahan, Beard called him "the son of a professor and swivel-chair tactician at West Point," who "served respectably, but without distinction, for a time in the navy" and "found an easy berth at the Naval War College." Actually, the occupation of Mahan's father has nothing to do with the validity of the son's arguments. But observe the sneer—which is meant to be transferred from father to son—in "professor" and "swivel-chair tactician." Beard's reference to Mahan's naval record is a good elementary instance of damning with faint praise. And whether or not Mahan's was "an easy berth" at the Naval War College (a matter of opinion), it too has no place in a discussion of the man's ideas or intellectual capacities.

16   Newspapers often use this device to imply more than they can state without risking a libel suit. In reporting the latest bit of gossip about celebrated members of the "jet set" or the "beautiful people" (what do the terms suggest about the habits and tastes of the people referred to?), a paper may mention the fact that "gorgeous movie actress A is a frequent companion of thrice-divorced playboy B" or that they "are seen constantly together at the Vegas night spots" or that they are "flitting from the Riviera to Sun Valley together." The inference suggested, however unfounded it may be, is that their relationship is not just that of good friends who happen to be in the same place at the same time. Similarly, newspapers which value sensationalism more than responsibility may describe an accused "child slayer" or "woman molester" as "dirty

and bearded" (implication: he is a suspicious-looking bum). His face may, in addition, be "scarred" (implication: he is physically violent). Such literal details may be true enough. But how much have they to do with the guilt or innocence of the person in this particular case? The effect on the reader is what courts of law term "prejudicial" and therefore inadmissible. Unfortunately the law does not extend to slanted writing, however powerfully it may sway public opinion.

17   Another instance of the way in which emotionally loaded language can be combined with unproved evidence to stir up prejudice may be taken from the field of art. A modern critic condemned certain paintings as "a conventional rehash of cubist patterns born among the wastrels of Paris forty years ago." In so doing, the critic attacked the art through the artist. The artistic merit of paintings has nothing to do with the private lives of the people who paint them. The painters referred to may well have been wastrels. But that fact—if it is a fact—has no bearing on the point at issue. The assumed connection between the personal virtues or shortcomings of artists and the artistic value of their productions has resulted in a great deal of confused thinking about literature, music, and the other arts.

18   Another diversionary tactic which introduces an irrelevant issue into a debate is the *red herring*. It too may involve shifting attention from principles to personalities, but without necessarily slinging mud or calling names. Since neither relaxing at a disco nor having a taste for serious books is yet sinful or criminal, a political party slings no mud when it portrays the other party's candidate as a playboy or an intellectual. Still, such matters are largely irrelevant to the main argument, which is whether one or the other candidate will better serve the interests of the people. The red-herring device need not involve personalities at all; it may take the form simply of substituting one issue for another. If a large corporation is under fire for alleged monopolistic practices, its public relations people may start an elaborate advertising campaign to show how well the company's workers are treated. Thus, if the campaign succeeds, the bad publicity suffered because of the assertions that the company has been trying to corner the market may be counteracted by the public's approval of its allegedly fine labor policy.

19   Unfortunately, most of us are eager to view questions in their simplest terms and to make our decisions on the basis of only a few of the many elements the problem may involve. The problem of minority groups in North America, for instance, is not simply one of abstract justice, as many would like to think. Rather, it involves complex and by no means easily resolvable issues of economics, sociology, politics, and psychology. Nor can one say with easy assurance, "The federal government should guarantee every farmer a decent income, even if the money comes from the pocketbooks of the citizens who are the farmer's own customers" or "It is the obligation of every educational institution to purge its faculty of all who hold radical sympathies." Perhaps each of these propositions is sound; perhaps neither is. But before either is adopted as a conviction, intelligent readers must canvass their full implications. … After the implications have been explored, more evidence may be found *against* the proposition than in support of it.

20   Countless reductive generalizations concerning parties, races, religions, and nations, to say nothing of individuals, are the result of the deep-seated human desire to reduce complicated ideas to their simplest terms. We saw the process working when we touched on stereotypes … and in our discussion of rhetorical induction. … Unfortunately, condemning with a few quick, perhaps indefensible assumptions is easier than recognizing the actual diversity in any social group. But every man and woman has an urgent obligation to analyze the basis of each judgment he or she makes: "Am I examining every aspect of the issue that needs to be examined? Do I understand the problem sufficiently to be able to make a fair decision? Or am I taking the easiest and simplest way out?"

Now answer the following questions. You may look back if necessary.

1. What two propaganda devices are used to stir up our prejudices? _____ ____

    _____

    _____

2. What part do our emotions play in the effectiveness of some propaganda tech-
    niques? __ _____ __ _____

    _____

    _____

    _____

3. What do the authors mean when they say that "advertisers often borrow the pres-
    tige of science and medicine to enhance the reputation of their products"?

    _____

    _____

    _____

4. What is meant by the term *transfer device*? Give some examples. _____ _____

    _____

    _____

    _____

5. Name the three devices or methods frequently used to attack a person rather than
    a principle. _____ __ _____ _____

    _____

    _____

6. Define the following terms: _____

    a. transfer devices _____

    _____

    b. testimonials _____ _____

    _____

    c. mudslinging _____ _____ _____

    _____

    d. innuendo _____ _____ _____ _____

    _____

    e. red herring _____ _____

    _____

    f. oversimplification _____ _____ _____

    _____

7. Why is it important to recognize and understand how propaganda is used? _____

    _____

    _____

    _____

Optional Exercise

To learn more about propaganda and its uses, type in *propaganda techniques* in a search engine and explore some of the sites listed.

Application I: Recognizing Propaganda at Work

Find an example of one of the seven propaganda techniques used in a current magazine or newspaper advertisement or essay. Write a brief explanation of how the technique is being used, attach it to the advertisement or essay, and share it in class.

D.   Putting It All Together

The next two practices give you the opportunity to use what you have learned about critical comprehension to distinguish fact from opinion, read opinions of others, and detect propaganda. Review your scores on the Student Record Sheet in the Appendix and try to match or do better than your scores for the previous reading selections. If you make mistakes, analyze errors and figure out how to improve the next time. The first practice follows an introduction to the author Ishmael Reed; the second practice is timed.

Now read about the following author, Ishmael Reed, to understand more about how an author's life affects his opinions. His views on reading and literacy may inspire you to develop different views. Another way to find current information, quotations, or pictures of this author is to use the World Wide Web. Type in the author's name in a search engine such as Google or AltaVista.

Introducing Ishmael Reed

Ishmael Reed has been called one of the most innovative and outspoken voices in contemporary literature. His work embodies seven novels, four books of poetry, three plays, several collections of essays, and book reviews. In addition

to these works, Reed is a songwriter, television producer, and magazine editor. Reed has taught at Harvard, Yale, Dartmouth, and the University of California–Berkeley.

Reed is a strong advocate of literacy and its power. In an essay that first appeared in the *San Francisco Examiner* and was later reprinted in his collection *Writin' Is Fightin'*, Reed spoke out against illiteracy:

If you're illiterate, people can do anything they want to you. Take your house through equity scams, cheat you, lie to you, bunko you, take your money, even take your life. …

As you go through life X-ing documents, unable to defend yourself against forces hostile to you, people can deprive you of your voting rights through ger-rymandering schemes, build a freeway next to your apartment building or open a retail crack operation on your block, with people coming and going as though you lived next door to Burger King—because you're not articulate enough to fight back, because you don't have sense enough to know what is happening to you, and so you're shoveled under at each turn in your life; you might as well be dead.

One of the joys of reading is the ability to plug into the shared wisdom of mankind. One of my favorite passages from the Bible is "Come, and let us reason together"—Isaiah 1:18. Being illiterate means that you often resort to violence, during the most trivial dispute…because you don't have the verbal skills to talk things out.…

I'm also convinced that illiteracy is a factor contributing to suicide becoming one of the leading causes of death among white middle-class youngsters, who allow their souls to atrophy from the steady diet of spiritual Wonder Bread: bad music and bad film, and the outrageous cheapness of superficial culture. When was the last time you saw a movie or TV program that was as good as the best book you've read, and I don't mean what imitation elitists call the classics. I'd settle for Truman Capote, John A. Williams, Cecil Brown, Lawson Inada, Paule Marshall, Xam Wilson Cartier, Victor Cruz, Howard Numerov, William Kennedy, Paula Gunn Allen, Margaret Atwood, Diane Johnson, Edward Field, Frank Chin, Rudolfo Anaya, Wesley Brown, Lucille Clifton, Al Young, Amiri Baraka, Simon Ortiz, Bob Callahan, David Metzer, Anna Castillo, Joyce Carol Oates and Harryette Mullen, a group of writers as good as any you'd find anywhere.…(From Ishmael Reed, "Killer Illiteracy," *Writin' Is Fightin'*, Atheneum, 1988, pp. 185–186.)

Reed's essay "America: The Multinational Society" offers his reasons for dis-agreeing with those who believe the United States "is part of Western civilization because our 'system of government' is derived from Europe."

PRACTICE D-1: Timed Reading

Directions: Before reading the following article, take a minute to survey it and the questions. Then time yourself as you begin to read the article. As you read, discover why the author believes America is a multinational society.

Begin timing : _____

AMERICA: THE MULTINATIONAL SOCIETY

ISHMAEL REED

1   At the annual Lower East Side Jewish Festival yesterday, a Chinese woman ate a pizza slice in front of Ty Thuan Duc's Vietnamese grocery store. Beside her a Spanish-speaking family patronized a cart with two signs: "Italian Ices" and "Kosher by Rabbi Alper." And after the pastrami ran out, everybody ate knishes.
—*New York Times*, 23 June 1983

2   On the day before Memorial Day, 1983, a poet called me to describe a city he had just visited. He said that one section included mosques, built by the Islamic people who dwelled there. Attending his reading, he said, were large numbers of Hispanic people, forty thousand of whom lived in the same city. He was not talking about a fabled city located in some mysterious region of the world. The city he'd visited was Detroit.

3   A few months before, as I was leaving Houston, Texas, I heard it announced on the radio that Texas's largest minority was Mexican American, and though a foundation recently issued a report critical of bilingual education, the taped voice used to guide the passengers on the air trams connecting terminals in Dallas Airport is in both Spanish and English. If the trend continues, a day will come when it will be difficult to travel through some sections of the country without hearing commands in both English and Spanish; after all, for some western states, Spanish was the first written language and the Spanish style lives on in the western way of life.

4   Shortly after my Texas trip, I sat in an auditorium located on the campus of the University of Wisconsin at Milwaukee as a Yale professor—whose original work on the influence of African cultures upon those of the Americas has led to his ostracism from some monocultural intellectual circles—walked up and down the aisle, like an old-time southern evangelist, dancing and drumming the top of the lectern, illustrating his points before some serious Afro-American intellectuals and artists who cheered and applauded his performance and his mastery of information. The professor was "white." After his lecture, he joined a group of Milwaukeeans in a conversation. All of the participants spoke Yoruban, though only the professor had ever traveled to Africa.

5   One of the artists told me that his paintings, which included African and Afro-American mythological symbols and imagery, were hanging in the local McDonald's restaurant. The next day I went to McDonald's and snapped pictures of smiling youngsters eating hamburgers below paintings that could grace the walls of any of the country's leading museums. The manager of the local McDonald's said, "I don't know what you boys are doing, but I like it," as he commissioned the local painters to exhibit in his restaurant.

6   Such blurring of cultural styles occurs in everyday life in the United States to a greater extent than anyone can imagine and is probably more prevalent than the sensational conflict between people of different backgrounds that is played up and often encouraged by the media. The result is what the Yale professor, Robert Thompson, referred to as a cultural bouillabaisse, yet members of the nation's present educational and cultural Elect still cling to the notion that the United States belongs to some vaguely defined entity they refer to as "Western civilization," by which they mean, presumably, a civilization created by the people of Europe, as if Europe can be viewed in monolithic terms. Is Beethoven's Ninth Symphony, which includes Turkish marches, a part of Western civilization, or the late nineteenth- and twentieth-century French paintings, whose creators were influenced by Japanese art? And what of the cubists, through whom the influence of African art changed modern painting, or the surrealists, who were so impressed with the art of the Pacific Northwest Indians that, in their map of North America, Alaska dwarfs the lower forty-eight in size?

7   Are the Russians, who are often criticized for their adoption of "Western" ways by Tsarist dissidents in exile, members of Western civilization? And what of the millions of Europeans who have black African and Asian ancestry, black Africans having occupied several countries for hundreds of years? Are these "Europeans" members of Western civilization, or the Hungarians, who originated across the Urals in a place called Greater Hungary, or the Irish, who came from the Iberian Peninsula?

8   Even the notion that North America is part of Western civilization because our "system of government" is derived from Europe is being challenged by Native American historians who say that the founding fathers, Benjamin Franklin especially, were actually influenced by the system of government that had been adopted by the Iroquois hundreds of years prior to the arrival of large numbers of Europeans.

9   Western civilization, then, becomes another confusing category like Third World, or Judeo-Christian culture, as man attempts to impose his small-screen view of political and cultural reality upon a complex world. Our most publicized novelist recently said that Western civilization was the greatest achievement of mankind, an attitude that flourishes on the street level as scribbles in public restrooms: "White Power," "Niggers and Spics Suck," or "Hitler was a prophet," the latter being the most telling for wasn't Adolph Hitler the archetypal monoculturalist who, in his pigheaded arrogance, believed that one way and one blood was so pure that it had to be protected from alien strains at all costs? Where did such an attitude, which has caused so much misery and depression in our national life, which has tainted even our noblest achievements, begin? An attitude that caused the incarceration of Japanese-American citizens during World War II, the persecution of Chicanos and Chinese Americans, the near-extermination of the Indians, and the murder and lynchings of thousands of Afro-Americans.

10   Virtuous, hardworking, pious, even though they occasionally would wander off after some fancy clothes, or rendezvous in the woods with the town prostitute, the Puritans are idealized in our schoolbooks as "a hardy band" of no-nonsense patriarchs whose discipline razed the forest and brought order to the New World (a term that annoys Native American historians). Industrious, responsible, it was their "Yankee ingenuity" and practicality that created the work ethic. They were simple folk who produced a number of good poets, and they set the tone for the American writing style, of lean and spare lines, long before Hemingway. They worshiped in churches whose colors blended in with the New England snow, churches with simple structures and ornate lecterns.

11   The Puritans were a daring lot, but they had a mean streak. They hated the theater and banned Christmas. They punished people in a cruel and inhuman manner. They killed children who disobeyed their parents. When they came in contact with those whom they considered heathens or aliens, they behaved in such a bizarre and irrational manner that this chapter in the American history comes down to us as a late-movie horror film. They exterminated the Indians, who taught them how to survive in a world unknown to them, and their encounter with the calypso culture of Barbados resulted in what the tourist guide in Salem's Witches' House refers to as the Witchcraft Hysteria.

12   The Puritan legacy of hard work and meticulous accounting led to the establishment of a great industrial society; it is no wonder that the American industrial revolution began in Lowell, Massachusetts, but there was the other side, the strange and paranoid attitudes toward those different from the Elect.

13   The cultural attitudes of that early Elect continue to be voiced in everyday life in the United States: the president of a distinguished university, writing a letter to the *Times*, belittling the study of African civilizations; the television network that promoted its show on the Vatican art with the boast that this art represented "the finest achievements of the human spirit." A modern up-tempo state of complex rhythms that depends upon contacts with an international community can no longer behave as if it dwelled in a "Zion Wilderness" surrounded by beasts and pagans.

14   When I heard a schoolteacher warn the other night about the invasion of the American educational system by foreign curriculums, I wanted to yell at the television

set, "Lady, they're already here." It has already begun because the world is here. The world has been arriving at these shores for at least ten thousand years from Europe, Africa, and Asia. In the late nineteenth and early twentieth centuries, large numbers of Europeans arrived, adding their cultures to those of the European, African, and Asian settlers who were already here, and recently millions have been entering the country from South America and the Caribbean, making Yale Professor Bob Thompson's bouillabaisse richer and thicker.

15   One of our most visionary politicians said that he envisioned a time when the United States could become the brain of the world, by which he meant the repository of all of the latest advanced information systems. I thought of that remark when an enterprising poet friend of mine called to say that he had just sold a poem to a computer magazine and that the editors were delighted to get it because they didn't carry fiction or poetry. Is that the kind of world we desire? A humdrum, homogeneous world of all brains but no heart, no fiction, no poetry; a world of robots with human attendants bereft of imagination, of culture? Or does North America deserve a more exciting destiny? To become a place where the cultures of the world crisscross. This is possible because the United States is unique in the world: The world is here.

Finish Timing: Record time here_____ and use the Timed Reading

Conversion Chart in the Appendix to figure your rate:_____wpm.

Comprehension Check

Directions: Answer the following questions without looking back.

1. List one fact about Detroit. _____

    _____

    _____

2. Is the following statement fact or opinion? "If the trend continues, a day will come when it will be difficult to travel through some sections of the country without hearing commands in both English and Spanish." _____

    _____

    _____

3. What is Reed's main argument about "Western civilization"? _____

    _____

    _____

4. List one of the facts he gives to support his argument. _____

    _____

    _____

5. List another fact he gives to support his argument._____

    _____

    _____

6. According to Reed, what are some of the problems in the United States because of the attitude that Western civilization is the greatest achievement of mankind? ____

    _____

    _____

7. What is Reed's overall opinion of the Puritans? _____ _ _

    _____

    _____

8. List one or two of the facts he uses to support this opinion. _____, _____

    _____

    _____

9. Are Reed's arguments in this article based more on fact or opinion? Explain. ____

    _____

    _____

10. Did the author convince you of his argument? Explain. _____ _____

    _____

    _____

Vocabulary Check

Directions: Define the following underlined words from the selection.

1. has led to his <u>ostracism</u> _____ _____

    _____

2. from some <u>monocultural</u> intellectual circles _____ _____

    _____

3. Afro-American <u>mythological</u> symbols ____ _____

    _____

4. referred to as a cultural <u>bouillabaisse</u> _____ - _____

    _____

5. as if Europe can be viewed in <u>monolithic</u> terms __ ____ _____

    _____

6. and what of the <u>cubists</u> _____

    ___ _____ - _____

7. Hitler, the <u>archetypal</u> monoculturist __ ____ _____

    _____

8. the <u>incarceration</u> of Japanese-American citizens ____ ___ _____

    _____

9. simple structures and <u>ornate</u> lecterns ____ _____

    _____

10. those whom they considered <u>heathens</u> _____ _____

_____

Record your rate and the results of the comprehension and vocabulary checks on the Student Record Chart in the Appendix. Each correct answer is worth 10 points, for a total of 100 points possible for comprehension and 100 points for vocabulary. An average score is around 250 wpm with 70 percent comprehension. Discuss any problems, concerns, or questions you have with your instructor.

Practice D-2: Timed Reading

Directions: Before reading the following article, take a minute to survey it and the questions. Then time yourself as you begin to read the article. As you read, notice the authors' opinion on the draft.

Begin timing : _____

BRING BACK THE DRAFT

WILLIAM L. HAUSER and JEROME SLATER

1   In the ongoing struggle between radical Islamism and Western democracy, military intervention by the United States may again be judged necessary as a last resort against particularly dangerous states or organizations. Although presidential candidate Barack Obama made drawing down U.S. forces in Iraq the centerpiece of his national security agenda, so as to focus on the "real fight" in Afghanistan, President Obama will find that even with a complete withdrawal from Iraq, the United States' current all-volunteer forces will be inadequate for accomplishing its worldwide national security goals. Regarding Afghanistan in particular, even the planned reinforcement of 20,000 to 30,000 troops will not begin to match the 1 to 10 troop-to-population ratio generally acknowledged to be necessary for success in counterinsurgency.

2   Moreover, as a result of the repetitive stresses of Afghanistan and Iraq, the human-resources quality of the U.S. military appears to be declining: recruitment and retention rates (by pre-Iraq standards) are slipping, forcing the armed services to lower their physical, educational, and psychological standards; to soften the rigors of initial training; and even to expand the moral waivers granted to some volunteers with criminal records. Generous inducements have also been needed to retain junior officers beyond the length-of-service payback requirements of their academy or ROTC educations. The economic downturn might help temporarily, but the problem cannot be resolved by continuing the present system. There will have to be a reinstitution, albeit in a significantly modified version, of universal military service—a "draft."

3   Our proposal is to combine a revived military draft with a broader public-service program as already practiced in some European states—a "domestic Peace Corps." Indeed, a crucial component of our proposal is that draftees be allowed to

William I. Hauser and Jerome Slater, "Bring Back the Draft," Foreign Policy.com, February 2009, http://www.foreignpolicy.com/story/cms.php?story_id=4659. Permission to reprint.

choose between military and nonmilitary service. A program structured along those lines would simultaneously increase the political appeal of conscription, defuse the opposition of those who disapprove of the use of military force, and serve such valuable national purposes as public health, public works, and the alleviation of shortages of teachers and social workers in disadvantaged regions of the country.

4   To be sure, an enlarged military can give rise to its own dangers, particularly an expansion of what some already consider excessive presidential power. It will be essential, therefore, that the creation of larger forces by means of conscription be accompanied by legal safeguards to prevent presidential unilateralism. First, Congress should use its constitutionally mandated role in decisions to go to war. Second, Congress should employ its appropriations powers—"the power of the purse"—to prohibit, limit, or end U.S. participation in unwise wars or military interventions by refusing to fund them. Third, to reduce political opposition to a revived draft as well as to provide another constraint against presidential unilateralism, a law establishing conscription should include a provision that draftees cannot be sent into combat without specific congressional authorization.

5   Of course, reinstating the draft will generate opposition from all parts of the political spectrum, on the left by civil libertarians and opponents of any use of force, in the center by classic libertarians and those who would regard conscription as an unfair "tax on youth," and even by some on the political right, who (as noted earlier) would correctly perceive that the modified draft proposed here would inherently constrain presidential unilateralism. The professional military, traditionally conservative, might initially resist such fundamental change, though we are confident the professional military will come to value its significant advantages.

6   The benefits of universal national service, however, far outweigh these resolvable objections. Aside from the strictly military advantages—larger and better-educated armed forces—there would be a number of positive social consequences. Conscription will enable the forces to reflect the full spectrum of American pluralism, in terms of both socioeconomic classes and racial/ethnic groups. It is unacceptable that less than 1 percent of the country's eligible population serves in the armed forces, with almost no war-relevant sacrifice being asked from the rest of society. It ought to be axiomatic that the hardships and dangers of military service be more widely shared.

7   A draft could also increase responsibility on the part of political decision-makers. There would surely be a greater likelihood of sound foreign and military policies if the sons and daughters of the United States' political and business elites also served in uniform—as so many did in the past, but so few do today.

8   These arguments would constitute a strong case for reinstating the draft at any time. But at the moment, the United States simply has no other option. The U.S. mission in Afghanistan, crucial in the global fight against Islamist terrorism, simply cannot be accomplished with current force levels. Looking beyond Afghanistan toward the long-term struggle with radical Islamism, the United States is going to need larger standing forces of considerable quality, with the educational, cultural, linguistic, and technical skills needed for modern military operations in foreign lands.

9   In the event of new terrorist attacks on U.S. soil on the scale of 9/11, let alone the unimaginable consequences if American cities were struck by nuclear or biological weapons, the arguments against conscription would vanish overnight, and there would be a crash program to build up the armed forces, similar to the aftermath of attack on Pearl Harbor. The country would be in a far stronger position if it put these forces in place now, rather than waiting until a catastrophe occurred. Moreover, if the United States had such larger standing forces, they would provide a credible deter-

rent against states that currently support, tolerate, or ineffectively suppress terrorist groups. Indeed, the reinstatement of the draft is not an invitation for more war; it may be the best chance for peace.

Finish Timing: Record time here _____ and use the Timed Reading Conversion Chart in the Appendix to figure your rate: _____ wpm.

Comprehension Check

Directions: Answer the following questions without looking back.

1. What type of draft system do the authors propose? _____

    _____

    _____ _____

2. Why do the authors believe a draft system is needed at this time? _____

    _____

    _____

3. Which of the following do the authors believe has occurred because of the stresses of fighting in Afghanistan and Iraq?
    a. Recruitment and retention rates in the military are slipping
    b. A lowering of physical, educational, and psychological enlistment standards
    c. A softening of initial military training
    d. Granting induction waivers to some criminals
    e. All of the above

4. What type of service would non-military draftees perform? _____

    _____

    _____

5. What dangers can arise from an enlarged military establishment? _____

    _____

    _____

6. Which of the following are proposed safeguards against a president misusing his power as commander-in-chief?
    a. Congress should use its constitutionally mandated role in decisions to go to war.
    b. Congress should use its "power of the purse" to prohibit participation in unwise wars or military intervention.
    c. A law should be passed establishing a provision that draftees cannot be sent into combat without specific congressional authority.
    d. All of the above.
    e. None of the above.

7. Reinstating the draft, according to the authors, will generate opposition from which of the following:

    a. Opponents of any use of force

    b. Those who would consider the draft as an unfair "tax on youth"

    c. Conservative professional military personnel

    d. All of the above

    e. None of the above

8. T/F According to the authors, there would be a greater likelihood of sound foreign and military policies if the children of political and business elites had to serve in the military.

9. Why do the authors believe that the draft should be instituted now rather than wait for a large scale attack or sudden emergency? _____ _____

_____ _____ _____ _____

_____ _____ _____

10. Is the article based mostly on fact or opinion? _____

_____ _____ _____

_____ _____ _____

Vocabulary Check

Directions: Define the following underlined words from the selection.

1. necessary for success in <u>counterinsurgency</u>

_____ _____ ___ _____

2. generous <u>inducements</u> have been needed

_____ _____

3. increase the political appeal of <u>conscription</u>

_____

4. the <u>alleviation</u> of shortages of teachers

_____ _____ _____

5. safeguards to prevent presidential <u>unilateralism</u>

_____ _____ _____ _____ _____ _____

6. use its <u>mandated</u> role in decisions

_____ _____ _____ _____

7. it ought to be <u>axiomatic</u> things be shared

_____ _____ _____

8. similar to the <u>aftermath</u> of attack on Pearl Harbor

_____

_____

9. employ its <u>appropriation</u> powers

_____ _____

10. a credible <u>deterrent</u> against states that support terrorism

_____ _____

Record your rate and the results of the comprehension and vocabulary checks on the Student Record Chart in the Appendix. Each correct answer is worth 10 points, for a total of 100 points possible for comprehension and 100 points for vocabulary. An average score is around 250 wpm with 70 percent comprehension. Discuss any problems, concerns, or questions you have with your instructor.

Questions for Group Discussion

1. Divide your group in two, one group arguing for conscription, the other group against. How much of each argument is based on facts and opinion?

2. As a group, discuss your opinions on the legalization of drugs. Make a list of facts expressed and a list for opinions expressed. Where might you go to research the subject for factual information?

3. As a group, see how many of you can use the following words in a sentence. Make certain you learn the ones you still may not be able to use or recognize by writing the definition in the blank space.

a. monolithic _____

b. archetypal _____

c. ornate _____

d. heathens _____

e. conscription _____

f. incarceration _____

g. ethical _____

h. deterrent _____

i. axiomatic _____

On Your Own

Pick ten new words you learned in this chapter, not necessarily those listed in question 4, and on a separate sheet of paper write a sentence for each word, using it correctly in context. Turn in the paper to your instructor.

CHAPTER FIVE

Recognizing Tone, Figurative Language, and Point of View

A.   Recognizing Intent, Attitude, and Tone

In addition to distinguishing fact from opinion, critical reading requires an awareness of an author's *intent*, *attitude*, and *tone*.

An author's **intent** is not always easy to recognize. Let's say, for instance, that you are reading Jonathan Swift's essay "A Modest Proposal," an essay that appears frequently in English literature anthologies. At the time he wrote this essay in the eighteenth century, many Irish people were dying from famine. To read his essay at the literal level, Swift would seem to be in favor of taking the profusion of children in Ireland and treating them as cattle, fattening up some for slaughter, exporting some to boost the economy, and raising some strictly for breeding. However, to accept his essay on the literal level would be to miss his intent. His essay is a satire, and his intent was to make his readers more aware of a social problem that existed in his day. His real purpose was to ridicule the people in power at the time. He intentionally wrote in a rather cold, uncompassionate way to shock his readers into action. Yet if you were not perceptive enough to understand Swift's intent, you could completely miss his point.

An author's intent may be to satirize a problem or condition; to amuse readers; to make them cry by arousing sympathy, pity, or fear; to argue a point that another writer has made; or to accuse someone of something. But whatever an author's intent may be, you, as a critical reader, need to be absolutely certain that you understand what it is.

An author's treatment of a subject reflects an **attitude** toward it. Swift, for instance, in the essay mentioned here, uses satire, but his attitude is serious. He is not serious about using children as an economic commodity, even though he provides a detailed plan for doing so. He was angry at the people of his day for allowing such deplorable conditions to exist. He was serious about wanting to change these conditions. An author's attitude, then, is the author's personal feeling about a subject. Attitudes can range from sad to happy, angry to delighted, sympathetic to unsympathetic, tolerant to furious.

The language an author uses is frequently a clue to that writer's attitude to both his or her subject and to the reader. In his book *Preface to Critical Reading*, Richard Altick provides a good example of how paying attention to the language a writer uses can reflect intent and attitude:

> Compare the two ways in which a person could express the desire [intent] to borrow some money: (1) "Hey, good buddy, how about loaning me a ten for a few days? I'm in a bind. You'll get it back on Friday." (2) "I'm very sorry to impose on you, but I'm in a bit of a predicament, and I need ten dollars just until payday. I'd be extremely grateful." The language of the first appeal suggests that slang is the normal means of expression for this speaker. The meaning of the second appeal is identical, and the general approach is the same. But whereas the first speaker is forthright and unembarrassed, the other seems hesitant and apologetic. The personalities of the two seem as different as the connotations of bind and predicament. (From Richard Altick, *Preface to Critical Reading*, 5th edition, Holt, Rinehart and Winston, 1960, p. 90.)

In other words, the intent of both appeals is the same; they want to borrow money. But the attitudes are different. Critical reading requires an ability to distinguish such differences.

How an author uses language creates what is called a **tone**. Tone in writing is similar to what we call a tone of voice. For instance, the phrase "Thanks a lot!" can have different meanings based on the tone of voice used to express it. If we are truly grateful, we will say it one way; if we want to be sarcastic, we'll say it another way; and if we are angry or disgusted, we'll say it still another way. When reading, however, we can't hear an author's tone of voice. But as critical readers, we must be able to recognize the true tone intended by the author.

Here are a few words that can be used to describe attitude, intent, and tone, depending on the context. Look up the ones you don't know.

angry	firm	ambivalent
disgruntled	confused	witty
humorous	furious	sad
light	antagonistic	lively
playful	outraged	resentful
positive	annoyed	amusing
negative	irritated	offended
harsh	troubled	disrespectful
sarcastic	somber	tyrannical
sardonic	delighted	compassionate
dismayed	favorable	sniveling
objective	troubled	bombastic
subjective	solemn	thankful
moderate	alarmed	
strident	rude	

The following practices will help you learn to recognize intent, attitude, and tone in various types of writing.

PRACTICE A-1

Directions: Read the following magazine article, looking for fact, opinion, intent, attitude, and tone.

BAN ATHLETES WHO DON'T USE STEROIDS

SIDNEY GENDIN

1   Governments and sports federations are wrong for continuing to ban the use of performance-enhancing drugs like steroids. Steroids are less hazardous to human health than smoking or drinking, and society has traditionally permitted people to engage in risky activities, such as mountain climbing, when the danger posed only affects the individual involved. In addition, ineffective and more costly dietary supplements, which falsely claim to work just like steroids, are legal. Steroid use by athletes should not be considered unnatural or cheating—the drugs simply allow athletes to perform at their very best.

2   Isn't it time for the brainwashed public to know the truth about steroids? In their ideological zeal to ban "performance enhancing" drugs, national governments and the various local and international sports federations have ignorantly and self-righteously declared that steroid use is cheating, dangerous, and stupid. In fact, in general, it is neither dangerous nor stupid and it is cheating only because it has been capriciously commanded to be so.

STEROID DANGERS ARE MINIMAL

3   In the first place, with respect to the alleged danger, people ought to know that there are dozens of steroids and it would be absurd to imagine that their risks are identical. Moreover, steroids come in two broad classes—the orals and the injectables. It is true that most of the orals have associated hazards but not a single one of them is as hazardous as smoking or drinking. The principal dangers of the injectables result from overdosing and, even so, they are mainly such alarming matters as acne and severe headache. Every legally obtainable prescription drug comes with a warning of dozens of worse side effects.

4   But what is that to you and me? Why should we legislate what risks people should run unless they can interfere with the rest of us? In our democratic, capitalist society many persons risk their last few dollars to start up businesses which will probably fail. We do not stop them. If and when they become multimillionaires we congratulate them. We don't permit people to drive without seatbelts because their accidents drive up insurance rates for the rest of us but we let people engage in the far riskier business of climbing mountains since the danger is mainly self-regarding. So enough virtue-parading preaching.

PRODUCT HYPOCRISY

5   As for the so-called cheating, who really are the cheaters? The average steroid user spends about $100–150 per month while the supplement industries grow rich on suckering in the hundreds of thousands, possibly millions, of foolish people spending up to $1,000 per month on a variety of mumbo jumbo: androstenedione, 4-androstenedione, 19-androstenedione, androstenediol and the several 4, 5, 17, and 19 varieties of androstenediol, tribulus terrestris, enzymatic conversion accelerators, growth hormone stimulators, hormone-releasing peptides, testosterone "boosters," dozens of magical herbs and a ridiculous number of "non drugs" with unpronounceable names so they are always abbreviated such as HMB and DHEA. On top of all this, these folks who tend to be more affluent than steroid users are pumping protein powders into their milk—$9 per day—and gobbling down protein candy bars—up to $3 each—while saving a bit of energy for screaming "Foul! Cheater!" at the poor steroid user. They are told by the manufacturers and distributors of these outlandish products that they look like steroids, feel like steroids and work like steroids. So? Why not ban them like steroids?

6   But I say ban them and only them. For one thing, they don't work as well as steroids. More importantly, what care I as a fan that someone sets a remarkable record because he used steroids? I pay money to see sporting events and I am entitled to an athlete's very best. Isaac Stern can afford a violin that few violinists and no high school orchestra player can afford. Is he taking unfair advantage of them? If I pay $60 to hear Stern and learn his tone was not up to par because he was too lazy to bring his own violin and borrowed a $50 one from a high school kid, I justifiably want my money back. What care I that he usually plays upon a $200,000

instrument? I am not bothered by this; I want his very best. Likewise, I want the very best an athlete can give me. I don't want to watch athletes who could have done better if only they had used steroids. Talk of steroid performance as unnatural is as ridiculous as complaining about artificial hearts. As for me I plan to have a T-shirt made for me that will read on its front: "Use steroids or go home. Enough of crying and whining."

Now answer the following questions.

1. T/F The main idea of this essay is that athletic use of steroids should not be banned.

2. T/F The main idea is based mostly on fact.

3. Which of the following best states the author's foremost intent?

   a. To show that there are dozens of steroids with various risk factors

   b. To show that the public has been brainwashed about the falsehoods of steroid use

   c. To show that the principal danger of steroid use is from overdosing

   d. To convince the reader that we should not make something illegal, like steroids, unless the risk interferes with the public

4. Which of the following best describes the author's attitude toward legislation banning steroid use among athletes?

   a. concerned   c. humorous

   b. open-minded   d. disgruntled

5. The tone of the essay is

   a. objective   c. apologetic.

   b. harsh.   d. respectful.

6. Based on the evidence provided, do you agree with the author? Explain.

   _____

   _____

   _____

Now let's look at your answers. The statement in question 1 is true. The statement in question 2 is false. The answer to question 3 is (d). For question 4, of the words offered, the best answer is (d), disgruntled. For question 5, the best choice is (b), harsh. This is not to say that other words might apply as well, but of the choices given, these are the best.

As to question 6, you've given your opinions; compare and discuss them in class.

PRACTICE A-2

Directions: As you read the following article, apply everything you've learned about main ideas and supporting details, considering especially the author's opinions on her topic, her attitude or point of view toward her topic, her intent in writing the essay, and her tone. Notice how they all work together.

IS HARRY POTTER EVIL?

JUDY BLUME

1   I happened to be in London last summer on the very day *Harry Potter and the Prisoner of Azkaban*, the third book in the wildly popular series by J. K. Rowling, was published. I couldn't believe my good fortune. I rushed to the bookstore to buy a copy, knowing this simple act would put me up there with the best grandmas in the world. The book was still months away from publication in the United States, and I have an 8-year-old grandson who is a big Harry Potter fan.

2   It's a good thing when children enjoy books, isn't it? Most of us think so. But like many children's books these days, the Harry Potter series has recently come under fire. In Minnesota, Michigan, New York, California and South Carolina, parents who feel the books promote interest in the occult have called for their removal from classrooms and school libraries.

3   I knew this was coming. The only surprise is that it took so long—as long as it took for the zealots who claim they're protecting children from evil (and evil can be found lurking everywhere these days) to discover that children actually like these books. If children are excited about a book, it must be suspect.

4   I'm not exactly unfamiliar with this line of thinking, having had various books of mine banned from schools over the last 20 years. In my books, it's reality that's seen as corrupting. With Harry Potter, the perceived danger is fantasy. After all, Harry and his classmates attend the celebrated Hogwarts School of Witchcraft and Wizardry. According to certain adults, these stories teach witchcraft, sorcery and satanism. But hey, if it's not one "ism," it's another. I mean Madeleine L'Engle's *A Wrinkle in Time* has been targeted by censors for promoting New Ageism, and Mark Twain's *Adventures of Huckleberry Finn* for promoting racism. Gee, where does that leave the kids?

5   The real danger is not in the books, but in laughing off those who would ban them. The protests against Harry Potter follow a tradition that has been growing since the early 1980's and often leaves school principals trembling with fear that is then passed down to teachers and librarians.

6   What began with the religious right has spread to the politically correct. (Remember the uproar in Brooklyn last year when a teacher was criticized for reading a book entitled "Nappy Hair" to her class?) And now the gate is open so wide that some parents believe they have the right to demand immediate removal of any book for any reason from school or classroom libraries. The list of gifted teachers and librarians who find their jobs in jeopardy for defending their students' right to read, to imagine, to question, grows every year.

7   My grandson was bewildered when I tried to explain why some adults don't want their children reading about Harry Potter. "But that doesn't make any sense!" he said. J. K. Rowling is on a book tour in America right now. She's probably befuddled by the brouhaha, too. After all, she was just trying to tell a good story.

Judy Blume, "Is Harry Potter Evil?" Reprinted with permission from Judy Blume. From the *New York Times* Op-Ed section, October 22, 1999.

8   My husband and I like to reminisce about how, when we were 9, we read straight through L. Frank Baum's Oz series, books filled with wizards and witches. And you know what those subversive tales taught us? That we loved to read! In those days I used to dream of flying. I may have been small and powerless in real life, but in my imagination I was able to soar.

9   At the rate we're going, I can imagine next year's headline: *"Goodnight Moon* Banned for Encouraging Children to Communicate With Furniture." And we all know where that can lead, don't we?

Now answer the following questions.

1. What is the thesis or main idea of this essay?

   a. Some people believe the Harry Potter books are evil and should not be available to children.

   b. The author has had various books of hers banned in some places.

   c. There is a growing danger that some parents believe they have a right to demand removal of books from schools and libraries for any reason.

   d. Parents should allow their children to read about wizards and witches if it gets them to enjoy reading.

2. T/F The opinions in this article are mostly based on factual accounts and reports.

3. Which of the following best describes the author's attitude toward book censorship?

   a. Concerned   **c.** Angry

   b. Open-minded   **d.** Pleased

4. Looking at the list on page 212, what word or words best describe the author's attitude and tone? _____

5. What is the author's intent?

   a. To caution readers about the growing attempts at book censorship by parents

   b. To show that reading books dealing with the occult are not harmful

   c. To defend the Harry Potter series against those who want it banned

   d. To laugh off those who want to ban certain books they find objectionable

Questions for Group Discussion

In small groups, pick one of the two essays, "Ban Athletes Who Don't Use Steroids" or "Is Harry Potter Evil?" Discuss your reactions to the author's intent, attitude, and tone. How do these reactions aid or hinder your acceptance of the author's thesis?

B.   Recognizing Figurative Language

Frequently, writers use **figurative language** to express their tone. Figurative language is used in an imaginative way rather than in a literal sense. For instance, when a writer says, "her eyes flashed fire," the intent is not for us to imagine real fire coming from someone's eyes but to realize that the character is angry. Or, when we read that a lawyer "dropped his client like a hot potato," we are given to understand that the lawyer's actions were quick, just as we'd be quick to drop a hot potato.

Figurative language is familiar to everyone. A great deal of our slang and ordinary speech is based on figurative language, as well as a great many works in literature. For example, many baseball terms have become part of our regular figurative speech:

> Keep your eye on the ball.
> What he said came out of left field.
> The salesman's pitch was off base.
> His friend went to bat for him.
> If you want to work here, you'll need to play ball with the manager.
> He got started right off the bat.
> The sales record knocked the ball out of the park.
> His bank account holds ballpark figures.

Without figures of speech, our language would be dull and mechanical. It becomes, therefore, important in developing reading comprehension to know the difference between literal and figurative language. It also becomes important to know the difference between literal and figurative language in developing your aesthetic understanding of what you read. More on that in later chapters.

One form of figurative language is the **metaphor**. A metaphor is a comparison of two things without the use of the word *like* or *as*. For instance, when you say someone "clammed up and wouldn't talk," you are comparing the person's closed mouth with the tightness of a closed clam. When you say someone has a "stone face," you are comparing their unchanging expression with the immobility of stone.

Dead metaphors are metaphors that have been used so frequently that we accept them almost literally. Terms such as "a tenderfoot," "hands" on a watch, the "head" of a cane, a "run" in a stocking, or an engine "knocking" are all dead metaphors, yet they help us convey meaning that is seldom misunderstood. S. I. Hayakawa says that metaphors are probably the most important of all the means by which language develops, changes, grows, and adapts itself to our changing needs.

A **simile** is another form of figurative language. It, like a metaphor, compares one thing with another but uses the word *like* or *as*. Examples of similes are "out like a light," "sparkles like a lake," "sounds like a machine gun," "cool as spring water," and "phony as a three-dollar bill."

When metaphors and similes are overused, they turn into **clichés**. Clichés are worn-out figures of speech such as "a blanket of snow covered the hill," "the silence was broken," or "my old lady." Such terms have been used so often in speech and writing that they lose their real effectiveness and seem stale.

Still another type of figurative language is **hyperbole**. Hyperbole is a deliberate exaggeration or overstatement used to emphasize a point being made. For instance, if a friend tells you she can't go to the movies because she has "mountains of homework" to do, she is using hyperbole. If someone tells you that the story was "so funny he almost died laughing," he's using hyperbole. If you "love someone to pieces," know someone who "talked your ear off," or couldn't get your work done because "the phone rang ten thousand times," then you have been dealing with hyperbole. Just as overused similes and metaphors can become clichés, it can happen with hyperbole, too.

Some writers use **puns**, a humorous use of words that involves a word or phrase that has more than one possible meaning. For example:

Two silk worms had a race; they ended in a tie.
No matter how much you push the envelope, it'll still be stationery.
A dog gave birth to puppies near the road and was cited for littering.
Time flies like an arrow. Fruit flies like a banana.
A chicken crossing the road is poultry in motion.

You get the picture.

Recognizing how authors use figurative language helps us clarify whether an author's attitude is serious, playful, sympathetic, outraged, sarcastic, bitter, humorous, and so on. Thus, attitude and tone are closely allied through the use of figures of speech.

PRACTICE B-1: Identifying Literal versus Figurative Language

Directions: The following statements are either literal or figurative. Place an *F* in the blank next to each statement that uses figurative speech. If you want more practice with the identification of figurative language, see Chapter Eight, Practice A-1.

_____   **1.** Mr. Timpkin went through the ceiling when his son told him that he had wrecked the car.

_____   **2.** Alyce waited eagerly for the show to start.

_____   **3.** Doreen's checks are bouncing all over town.

_____   **4.** The crowd was getting increasingly angry waiting for the musicians to show up.

_____   **5.** The battery is dead as a doornail.

_____   **6.** Prices are being slashed to rock bottom.

_____   **7.** Mom really stuck her neck out for you this time.

_____   **8.** I find myself out on a limb.

_____   **9.** When Jimmy screamed, her hair stood on end.

_____   **10.** The Giants were defeated 18–4 in the last game.

PRACTICE B-2: Recognizing Tone through Figurative Language

Directions: Read the following paragraphs and answer the questions that follow.

1. There is an appalling cloud of illiteracy shadowing America's pride. We would do well to attack some basic causes for the lack of literacy facing us. Instead, we seem to throw more money down the drain for more grants and studies.

   a. The expression "cloud of illiteracy shadowing America's pride" means _____

   _____

    b. T/F The literary term for the phrase in question 1(a) is *simile*.

    c. T/F Using the phrase "money down the drain" lets us know the author is happy with what efforts are taking place.

    d. The tone of this passage is best described as

_____ serious concern.	_____ concerned displeasure.
_____ humorous concern.	_____ sarcastic.

2. My job was really starting to get to me. It seemed a dead end, a treadmill taking me nowhere. If I was to keep from blowing a fuse, I had to somehow shatter my negativity toward my work or go for broke and resign. After what seemed like centuries of indecisiveness, one day I plunked myself down at the typewriter, quickly tossed off my resignation, and boldly signed it with great flair. So I wouldn't chicken out at the last minute, I sailed into my boss's office and slapped it down on her desk.

    a. The tone of this passage is best described as

_____ one of relief.	_____ frustration.
_____ fear of losing a job.	_____ indecision.

    b. The phrase "go for broke" here means _____

    _____

    c. T/F "My treadmill job was a dead end" is an example of a metaphor.

    d. T/F It is possible to literally shatter a negative attitude.

3. Out deeper, in cooler water, where trout live, floating on one's back is a kind of free ride, like being fifteen again, like being afloat upon another sky. Perhaps there is a bit of Tom Sawyer's pleasure at watching his own bogus funeral in this, but before we get overly morbid, a fish begins nibbling our toes. Floating on one's back is like riding between two skies. (From Edward Hoagland, "Summer Pond," *New York Times*, August 1, 1979.)

    a. T/F The author mostly uses similes in the preceding passage.

    b. The tone of the paragraph is best described as

_____ lazy.	_____ morbid.
_____ pleasant.	_____ sad.

    c. T/F The intent of the passage is to relive the joys of swimming in a pond or lake.

4. "C'mon, we're supposed to be having fun," snaps her companion, a clone. In razor-crease jeans and stiletto heels they stamp into the ladies room, flounce around the corner past the polished washbasins and disappear into the two long rows of toilet stalls. They are the kind of girls who obey their mothers' warnings never to sit on strange toilet seats. Attendants have to nip in after that type, making sure the next woman will have no unpleasant surprises. (From Jane O'Reilly, "In Las Vegas: Working Hard for the Money," *Time*, January 9, 1984.)

    a. T/F The phrase "razor-crease jeans and stiletto heels" reflects a negative attitude toward the girls.

    b. T/F The intent of the passage is to gain sympathy for the two girls.

    c. The tone of the passage can best be described as

_____ humorous.	_____ sweet.
_____ sarcastic.	_____ apathetic.

5. There had been some change in the kitchen staff since my last visit and somehow the perfect little salad had become a Plain Jane. The tortilla soup was a bowl of monotone flavor and tasted like tortilla chips thrown into a blender. This soup compared to the previous soup was like comparing a No. 2 pencil against a Mont Blanc pen. The grilled cheese with apple, Gruyere, and whole-grain mustard was disappointing. In trying to be original, a grilled cheese got whiplashed into a sloppy, runny junket of sweet, mustard and cheese flavors, all coming together like a blind date. Worse is the heavy-scented sweet vanilla deodorizer in the gas-station-like loo, which is reminiscent of walking down the candle aisle at Pier 1. (From Arthur von Wiesenberger, "A Mixed Harvest," *Santa Barbara News-Press*, March 10, 2006, p. 33.)

   a. T/F The intent of this passage is to compare the food of a previous restaurant visit with the latest visit.

   b. The tone of the passage is mostly
      _____ humorous.   _____ objective.
      _____ disappointment.   _____ frustration.

   c. What does the author mean by the phrase "Plain Jane"?

      _____

      _____

   d. What effect does the author create with the use of the term "whiplashed"?

      _____

      _____

   e. The author uses several similes. Write down two of them.

      _____

      _____

6. Three decades after bursting into pool halls and living rooms, video games are tak-ing a place in academia.... Traditionalists in both education and the video game industry pooh-pooh the trend, calling it a bald bid by colleges to cash in on a fad. But others believe that video games—which already rival movie tickets in sales—are poised to become one of the dominant media of the new century. Certainly, the burgeoning game industry is famished for new talent. And now, universities are stocked with both students and young faculty members who grew up with joystick in hand. (Seth Schiesel, "Video Games Are Their Major," *New York Times*, November 22, 2005.)

   Explain how these words and phrases are used figuratively:

   a. bursting into

      _____

   b. pooh-pooh

      _____

   c. a bald bid

      _____

d. famished for

_____

e. stocked with

_____

PRACTICE B-3

Directions: Read the following essay, looking for intent, attitude, tone, and figurative language.

THIRST FOR A HERO CAN GET US IN HOT WATER

PHILADELPHIA INQUIRER

1   At a low point of the Iraq war, when unexpected Iraqi opposition seemed to threaten U.S. troops with a morass, America badly needed a hero.

2   And it found one.

3   This was the story, and a compelling one it was. Pfc. Jessica Lynch, a fresh-faced, 19-year-old Army supply clerk from West Virginia, was miraculously rescued from a hospital in Nasiriyah where, gravely injured, she was being held captive.

4   The *Washington Post* quoted unnamed U.S. officials recounting that Ms. Lynch had engaged in a "fierce" firefight after her unit was ambushed following a wrong turn. She shot several enemy soldiers before her ammo ran out and she was captured.

5   "She was fighting to the death" and has multiple gunshot wounds, said an unnamed U.S. official in the story.

6   The most exciting part of the tale came next: Ms. Lynch's rescue.

7   The defense sources described for the *Post* a classic Special Operations raid, with commandos in Black Hawk helicopters engaging Iraqi forces on their way into and out of Ms. Lynch's medical compound.

8   The commandos had been directed there by a heroic Iraqi lawyer who was appalled to see the bedridden Ms. Lynch slapped twice in the face by one of her captors. This account was trumpeted by U.S. print and broadcast outlets far and wide.

9   The story was a balm to American hearts.

10   Except that much of it now appears to be untrue. The British Broadcasting Corp. cast cold water on the tale two weeks ago: Ms. Lynch's injuries were probably caused by a road crash; she had received good treatment at the hospital; there wasn't a single armed opposition soldier in the hospital when the U.S. troops burst in, John Wayne style.

11   Later—too much later—the American media have begun examining the story they had so eagerly swallowed in April.

12   Thursday, a lengthy *Chicago Tribune* story quoted Iraqis on the scene who said that much of the Lynch hero/rescue story was, basically, bunk. (Ms. Lynch herself has no memory of events.)

13   Now this glorious tale must be traded for some complicated questions about the sticky entanglements of a rah-rah Pentagon, a thirsty press, and a public desperate for good news.

14   Those questions don't just concern the story of Jessica Lynch.

15   Early reports of her rescue were, as the saying goes, the first, rough-draft history. But, then, so too are all the accounts so far of this fast-moving war.

16   Stay tuned—perhaps decades from now—for the real story. What really did become of those weapons of mass destruction, if they existed at all? Where is Saddam Hussein? Exactly how many Iraqi civilians suffered and died?

17   It's too easy just to blame a sloppy press for overdramatizing the Jessica Lynch story initially. In the fog of war, most reporting is quick and dirty, with virtually no chance for outside corroboration. Clearly, in this case, at least some in the military were eager to peddle the more heroic narrative. And, to journalism's credit, the original, faulty stories usually get revised when facts finally become clear.

18   Is Pfc. Lynch indeed a hero?

19   For volunteering to serve the way she did, and enduring the way she did, she is. There are no doubt thousands more untold stories about the heroism of individual American and British soldiers in Iraq.

20   But a search for the perfect heroic story—and eager acceptance of any "facts" that enhance the tale—does a disservice to both heroes and the truth.

Comprehension Check

Directions: Answer the following questions without looking back.

1. What is the intent of this article? _____

    _____

2. Which of the following best describes the author's attitude toward the media's coverage of the Jessica Lynch story?

    a. sympathetic

    b. tolerant

    c. furious

    d. alarmed

3. Which of the following best describes the author's attitude toward the U.S. official who gave the story to the press?

    a. praise

    b. disturbed

    c. accepting

    d. can't tell

4. The tone of the essay is mostly

    a. humorous.

    b. nasty.

    c. sarcastic.

    d. troublesome.

   5. The tone of paragraph 13 can best be described as

       a. mean.

       b. sarcastic.

       c. serious.

       d. ecstatic.

   6. Rewrite paragraph 11 without using any figurative language.

   _____

   _____.

   7. T/F The phrases "a rah-rah Pentagon" and "a thirsty press" in paragraph 13 are examples of figurative language.

   8. Reread paragraph 10. What, if any, figurative language is being used? _____

   _____

   9. What examples of figurative language are used in paragraph 17?

   _____

   _____

   10. Why does the author believe that the press reported the Jessica Lynch story without checking on the "unnamed U.S. official"?

   _____

   _____

Vocabulary Check

Directions: Define the following underlined words from the selection.

   1. opposition seemed to threaten troops with a <u>morass</u>

   _____

   2. and a <u>compelling</u> one it was

   _____

   3. was <u>appalled</u> to see

   _____

   4. this account was <u>trumpeted</u> by U.S. print and broadcast outlets

   _____

   5. perhaps <u>decades</u> from now

   _____

   6. about the sticky <u>entanglements</u>

   _____

   7. no chance for outside <u>corroboration</u>

   _____

8. <u>enduring</u> the way she did

_____

9. "facts" that <u>enhance</u> the tale

_____

10. a <u>disservice</u> to both heroes and the truth

_____

Record the results of the comprehension and vocabulary checks on the Student Record Chart in the Appendix. Each correct answer is worth 10 points, for a total of 100 points possible for comprehension and 100 points for vocabulary.

PRACTICE B-4

Directions: Read the following essay, looking for intent, attitude, tone, and figurative language.

DO AWAY WITH PUBLIC SCHOOLS

JONAH GOLDBERG

1   Here's a good question for you: Why have public schools at all?

2   OK, cue the marching music. We need public schools because blah blah blah and yada yada yada. We could say blah is common culture and yada is the government's interest in promoting the general welfare. Or that children are the future. And a mind is a terrible thing to waste. Because we can't leave any child behind.

3   The problem with all these bromides is that they leave out the simple fact that one of the surest ways to leave a kid "behind" is to hand him over to the government. Americans want universal education, just as they want universally safe food. But nobody believes that the government should run nearly all of the restaurants, farms and supermarkets. Why should it run the vast majority of the schools—particularly when it gets terrible results?

4   Consider Washington, home of the nation's most devoted government-lovers and, ironically, the city with arguably the worst public schools in the country. Out of the 100 largest school districts, according to _The Washington Post_, the District of Columbia ranks third in spending for each pupil ($12,979) but last in spending on instruction. Fifty-six cents of every dollar go to administrators who, it's no secret, do a miserable job administrating, even though D.C. schools have been in a state of "reform" for nearly 40 years.

5   In a blistering series, the _Post_ has documented how badly the bureaucrats have run public education. More than half of Washington's teenagers spend their days in "persistently dangerous" schools, with an average of nine violent incidents a day in a system with 135 schools. "Principals reporting dangerous conditions or urgently needed repairs in their buildings wait, on average, 379 days...for the problems to be fixed," according to the _Post_. But hey, at least the kids are getting a lousy education. A mere 19 schools managed to get "proficient" scores or better for a majority of students on the district's Comprehensive Assessment Test.

6   A standard response to such criticisms is to say we don't spend enough on public education. But if money were the solution, wouldn't the district, which spends nearly $13,000 on every kid, rank near the top? If you think more money will fix the schools, make your checks out to "cash" and send them to me. Private, parochial and charter schools get better results. Parents know this. Applications for vouchers in the district dwarf the available supply, and home schooling has exploded.

7   As for schools teaching kids about the common culture and all that, as a conservative, I couldn't agree more. But is there evidence that public schools are better at it? The results of the 2006 National Assessment of Educational Progress history and civics exams showed that two-thirds of U.S. high school seniors couldn't identify the significance of a photo of a theater with a sign reading "Colored Entrance." And keep in mind, political correctness pretty much guarantees that Jim Crow and the civil rights movement are included in syllabi. Imagine how few kids can intelligently discuss Manifest Destiny or free silver.

8   Right now, there's a renewed debate about providing "universal" health insurance. For some liberals, this means replicating the public school model for health care. (Stop laughing.) But for others, this means mandating that everyone have health insurance—just as we mandate that all drivers have car insurance—and then throwing tax dollars at poorer folks to make sure no one falls through the cracks.

9   There's a consensus in America that every child should get an education, but as David Gelernter noted recently in *The Weekly Standard*, there's no such consensus that public schools need to do the educating.

10   Really, what would be so terrible about government mandating that every kid has to go to school and providing subsidies and oversight when necessary, but then getting out of the way?

11   Milton Friedman noted long ago that the government is bad at providing services—that's why he wanted public schools to be called "government schools"—but that it's good at writing checks. So why not cut checks to people so they can send their kids to school?

12   What about the good public schools? Well, the reason good public schools are good has nothing to do with government's special expertise and everything to do with the fact that parents care enough to ensure their kids get a good education. That wouldn't change if the government got out of the school business. What would change is that fewer kids would get left behind.

Comprehension Check

Directions: Answer the following questions without looking back.

1. What is the author's thesis or main idea? _____

_____

_____

2. The tone of paragraph 2 is
   a. serious.
   b. playful.
   c. angry.
   d. sarcastic.

3. Explain how paragraph 2 sets up the tone of the essay. _____
   _____
   _____

4. Which of the following describes Goldberg's attitude toward those in control of public school education and funding?

   a. pleased

   b. angry

   c. favorable

   d. disapproving

5. Goldberg's intent is to

   a. offer ideas that would better serve public schools.

   b. criticize the public school system.

   c. show we don't spend enough on public education.

   d. praise private schools.

6. On what school district does Goldberg mostly base his argument?

   _____

7. Goldberg states a study that revealed two-thirds of U.S. high school seniors could not identify the significance of a photo of a theater with a sign reading "Colored Entrance." What point is he making by quoting this study?

   _____
   _____

8. T/F Goldberg does not blame or find fault with the school administrators but feels the real problem is the lack of funding for schools.

9. T/F Goldberg uses a metaphor in the last sentence of paragraph 9.

10. Goldberg believes that the government should mandate that every child has to go to school and then _____
    _____

Vocabulary Check

Directions: Define the following underlined words from the selection.

1. the problem with all these bromides...

   _____

2. in a blistering series

   _____

3. to get proficient scores

   _____

4. private, parochial and charter schools

   _____

5. application for <u>vouchers</u>

_____

6. home schooling has <u>exploded</u>

_____

7. <u>Jim Crow</u> and the civil rights

_____

_____

_____

8. included in <u>syllabi</u>

_____

9. intelligently discuss <u>Manifest Destiny</u>

_____

_____

_____

10. this means <u>replicating</u> the public schools

_____

Record the results of the comprehension and vocabulary checks on the Student Record Chart in the Appendix. Each correct answer is worth 10 points, for a total of 100 points possible for comprehension and 100 points for vocabulary.

Class discussion questions:

1. Should we do away with public school education and let the government provide vouchers or subsidies to send children to private schools?

2. Discuss group attitudes toward their own education. Who went to public schools? Who went to private schools? How does each person value the education they received?

Application 1: Finding Figurative Language in Other Materials

In magazines, newspapers, or textbooks, find at least two examples of metaphors or similes and underline them. Write a sentence about how the figurative language shows the author's tone and attitude.

C.   Comparing Biased Points of View

A writer's attitude toward a subject may not be ours. However, as critical readers, it is important not to let either the author's **bias** or our own interfere with critical comprehension. Being biased means being prejudiced about or having a special leaning toward something. For instance, you may be biased about the type of music you listen to. Maybe you have no patience with classical music and prefer hard rock. That is a bias. Perhaps you are biased when it comes to food and would rather eat vegetables than meat. Everyone is biased about something, whether it's music, food, religion, politics, or people. Many of our biases are unconsciously learned from parents, friends, people we admire, or teachers. Reading critically can help us examine our own biases for their value.

While we are free to make up our own minds about a subject, we must still examine carefully the arguments and reasons of an author with opinions different from ours. We must recognize those biases of the author and not allow our own biases to interfere with or shut out those of the author. Once we critically examine what we read, we should reflect on its worth before accepting or rejecting it.

Most of us tend to accept readily the ideas of writers who have the same biases we do, and we tend to reject the views of those we have biases against. To do so is to be closed minded. As critical readers, we must be willing to make critical judgments based on reason rather than emotion.

As you learn to read critically, you need to recognize bias in writing. If you don't, you may become the victim of an author's propaganda. You may miss seeing how an author misrepresents facts. You may not see that an author is being more subjective (using personal opinions) than objective (using undistorted facts). Or you may be unaware of how one-sided some writing is.

Sometimes recognizing an author's bias is easy; at other times it isn't. Bias is likely to be present in advertisements, newspaper and magazine editorials, and religious and political pamphlets. You generally pay little attention to an author's bias when it matches your own. When you don't agree with an author, the reverse is true. To read critically requires real involvement in the text and in thinking through what is being read. In effect, critical reading *is* thinking.

The following passage appeared in *Consumer Reports*, a publication of Consumers Union, a nonprofit organization. Read it and then answer the questions that follow.

> The letter, marked "confidential," was from the R. I. Research Special Human Being Laboratory in New York City and was signed by one Dr. Roger Grimstone. It informed the recipient that, based on the date and hour of her birth, she was an extraordinary individual, "apart from the rest of humanity," a "Beyonder."
>
> "Owing to some cosmic quirk," the letter went on, "your destiny operates independently of any stars.... Why have you suffered so much? *Why has true happiness, true love, wealth, a happy home always been out of your reach?* Why have the things you've yearned for most been snatched away?"
>
> Simple. According to the good Dr. Grimstone, it's because the recipient has yet to send him 20 bucks for something entitled "The Guide."
>
> The reader who sent us Dr. Grimstone's solicitation has a different theory, however. He believes that his daughter, the recipient of the letter, has yet to find happiness, companionship, and financial security because she is only four months old. (From "Selling It," copyright © 1987 by Consumers Union of U.S., Inc., Yonkers, NY 10703-1057, a nonprofit organization. Reprinted with permission from the September 1987 issue of Consumer Reports © for educational purposes only. No commercial use or photocopying permitted. Log onto: *www.ConsumerReports.org*.)

1. What is the intent of the "confidential" letter sent by the R. I. Research Special Human Being Laboratory? _____

   _____

   _____

   _____

2. What is the intent of the article from *Consumer Reports*? _____

   _____

   _____

   _____

3. What attitude toward the recipient is implied by the originators of the letter?

   _____

   _____

4. What is *Consumer Reports*'s attitude toward the Laboratory?

   _____

   _____

   _____

5. What is the tone of the letter sent by Dr. Grimstone? _____

   _____

   _____

6. What is the tone of the passage from *Consumer Reports*? _____

   _____

   _____

Your answers to the questions may be worded differently from the following, but see if they match up. The answer to the first question is to sell "The Guide" for twenty dollars by appealing to the recipient's "uniqueness" and desire for more wealth, happiness, and health, things most all of us want more of. The intent of *Consumer Reports*, the second question, is to expose the "Laboratory" as a fraud.

The third question can be answered by looking at such phrases as "apart from the rest of humanity," "owing to some cosmic quirk," and "Beyonder." The Laboratory believes there are enough people (suckers?) who believe in astrology and who are dissatisfied enough with their lives (or curious enough) that they are willing to spend twenty dollars to find "the answer." *Consumer Reports*'s attitude is that the whole thing is phony.

The tone of the letter is tied in with attitude. The letter's tone, based on what quotes are given, seems serious about wanting to help. Even the "doctor's" name is serious sounding—Grimstone (or is it a subtle touch of humor on the sender's part?). *Consumer Reports*'s tone is humorous. Waiting until the end of the passage to let us know that the "confidential" letter was sent to a four-month-old makes us chuckle. We realize that phrases such as "the good Dr. Grimstone" and "20 bucks" provide a light, playful tone.

Critical reading requires identifying an author's point of view and motives. Nearly all controversial subjects are written from a particular point of view or bias.

By their very nature, such controversial subjects cannot be written about with complete objectivity. For instance, if a Catholic priest were to write about abortion, chances are his point of view would reflect opposition by the very nature of his training and religious beliefs. On the other hand, a social worker who has seen many teenage lives destroyed because of unwanted pregnancies might very well speak in favor of abortion. Even though the priest and the social worker have different points of view, their motives are the same—to convince us that their particular viewpoint is the correct one. As critical readers—and thinkers—we need to be alert to as many points of view as possible before making up our own minds on controversial issues. Then we need to examine the reasoning used to support those viewpoints.

Here are a few guidelines to follow so that you don't fall victim to poor reasoning. Watch out for:

1. Statements that oversimplify or distort the issue being discussed.
2. Irrelevant or unsupported evidence.
3. Left-out or suppressed information or evidence.
4. Appeals to the emotions rather than reasonable evidence.
5. Mudslinging, or attacks on people or groups rather than the issue itself.
6. References to or quotations from the Bible or historical figures even though there is no connection to the issue.

These are the most frequent, although not all, of the devices used to sway people to accept a particular point of view. They appear in advertisements, political campaigns, newspaper and magazine columns, editorials, and television commentaries.

PRACTICE C-1: Recognizing Opinions

The next reading is a syndicated column from the *Boston Globe* that appeared in hundreds of newspapers around the country. The subject has to do with the censorship of movies, videocassettes, television programs, and rock music. Before you read it, answer the following questions about your own biases regarding censorship.

1. Do you believe in censorship of any kind? _____ Explain._____

   _____

   _____

   _____

2. Do you believe that the electronic media (TV, VHS and DVD recordings, music CDs, radio) are generally responsible for the rise in drug addiction, adolescent suicides, and a decline in SAT scores? _____ Explain._____

   _____

   _____

   _____

   _____

   _____

Now read the following essay, using the six previously listed guidelines that outlined what you should watch for when reading about controversial issues.

SHIELD OUR YOUTH WITH CENSORSHIP

WILLIAM SHANNON

1   The United States today has a popular culture at war against the nation's children and youth. Movies, video cassettes, television programs, and rock music have produced what the late Harvard sociologist Pitirim Sorokin called a "sensate culture." The message of this popular culture is "Feel good." What one thinks hardly matters.

2   These media bombard young people with sounds and images for several hours each day. The two dominant themes are sexual pleasure and sadistic violence. The indescribable "highs" and mysterious charms of using drugs also lurk as subsidiary themes.

3   The effect of this non-stop sensual assault is anti-intellectual and anti-academic. It is difficult for any classroom teacher to compete with the exciting images projected by television and films. Serious use of the mind requires patience, self-discipline, and the ability to defer present gratification in favor of future achievement. Very little in our culture supports these serious values. On the contrary, the fast pace and pounding rhythms of rock music and violent films tell impressionable youngsters "Go, go, go...now, now, now."

4   Parents are engaged in an uneven battle against this popular culture. There are still young persons who read for pleasure and who do well in school, but their number dwindles. The middle range of children muddles through high school and some go through college, but the general level of their academic achievement is significantly below what it was 30 years ago. The number of vulnerable youngsters cruelly damaged or destroyed by this culture grows. Victims are at every level of intelligence and family income. Their vulnerability is a matter of temperament, family history, and perhaps genetic endowment.

5   The casualty figures in this uneven battle between conscientious parents and the popular culture appear in the form of a rising number of adolescent suicides and drug addicts and in the Scholastic Aptitude Test scores, which have fallen significantly from their levels of 20 years ago. Parents try various expedients. Wealthy families send their children to private boarding schools in the hope that tight scheduling of time and close supervision by teachers will reduce the risks.

6   Other families—some of them non-Catholic—turn to the Catholic schools, in the hope that the schools' traditionally stricter discipline and the greater respect for authority that they inculcate will save their children.

7   No place in this society is a sanctuary, however, from the brutal and corrupting pressures of our popular culture. Schools of every kind, public and private, secular and religious, struggle valiantly to instill good work habits and encourage intellectual values, but the opposing cultural pressures are too pervasive.

8   The film industry makes much of ratings such as "R" for restricted to adults, and "PG" for parental guidance suggested, but these ratings are close to useless.

9   The only solution is to restore prior censorship over the electronic media. Everyone older than 50 grew up in a time when Hollywood films were strictly censored by

the industry itself to exclude explicit sexual scenes, gruesome violence, and vulgar language. The Supreme Court in the 1950s struck down movie censorship. It extended to film makers the First Amendment protection traditionally enjoyed by newspapers and book publishers. The court also redefined the anti-pornography and anti-obscenity statutes into meaninglessness.

10   Those decisions were praised as liberal advances, but their consequences were unforeseen and disastrous. It would require a constitutional amendment to reverse those decisions. Unless they are reversed, the coarsening and corrupting of the nation's youth will continue.

Now answer the following questions.

1. What is the author's point of view toward censorship? _____
   _____

2. What is his attitude toward movies, videocassettes, and rock music?
   _____

3. What is his intent in writing this essay?
   _____

4. The statements made in paragraph 3 are factual.
   a. True, because_____
   b. False, because_____

5. The statements made in paragraph 3 are supported with evidence.
   a. True, because_____
   b. False, because_____

6. Statements such as "The only solution is to restore prior censorship over the electronic media" oversimplify the issue being discussed.
   a. True, because_____
   b. False, because_____

7. By blaming today's problems on the Supreme Court of the 1950s, the author is mudslinging rather than dealing rationally with the issue.
   a. True, because_____
   b. False, because_____

8. Circle any of the following that you feel the author does:
   a. Makes irrelevant or unsupported statements_____
   b. Oversimplifies the problem and solution_____
   c. Refers to the Bible for support_____
   d. Appeals to the emotions rather than providing reasonable evidence_____

9. For each of the items you circled in question 8, find a passage in the essay that serves as an example.
   _____
   _____

It's not too difficult to answer the first question. The title of the essay provides us with our first clue: "Shield Our Youth with Censorship." As we read through the essay, the author makes it clear that he blames the electronic media as the corrupting pressure on today's youth. Thus, his attitude is negative. His intent seems to be to push for censorship of some kind, to bring a constitutional amendment that would reverse the Supreme Court's earlier decision. Otherwise, he says in the last paragraph, "the coarsening and corrupting of the nation's youth will continue."

The statements in questions 4 and 5 are both false. The author makes three statements in paragraph 3, each one an opinion as stated. Though he may be correct, he needs facts to support his opinions. But instead of providing facts, he moves on to "the effects of this non-stop sensual assault."

The statements in questions 6 and 7 are both true. The issue is too complex for such a simple solution. When he blames the Supreme Court of the 1950s for today's problems, he not only simplifies the issue again but also enters into what is called "mudslinging," attacking the Court rather than the problem he claims the electronic media are causing.

As to questions 8 and 9, he uses all but (c). We've already seen that paragraph 3 is full of unsupported statements. Another example is the last sentence in paragraph 3. The last three sentences in paragraph 4 are also unsupported. Then in paragraph 5, he links adolescent suicides, drug addiction, and a decline in SAT scores together as though all of these are related to the electronic media. Admittedly, he could be correct, but his argument is not very convincing. His tone is frequently emotional. Wording and phrases such as "vulnerable youngsters cruelly damaged," "no place is a sanctuary," and "a popular culture at war against the nation's children" all appeal to our emotions. Censorship of any type is a serious matter. To accept the author's premise and solution as written is to do so without solid facts or rational reasoning.

It's important to remember that Shannon may be right. What we as critical readers must do is recognize his point of view or bias, then see what facts he provides to support his thesis. If his facts or supporting arguments are valid, then we should consider his point of view before making up our minds, especially if we disagree with him. If we already agree with him, but have no more facts or reasons to support our point of view than he has, then we need to critically evaluate our own reasons for having the views we do. One of the primary reasons for reading a wide range of viewpoints is to acquire, broaden, and strengthen intelligent views of our own.

Too often we tend to accept the views of others we trust or admire without examining the logic or reasoning behind them. Many people practice the religion they do not because they have truly examined the creeds but because parents or friends are members of that religion. Many politicians have been elected to office not because they are the best qualified but because they make a good impression in public. Many countries have gone to war not because it was the right thing to do but because people were led to believe it was the only solution to a problem.

The next set of practices will help you develop your critical reading skills in these areas.

PRACTICE C-2: A Controversy: Should the Bible Be Taught in Schools?

Directions: Before reading the following selection, answer the questions that follow:

1. I believe that teaching the Bible in schools is

    a. important, because _____

_____

    b. unimportant, because _____

2. I believe in separation of church and state.

    a. Yes, because _____

    b. No, because _____

3. We should not talk about politics and religion in public.

    a. True, because _____

    b. False, because _____

Now read the following essay.

TEACH, DON'T PREACH, THE BIBLE

BRUCE FEILER

1   Yesterday's ruling by a federal judge that "intelligent design" cannot be taught in biology classes in a Pennsylvania public school district has the potential to put the teaching of the Bible back where it belongs in our schools: not in the science laboratory, but in its proper historical and literary context. An elective, nonsectarian high school Bible class would allow students to explore one of the most influential books of all time and would do so in a manner that clearly falls within Supreme Court rulings.

2   In the landmark 1963 Abington case (which also involved Pennsylvania public schools), the Supreme Court outlawed reading the Bible as part of morning prayers but left the door open for studying the Bible. Writing for the 8–1 majority, Justice Thomas Clark stated that the Bible is "worthy of study for its literary and historic qualities," and added, "Nothing we have said here indicates that such study of the Bible or of religion, when presented objectively as part of a secular program of education, may not be effected consistent with the First Amendment."

3   Though the far right may complain that this academic approach to teaching the Bible locks God out of the classroom, and the far left may complain that it sneaks God in, the vast majority of Americans would embrace it. But the devil, as some might say, is in the details. School board officials in Odessa, Tex., for example, have been embroiled in a running controversy over their choice of a curriculum for an elective high school Bible class. While the board's choice is now between two competing curriculums, pressure from civil liberties groups has prompted changes in even the more conservative alternative.

4   By helping to design an academic course in the Bible, moderates can show that the Bible is not composed entirely of talking points for the religious right. In fact, on a wide range of topics, including respecting the value of other faiths, shielding religion from politics, serving the poor and protecting the environment, the Bible offers powerful arguments in support of moderate and liberal causes.

5   In the story of David, the ruthless Israelite king who unites the tribes of Israel around 1000 B.C.E. but is rebuked by God when he wants to build a temple, the Bible makes a stirring argument in favor of separating religion and politics, or church and state to use contemporary terms.

6   In the Book of Isaiah, God embraces the Persian king Cyrus and his respect for different religions, even though Cyrus does not know God's name and does not

practice Judaism. By calling Cyrus "the anointed one," or messiah, God signals his tolerance for people who share his moral vision, no matter their nationality or faith.

7   In the Book of Jonah, God offers a message of forgiveness and tolerance when he denounces his own prophet and spares his former enemies, the Ninevehites, when they repent and turn toward him.

8   In recent decades, the debate over religion has been characterized as a struggle between two groups that Noah Feldman calls "values evangelicals," like Roy Moore, who placed the Ten Commandments in the Alabama Supreme Court, and "legal secularists," like Michael Newdow, who attacked the use of "under God" in the Pledge of Allegiance. This debate does not represent reality.

9   The Fourth National Survey of Religion and Politics, completed in 2004 by the University of Akron, shows that only 12.6 percent of Americans consider themselves "traditionalist evangelical Protestants," which the survey equates with the term "religious right." A mere 10.7 percent of Americans define themselves as "secular" or "atheist, agnostic." The vast majority of Americans are what survey-takers term centrist or modernist in their religious views.

10   These mainstream believers represent to their religiously liberal and conservative neighbors what independents do to Republicans and Democrats in the political arena. They are the under-discussed "swing voters" in the values debate who, the survey shows, are slightly pro-choice, believe in the death penalty, support stem-cell research and favor gay rights but oppose gay marriage.

11   Above all, they welcome religion in public life but are turned off by efforts to claim exclusive access to God.

12   At a time when religion dominates the headlines—from Iraq to terrorism to stem cells—finding a way to educate young people about faith should become a national imperative. Achieving this goal in a legal, nonsectarian manner requires Americans to get over the kitchen-table bromide, "Don't talk about politics and religion in public."

13   The extremists talk about religion—and spew messages of hate. Religious moderates must denounce this bigotry and reclaim Scripture as the shared document of all. When flamethrowers hold up Scripture and say, "It says this," moderates must hold up the same text and say, "Yes, but it also says this." The Bible is simply too important to the history of Western civilization—and too vital to its future—to be ceded to one side in the debate over values.

"Now answer the following questions." with the following head and text:

Comprehension Check

Answer the following questions.

1. Circle the best statement of the main point or thesis of Feiler's essay.
   a. The Bible should be taught in schools.
   b. The Bible should not be taught in schools.
   c. The Bible should be taught in schools as a historical and literary work.
   d. The Bible offers powerful arguments in support of moderate and liberal causes.

2. The author's basic intent is
   a. to persuade school boards to develop a Bible studies curriculum.
   b. to show that teaching religious faith in our schools should become a national imperative.

    c. to persuade religious moderates to denounce the bigotry of extremists' religious views and reclaim Scripture as the document of all.

    d. to show religious extremists and moderates that the Bible is too important to the history of Western civilization to leave out of a school curriculum.

3. The author's attitude is

    a. sarcastic.   **c.** sincere.

    b. condescending.   **d.** humorous.

4. The author's tone is one of

    a. anger.   **c.** concern.

    b. sadness.   **d.** sympathy.

5. The essay is mostly factual.

    a. True

    b. False, because_____

6. The author is biased toward the value of the Bible and its place in the school curriculum.

    a. True

    b. False, because_____

7. The author believes the Bible offers powerful arguments in support of both moderate and liberal causes.

    a. True

    b. False, because_____

8. What is the author's attitude toward publicly discussing politics and religion?

    _____

9. Is the essay mostly objective or subjective? Explain.

    _____

10. Explain how your own bias toward the subject may affect your reaction to the essay.

    _____

    _____

    _____

Vocabulary Check

Directions: Define the following words from the selection. The number in the parentheses is the paragraph in which the word appears.

    1. nonsectarian (1) _____

    2. landmark (2) _____

    3. embroiled (3) _____

    4. rebuked (5) _____

5. anointed (6) _____

6. evangelicals (8) _____

_____

7. secularists (8) _____

8. agnostic (9) _____

9. imperative (12) _____

10. ceded (13) _____

Record the results of the comprehension and vocabulary checks on the Student Record Chart in the Appendix. Each correct answer is worth 10 points for a total of 100 points possible for comprehension and 100 points for vocabulary. Make certain you understand any reading or comprehension problems you may have had before going on.

PRACTICE C-3: A Controversy: Should Religion Be Separate from Government?

Directions: As you read the following selection, look for the author's thesis, supporting points, opinions, intent, attitude, and tone. How does this author's opinion of the Bible differ from the previous selection, "Teach, Don't Preach the Bible"?

GODS ARE CREATED IN OUR OWN IMAGE

RANDY ALCORN

1   Because religion has been an essential part of man's psychology, priests historically have wielded tremendous influence in affairs of state. The principle of keeping religion separate from government is a rather recent development in human history, and some folks haven't quite caught up yet.

2   There is growing pressure from some Americans to involve religion more deeply and directly into secular policy. Recently, we have seen Catholic bishops threatening to excommunicate Catholic politicians who, when conducting governmental duties, do not adhere to the tenets of their faith. We have seen an Alabama Supreme Court justice lose his job over his insistence on keeping the Biblical Ten Commandments displayed in stone in the lobby of that state's courthouse. We have seen the previous president of the United States exercising executive fiat to draw the church and government closer together to affect public policy.

3   Perhaps this atavistic behavior is to be expected. As soon as human creatures developed self-awareness they developed religions. Religion is man's way of explaining the mystery of his own existence, and reflects his own hopes and fears. The prehistoric talismans of plumply pregnant women represented the importance of female fertility and mirrored the overwhelming concern prehistoric man had for survival of

his species. The gods of ancient Egypt ruled over the annual cycle of Nile flooding so vital to food production. Matters of life and death have long been considered the province of the divine, so why shouldn't the divine be dictating the affairs of men on earth?

4   There are those who staunchly believe this should be so, and while it is the right of every human to believe in the religion of his or her choice, it's not the right of any human to dictate religious beliefs to, or interfere with the harmless behavior of, others. The consequences of governing with or through religion include such horrors as human sacrifice, mass murder, torture, and a variety of state-sanctioned persecutions and confiscations.

5   One of the vexing problems with religion is there are so many of them, and the followers of all these mythical explanations of existence unquestionably believe in the absolute truth of their particular explanation. Even within a particular religion, like Islam or Christianity, there can be a multitude of denominations and sects all devoted to a unique version of the "truth" that makes all others "infidels."

6   Christianity and Islam are founded on remarkably malleable, if not inconsistent, ancient documents. The Christian Bible has a curious capacity for contradiction frequently condoning and condemning the same behavior. Its variety of interpretations has not only provided the genesis of a multitude of sects and denominations, but has also proved useful in supporting conflicting positions on many issues. Quoting the Bible to support one's position becomes a form of verbal fencing that can even be amusing, except when it enters the arena of public policy: then it can become oppressive, even deadly.

Reprinted by permission of Don Addis

Don Addis. Reprinted by permission of the St. Petersburg Times.

7   The debate on marriage rights for homosexuals now swirls in the swill cooked up when religion becomes a primary ingredient in public policy. Christians in politics assert that their Bible clearly labels homosexuality as sin and an affront to God. Therefore government should not recognize or even permit legal matrimony between same-sex couples. Some good Christians don't want same-sex couples adopting and raising children for fear that the "unholy perversion" of homosexuality will be propagated among the innocent young. Have children been any safer in the care of Catholic clerics?

8   When religion infects government a nation can suffer some weirdly irresponsible public policy. Recall James Watt, interior secretary under President Reagan, who when questioned about the alarming depletion of natural resources, including clean water, forests, and topsoil, cavalierly responded that it didn't matter because Jesus is coming back soon anyway. Coming back to what?

9   Perverse notions of morality based on religion certainly are not peculiar to Christianity. Muslim terrorists interpret their religion's doctrine in a way that justifies mass murder and suicide, even of children. Nations ruled by theocracies or "holy" laws, such as Iran and Saudi Arabia, can in good conscience punish, persecute, even murder in the name of God. In nations brainwashed by religious dogma, what greater claim to legitimacy can those in power have than to be enforcing the will of God?

10   Why would the omnipotent creator of the universe require that fallible mortals record and enforce Its will? Why wouldn't God just come grab us by the lapels and say, "Listen buddy, this is what I want you to understand"? That would quickly silence the cacophony of religious opinions and eliminate the interpreters.

11   At the least, Christianity ought to retire the Bible as its doctrinal document and replace it with a primer, "The Essential Jesus Christ," containing only the profound fundamentals of moral behavior as Christ taught them. Then, there might be fewer opportunities for conveniently idiosyncratic interpretations of God's will.

12   Too many Christians are better at preaching what Christ practiced, than practicing what he preached. Christian doctrine affords an excuse for this failure—Christ, after all, was not mortal; he was a god divinely capable of perfect moral behavior. Mere mortals can never be. What an accommodating abrogation of responsibility.

13   But then, the Christian god has a divine plan that allows Its flawed human creatures to freely decide which myth is the correct one. Guess wrong and the loving Christian god condemns Its creatures to eternal torment. The notion that the creator of the vast infinite universe, with all its miraculous interconnectivity and perfect balance, now amuses Itself by playing a deadly game of cosmic Jeopardy with sentient creatures on some speck of a planet is accepted as reality by many folks, including some who hold power in our government.

14   The human capacity for mass delusion can never be underestimated. Five centuries ago, most people, following the dictates of religion, believed the Earth was the center of the universe. What nonsense passes as divine truth these days?

15   Gods are created in man's own image, not the other way around. Responsibility for determining morality is ultimately our own, not derived from or deflected to mythical deities. Religious beliefs are personal, and all the conversions to faith, forced or voluntary, do not make a myth a fact. In a free, rational nation with impartial justice for all, religious myths should not determine public policy.

Comprehension Check

Directions: Answer the following questions without looking back. Try to answer using complete sentences.

1. What is Alcorn's thesis or main point? _____

   _____

   _____

2. The author's attitude toward those who wish to inject religious beliefs into govern-mental policy can best be described as

   a. tolerant.

   b. bitter.

   c. angry.

   d. cautionary.

   e. negative.

3. T/F Alcorn's intent is to show how religion is humankind's way of explaining the mystery of its own existence.

4. Alcorn asks, "Matters of life and death have long been considered the province of the divine, so why shouldn't the divine be dictating the affairs of men on earth?" How would he answer his own question? _____

   _____

   _____

5. Which of the following reasons does Alcorn offer as a way of showing the growing pressure from some Americans to involve religion more deeply into civil policy?

   a. Catholic bishops threatening to excommunicate Catholic politicians who do not conduct their governmental duties according to Catholic beliefs

   b. An Alabama Supreme Court justice losing his job because he insisted on keep-ing the biblical Ten Commandments displayed in stone in the lobby of the state's courthouse

   c. The president of the United States using executive powers to pull the church and government closer together to affect public policy

   d. All of the above

   e. None of the above

6. What is Alcorn's opinion of the Christian Bible? On what does he base his opinion?

   _____

   _____

7. Reread paragraph 9. What is the intent of this paragraph? _____

   _____

   _____

8. Reread paragraph 14. What is the intent of this paragraph? _____

   _____

   _____

9. According to Alcorn, what are some of the consequences of governing with or through religion? _____

   _____

   _____

10. Alcorn says, "Gods are created in our own image, not the other way around." Explain what he means. _____

_____

_____

Vocabulary Check

Directions: Define the following underlined words from the selection.

1. priests historically have <u>wielded</u> tremendous influence

_____

2. <u>secular policy</u>

_____

3. this <u>atavistic</u> behavior is to be expected

_____

4. founded on remarkably <u>malleable</u>...ancient documents

_____

5. a form of <u>verbal fencing</u>

_____

6. will be <u>propagated</u> among the innocent

_____

7. silence the <u>cacophony</u> of religious opinions

_____

8. might be fewer...<u>idiosyncratic</u> interpretations

_____

9. <u>abrogation</u> of responsibility

_____

10. playing cosmic Jeopardy with <u>sentient</u> creatures

_____

Record the results of the comprehension and vocabulary checks on the Student Record Chart in the Appendix. Each correct answer is worth 10 points for a total of 100 points possible for comprehension and 100 points for vocabulary. Make certain you understand any reading or comprehension problems you may have had before going on.

Put It in Writing

Directions: Pick one of the following questions, write a response, and turn it in to your instructor.

1. Of the two reading selections, "Shield Our Youth with Censorship" (page 231) and "Teach, Don't Preach, the Bible" (page 234), which author best supports his thesis? Support your answer with evidence from the reading selection.

2. How, if at all, have your opinions about the teaching of the Bible in public schools changed? What has either author said to change or support your opinion?

PRACTICE C-4: Timed Readings Comparing Two Authors

The next two reading practices offer opinions on the fate of newspapers. Editor and journalist Neil Morton argues that most people now get their news on the Internet and that newspapers are losing audience and influence. Arguing against this idea is Mark Briggs, an editor for the *Everett Herald*, a newspaper serving the northwest region of the state of Washington. Briggs believes that newspapers will continue to be indispensable. Time your reading on both practices.

An Argument against the Survival of Newspapers

Begin Timing: _____

ALL THE NEWS THAT'S FIT TO POST

NEIL MORTON

1   Growing up in Peterborough, Ontario (pop: 70,000), my parents, voracious readers, always had three newspapers delivered to their front door: the *Toronto Star*, the *Globe and Mail* (at the time, Canada's only national newspaper), and our local paper, the *Peterborough Examiner*.

2   This being the late '80s, meaning pre-web, the *Star* and *Globe* were my gateway to the outside world—to nearby Toronto, to Ontario, to Canada, to North America, to the rest of Planet Earth. My parents encouraged me to read them from cover to cover—"Not just the sports, Neil!"—and I did, including the Op-Ed pages on occasion.

3   As for the *Examiner* (for which, incidentally, novelist Robertson Davies served as editor and publisher in the 1940s, 1950s and 1960s), it was my resource for local politics (the heated planning board sessions were always exhaustively covered), entertainment (anything from local theater to bar fights that escalated into assault causing bodily harm charges) and sports, including the Ontario Hockey League's Peterborough Petes (and hey, once in a blue moon, me scoring 12 points to lead my Adam Scott Lions' b-ball senior team to victory).

4   Fast forward to 2002: My folks still turn to the papers as their primary source for news and analysis (they do go online, but it's primarily for email). Although I'll still buy a paper occasionally or grab one that's lying around the office (for Canadian news or a Canadian perspective on an international event), I don't turn to the papers much these days. For the most part, I rely on the Internet to let me know what's happening out there.

5   The *New York Times* on the Web, Slashdot, USAToday.com, Google News Headlines, NewScientist.com, Technology Review, Salon, CNN.com, Wired News, BBC.co.uk, Guardian Unlimited, Slate, LATimes.com, The Smoking Gun, PopBitch, Feed and Suck (when they were still alive and updating), the *Onion*, Modern Humorist and

an assortment of weblogs (Metafilter, Fark, Plastic, Shift.com's Filter section)—that's where I get my daily dose of news, analysis and humor.

6   I know many many others in their twenties, thirties and even forties who are in exactly the same boat.

7   So what does this all mean? Well, quite simply, it points to a significant shift—one that has many newspaper publishers squirming—away from papers as we know them. I fall in between the old and new vanguard of media in that I was raised on newspapers and am now weaning myself on the web, so I'm loyal to both. But a new generation is growing up on the net and for many of them, the print papers aren't even an option; even if they do read the papers, they tend to end up on the online version—adn.com, say, rather than the *Anchorage Daily News*—through a referral.

8   Newspapers have always been in the business of reporting news, breaking news, analyzing news, but now that job is done adequately, and with much more immediacy, on the Internet. For example, people flocked to the web in droves on 9/11 to learn everything they could about the disaster and to connect with others. Most of the print papers were light-years behind in their coverage of the biggest event of our generation—though some did put out special second editions that day, and of course their online versions were all over it.

9   Many 12- to 35-year-olds now view Salon and Slashdot as seminal news sources, news sources their parents likely haven't even heard of. With the net, now we go and find the news; editors and writers don't select the news for us. We go out and discuss various viewpoints on political events in threads and discussion boards rather than having them dictated to us by op-ed pages with their own agenda.

10   While many mainstream media outlets were feeding us their pro-U.S. version of the war in Afghanistan and American foreign policy, we could find blogs like Metafilter and Plastic discussing the flip-side of the coin and linking to superb articles at places like the *Guardian* that were giving us the Bigger Picture (for example, that the number of civilian casualties in Afghanistan has now overtaken the lives lost on 9/11).

11   There are countless other examples of what the web offers us that the print papers don't:

12   If you just couldn't get enough of the manslaughter trial of Boston hockey dad Thomas Junta, you could go to *Boston Globe* Online for expanded coverage. Similarly, for those that wanted more on the Gary Condit/Chandra Levy case last year, sites like WashingtonPost.com were the place to go. When Orlando Magic star Grant Hill went down with yet another season-ending injury late last year, hardcore basketball fans were able go online to get in-depth coverage of team—and community—reaction at OrlandoSentinel.com or ESPN.com. If you want to see celebrity divorce petitions for the likes of Pamela Lee, Janet Jackson and Michael Jordan, you can go to Smoking Gun.com.

13   The *Peterborough Examiner* has a tiny section called the Odd Spot on their cover page, which points to a ludicrous news story. Many other papers have similar sections. On the net, however, there's a gigantic and wonderful 24/7 Odd Spot at Fark. (For more info, take a look at Shift.com's recent profile of the blog.) Newspapers do a horrible job of covering videogames, now a mainstream phenomenon. On the Internet, there are plenty of webzines like GameCritics.com, Joystick101.org, RobotStreet Gang.com and Womengamers.com that are covering their cultural impact.

14   As a kid, I didn't have the option to turn to other sources for other viewpoints or peripheral information. I pretty much took as gospel what our national newspaper was saying. I thought the *Globe* was giving me 99 percent of the "news," but in truth, as I've discovered via the web, it's more like five to 10 percent of what's really going on. If I had had the choice to go online, I would likely have gravitated toward the Internet and away from the coffee table, like so many teens and young adults are doing now.

15   As cliché as it sounds, the world is your oyster on the net in the way it can never be in newspapers, which, by no fault of their own, have been overtaken by technology in the way radio was by TV.

16   Over the next 10 to 20 years—and this is a conservative estimate—newspapers will have to substantially re-invent themselves or they will perish. In some cases, maybe only the online version will exist; I already know many people—and this has to be considered a major concern among newspaper publishers—who used to buy or subscribe to a daily that now just check out the (free) online version. If the print version does survive, it will look much different—perhaps it will primarily be service-oriented, like a gigantic Life section or something.

17   Newspaper bigwigs are doing their strategizing behind closed doors, but they'll have to really have their thinking caps on. Soon, new wireless technologies will enable us to access the net whenever, wherever: in the kitchen, on the subway, on the toilet, at the cottage, in the car (an in-car web browser with text-to-speech synthesis can't be that far off), in the pool, at the Laundromat, at the hairdresser, on the treadmill. If I have the choice between reading a big clunky paper that leaves my hands stained with black ink and a portable Internet that offers insane amounts of legible news content and clean design, guess who's going to win out?

18   The web—still very much in its infancy but maturing rapidly as a new mass medium—is fast becoming the number one resource for news. It can disseminate information the way no other medium can. And that's where the next generation of Moms and Dads will be going with their morning cup of coffee.

Finish Timing: Record time here _____ and use the Timed Reading Conversion Chart in the Appendix to figure your rate: _____ wpm.

Comprehension Check

Directions: Answer the following questions without looking back.

1. Which of the following were Morton's sources of information in his youth?

    a. three newspapers

    b. television

    c. radio

    d. his hometown newspaper

2. T/F The author believes that people in their twenties, thirties, and forties get their news through the Internet rather than the newspaper brought to their doors.

3. T/F Morton's parents are gradually turning from the newspaper to the Internet.

4. T/F According to Morton, even if young people read newspapers, they do it on the Web.

5. T/F Most of the print papers are unable to keep up with the immediacy of current events as quickly as many sites on the Internet.

6. Which of the following are Internet sites Morton frequents?

    a. Salon

    b. Slashdot

    c. Metafilter

    d. Plastic

    e. BiggerPicture

7. T/F Many online newspapers, such as the *Washington Post* and the *New York Times*, offer expanded coverage on the Internet beyond what the print version offers.

8. T/F Morton admits that it will be a long time before the Internet offers what print papers do.

9. Morton bases his thesis mostly on

    a. facts.

    b. opinion.

10. What is the intent of the essay? _____

_____

Vocabulary Check

Directions: Define the following underlined words from the selection.

1. fights that <u>escalated</u> into assaults

_____

2. a Canadian <u>perspective</u> on an international event

_____

3. an assortment of <u>weblogs</u>

_____

4. Between the old and the new <u>vanguard</u> of media

_____

5. as <u>seminal</u> news sources

_____

6. which points to a <u>ludicrous</u> news story

_____

7. there are plenty of <u>webzines</u>

_____

8. would likely have <u>gravitated</u> toward

_____

9. as <u>cliché</u> as it sounds

_____

10. it can <u>disseminate</u> information

_____

_____

Record your rate and the results of the comprehension and vocabulary checks on the Student Record Chart in the Appendix. Each correct answer is worth 10 points, for a total of 100 points possible for comprehension and 100 points for vocabulary. Make certain you understand any reading or comprehension problems you may have had before going on.

An Argument for the Survival of Newspapers

Begin Timing: _____

VOX HUMANA

MARK BRIGGS

1   Television was supposed to kill the radio and the Internet was supposed to kill newspapers, so what happened? Most people today get some news from all four media, proving that Americans have an apparently insatiable appetite for news. More than 50 million newspapers will be delivered in the United States daily in 2001.

2   The past 100 years have seen great advancement at *The Herald*, and in newspapering in the United States. As we take time on *The Herald*'s 100th anniversary to look back, it's also worth a glance forward. We may not be able to accurately predict how (some would say if) newspapers will progress to the year 2101, but we do know *The Herald* and other newspapers will be around for many years to come.

A NEWSPAPER'S CORE MISSION

3   Technology will obviously be the greatest influence of change in newspapering in the future. But no technological advancement will change *The Herald*'s core mission: delivering timely, relevant, interesting and important news and advertising to Snohomish and Island counties. It will be the delivery of that news and advertising, however, that is likely to change the most through new technology.

4   Here's a look at where *The Herald* and the business of newspapering will travel during the next 100 years.

5   In five years: Currently, most newspapers publish a Web site that closely mirrors the printed newspaper. In 2006, there will be more reliance among readers on electronically delivered news content than today [2001].

6   The good news for readers is that news publishers will respond to this need, publishing their news for all kinds of wireless, digital and portable devices. The bad news is that the day of free content on the Web—or anywhere else in the wireless world—will have ended.

PAYING FOR CONTENT

7   News consumers will pay for content they receive—on the Web, on a cellular phone, on a handheld computer—but that content will be specifically tailored to their needs and tastes. The number of copies printed by news publishers will diminish, but the number of people who read the news and advertising will continue to grow.

8   Newspapers, TV stations and radio stations will have jettisoned their single-purpose identities and transformed into broad-reaching news companies. Internet and satellite radio will be common in new cars, forever changing the radio broadcast game in the same manner the World Wide Web altered the content publishing world in the late 1990s.

9   For newspapers, this will mean a new opportunity: to reach people in their cars. Newspaper reporters will routinely file audio reports of the stories they write for the paper. Around here, people will listen to *The Herald* in their cars and at work. We'll bring the newspaper to life.

10   In 10 years: The profession of news reporting became much more efficient with telephones, tape recorders and computers over the years. In the year 2011, the tools for news gathering will make the advent of the Internet look like the Stone Age.

11   Instead of a steno notebook and a pen, reporters will use a handheld, digital, wireless computer that will record interviews, shoot photographs, work as a cellular phone and connect to the Internet. This will be part of a 24-hour publishing cycle that will connect news consumers to the news.

12   With reporters wirelessly connected, readers won't have to wait for the morning paper to find out who won a high school football game or how the jury decided a big case. The morning newspaper will continue to be a valued product, however, since the immediacy of news consumption will not usurp the desire for great depth in news coverage.

CHANGING NEWSPRINT

13   In 20 years: Newsprint will evolve, finally, into a synthetically enhanced product that will look and feel just like the paper of the previous century. The Herald will install a new printing press that prints more efficiently on this new material.

14   The printing of newspapers will take only 20 percent of actual paper from trees. The rest will be manufactured out of a new-age plastic that is completely recyclable. To ensure the rate of recycling, *The Herald* will pick up old newspapers from subscribers' homes once a week, bringing the material back to the printing plant where the newspapers will be wiped clean and folded for reuse.

15   By cutting out the waste management companies in the recycling process, *The Herald* will dramatically increase the efficiency of the entire process. After years of electronic reader experiments that were supposed to doom the daily newspaper, subscriptions will increase dramatically with the introduction of this new synthetic "news-plastic."

A CENTURY FROM NOW

16   In 100 years: Will newspapers still exist in the year 2101? Yes, although you wouldn't recognize them today. Newsprint—and "news-plastic"—will be replaced by a reusable yet durable form of e-paper that will allow readers to "download" the new version of *The Herald* each morning as soon as they want it.

17   This e-paper will likely resemble today's newsprint: It will be flexible, foldable and very portable. Newspaper carriers will no longer go door-to-door each morning. Instead, they will deliver and service the electronic port machines that will receive and "print" the paper each morning. A subscription to *The Herald* will include this service.

18   The news will be gathered in fundamentally the same fashion, with professional reporters following leads, interviewing, researching and writing. It was essentially the same process in 1801, 1901 and today, in 2001, so there's no reason to think people won't desire well-reported, well-written and well-edited stories in 2101. The narrative story was with us long before newsprint, and it will remain with us long after.

19   Despite the challenges that newspapers have faced in recent years, including skyrocketing newsprint costs and massive mergers across the country, the newspaper is still the most respected source of news and information in the United States.

20   Will that ring true 100 years from now? Yes, but the process of printing the newspaper will change dramatically, and the ritual of walking out on the doorstep with a cup of coffee to pick up the morning paper will seem as antiquated as milk delivery on your doorstep seems today.

21   The year 2101 will be an even more wired world than the one we live in today, but *The Herald* will still be producing a product indispensable to those in and around Snohomish and Island counties.

Finish Timing: Record time here _____ and use the Timed Reading Conversion Chart in the Appendix to figure your rate: _____ wpm.

Comprehension Check

Directions: Answer the following questions.

1. T/F Most people today get their news from television, radio, newspapers, and the Internet.

2. T/F The core mission of a newspaper is to deliver timely, relevant, interesting, and important news and advertising.

3. T/F Only a few newspapers currently publish a Web site that closely mirrors the printed newspaper.

4. Which of the following does the author predict for the future?

    a. More people will rely on electronically delivered news.

    b. Free news content on the Web will end.

    c. The number of printed copies of newspapers will diminish, but the number of people who read news and advertising will continue to grow.

    d. Internet and satellite radio will be common in new cars.

    e. Newsprint will evolve into a synthetically enhanced recyclable product that will look and feel just like the present paper.

5. Briggs believes that in the year 2011, the tools for news gathering will make the advent of the Internet look like the _____

    _____

6. Instead of a steno pad and a pen, reporters of the future will use a

    _____

7. T/F In twenty years, newspaper companies will pick up old newspapers from homes once a week and recycle them, reducing the number of trees used for newsprint.

8. T/F Subscriptions to newspapers will increase in the next twenty years because of the introduction of a new synthetic "news plastic."

9. The "news plastic" will become outmoded in 100 years and be replaced by a durable but reusable form of _____ that will allow subscribers to download and print their paper each morning.

10. T/F In 100 years, newspapers will still be in demand because people have always wanted and always will want well-written and well-edited stories.

Vocabulary Check

Directions: Define the following underlined words from the selection.

1. have an <u>insatiable</u> appetite for news

   _____

2. a newspaper's <u>core</u> mission

   _____

3. more <u>reliance</u> among readers on electronically delivered news

   _____

4. will have <u>jettisoned</u> their identities

   _____

5. the <u>advent</u> of the Internet

   _____

6. will not <u>usurp</u> the desire for

   _____

7. reusable but <u>durable</u> form

   _____

8. the <u>narrative</u> story was with us long before newsprint

   _____

9. a product <u>indispensable</u> to readers

   _____

10. *vox humana*

    _____

Record your rate and the results of the comprehension and vocabulary checks on the Student Record Chart in the Appendix. Each correct answer is worth 10 points, for a total of 100 points possible for comprehension and 100 points for vocabulary. Make certain you understand any reading or comprehension problems you may have had before going on.

PRACTICE C-5: Put It in Writing

Directions: Pick one of the following to write about and turn in your paper to your instructor.

1. Summarize the two essays you read in Practice C-4: "All the News That's Fit to Post" (page 242) and "*Vox Humana*" (page 246). Then explain which essay best expresses what you think is the future of newspapers.

2. Discuss your newspaper reading habits. Do you read a newspaper regularly? Do you read newsprint or online news? What information are you most interested in reading? What value do you find in the newspaper? Do you care about the future of the newspaper?

Questions for Group Discussion

1. Discuss Briggs's predictions regarding the technological changes he thinks will be made ten, twenty, and a hundred years from now.

2. As a group, discuss your various newspaper reading habits. How many of you read the newspapers regularly? How many of you don't read the newspaper? How many of you use the Internet as your source for news?

On Your Own

If you have access to a computer, do one of the following:

1. Go to http://www.onlinenewspapers.com.

2. Type "newspapers" into a search engine and explore the list of results.

3. Type the name of your local newspaper in a search engine and see if it has an online version.

D.   Putting It All Together

The next two reading selections provide practice in using what you have learned in this and previous chapters.

PRACTICE D-1 – TIMED READING

Directions: Read the following newspaper commentary. Because this selection appeared in a newspaper, you will notice many one- and two-sentence paragraphs. Apply what you have learned about reading, looking for the author's thesis, intent, attitude, tone, facts, and opinions. This is a timed reading. Try to read faster than your last timed reading rate without a loss in comprehension. Record your starting time and your finishing time.

Begin Timing: _____

TALK, NOT TORTURE GETS THE INFORMATION

MATTHEW ALEXANDER (written under a pseudonym for security reasons)

1   He was only 12 years old, but he knew how to sling invective.

2   "You Americans are infidels, and you deserve to die." A skinny kid with a black head of hair and soft brown eyes, Naji had been brought to the Iraqi prison where I

worked as an interrogator after his parents were killed. They died when the suicide bombers they'd been hosting blew themselves up to avoid being arrested. But Naji didn't yet know that he was an orphan, and he was furious at having been captured by the Americans.

3   Steve, one of a team of interrogators who worked for me, responded to the boy's tirade politely.

4   "Don't you think we're all just people and we need to get along?" Steve asked, speaking through our interpreter, Biggie. Naji, who's name I have changed to protect his identity, shook his head violently.

5   "No," Biggie translated. "You're all infidel pigs! I can't wait until I'm old enough to cut your heads off!"

6   There is more than one approach to extracting information from a captive. Interrogators are often encouraged to use threats and intimidation—and even harsher methods. But my small group of Air Force investigators, along with several military and civilian interrogators on my team, were committed to a different way. We believed that interrogation methods based on building a relationship and on intellectual engagement were far more effective than intimidation and coercion.

7   As I watched the interrogation from the monitoring room, Naji's invective seemed almost funny coming from such a scrawny kid. But it was a sign of how thoroughly he had embraced the Al Qaeda propaganda he had heard at home. We had to hope he was not the face of Iraq's future.

8   "Do you know who this is?" Steve asked, showing Naji a photo of Abu Musab Zarqawi, the leader of Al Qaeda in Iraq.

9   "Of course, that is Abu Musab Zarqawi. He is our hero."

10   "Your hero?"

11   "Of course! When we play, the tallest, biggest kid gets to be Zarqawi."

12   In response to Steve's probing questions, Naji proudly explained that his father was grooming him to be a mujahedin and a future leader of Al Qaeda. He also said that his father took him to important meetings.

13   A veteran interrogator the night before had told us we "should show the little punk who's in charge." This was the attitude of many of the old guard, the interrogators who had been at Guantanamo Bay and in Afghanistan and Iraq early in the war, when the "gloves were off." They mocked those of us who didn't imitate their methods of interrogation, which were based on fear and control. There was tremendous peer pressure to follow in their footsteps and not appear soft on our enemies.

14   We ignored the pressure. We believed that, particularly with a child, interviewing rather than interrogation got better results. Steve had been trained in interviewing children, and he used those skills with Naji, gently stroking the child's ego and noting that he must have been a very important boy to have attended meetings. Soon, Naji started rattling off places where meetings had taken place. He detailed who was at the gatherings, how many guns were stored at the houses, what was discussed and what plans were made. Naji talked because Steve was sympathetic and made him feel good.

15   From the information he provided, it was clear that Naji's father had been a mid- to high-level Al Qaeda leader with connections throughout Yousifiya and Al Anbar province. By the time the interview ended after an hour, Steve had filled up pages in his notebook with detailed information about Naji's father's network.

16   Back in our office, Steve and I marveled at all the intelligence Naji had provided—the names, the locations. He'd pinpointed the better part of Al Qaeda's operations around Yousifiya. In the two weeks that followed, our soldiers put this information to good use and took out a significant portion of Al Qaeda's suicide-bombing network in the area. For two weeks, violence dropped and many lives were saved.

17   During my time in Iraq, I personally conducted 300 interrogations and supervised more than 1,000. Naji was the most committed Al Qaeda member I met during that time. He and his father, who had clearly joined the group because they bought into the ideology, represented a very small percentage of the Sunni Iraqis. The overwhelming majority of Sunni Iraqis I interviewed joined for other reasons—economic need, to meet tribal obligations or, most common of all, to get protection from Shiite militias.

18   I interviewed Naji twice during the week after his first interview. By the end of his stay with us, after we had coddled him, ensured his comfort and treated him with affection despite his contempt for us, he started to warm up. By the day before he left, his vituperative speech had disappeared completely.

19   Good interrogation is not an exercise in domination or control. It's an opportunity for negotiation and compromise. It's a common ground where the two sides in this war meet, and it's a grand stage where words become giants, tears flow like rivers and emotions rage like wildfires. It is a forum in which we should always display America's strengths—cultural understanding, tolerance, compassion and intellect. But that's not how all interrogators see their role.

20   According to a recent report from the bipartisan Senate Armed Services Committee, "The abuse of detainees in U.S. custody cannot be attributed to the actions of a 'few bad apples' acting on their own." The effects of the policy that allowed torture to happen at Guantanamo Bay, the report concluded, spread to Iraq through the interrogators who had first been at Guantanamo. The preference for harsh interrogation techniques was extremely counterproductive and harmed our ability to obtain cooperation from Al Qaeda detainees. Even after the old guard interrogators were forced to play by the rules of the Geneva Convention, there was still plenty of leeway for interrogation methods based on fear and control. I believe their continued reliance on such techniques has severely hampered our ability to stop terrorist attacks against U.S. forces and Iraqi civilians.

21   We will win this war by being smarter, not harsher. For those who would accuse me of being too nice to our enemies, I encourage you to examine our success in hunting down Zarqawi and his network. The drop in suicide bombings in Iraq at two points in the spring and summer of 2006 was a direct result of our smarter interrogation methods.

22   I used to tell my team in Iraq: "The things that make you a good American are the things that will make you a good interrogator." We must outlaw torture across every agency of our government, restore our adherence to the American principles passed down to us and, in doing so, better protect Americans from future terrorist attacks.

Finish Timing: Record time here _____ and use the Timed Reading Conversion Chart in the Appendix to figure your rate: _____ wpm.

Comprehension Check

Directions: Answer the following questions without looking back.

1. Which best states the author's subject?

    a. Al Qaeda propaganda

    b. Zarqawi, leader of Al Qaeda in Iraq

    c. the abuse of detainees in U.S. custody

    d. proper interrogation techniques

2. What is the author's thesis?

_____

_____

3. T/F The author's thesis is based mostly on facts.

4. What is the author's attitude toward his subject?

   a. angry

   b. outraged

   c. annoyed

   d. troubled

   e. serious

5. Which of the following best states the overall tone of the selection?

   a. frustration

   b. apathetic

   c. morbid

   d. concerned

   e. sarcastic

6. Who is Naji? _____

_____

7. Which of the following are examples of figurative language?

   a. a grand stage where words become giants

   b. tears flow like rivers

   c. emotions rage like wildfires

   d. made him feel good

   e. gently stroking the child's ego

8. T/F The author personally conducted 300 interrogations and supervised more than a thousand.

9. T/F The author and his group of Air Force interrogators were pressured by those who had conducted interrogations in Guantanamo Bay and Iraq prisons to go more gently in their interviewing techniques.

10. What evidence does the author point to as support for his team's methods of interrogation? _____

Vocabulary Check

Directions: Define the following underlined words from the selection.

1. knew how to sling <u>invective</u>

_____

2. you Americans are <u>infidels</u>

_____

3. the boy's <u>tirade</u>

_____

4. his father was <u>grooming</u> him to be

_____

5. after we had <u>coddled</u> him

_____

6. his <u>vituperative</u> speech

_____

7. was extremely <u>counterproductive</u>

_____

8. bought into the <u>ideology</u>

_____

9. plenty of <u>leeway</u> for interrogation

_____

10. restore our <u>adherence</u> to principles

_____

Practice D-2: Timed Reading

Directions: Read the following newspaper editorial. Apply what you have learned about reading, looking for the author's thesis, intent, attitude, tone, facts, and opinions. This is a timed reading. Try to read faster than your last timed reading rate without a loss in comprehension. Record your starting time and your finishing time.

Begin Timing: _____

WHAT'S ON TV TONIGHT? HUMILIATION TO THE POINT OF SUICIDE

ADAM COHEN

1   In November 2006, a camera crew from "Dateline NBC" and a police SWAT team descended on the Texas home of Louis William Conradt Jr., a 56-year-old assistant district attorney. The series' "To Catch a Predator" team had allegedly caught Mr. Conradt making online advances to a decoy who pretended to be a 13-year-old boy. When the police and TV crew stormed Mr. Conradt's home, he took out a handgun and shot himself to death.

2   "That'll make good TV," one of the police officers on the scene reportedly told an NBC producer. Deeply cynical, perhaps, but prescient. "Dateline" aired a segment

based on the grim encounter. After telling the ghoulish tale, it ended with Mr. Conradt's sister decrying the "reckless actions of a self-appointed group acting as judge, jury and executioner, that was encouraged by an out-of-control reality show."

3   Mr. Conradt's sister sued NBC for more than $100 million. Last month, Judge Denny Chin of Federal District Court in New York ruled that her suit could go forward. Judge Chin's thoughtful ruling sends an important message at a time when humiliation television is ubiquitous, and plumbing ever lower depths of depravity in search of ratings.

4   NBC's "To Catch a Predator" franchise is based on an ugly premise. The show lures people into engaging in loathsome activities. It then teams up with the police to stage a humiliating, televised arrest, while the accused still has the presumption of innocence.

5   Each party to the bargain compromises its professional standards. Rather than hold police accountable, "Dateline" becomes their partners—and may well prod them to more invasive and outrageous actions than they had planned. When Mr. Conradt did not show up at the "sting house"—the usual "To Catch a Predator" format — producers allegedly asked police as a "favor" to storm his home. Ms. Conradt contends that the show encourages police "to give a special intensity to any arrests, so as to enhance the camera effect."

6   The police make their own corrupt bargain, ceding law enforcement to TV producers. Could Mr. Conradt have been taken alive if he had been arrested in more conventional fashion, without SWAT agents, cameras and television producers swarming his home? Judge Chin said a jury could plausibly find that it was the television circus, in which the police acted as the ringleader, that led to his suicide.

7   "To Catch a Predator" is part of an ever-growing lineup of shows that calculatingly appeal to their audience's worst instincts. The common theme is indulging the audience's voyeuristic pleasure at someone else's humiliation, and the nastiness of the put-down has become the whole point of the shows.

8   Humiliation TV has been around for some time. "The Weakest Link" updated the conventional quiz show by installing a viciously insulting host, and putting the focus on the contestants' decision about which of their competitors is the most worthless. "The Apprentice" purported to be about young people getting a start in business, but the whole hour built up to a single moment: when Donald Trump barked "You're fired."

9   But to hold viewers' interest, the levels of shame have inevitably kept growing. A new Fox show, "Moment of Truth," in a coveted time slot after "American Idol," dispenses cash prizes for truthfully (based on a lie-detector test) answering intensely private questions. Sample: "Since you've been married, have you ever had sexual relations with someone other than your husband?" If the show is as true as it says it is, questions in two recent episodes seemed carefully designed to break up contestants' marriages.

10   There are First Amendment concerns, of course, when courts consider suits over TV shows. But when the media act more as police than as journalists, and actually push the police into more extreme violations of rights than the police would come up with themselves, the free speech defense begins to weaken.

11   Ms. Conradt's suit contains several legal claims, including "intentional infliction of emotional distress," for which the bar is very high: conduct "so outrageous in character, and so extreme in degree, as to go beyond all possible bounds of decency, and to be regarded as atrocious, and utterly intolerable in a civilized community."

12   Reprehensible as "Moment of Truth" is, it doubtless falls into the venerable category of verbal grotesquery protected by the First Amendment. The producers of "To Catch a Predator," however, appear to be on the verge—if not over it—of becoming brown shirts with television cameras. If you are going into the business of storming

people's homes and humiliating them to the point of suicide, you should be sure to have some good lawyers on retainer.

Finish Timing: Record time here _____ and use the Timed Reading Conversion Chart in the Appendix to figure your rate: _____ wpm.

Comprehension Check

Directions: Answer the following questions without looking back.

1. Which best states the author's subject?

    a. A televised arrest ending in suicide

    b. NBC's television program *Dateline*

    c. The First Amendment versus television censorship

    d. Television freedom

    e. Out-of-control reality television shows

2. Which best states the author's thesis or main idea about his topic?

    a. Some television shows intentionally go beyond the bounds of decency.

    b. The arrest of a suspect on the television series *To Catch a Predator* caused the suspect to commit suicide.

    c. The police often aid television producers in pursuing televised arrests.

    d. There is an ever-growing lineup of reality shows that appeal to an audience's worst instincts at seeing someone humiliated.

3. What is the author's attitude toward many reality television programs?

    a. favorable

    b. unfavorable

4. Which best describes the author's tone?

    a. humorous

    b. sarcastic

    c. serious

    d. playful

    e. angry

5. T/F The article is based mostly on supporting facts.

6. What is the author's opinion of the claims being made in Patricia Conradt's lawsuit?

    a. agrees

    b. disagrees

7. Which of the following are mentioned in the article?

    a. *The Apprentice*

    b. *The Weakest Link*

     c. *Moment of Truth*

     d. *To Catch a Predator*

     e. All of the above

8. To whom is the author referring when he says "The producers…appear to be on the verge—if not over it—of becoming brown shirts with television cameras…storming people's homes…"? _____

9. Why does the author believe the program *Moment of Truth* is deserving of censure?

_____

_____

10. T/F The author believes that the police should not take part in reality television shows.

Vocabulary Check

Directions: Define the following underlined words from the selection.

1. allegedly caught him

_____

2. cynical perhaps, but prescient

_____

3. humiliation television is ubiquitous

_____

4. depths of depravity in search of ratings

_____

5. prod them to more invasive actions

_____

6. the audience's voyeuristic pleasure

_____

_____

7. a coveted time slot

_____

8. First Amendment concerns

_____

9. regarded as atrocious

_____

10. it doubtless falls into the venerable category

_____

Be sure to record your rate and the results of the comprehension and vocabulary checks on the Student Record Sheet in the Appendix. Each correct answer is worth

10 points, for a total of 100 points possible for comprehension and 100 points for vocabulary. Understand any errors before you go on. Make certain you understand any reading or comprehension problems you may have had before going on.

Questions for Group Discussion

1. Discuss William Shannon's opinions about popular culture and its effects on youth (pp. 231–232). With what opinions do you as a group agree and disagree?

2. Discuss as a group your opinions about censorship. Is there a case for censorship? If so, under what circumstances?

3. Discuss Randy Alcorn's essay (pp. 237–239). On what issues does your group agree or disagree with Alcorn? Argue the pros and cons of Alcorn's last sentence.

4. As a group, see how many of you can use the following words in a sentence. Make certain you learn the ones you still may not be able to use or recognize by writing the definition in the blank space.

   a. escalated _____

   b. vanguard _____

   c. seminal _____

   d. ludicrous _____

   e. webzines _____

   f. disseminate _____

   g. insatiable _____

   h. usurp _____

   i. secular _____

   j. malleable _____

On Your Own

Pick ten new words you learned in this chapter, not necessarily those listed in question 4, and on a separate sheet of paper write a sentence for each word, using it correctly in context. Turn in the paper to your instructor.

CHAPTER SIX

Recognizing Inferences, Drawing Conclusions, and Evaluating Arguments

A.   Recognizing Inferences

All the skills you have been practicing in this unit are a basis for making critical judgments. You have been learning to recognize an author's attitude, intent, tone, and bias. Here's another important aspect of reading critically: recognizing **inferences**. An inference is a conclusion or an opinion drawn from reasoning based on known facts or events. For instance, when people smile we infer that they are happy. We base our inference on the fact that most smiles are from happiness or pleasure. A frown, we know from experience, generally means displeasure or pain. Thus, when someone frowns, we infer that the person is displeased. Our inferences are based on experience and/or knowledge. In his famous book *Language in Thought and Action*, S. I. Hayakawa defines an inference as "a statement about the unknown made on the basis of the known."

Drawing inferences is something we do every day. For instance, if you met a woman wearing a large diamond necklace and three platinum rings with rubies and pearls, you would no doubt infer that she is wealthy. You may not be right; the jewelry could belong to someone else or it could be fake. But because we know from experience that the type of jewelry she is wearing is expensive, it is natural to assume she is wealthy. It's a good educated guess based on experience and knowledge. Without experience or knowledge, however, any inferences we make are based on shaky ground.

Complete the following statements by drawing inferences from what is known in each case:

1. We may infer from a boy's crying and a melting ice cream cone on the ground that the boy _____

_____

2. We may infer from a woman's grease-stained hands and fingernails that she probably has been _____

_____

3. We may infer from the many whitecaps on the ocean that sailing would be _____

_____

4. We may infer from the way a man threw his food on the floor and refused to pay the restaurant bill that he was _____

_____

5. We may infer from an F grade on a test that we _____

_____

Let's look now at some of the possible inferences. In item 1, we can assume that the boy dropped his ice cream cone; however, we don't know for a fact that this is what happened. Someone may have knocked it out of his hands, or even thrown it at him. But based on the circumstances described, a good inference to draw is that he dropped it and is unhappy.

In item 2, we can infer that the woman has been working on something mechanical, such as an oily engine. Because we know that our hands and fingernails get greasy from such work, it's a good inference to make.

The circumstances in item 3 lead us to believe that sailing conditions might be rough, because whitecaps are caused by strong winds. However, a good sailor might like the conditions and think of it as a challenge. Of course, if you have never been around the sea, whitecaps might provide no information for drawing any kind of inference.

The man in item 4 might be angry, drunk, or "high" on something. We might further infer that he didn't like the food, didn't get what he ordered, or hated the service. Most of us don't make a habit of throwing our food on the floor and making a scene, so we can infer that something is greatly upsetting him to act this way.

In item 5, we probably infer that we failed. But is that technically an inference? The F grade is a symbol for failure. No inference need be drawn. But *why* did we fail? Maybe we didn't study hard enough, misunderstood the directions, or studied the wrong material; the test was a poor one; or the instructor made a mistake.

Drawing inferences while we read critically is no different from the kind of thinking done in the preceding examples. For example, read the following passage and then answer the questions that follow.

> If we compare college textbooks of just two decades ago with those of today, we see a dramatic decrease in the number of words, vocabulary level, and specificity of detail, but a sharp increase of graphics and, particularly, illustrations. Such textbook pictures can scarcely convey as well as words the subtle distinctions that emerge from scholarly or scientific work.

1. What is being compared in this paragraph? _____

   _____

2. What inference can be drawn about the author's attitude toward college textbooks today? _____

   _____

3. What inference can be drawn about today's college students? _____

   _____

Notice that the first question has nothing to do with inference, but it reminds you that in order to read critically you also have to use literal comprehension skills. The paragraph contrasts college textbooks of today with those published twenty years ago. In order to draw inferences, you have to understand that first. The answer to question 2 is that the author's attitude is negative. We can infer that because of the last sentence of the paragraph. The answer to question 3 is that today's college students' reading levels are probably lower than they were twenty years ago. Because of the decrease in words, lower vocabulary level, and more pictures, we can infer that today's students don't read as well. However, we could also infer that publishers are merely changing their way of publishing, but chances are that's not the author's intent here.

Here's a passage taken from a short story. Read it and answer the questions that follow.

> In walks these three girls in nothing but bathing suits. I'm in the third checkout slot, with my back to the door, so I don't see them until they're over by the bread. The one that caught my eye first was the one in the plaid green two-piece. She was a chunky kid, with a good tan and a sweet broad soft-looking

can with those two crescents of white just under it, where the sun never seems to hit, at the top of the back of her legs. I stood there with my hand on a box of HiHo crackers trying to remember if I rang it up or not. I ring it up again and the customer starts giving me hell. She's one of those cash-register-watchers, a witch about fifty with rouge on her cheekbones and no eyebrows, and I know it made her day to trip me up. She'd been watching cash registers for fifty years and probably never seen a mistake before. (From John Updike, "A & P" from Pigeon Feathers and Other Stories, Knopf, 1962. Reprinted by permission of the author and Alfred A. Knopf, a Division of Random House, Inc., Copyright © 1962.)

Based on the information provided, answer the following questions by drawing inferences:

1. How old and what sex is the narrator or person telling the story? What makes you think so? _____

   _____

2. Where is the story taking place? _____

   _____

3. People in bathing suits coming into the place where the narrator is working is not an everyday occurrence.

   a. True, because _____

   _____

   b. False, because _____

   _____

4. The narrator is not distracted by the girls.

   a. True, because _____

   _____

   b. False, because _____

   _____

5. The narrator is very observant.

   a. True, because _____

   _____

   b. False, because _____

   _____

As we find out later in the story, the answer to question 1 is "a nineteen-year-old male." But we can guess from the passage that the narrator is male because of his reaction to the girls, because of the language he uses, and because of his comments about the "witch about fifty" who catches his mistake. The tone has a youthful, informal quality about it.

In question 2, it's not too difficult to infer that the story is taking place in a supermarket of some type, probably a grocery store. He is working at a checkout slot ringing up HiHo crackers, and he comments that the girls were "over by the bread" before he saw them. These are clues to us.

The statement in question 3 is probably true, making the statement in question 4 false. He is distracted by the girls. No doubt girls come into the store all the time, but in this case they are wearing "nothing but bathing suits," making this an unusual event. It causes him to forget whether he has already rung up the crackers.

The statement in question 5 is true; he is very observant. His description of the one girl and the "cash-register-watcher" are full of details, reflecting an observant person.

The word *critical* often connotes finding fault with something. But making valid critical judgments, in its strictest sense, implies an attempt at objective judging so as to determine both merits and faults. Critical reading is thoughtful reading because it requires that the reader not only recognize what is being said at the literal level but also distinguish facts from opinions; recognize an author's intent, attitude, and biases; and draw inferences. A reader who is not actively involved is not reading critically.

PRACTICE A-1: Drawing Inferences

Part A

Directions: An inference, remember, is "a statement about the unknown made on the basis of the known." Complete the following statements, drawing inferences from what is known.

1. We may infer from the smile on the professor's face as he passed back the exams that _____

   _____

2. We may infer from the large turnout at our college orientation session that _____

   _____

3. We may infer from the fact that a student in a college English class is consistently late for class that _____

   _____

4. We may infer from the number of Academy Awards a movie won that _____

   _____

5. We may infer from the extreme thinness of some current models and actresses that

   _____

   _____

Part B

Directions: Read the following passages and answer the questions that follow.

1.   The word *concerto* originally meant a group of performers playing or singing together, as "in concert" or making a "concerted effort" of entertaining. The Gabrielis of sixteenth-century Venice called their motets, scored for choir and organ,

concerti ecclesiastici. Heinrich Schultz, a seventeenth-century German composer, titled his similar works *Kleine geistliche Konzerte.*

a. What is the intent of this paragraph? _____

_____

b. T/F The German word *Konzerte* probably means "concerto."

c. T/F We can infer that the author probably knows some history of music.

2.   He had a direct and unassuming manner and a candid way of speaking in a soft Minnesota voice. The interviewer rushed right in with questions, but he turned all the questions around and wanted first to know some things about the interviewer. She had a hard time getting the conversation centered on him until he was ready. He was a bright, insightful man who seemed oblivious to his genius.

a. What words best describe the man in the preceding passage? _____

_____

b. T/F The man is important or famous.

c. T/F The interviewer was impressed with this man.

d. T/F We can infer that the man is talkative and open.

3.   Infer as much as you can from each of the following statements:

a. The evening has proved to be most entertaining. I extend my deepest appreciation. _____

_____

b. Tonight's been a real blast! Thanks a bunch. _____

_____

c. Like, I mean, funwise, this night has blown me away, babe. _____

_____

4.   There are all kinds of rumors about Ed Cantrell. Some say he can ride a horse for days without eating and still bring down a man at a thousand yards with a rifle. Some say he is almost deaf from practicing every day with a .38. Others say he can quote long passages from Hemingway's novels. And still others claim he has the eyes of a rattlesnake and faster hands. Most all who know him claim he is the last of the hired guns.

a. What is Ed Cantrell's occupation?

_____

b. T/F Based on the rumors, most people seem to admire him.

c. T/F Cantrell probably lives somewhere in the Western states.

d. What can we infer about Cantrell if it is true that he can quote long passages from Hemingway's works? _____

_____

e. Why would a man such as Cantrell be interested in Hemingway's works?

_____

5.   During the Middle Ages, many scholars regarded printed books with apprehension. They felt that books would destroy the monopoly on knowledge. Books

would permit the masses to learn to improve their lives and to realize that no man is better than another. And not too long ago, slaves were strictly forbidden to learn to read and had to pretend that they were illiterate if they had learned how. Societies based on ignorance or repression cannot tolerate general education.

a. T/F The first sentence is fact.

b. What is the author's attitude toward education? _____

_____

c. What is the intent of the statement? _____

_____

PRACTICE A-2: Recognizing Inferences

Directions: Read the following passages and answer the questions that follow.

1.   "Social science" in cold print gives rise to images of some robot in a statistics laboratory reducing human activity to bloodless digits and simplified formulas. Research reports filled with mechanical sounding words like "empirical," "quantitative," "operational," "inverse," and "correlative" aren't very poetic. Yet the stereotypes of social science created by these images are, I will try to show, wrong.

Like any other mode of knowing, social science can be used for perverse ends; however, it can also be used for humane personal understanding. By testing thoughts against reality, science helps liberate inquiry from bias, prejudice, and just plain muddleheadedness. So it is unwise to be put off by simple stereotypes—too many people accept these stereotypes and deny themselves the power of social scientific understanding. (From Rodney Stark, *Sociology*, 2nd edition, Wadsworth, 1987, p. 28.)

a. The author's intent in this passage is to __ _____ _____

_____   _____

b. T/F We can infer that the author feels that some of his readers have a negative attitude toward social science.

c. T/F The author believes strongly in the scientific method of inquiry.

d. T/F The author is probably a social science teacher.

2.   On July 10, 1985, the following events worth reporting occurred around the world:

— An Israeli court convicted fifteen Jewish terrorists of murder and violence against the Arabs.
— Bishop Desmond Tutu, Nobel laureate, pushed himself through an angry mob to save an alleged police informer from being burned alive.
— An Iraqi missile struck and heavily damaged a Turkish supertanker.
— A ship photographer was killed when a Greenpeace protest ship was blown up in New Zealand.
— The Nuclear Regulatory Commission (NRC) was accused of not properly considering earthquake hazards at the Diablo Canyon, California, atomic energy plant.
— Numerous major fires in Northern California burned more than 300,000 acres of forests and destroyed many homes.

Yet the lead story of the day on two of the three major American television news broadcasts that evening had to do with the Coca-Cola Company's decision to return to its original formula after experimenting with a new taste that few seemed to like. Even the country's major newspapers featured the Coke story on their front pages at the expense of more newsworthy events. The headline of the *Denver Post*, for example, stated, "'The Real Thing' Is Back." In addition, a six-square-inch picture of a can of Coke in two colors appeared next to the column.

a. The intent of the passage is to _____

_____

_____

b. T/F The passage is mostly opinion.

c. T/F The author feels that the type of news reporting described reflects an erosion of values in our society.

d. T/F The author of the passage would probably agree with this statement: Coca-Cola has become a national institution of sorts and what it does is of interest to almost all Americans.

e. State the author's attitude toward the reporting he describes. _____

_____

3.   The United States Atomic Energy Commission, created by Congress in 1946, grew into a uniquely powerful, mission-oriented bureaucracy. One of its main goals, which it pursued with exceptional zeal, was the creation of a flourishing commercial nuclear power program.

By the late 1950s, the AEC began to acquire frightening data about the potential hazards of nuclear technology. It decided, nevertheless, to push ahead with ambitious plans to make nuclear energy the dominant source of the nation's electric power by the end of the century. The AEC proceeded to authorize the construction of larger and larger nuclear reactors all around the country, the dangers notwithstanding.

The AEC gambled that its scientists would, in time, find deft solutions to all the complex safety difficulties. The answers were slow in coming, however. According to the AEC secret files [obtained through the Freedom of Information Act], government experts continued to find additional problems rather than the safety assurances the agency wanted. There were potential flaws in the plants being built, AEC experts said, that could lead to "catastrophic" nuclear-radiation accidents—peacetime disasters that could dwarf any the nation had ever experienced.

Senior officials at the AEC responded to the warnings from their own scientists by suppressing the alarming reports and pressuring the authors to keep quiet. Meanwhile, the agency continued to license mammoth nuclear power stations and to offer the public soothing reassurances about safety. (From Daniel Ford, *The Cult of the Atom: The Secret Papers of the Atomic Energy Commission.* New York: Simon & Schuster, 1982). Copyright © 1982, 1984 by Daniel Ford. Reprinted by permission of Simon & Schuster, Inc.)

a. The intent of the passage is to _____

_____

b. Describe the author's attitude toward the AEC. _____ _____

_____

   c. T/F The passage is mostly opinion rather than factual.

   d. T/F We can infer from the passage that the author is probably not worried about the number of atomic energy plants that have been built and are being built.

   e. T/F The author implies that the AEC placed its own commercial desires over the safety of the American people.

   f. What is your reaction to this passage and why? _____

   _____

4.   Futurists generally assume that twenty-first-century medicine will include new and more powerful drugs and technologies to fight diseases. They tend to forget, however, the serious problems presently arising from conventional medication prescribed by the average doctor. According to 1987 statistics, the average American receives 7.5 prescriptions per year. This is even more frightening when we realize that many people have not been prescribed any medication at all. This means that someone else is getting *their* 7.5 medications.

   Most drugs have serious side effects, some quite serious. Since the sick person is often prescribed several drugs at the same time, there is often unfavorable reaction or illness from the drugs themselves. Studies also show that 25 to 90 percent of the time, patients make errors when taking their prescribed drug dosage. Despite the respect that people generally have for present-day doctors, there doesn't seem to be equal confidence in the treatments they prescribe because 50 percent of the time people do not even get their prescriptions filled.

   Homeopathic medicine (using natural means to help the body build immune systems) offers an alternative. Instead of giving a person one medicine for headache, one for constipation, one for irritability, and so on, the homeopathic physician prescribes one medicine at a time to stimulate the person's immune system and defense capacity to bring about overall improvement in health. The procedure by which the homeopath finds the precise substance is the very science and art of homeopathy. (From Dana Ullman, "Royal Medicine," *New Age Journal*, September/October 1987, p. 46.)

   a. The intent of the passage is to _____ _____ _____

   _____

   b. T/F The author's attitude toward conventional doctors and homeopathic doctors is equal.

   c. T/F The passage is mostly opinion.

   d. T/F We can infer from the passage that the author is biased against homeopathic medicine.

   e. T/F The author implies that many patients do not trust or want to take the medications prescribed by their doctors.

   f. Would you be willing to go to a homeopathic doctor rather than a conventionally trained physician? _____

   Explain. _____

   _____

   _____

   _____

   _____

B.   Recognizing Inferences and Facts

When inferences are based on facts, much useful information can be obtained. Scientists and historians, to name a few, have been able to infer from facts and observation most of the knowledge we have today. The following passage is based on fact, with many inferences that are probably true. As you read, note the inferences and the facts.

1   Nine hundred years ago, in what is now north-central Arizona, a volcano erupted and spewed fine cinders and ash over an area of about 800 square miles. The porous cinder layer formed a moisture-retaining agent that transformed the marginal farmland into a country of rich farmland.

2   Word of this new oasis spread among the Indians of the Southwest, setting off a prehistoric land rush that brought together the Pueblo dry farmers from the east and north, the Hohokam irrigation farmers from the south, and probably Mogollon groups from the south and east and Cohonino groups from the west. Focal points of the immigrants were the stretches of land lying some 15 miles northeast and southeast of the volcano, bordering territory already occupied by the Sinagua Indians.

3   Nudged out of their now-crowded corner by the newcomers, some of the Sinagua moved to the south of the volcano to a canyon that offered building sites and a means of livelihood. Here they made their homes.

4   Remains of the Sinagua's new homes, built in the early 1100s, are now preserved in Walnut Canyon National Monument; the cone of the benevolent volcano, in Sunset Crater National Monument; and part of the focal points of the immigrants, in Wupatki National Monument. (From the brochure *Walnut Canyon*, 1968-306-122/97, revised 1982, Superintendent of Documents, Washington, D.C.)

Now answer these questions.

1. T/F Paragraph 1 is mainly fact rather than inference.
2. T/F The first sentence of paragraph 2 is inference.
3. T/F The information in the last sentence of paragraph 2 is based on inference.
4. T/F Paragraph 3 is mostly inference.
5. T/F Paragraph 4 is mostly inference.
6. T/F Chances are that someday this information will prove to be in error.

The answer to question 1 is false; it's mainly inference based on facts or evidence that when put together leads scientists to believe that the events described happened eight hundred years ago. We have no way to prove that the eruption occurred as stated, yet scientists basically agree that this is what did happen.

The statements in questions 2 and 3 are true. Again, no one was around to verify these statements, but the inference that it happened can be made from present-day evidence.

While the statement in question 4 is basically true, at least the first part, the last part is fact because the remains are still there to see. The statement in question 5 is false, because all statements can be verified by visiting the places mentioned.

The statement in question 6 is false; it's possible, but highly unlikely because of present-day facts and remains. However, in the future, this might be a "slippery fact," like the atom's being thought of as the smallest particle at one time. But based on all the known facts we have at present, the best answer is false.

You can see that much of what we call "fact" today is based on inferences. When scientists agree on inferences that are drawn from what is known, we tend to accept as fact their conclusions until more evidence shows that the inferences drawn were wrong.

The following practices will help you recognize the difference between facts and inferences.

PRACTICE B-1: Drawing Inferences from Facts

Directions: Read the following passages and answer the questions that follow.

1.   The unit that is used to measure the absorption of energy from radiation in biological materials is the rem, usually abbreviated R. It stands for "roentgen equivalent in man." There is a unit called the rad, which corresponds to an amount of radiation that deposits 100 ergs of energy in one gram of material. The rem is defined as the radiation dose to biological tissue that will cause the same amount of energy to be deposited as would one rad of X-rays.

A millirem (abbreviated mrem) is one thousandth of a rem. To give some idea of the size of the things we are discussing, you get about 1 mrem of radiation from a dental X-ray, about 25 mrem of radiation from a chest X-ray. Since the average dose of radiation to the average American is about 360 mrem, it is not hard to see that it would be very easy to absorb in medical and dental X-rays more radiation than one absorbs from natural causes.

The "average" dose of radiation, of course, varies as much as 150 or so mrem per year depending on where one lives. For example, in Colorado and Wyoming the average mrem dose is about 250 per year, while in Texas the average dose is 100 mrem. It is higher in the mountains because there is less air to shield us from cosmic rays and because there are more radioactive elements in the soil.

According to federal requirements in effect, the radiation dose at the fence of a nuclear plant can be no more than 5 mrem per year. We can see that based on the average dose most of us receive, living near a nuclear plant offers relatively little dosage risk.

a.   The intent of this passage is to _____

_____

_____

b.   T/F The first paragraph is mostly factual.

c.   T/F Living in higher altitudes is safer from radiation doses than living at sea level, based on the information in the passage.

d.   T/F We can infer that the author is opposed to nuclear power plants.

e.   T/F The last sentence in the passage is factual.

2.   In the 1980s, in an ebullient bid to curtail drunk driving by teenagers, the government imposed a nationwide minimum drinking age of 21. It was a kind of second Prohibition, albeit for young adults only. The law's goal, of course, was to make young people happier, healthier, and safer.

By now it is obvious that the law has not succeeded in preventing the under-21 group from drinking. The popular press and higher-education media are filled with reports of high-visibility, alcohol-related troubles on our campuses. Serious riots by students who want to do their boozing unhindered have broken out at many institutions. Some of the melees, such as those at Ohio University, the University of Colorado, and Pennsylvania State University, have involved significant injuries and many arrests.

Reports of binge drinking come from all types of campuses across the country. In 1992, researchers reported that more college students were drinking to get drunk than their counterparts a decade earlier, and one recent study reported an increase, just since 1994, in the number of students who drink deliberately to get drunk. Of particular pertinence, in another national study, Ruth Engs and Beth Diebold of Indiana University and David Hanson of the State University of New York at Potsdam reported in 1996 in the *Journal of Alcohol and Drug Education* that, compared with those of legal age, a significantly higher percentage of students under age 21 were heavy drinkers.

Worst of all are the reports of drinking-related deaths. In 1997, at least two fraternity pledges died of alcohol poisoning, and in 1995 a third choked to death on his own vomit, all after initiation-night parties. One informal survey of alcohol-related deaths among college students during 1997 turned up 11 more fatalities: Three students fell from dormitory windows, one darted into the path of a motorcycle, one fell through a greenhouse roof, another was asphyxiated, and five died in highway crashes. At Frostburg State University, seven students were charged with manslaughter in 1997 in connection with the death of a freshman who guzzled beer and 12 to 14 shots of vodka in two hours at a fraternity party.

American's second experiment with Prohibition seems to have been no more effective than the first one. (From Document X3010 2152230, Opposing Viewpoints Resource Center, Gale Group, 2003. http://www.galenet.com/servlet/OVRC.)

a. The intent of this passage is to ___show readers that the law isn't working___

b. ⓣ/F The passage is mostly factual.

c. T/Ⓕ We can infer that the author believes the legal drinking age should be lowered from 21.

d. T/Ⓕ We can infer that the author believes the drinking age of 21 has driven college students to partying less in public and into more dangerous places.

3.   To understand the debate over global warming, it is important to understand the scientific concept known as the greenhouse effect. The greenhouse effect is a natural phenomenon involving the interaction of the sun's energy with atmospheric gases. After the sun's energy, or solar radiation, enters the atmosphere, the earth absorbs most of it while the rest is reflected back into space. Atmospheric gases, known as greenhouse gases, absorb a portion of this reflected energy. The energy trapped by these gases warms the planet's surface, creating the greenhouse effect. This natural process keeps Earth's atmosphere warm enough to support life. However, as the amount of greenhouse gases in the atmosphere increases, so too does the amount of heat they absorb: Global warming is the result.

The atmospheric concentrations of greenhouse gases have increased dramatically in the past century. Concentrations of carbon dioxide (CO_2), the primary greenhouse gas, have increased 30 percent, according to the Intergovernmental Panel on Climate Change (IPCC), a group of about 2,000 scientists from

116 countries assembled to address the problem of climate change. Concentrations of the other main culprits, methane and nitrous oxide, have risen 145 percent and 15 percent, respectively. At the same time, the average atmospheric temperature has also risen between 0.3 and 0.6 degrees Celsius. Most scientists agree that human activity is the cause of the rise in greenhouse gases, which are in turn responsible for global warming. Thus, in its definitive 1995 report, the IPCC concluded, "The balance of evidence suggests that there is a discernible human influence on global climate." (From Document X3010101223, Opposing Viewpoints Resource Center, Gale Group, 2003. http://www.galenet.com/servlet/OVRC.)

a. The intent of this passage is to _let you know that climate change is result of gl wrm_

b. (T)/F   The passage is mostly factual.

c. (T)/F   We can infer that the author is concerned with the increase of greenhouse gases in the atmosphere.

d. (T)/F   We can infer that the author agrees with scientists who claim that human activity is the cause for the increase of global warming.

4.   From the seller's viewpoint advertising is persuasion; from the buyer's viewpoint it is education. No single group of people spends as much time or money per lesson to educate the masses as do the creators of ads.

Ads participate in a feedback loop. They reflect a society they have helped to educate, and part of the advertising reflection is the effect of the advertising itself. Every ad that exploits a personality hole educates the audience toward using a particular product to fill that hole. Just as drug ads teach a crude and sometimes dangerous form of self-medication, psychosell ads teach a form of self-analysis and cure for psychological problems.

An ad that stirs a hidden doubt, that causes a person to ask, "Why does no one love me?"; "Why don't I have more friends?"; "Why am I lonely?" invariably goes on to suggest a partial cure—use our product. If an announcer for Pepsi would appear on screen and say:

> Are you lonely? Do you feel left out? Do you sometimes feel that everybody else has all the fun in life? Are you bored and isolated? Well, if you are, drink Pepsi and find yourself instantly a part of all those energetic, joyful, young-at-heart people who also drink Pepsi.

Such an ad would be greeted as either laughable or insulting by the viewing audience. Yet the old "Pepsi generation" campaign used pictures and a jingle to make exactly such a point.

The danger in psychosell techniques is not that people might switch from Coke to Pepsi in soft-drink loyalties or abandon Scope for Listerine. The danger is that millions learn (especially if the message is repeated often enough, as ads are) that problems in self-acceptance and boredom can be alleviated by corporate products. Which brand to buy is secondary to ads as education; the primary lesson is that the product itself satisfies psychological needs. (From Jeffrey Schrank, *Snap, Crackle and Popular Taste: The Illusion of Free Choice in America*, Delacorte, 1977.)

a. What is the intent of the author? _____

_____

b. Is the passage primarily fact or opinion? _____

Explain. _____

_____

c. T/F The author thinks ads may be silly and repetitive, but basically harmless.

Explain. _____

_____

d. T/F The author believes that some advertising is a dangerous form of education because it brainwashes us into thinking we can solve many of our personal
problems by buying corporate products.

Explain. _____

_____

e. T/F The author's bias is easy to identify.

Explain. _____

_____

PRACTICE B-2: Drawing Inferences from Descriptive Passages

Directions: Read the following passages and answer the questions that follow.

1.   Daddy's genial voice sometimes traveled slowly through sentences, shaping
each syllable correctly. He was polishing the skin of a second language. He would
come to speak it much more eloquently than most people who grew up speaking only English. Sometimes he slipped Arabic words into our days like secret gift
coins into a pocket, but we didn't learn his first language because we were too busy
learning our own. I regret that now.

When someone else who spoke Arabic came to visit us, their language ignited
the air of our living room, dancing, dipping and whirling. I would realize: all those
sounds had been waiting inside our father! He carried a whole different world of
sounds—only now did they get to come out! (From Naomi Shihab Nye, "Wealthy
with Words," *The Most Wonderful Books,* Milkweed Editions, 1997, p. 193.)

a. T/F We can infer that the author's father's first language was Arabic.

b. T/F We can infer that her father learned to speak English well.

c. T/F We can infer that the author did not like the sound of Arabic being
spoken.

d. T/F The author is bilingual.

e. What do you infer about the author's view of language? _____ likes it _____

2.   My van (and the passage of nearly 200 years) had made my journey both faster
and easier than theirs. For much of their journey west—as they fought the Missouri's relentless current for its entire 2,400-mile length, then trudged through the
snowy Bitterroot Range—Lewis and Clark would have defined substantial progress
as making 12 miles a day. Shooting down the Snake and Columbia Rivers in their

dugout canoes for the final stretch must have seemed like hyperdrive, although in fact it only increased their speed to 30 or 40 miles per day. No wonder it took them a year and a half to reach Cape Disappointment. Allowing plenty of time for unhurried stops and side trips, my camper covered the same distance in 60 days.

Needless to say, I also hadn't suffered the hardships the Corps of Discovery routinely faced: backbreaking toil, loss of a comrade to illness, encounters with enraged grizzlies, near-starvation in the ordeal across the Bitterroots, demoralizing coastal rains that rotted the clothes on their backs, and so much more. They had been making history; I was merely retracing it. (From Dayton Duncan, "American Odyssey," *Land's End Catalog*, July/August 2003.)

a. (T)/F We can infer that the author followed the same route as the Lewis and Clark expedition in the early 1800s.

b. (T)/F We can infer that the author admires what the Corps of Discovery went through.

c. T/(F) The author feels proud of himself for having retraced the Corps of Discovery's route in only sixty days.

d. What do you infer about the author, based on this passage? _____

_____

3. With that thought in mind, I raised my head, squared my shoulders, and set off in the direction of my dorm, glancing twice (and then ever so discreetly) at the campus map clutched in my hand. It took everything I had not to stare when I caught my first glimpse of a real live football player. What confidence, what reserve, what muscles! I only hoped his attention was drawn to my air of assurance rather than to my shaking knees. I spent the afternoon seeking out each of my classrooms so that I could make a perfectly timed entrance before each lecture without having to ask dumb questions about its whereabouts.

The next morning I found my first class and marched in. Once I was in the room, however, another problem awaited me. Where to sit? ... After much deliberation I chose a seat in the first row and to the side. I was in the foreground (as advised), but out of the professor's direct line of vision.

I cracked my anthology of American literature and scribbled the date on the top of the crisp ruled page. "Welcome to Biology 101," the professor began. A cold sweat broke out at the back of my neck. (From Evelyn Herald, "Fresh Start," *Nutshell* magazine, 1989.)

a. Where can we infer that the event described in the passage is taking place?
_____ first day of college _____
How can you tell? _____ dorms _____
_____

b. (T)/F The narrator telling the story is female. Explain. _____

_____

c. (T)/F We can infer from the author's tone that the author has a sense of humor. Explain. _____ _____

_____

d. Why did the author break out in a cold sweat when the professor greeted the class? _____Wrong class_____

_____

e. T/F We can infer that the author is not trying to conceal her true feelings. Explain. _____

_____

C.   Drawing Conclusions Using Induction and Deduction

A big part of critical reading is being able to draw conclusions based on the information authors provide. Once you understand the thesis or main idea of a reading selection, recognize fact from opinion, and understand intent, attitude, and inference, you almost automatically draw conclusions of your own. In fact, some of the questions you have been answering in the preceding practices require drawing conclusions based on the evidence provided.

Drawing conclusions is based on making **reasoned judgments**. Reasoned judgments usually come from two basic methods of reasoning: **deductive reasoning** and **inductive reasoning**. Deductive reasoning occurs when you begin with a general statement of truth and infer a conclusion about a particular specific. For instance, the old standby definition of deductive reasoning is shown through a **syllogism**, a three-step statement that begins with a general statement recognized as a truth and moves to a specific statement:

> All humans are mortal.
> Britney Spears is a human.
> Therefore, Britney Spears is mortal.

Deductive reasoning is the subject of formal logic courses and involves a process of stating a series of carefully worded statements, such as the example just given, each related to the other statements. Deductive reasoning begins with a generalization:

> All dogs are animals.   *or*   Athletes are physically strong.

The next statement identifies something as belonging (or not belonging) to that class:

> _____ is a dog.

What would be a second statement for the athlete generalization?

_____

For the first example, you should have given the name of a dog you know or a famous dog. For example, Lassie is a dog. For the second statement, you should have named an athlete. "Lance Armstrong is an athlete" would be one example.

The third statement of deductive reasoning is the inference you arrive at if the first two statements are true:

All dogs are animals.	Athletes are physically strong.
Lassie is a dog.	Lance Armstrong is an athlete.
Lassie is an animal.	Lance Armstrong is physically strong.

Fully understanding deductive reasoning takes a lot of study but, for the purpose of this introduction, you should be aware that you start with a generalization and use a careful reasoning process to arrive at a conclusion.

You can make errors with deductive reasoning if you start with faulty generalizations or premises. If you started with the generalization that "all college students have high IQs," you would be starting with a false premise. Some college students have high IQs; others may be conscientious workers with average IQs.

Inductive reasoning works in the opposite way of deductive reasoning. With inductive reasoning, you begin with observing specifics and draw a general conclusion. You might move to a new town and notice that every time you see police officers they are wearing bright green uniforms. After seeing no police officer wearing anything other than this color, you might inductively reason that in this particular town the official police uniform is bright green.

Inductive reasoning is often used when you can't examine all the data but need to come to conclusions based on what you know. Political polls do this when they look at some voters and base conclusions on what "the people" want by that sample. You may come to inductive conclusions based on sensory observations (what you see or hear), lists or groups, cause-effect thinking, or pattern recognition.

Sensory observation: Using your eyes, ears, taste, touch, or smell involves sensory observation. The police uniform example in the previous paragraph is an example of sensory observation.

Lists or enumeration: Often we look at lists of items and come to conclusions based on those lists. You may look at lists of what prevents heart problems and conclude that you will not smoke and will exercise every day.

Cause-effect: When two events happen, we may decide that the first one was the cause of the second one (effect). Historians use this kind of reasoning. Cause-effect thinking means you notice that every time you run a red light, you are almost in an accident. The cause (running the red light) has a certain effect (near accident).

Pattern recognition: Pattern recognition involves looking at parts and drawing conclusions. A professor may notice one student who is rarely in class, doesn't turn in work, and flunks the midterm. That professor is likely to conclude that the student is a poor college student.

The conclusion you draw in inductive reasoning is usually called a hypothesis. Scientists use this method all the time.

As with deductive reasoning, you can make many errors with inductive reasoning. Some of these are listed in Practice C-3 of this chapter and include such obvious errors as oversimplification and using the wrong facts to come to your conclusion.

Perhaps the best way to explain these two types of reasoning is to quote Robert M. Pirsig in a passage from his book *Zen and the Art of Motorcycle Maintenance*:

> If the cycle goes over a bump and the engine misfires, and then goes over another bump and the engine misfires, and then goes over another bump and the engine misfires, and then goes over a long smooth stretch of road and there is no misfiring, and then goes over a fourth bump and the engine misfires again, one can logically conclude that the misfiring is caused by the bumps. That is induction: reasoning from particular experiences to general truths.

Deductive inferences do the reverse. They start with general knowledge and predict a specific observation. For example if, from reading the hierarchy of facts about the machine, the mechanic knows the horn on the cycle is powered exclusively by electricity from the battery, then he can logically infer that if the battery is dead the horn will not work. That is deduction. (From Robert M. Pirsig, *Zen and the Art of Motorcycle Maintenance,* Morrow, 1974, p. 107.)

We use these two types of reasoning every day, often without even knowing it.

To look more closely at how we draw conclusions, read the following passage and then answer the questions that follow.

In 1832, a twenty-four-old Englishman named Charles Darwin, aboard the HMS Beagle on a surveying expedition around the world, was collecting beetles in a rain forest near Rio de Janeiro. In one day, in one small area, he found over sixty-eight different species of small beetles. That there could be such a variety of species of one kind of creature astounded him. In his journal he wrote that such a find "… is sufficient to disturb the composure of an entomologist's mind…." The conventional view of his day was that all species were unchangeable and that each had been individually and separately created by God. Far from being an atheist, Darwin had taken a degree in divinity in Cambridge. But he was deeply puzzled by his find. (Adapted from James Burke, *The Day the Universe Changed,* Little, Brown, 1985, p. 267.)

1. T/F We can draw the conclusion that Darwin was not actually out searching for what he found.

2. T/F The evidence provided for our conclusion is based partly on Darwin's journal.

3. T/F What Darwin discovered was contrary to the beliefs of his day.

4. T/F Darwin's later "theory of evolution," that species were not fixed forever, probably began with his discovery about the beetle.

All of the answers to these questions are true. Based on his journal statement that the find was "sufficient to disturb" his composure, the statement that he was "deeply puzzled," and the fact that what he found was contrary to what he had been taught to believe all provide evidence to support our conclusions that he was not looking for what he found.

Even though no one living today was with Darwin in 1832, his journal notes leave evidence to help answer question 2 as true. As to question 3, if Darwin had a degree in divinity from Cambridge, he would have been taught to believe what was accepted as "fact" in his day: that God individually and separately created all species. The fact that he found sixty-eight different species is contrary to such a belief.

The statement in question 4 is true, but unless you know what Charles Darwin's "theory of evolution" is, you might have difficulty drawing such a conclusion. If you know that he continued to pursue the suspicion in his mind that all species were not fixed forever, and that he eventually wrote *On the Origin of Species by Means of Natural Selection,* then there's no problem in answering this question as true.

The following practices are designed to help you develop your ability to draw conclusions from what you read.

PRACTICE C-1: Drawing Conclusions from Paragraphs

Directions: Read the following paragraphs and answer the questions that follow.

1.　Look for a moment at the situation in those nations that most of us prefer to label with the euphemism "underdeveloped," but which might just as accurately be described as "hungry." In general, underdeveloped countries (UDCs) differ from developed countries (DCs) in a number of ways. UDCs are not industrialized. They tend to have inefficient, usually subsistence agricultural systems, extremely low gross national products and per capita incomes, high illiteracy rates, and incredibly high rates of population growth.... Most of these countries will never, under conceivable circumstance, be "developed" in the sense in which the United States is today. They could accurately be called "never-to-be-developed" countries. (From Paul Ehrlich and Anne Ehrlich, *Ecoscience: Population, Resources and Environment*, Freeman, 1977.)

   a. The intent of the passage is to _____

   _____

   b. T/F The authors of the passage have drawn the conclusion that UDCs exist because they are not industrialized and have poor agricultural systems, high illiteracy rates, low incomes, and too much population growth.

   c. T/F If a UDC has a population growth that is too high for its agricultural system, we can draw the conclusion that it will never become a DC.

   d. T/F We can draw the conclusion from the information in the passage that the authors feel UDCs can eventually become DCs.

   e. Identify what kind of reasoning (inductive or deductive) is required to answer question 1 (d). _____

   _____

2.　Science is sometimes confused with technology, which is the application of science to various tasks. Grade-school texts that caption pictures of rockets on the moon with the title, "Science Marches On!" aid such confusion. The technology that makes landing on the moon possible emerged from the use of scientific strategies in the study of propulsion, electronics, and numerous other fields. It is the mode of inquiry that is scientific; the rocket is a piece of technology.

   Just as science is not technology, neither is it some specific body of knowledge. The popular phrase "Science tells us that smoking is bad for your health" really misleads. "Science" doesn't tell us anything; people tell us things, in this case people who have used scientific strategies to investigate the relationship of smoking to health. Science, as a way of thought and investigation, is best conceived of as existing not in books, or in machinery, or in reports containing numbers, but rather in that invisible world of the mind. Science has to do with the way questions are formulated and answered; it is a set of rules and forms for inquiry created by people who want reliable answers. (From Kenneth R. Hoover, *The Elements of Social Scientific Thinking*, 3rd edition, St. Martin's, 1984, pp. 4–5.)

   a. The intent of the passage is to _____

   _____

b. T/F According to the author, some grade-school textbooks contribute to the confusion between science and technology.

c. T/F The author does not think there is much difference between the terms *science* and *technology*.

d. T/F The author does not believe that science is something that cannot be written down.

e. T/F The author would agree with the statement, "Science has proven that too much sun causes skin cancer."

f. T/F The author has respect for scientific thinking.

g. What kind of reasoning (inductive or deductive) did you use to answer question 2 (f)? _____

_____

3.   Some years ago, I ran into an economist friend at the University of Michigan in Ann Arbor who told me, with concern bordering on shock, that assembly-line workers at the nearby Ford plant in Dearborn were making more money than an assistant professor at the University. It occurred to me that quite a few at Ford might prefer the more leisured life of a young professor: Certainly there seemed no need to fear any major movement of academic talent from Ann Arbor to the noisome shops in Dearborn. (From John Kenneth Galbraith, "When Work Isn't Work," *Parade*, February 10, 1985.)

a. T/F The author's economist friend believes that a university professor should be paid more than an assembly-line worker.

b. T/F The author agrees with his friend.

c. T/F The author feels that a university professor's work is easier than factory work.

d. T/F Because the pay is better for factory work, many professors will probably leave the university to seek factory jobs.

e. T/F The author probably believes that the usual definition of *work* can be misleading when comparing various types of jobs.

4.   Almost everyone in the middle class has a college degree, and most have an advanced degree of some kind. Those of us who can look back to the humble stations of our parents or grandparents, who never saw the inside of an institution of higher learning, can have cause for self-congratulation. But—inevitably but—the impression that our general populace is better educated depends on an ambiguity in the meaning of the word education, or fudging of the distinction between liberal and technical education. A highly trained computer specialist need not have any more learning about morals, politics or religion than the most ignorant of persons.... It is not evident to me that someone whose regular reading consists of *Time, Playboy* and *Scientific American* has any profounder wisdom about the world than the rural schoolboy of yore with his McGuffey's reader. (From Allan Bloom, *The Closing of the American Mind*, Simon and Schuster, 1987, p. 59.)

a. T/F The author believes that the general public today is better educated than before.

b. T/F The "McGuffey's reader" must have been a widely used textbook in schools at one time.

c. T/F The author believes that learning about morals, politics, and religion is not the function of institutions of higher learning.

    d. T/F The author favors a technical education over a liberal one.

    e. T/F The passage suggests that the author is pleased with the direction education is taking and thinks it is much better than it was in his grandparents' day.

    f. Identify the type of reasoning (*inductive* or *deductive*) the author uses to come to his conclusion. _____

PRACTICE C-2: Arguments and Responses

Directions: The legal drinking age in the United States is 21. Some people want to lower the age, in most cases to age 18. Presented here are some argumentative statements or claims as reasons for lowering the legal age to 21. Responses to those arguments follow. Read each argument and response, then answer the questions that follow.

Statement 1

Argument

Lowering the drinking age will reduce the allure of alcohol as a "forbidden fruit" for minors.

Response

Lowering the drinking age will make alcohol more available to an even younger population, replacing "forbidden fruit" with "low-hanging fruit."

The practices and behaviors of 18-year-olds are particularly influential on 15–17-year-olds. If 18-year-olds get the OK to drink, they will be modeling drinking for younger teens. Legal access to alcohol for 18-year-olds will provide more opportunities for younger teens to obtain it illegally from older peers.

Age-21 has resulted in decreases, not increases in youth drinking, an outcome inconsistent with an increased allure of alcohol. In 1983, one year before the National Minimum Purchase Age Act was passed, 88% of high school seniors reported any alcohol use in the past year and 41% reported binge drinking. By 1997, alcohol use by seniors had dropped to 75% and the percentage of binge drinkers had fallen to 31%. (From Opposing Viewpoints Resource Center, document X3010084223, http://www.galenet.galegroup.com/servlet/OVRC.)

    a. The argument for lowering the drinking age uses the term "forbidden fruit." Explain what is meant. _____

        _____

    b. T/F The argument is based mostly on fact.

    c. T/F The response to the argument is based mostly on facts.

    d. Draw your own reasoned conclusion on the argument. If you support the argument, what reasons do you have? _____

        _____

        _____

Statement 2

Argument

At 18, kids can vote, join the military, sign contracts, and even smoke. Why shouldn't they be able to drink?

Response

Ages of initiation vary—one may vote at 18, drink at 21, rent a car at 25, and run for president at 35. These ages may appear arbitrary, but they take into account the requirements, risks, and benefits of each act.

When age-21 was challenged in Louisiana's State Supreme Court, the Court upheld the law, ruling that "statutes establishing the minimum drinking age at a higher level than the age of majority are not arbitrary because they substantially further the appropriate governmental purpose of improving highway safety, and thus are constitutional."

Age-21 laws help keep kids healthy by postponing the onset of alcohol use. Deferred drinking reduces the risks of:

- developing alcohol dependence or abuse later in life.
- harming the developing brain.
- engaging in current and adult drug use.
- suffering alcohol-related problems, such as trouble at work, with friends, family, and police. (From Opposing Viewpoints Resource Center, document X3010084223, http://www.galenet.galegroup.com/servlet/OVRC.)

    a. T/F As stated, the argument is mostly opinion.

    b. Explain why you agree or disagree with the argument. _____

_____

    c. T/F The response uses more facts than opinions.

    d. State your own conclusion regarding the argument and what reasoning you used. _____

_____

Statement 3

Argument

Minors still drink, so age-21 laws clearly don't work.

Response

Age-21 laws work. Young people drink less in response. The laws have saved an estimated 17,000 lives since states began implementing them in 1975, and they've decreased the number of alcohol-related youth fatalities among drivers by 63% since 1982.

Stricter enforcement of age-21 laws against commercial sellers would make those laws even more effective at reducing youth access to alcohol. The ease with which young people acquire alcohol—three-quarters of 8th graders say that it is "fairly easy" or "very easy" to get—indicates that more must be done. Current laws against sales to minors need stiff penalties to deter violations. Better education and prevention-oriented laws are needed to reduce the commercial pressures on kids to drink. (From Opposing Viewpoints Resource Center, document X3010084223, http://www.galenet.galegroup.com/servlet/OVRC.)

    a. T/F As stated, the argument is mostly opinion, but true.

    b. Explain why you agree or disagree with the argument. _____

_____

    c. T/F The response uses more facts than opinions.

    d. State your own conclusion regarding the argument and what reasoning you used.

Questions for Group Discussion

1. As a group, discuss your views on lowering the drinking age. Are your views and conclusions based on reasoned judgment? Review pages 274–276 on reasoning.

2. Of late, "binge drinking" on college campuses has received widespread coverage. Does this occur on your campus? Why does drinking seem to attract many students?

3. If your group has access to the online Opposing Viewpoints Research Center, go there and read the article "The Drinking Age Should Be Lowered" by Michael Clay Smith and compare it with what you just read. Is it mostly facts or opinions? Is the argument based on reasoned judgments?

Logical Fallacies

Of course, we can make mistakes in our reasoning. Sometimes we make statements that draw the wrong conclusions. These are called **logical fallacies**. Here are some of the more common fallacies that you should avoid making and that you should look for when you are reading:

1. *Either-or thinking* or *oversimplification* occurs when a simplistic answer is given to a large problem: "You want to get rid of abortion clinics? Let's blow them up." Either-or thinking is also oversimplifying issues: "Let's either get rid of all the nuclear weapons in the world, or learn to live with the bomb." Such thinking ignores or covers up other possible answers to a problem.

2. *Stereotyping* ignores individuality. There are stereotypes about political parties (Republicans are pro-rich people; Democrats are pro-poor people), stereotypes about Jews (they always look for bargains), stereotypes about blacks (they are better athletes), and so on. Stereotyping disallows looking at people, groups, or ideas on individual merit.

3. *Attacking a person's character* (the Latin term for this reasoning is *ad hominem*) to discredit someone's views is also a faulty way to reason: "Sure, Senator Nicely favors a bill to stop acid rain from being carried to Canada. Why shouldn't he? He owns a big farm in Canada and probably plans to retire there."

4. *Non sequiturs* (just a fancy Latin name for "it does not follow") occur when a logical reason is not provided for the argument being made. It's a contradiction when a person says, "Clint Eastwood would make a good president; his Dirty Harry movies show you how tough he'd be on crime." The two assertions don't logically follow, since one has nothing to do with the other.

5. *Arguments because of doubtful sources* occur when an unknown source or a source lacking authority is cited: "The government doesn't want us to know about UFOs, but the *National Enquirer* has been providing a lot of evidence that proves contrary." While it might be true that the government is hiding something, the *National Enquirer*'s reputation for sensationalism does not make it a good source to use as a convincing argument. Also, be careful when you read that a story comes from an unnamed "high-level official."

6. *Begging the question* occurs when an argument uses circular reasoning. An argument is circular if its premise assumes that its central point is already proven and uses this in support of itself. Arguing that drunken drivers are a menace is begging the question since it's already been proven that they are.

7. *Irrational appeal* occurs when appeals to our emotions, to our religious faith, or to authority are made rather than appeals or reasons based on logic. "Of course you'll vote Republican; our family always has." "I'll get even. The Bible says 'an eye for an eye.'" "My country, right or wrong."

8. *Mistaking the reason for an occurrence* happens when we fail to see there may be other causes or we are misled. "John is a naturally brilliant student." (Is John brilliant, or does he do well in school because his parents make him study more than others? Maybe he's trying to impress a girl in his class.) "Karla is absent from class again. She must not be a serious student." (Maybe Karla has a health problem, or a small child to attend, or lacks transportation to campus on certain days.)

There are many kinds of faulty reasoning, but the ones described in this chapter are some of the more common ones you should begin to look for and avoid using when you draw conclusions or make inferences.

PRACTICE C-3: Identifying Logical Fallacies

Directions: Read the following dialogues and determine which of the following logical fallacies or errors in reasoning appear in the argument. There may be more than one type in a dialogue.

a. either-or thinking (oversimplification)   e. doubtful sources

b. stereotyping   f. begging the question

c. attacking character   g. irrational appeal

d. non sequitur (contradiction)   h. mistaking the reason

1. SAM: There's only one real aim of education—to learn all you can while going to school.

   GEORGE: Nonsense. Today, the only real reason to go to college is to get the skills necessary for a good job.

   Error in reasoning: _attacking situation_

   Explain: _____

2. PAULA: Let's go hear the Nicaraguan ambassador at Fraley Hall tonight. It should be interesting to hear his views.

   SUE: There's nothing that little commie's got to say that I want to hear.

   Error in reasoning: _~~the~~ attacking character_

   Explain: _____

3. HARRY: George is forming an organization to protest the dumping of toxic waste near the bird wildlife sanctuary. He really seems concerned about this. Quite a few people I know are joining with him. I think I will, too.

SALLY: Don't be a sucker: George's just doing it to bring attention to himself. He plans to run for president of the student body next term and wants to look good. Anyway, I dated him once and he came on too strong for me.

Error in reasoning: _____ non sequitter _____

Explain: _____

4. KIP: You going to vote for Sally? She'd make a good school representative on the board of education. She gets As in all her classes.

PIP: You kidding? What does she know about politics? Anyway, a female's place is in the home, not running for office.

Error in reasoning: _____ stereotype _____

Explain: _____

5. DALE: Did you hear that Sue is moving to the Midwest? She's convinced a major earthquake is going to hit us any day now.

FRED: She may be right. Have you been reading that series on natural disasters in the local newspaper? They predict an 8.8 earthquake will occur here in the next two years. The Midwest is a lot safer, that's for sure.

Error in reasoning: _____

Explain: _____

6. RAUL: Did you read about the junior high kid who stabbed and killed his friend after they watched the movie *Friday the 13th* on TV?

PAM: Isn't that terrible? Maybe now they'll stop showing that worthless junk on television. Everybody knows what a big influence TV viewing has on kids.

RAUL: But how will this incident change anything?

PAM: Now there's proof of the harm.

Error in reasoning: _____ mistaking the reasoning _____

Explain: _____

PRACTICE C-4: Evaluating Pros and Cons of an Argument

Directions: Disagreements on what type of sex education should be provided in public schools continues. One camp believes that teenagers should be taught abstinence only. Another camp believes teaching abstinence only does not work alone and that teaching comprehensive safe sex and contraception methods should be part of a sex education program for teens. One of the following selections advocates abstinence-only programs, the other argues for comprehensive sex education programs. Apply all the reading skills you have learned as you read each one. How well is each opinion supported?

Pro Argument

At the time she wrote the following selection, Kathleen Tsubata was codirector of the Washington AIDS International Foundation and taught HIV/AIDS prevention.

ABSTINENCE-ONLY PROGRAMS BENEFIT YOUTHS

KATHLEEN TSUBATA

1   The current tug-of-war between "abstinence-only" and "comprehensive" sexual-education advocates is distracting us from the real issue. We are in a war against forces far more unforgiving than we ever have encountered. We must look at what works to save lives. My work brings me to deal with teens every day, in public schools, churches and community organizations, teaching HIV/AIDS prevention. I train teens to teach others about this genocidal plague that is sweeping nations around the world and depleting continents of their most-productive population. I can tell you that most teens have a very superficial understanding of HIV and that many are putting themselves at risk in a wide variety of ways.

2   While teen pregnancy is serious, it is still, in one sense, the lesser evil. It's a difficult thing to bear a child out of wedlock, with the accompanying loss of education, financial stability and freedom. However, compared to HIV, it's a walk in the park. Make no mistake about it: The choice of sexual activity is a life-and-death matter, as Third World nations are finding out in stark terms.

THE PROBLEM WITH CONDOMS

3   Having multiple sexual partners is the No. 1 risk factor for contracting HIV and 19 percent of teens have had four or more sexual partners.

4   "So teach them to use condoms!" we are told. Studies indicate that condoms, if used correctly and consistently, may lower the transmission rate to 15 to 25 percent. That's not a fail-safe guarantee, as any condom manufacturer under litigation quickly would point out.

5   But there are two additional problems with condoms being the central pillar of HIV prevention. First, correct usage of condoms is hard to achieve in the dimly lit, cramped back seat of a car. Second, and more importantly, kids simply make decisions differently than adults. Janet St. Lawrence, of the Centers for Disease Control and Prevention (CDC), related the results of one behavioral study to me in a phone conversation [in 2002]. In that study, teens reported using a condom for their first sexual contact with someone, and subsequent contacts, "until they felt the relationship was permanent," St. Lawrence said. Then they stopped using condoms. These teens were asked what defines a "permanent" relationship. "Lasting 21 days or longer," was their response. In other words, such a teen could start a relationship, initiate sex using a condom, decide ater three weeks that it is "safe" to stop using a condom, break up and replay the whole cycle, convinced that this was responsible sexual behavior.

6   Teens are not realistic because they are young and not fully developed in key mental and emotional areas. They tend to imbue love with magical properties, as if the emotion is a sanitizing force, and that their trust can be shown by the willingness to take risks. Kids process information differently than adults. Parents know this. Saying "It's best not to have sex, but if you do, use a condom" is translated in their minds to "It's okay to have sex if you use a condom." Then, if they feel "this is true love," they convince themselves that even that is unnecessary. That's why during four decades of sex education we witnessed steep increases in sexual activity and the consequential increases in teen pregnancy, sexually transmitted diseases and poverty.

From "Insight in the News." Used with permission.

THE BENEFITS OF ABSTINENCE EDUCATION

7   Only when abstinence education began in recent years did the numbers of sexually active teens go down a full 8 percentage points from 54 percent of teens to 46 percent, according to the 2001 *Youth Risk Behavior Surveillance*, published by the CDC. Simultaneously, teen pregnancies went down, abortions went down and condom use went up among those who were sexually active. Raising the bar to establish abstinence as the best method indirectly resulted in more-responsible behavior in general.

8   You would think such good news would have people dancing in the aisles. Instead, the safe-sex gurus grimly predict that increased abstinence education will result in teens giving in to natural urges without the benefit of latex. Or, the critics of abstinence-until-marriage education insisted that their programs (which pay lip service to abstinence) somehow reached teens more effectively than the programs that focused on abstinence. A third interpretation is that contraception, not abstinence, has lowered the numbers.

9   However, a study of lowered teen-pregnancy rates between 1991 and 1995 (published in *Adolescent and Family Health* by Mohn, Tingle et al., April 2003) showed that abstinence, not contraceptives, was the major cause of the lowered pregnancy rate. Another 1996 study, by John Vessey, of Northwestern University Medical School, followed up on 2,541 teens, ages 13 to 16, who completed an abstinence-education program. He reported that one year after completing the program, 54 percent of formerly sexually active teens no longer were sexually active. This puts to rest the idea that "once a teen has sex, they will continue to be sexually active."

10   It often is claimed that most parents want pro-contraceptive education for their kids. In fact, a nationwide Zogby International poll of 1,245 parents in February [2003] (see poll results at www.whatparentsthink.com) commissioned by the pro-abstinence Coalition for Adolescent Sexual Health found that when shown the actual content of both comprehensive and abstinence-only sex-education programs, 73 percent of parents supported abstinence education and 75 percent opposed the condom-based education, with 61 percent opposing the comprehensive sex-ed programs.

11   But what do teens themselves think? In a 2000 study by the National Campaign to Prevent Teen Pregnancy, 93 percent of the teens surveyed said there should be a strong message from society not to engage in sex at least until graduation from high school. Will abstinence education cause sexually active teens to be unable to find out about contraception? The small amount in abstinence-education funding requested by Congress ($135 million among three programs) is miniscule compared with the $379 million funding of only six of the 25 federal programs teaching contraceptive-based education. This is Goliath complaining that David is using up all the rocks.

12   But, in all good conscience, can we teach something that would put kids in danger of contracting HIV, even if at a somewhat-reduced risk? Can we glibly decide, "Oh, only 15 percent of users will die?" That's acceptable? The stakes simply are too high. Even one life is too important to lose. When we're talking about life and death, we can't settle for the soggy argument of "Kids are going to do it anyway." That's what used to be said about racial discrimination, drunk driving and cigarette smoking, but when people became serious about countering these behaviors, they receded. If we realize the necessity of saving every teen's life, we can't help but teach them that because sex is wonderful, powerful and life-changing, it must be treated with great care.

THE NEED TO LIMIT SEXUALITY

13   Sex is most pleasurable and joyful when there is no fear of disease, when both partners feel absolute trust in the other, when the possibility of a pregnancy is not a destructive

one and when each person truly wants the best for the other. This takes self-development, investment, emotional growth, responsibility and a whole host of other elements a typical teen doesn't possess, unless they are guided. In reality, every person already is aware of the need to limit sexuality to certain times and places, like many activities. Sexuality is far more complex than the physical mechanics of orgasm. That stuff is pretty much automatic. It's far more important to know that orgasm is the perfectly engineered system for creating life, and for experiencing the fulfillment of love.

14   Abstinence isn't a vague ideal but a practical, feasible life skill. Studies show that kids who are able to say no to sex also can say no to drugs, alcohol and tobacco. The skills in one area automatically transfer to other areas of health. Learning to delay gratification can have positive impacts on academic goals and athletic accomplishments.

15   Without the soap-opera distractions of sex, kids feel more confident and free to enjoy the process of making friends, developing their own individuality and working on their dreams. That's why virtually no one looks back on the decision to be sexually abstinent and says "I wish I had never done that," But 63 percent of teen respondents who have had sex regretted it and said they wish they had waited, according to an International Communications Research of Media survey in June 2000 commissioned by the National Campaign to Prevent Teen Pregnancy. Further, 78 percent of the 12- to 17-year-old respondents said teens should not be sexually active, and only 21 percent thought sex for teens was okay if they used birth control.

YOUTHS WANT SUPPORT

16   Teens are telling us that they need support to resist the pressure to have sex. Even just making an abstinence pledge was found to delay sexual debut by 18 months on average, according to the National Longitudinal Study on Adolescent Health in 1997. And teens who know their parents have a strong belief and expectation of abstinence are far more likely to abstain, as shown in two 2002 studies released by the University of Minnesota Center for Adolescent Health and Development in which more than 80 percent of teens stayed abstinent when they knew their mothers strongly disapproved of premarital sex.

17   Even if it were only to end the spread of HIV/AIDS, that would be a valid reason to support abstinence education.

18   But teaching abstinence goes beyond preventing disease and unwanted pregnancy. It helps kids improve in the areas of self-esteem, academic attainments and future careers. It increases refusal skills toward drugs, alcohol and smoking. It equips teens with tools that they will use successfully through-out life, especially in their eventual marriage and family life. In other words, it has a positive ripple effect both in terms of their current and future life courses.

19   In my estimation, that definitely is worth funding.

Now answer the following questions. You may need to skim the selection for the answers.

1. What does Tsubata believe has helped lower teen pregnancy rates and can help protect youths from life-threatening diseases? _____

   _____

2. What two reasons does the author see as a problem with teaching the use of condoms? _____

   _____

3. What proof does the author provide for her statement that abstinence, not contra-ception, has lowered teen pregnancy rates? _____

_____

4. Besides health benefits, the author feels that by practicing sexual abstinence, teens improve in self-esteem and academic attainments; learn refusal toward drugs, alcohol and smoking; and acquire tools used successfully throughout life. What factual evidence does the author give to support the benefits? _____

_____

5. Why does Tsubata mention that she works with teens everyday in public schools, churches, and community organizations, teaching HIV prevention? _____

_____

6. Is the author's argument logical and balanced? _____

_____

Con Argument

The following essay was published by the American Civil Liberties Union (ACLU), a civil rights and individual liberties advocacy group.

As you read, look for the arguments used to counter the previous selection on sex education.

ABSTINENCE-ONLY PROGRAMS DO NOT WORK

American Civil Liberties Union

1
- Nearly two-thirds of all high school seniors in the U.S. have had sexual inter-course.
- Each year, approximately 9.1 million 15–24 year olds are infected with sexu-ally transmitted diseases (STDs), accounting for almost one-half of the total new STDs occurring annually in the U.S.
- The Centers for Disease Control and Prevention estimate that one-half of all new HIV infections occur among people under age 25, with the majority contracted through sexual intercourse.
- An estimated 757,000 pregnancies occurred among 15–19 year olds in 2002.

2   These statistics demonstrate a high level of sexual activity and risk taking among U.S. teens. Indeed, the U.S. has one of the highest teen pregnancy rates in the devel-oped world. The good news is that in recent years this rate dropped. From 1995–2002, the pregnancy rate among 15–19 years olds declined by nearly 24 percent. Researchers attribute 86 percent of this decline to improved contraceptive use and only 14 percent to teens choosing not to have sexual intercourse. Despite this reality, Congress has allo-cated more than a billion dollars since 1996 for programs that focus exclusively on absti-nence until marriage and censor vital health care information about contraceptives.

3   The ACLU supports programs that give teens the information they need to make healthy and responsible decisions about sex. Evidence shows that stressing

American Civil Liberties Union, "Abstinence-Only-Until-Marriage Programs Censor Vital Health Care Information," August 2007, http://www.aclu.org/reproductiverights/sexed/12670res20070319.html.

the importance of waiting to have sex while providing accurate, age-appropriate, and complete information about how to use contraceptives can help teens delay sex and reduce sexual risk taking. In addition to censoring vital health care information, abstinence-only-until-marriage programs raise other serious civil liberties concerns: They create a hostile environment for gay and lesbian teens; reinforce gender stereotypes; and in some instances use taxpayer dollars to promote one religious perspective.

Abstinence-Only-Until-Marriage Programs Censor Vital Health Information

4   Currently, there are three federal programs dedicated to funding abstinence-only-until-marriage programs. Each requires eligible programs to censor critical information that teens need to make healthy and responsible life decisions.

5   To receive funds under any of the federal programs, grantees must offer curricula that have as their "exclusive purpose" teaching the benefits of abstinence. In addition, recipients of abstinence-only-until-marriage dollars may not advocate contraceptive use or teach contraceptive methods except to emphasize their failure rates.

6   Thus, recipients of federal abstinence-only-until-marriage funds operate under a gag order that censors vitally needed information. Grantees are forced either to omit any mention of topics such as contraception, abortion, homosexuality, and AIDS or to present these subjects in an incomplete and thus inaccurate fashion.

7   **Research Shows that Abstinence-Only-Until-Marriage Programs Don't Work** A rigorous, multi-year, scientific evaluation authorized by Congress and released in April 2007 presents clear evidence that abstinence-only-until-marriage programs don't work. The study by Mathematica Policy Research, Inc., which looked at four federally funded programs and studied more than 2,000 students, found that abstinence-only program participants were just as likely to have sex before marriage as teens who did not participate. Furthermore, program participants had first intercourse at the same mean age and the same number of sexual partners as teens who did not participate in the federally funded programs.

8   In addition, an academic study of virginity pledge programs—which encourage students to make a pledge to abstain from sex until marriage and are often a component of abstinence-only-until-marriage curricula—found that while in limited circumstances virginity-pledgers may delay first intercourse, they still have sex before marriage and are less likely than non-pledgers to use contraception at first intercourse and to get tested for STDs when they become sexually active.

9   On the other hand, there is ample evidence that programs that include information about both abstinence and how to use contraceptives effectively delay sex and reduce sexual risk taking among teens. Many of these programs have been shown to "delay the onset of sex, reduce the frequency of sex, reduce the number of sexual partners among teens, or increase the use of condoms and other forms of contraception" among sexually active teens. Research also shows that sex education curricula that discuss contraception—by presenting accurate information about contraceptive options, effectiveness, and use—do not increase sexual activity.

Abstinence-Only-Until-Marriage Programs Withhold Information Teens Need to Make Healthy and Responsible Life Decision

10   Abstinence-only-until-marriage programs are increasingly replacing other forms of sex education in high schools. Between 1995 and 2002, "[t]he proportion of adolescents who had received any formal instruction about methods of birth control declined significantly," and by 2002, one-third of adolescents had not received any instruction on contraception. At the same time, in 1999, 23 percent of secondary school sexuality

education teachers taught abstinence as the only way of avoiding STDs and pregnancy, up from 2 percent in 1988. When abstinence-only-until-marriage programs do present information about pregnancy prevention and testing and treatment of STDs, they do so incompletely and/or inaccurately. For example, a 2004 congressional report concluded that many federally funded abstinence-only-until-marriage curricula "misrepresent the effectiveness of condoms in preventing sexually transmitted diseases and pregnancy" by exaggerating their failure rates.

11   We need to help teenagers make healthy and responsible life decisions by giving them full and accurate information about the transmission and treatment of STDs, and how to use contraception effectively. Abstinence-only-until-marriage programs jeopardize the health of sexually active teens and leave those who become sexually active unprepared.

Abstinence-Only-Until-Marriage Programs Create a Hostile Environment for Lesbian and Gay Teens

12   Many abstinence-only-until-marriage programs use curricula that discriminate against gay and lesbian students and stigmatize homosexuality. The federal guidelines governing these programs state that they must teach that a "mutually faithful monogamous relationship in [the] context of marriage is the expected standard of human sexual activity." In a society that generally prohibits gays and lesbians from marrying, such a message rejects the idea of sexual intimacy for lesbians and gays and ignores their need for critical information about protecting themselves from STDs in same-sex relationships.

13   A review of the leading abstinence-only-until-marriage curricula found that most address same-sex sexual behavior only within the context of promiscuity and disease, and several are overtly hostile to lesbians and gay men. For example, materials from an abstinence-only-until-marriage program used recently in Alabama state, "[S]ame sex 'unions' cannot provide an adequate means of achieving a genuine physical relationship with another human being because this type of 'union' is contrary to the laws of nature."

14   By talking only about sex within marriage and teaching about STDs as a form of moral punishment for homosexuality, abstinence-only-until-marriage programs not only undermine efforts to educate teens about protecting their health, but create a hostile learning environment for lesbian and gay students and the children of lesbian and gay and/or single parents.

Many Abstinence-Only-Until-Marriage Programs Feature Harmful Gender Stereotypes

15   In addition to false and misleading information, many abstinence-only-untilmarriage programs present stereotypes about men and women as scientific facts. In an attempt to demonstrate differences between men and women, one popular program, WAIT Training, instructs teachers to "[b]ring to class frozen waffles and a bowl of spaghetti noodles without sauce. Using these as visual aids, explain how research has found that men's brains are more like the waffle, in that their design enables them to more easily compartmentalize information. Women's minds, on the other hand, are interrelated due to increased brain connectors." Similarly, the teacher's manual for Why Know Abstinence Education Programs suggests that girls are responsible for boys' inability to control their sexual urges: "One subtle form of pressure can be the way in which a girl acts toward her boyfriend. If the girlfriend is constantly touching him and pressing against him, or wearing clothing which is tight or revealing of her body, this will cause the guy to think more about her body than her person, and he may be incited toward more sexual thoughts."

16   Many abstinence-only-until-marriage programs are riddled with similarly troubling discussions of gender. Such stereotypes and false information undermine women's equality and promote an outmoded and discredited view of women's and men's roles and abilities.

Some Abstinence-Only-Until-Marriage Programs Use Taxpayer Dollars to Promote One Religious Perspective

17   Although the U.S. Constitution guarantees that the government will neither promote nor interfere with religious belief, some abstinence-only-until-marriage grantees violate this core freedom by using public dollars to convey overt religious messages or to impose religious viewpoints. The ACLU has successfully challenged this misuse of taxpayer dollars:

- In May 2005, the ACLU filed a lawsuit challenging the federally funded promotion of religion by a nationwide abstinence-only-until-marriage program called the Silver Ring Thing. The program was rife with religion. In its own words, "The mission of Silver Ring is to saturate the United States with a generation of young people who have taken a vow of sexual abstinence until marriage.... This mission can only be achieved by offering a personal relationship with Jesus Christ as the best way to live a sexually pure life." The lawsuit, *ACLU of Massachusetts v. Leavitt*, brought swift results: In August 2005, the U.S. Department of Health and Human Services (HHS) suspended the Silver Ring Thing's funding, pending corrective or other action. And in February 2006, the parties reached a settlement in which HHS agreed that any future funding would be contingent on the Silver Ring Thing's compliance with federal law prohibiting the use of federal funds to support religious activities. Soon after, HHS released new guidelines for all abstinence-only-until-marriage grantees to ensure that government funds will not be used to promote religion. These guidelines were modeled after the settlement agreement in *ACLU of Massachusetts v. Leavitt*.

- In 2002, the ACLU challenged the use of taxpayer dollars to support religious activities in the Louisiana Governor's Program on Abstinence (GPA), a program run on federal and state funds. Over the course of several years, the GPA had funded programs that, among other things, presented "Christ-centered" theater skits, held a religious youth revival, and produced radio shows that "share abstinence as part of the gospel message." In violation of the Constitution, a federal district court found that GPA funds were being used to convey religious messages and advance religion. The court ordered Louisiana officials to stop this misuse of taxpayer dollars. The case was on appeal when the parties settled. The GPA agreed to closely monitor the activities of the programs it funds and to stop using GPA dollars to "convey religious messages or otherwise advance religion in any way."

Parents, Teachers, and Major Medical Groups Support Comprehensive Sexuality Education

18   The vast majority of U.S. parents, teachers, and leading medical groups believe that teens should receive complete and accurate information about abstinence and contraception.

- In a nationwide poll conducted in 2004 for the Kaiser Family Foundation, National Public Radio, and the Kennedy School of Government, researchers found that an overwhelming majority of parents want sex education curricula to cover topics such as abortion and sexual orientation, as well as how to use and where to get contraceptives, including condoms.

- A 1999 nationally representative survey of 7th-12th grade teachers in the five specialties most often responsible for sex education found that a strong majority believed that sexuality education courses should cover birth control methods (93.4%), factual information about abortion (89%), where to go for birth control (88.8%), the correct way to use a condom (82%), and sexual orientation (77.8%), among other topics.
- Similarly, major medical organizations have advocated for and/or endorsed comprehensive sexuality education, including the American Medical Association, the American Academy of Pediatrics, the American College of Obstetrics and Gynecology, and the Society for Adolescent Medicine.

Now answer the following questions.

1. What position does the ACLU take regarding abstinence-only education programs?

    _____

    _____

2. T/F The ACLU believes that federal funds should support comprehensive sex education in high school courses which includes teaching contraceptive methods.

3. On what sources does the ACLU base its information stating there is no link between abstinence-only education with a downward trend in teens reporting they have had sex? _____

    _____

4. Does the ACLU provide sources for their statement that parents, teachers, and medical groups believe students should receive comprehensive sex education?

    _____

5. Is the ACLU's argument well balanced and logical? _____

    _____

    _____

Considering the Pros and Cons of Both Arguments

1. Whether or not you are for or against comprehensive sex education, which argument is most persuasive? Why? _____

    _____

2. Even if you agree with her, what might Tsubata have done to be more convincing?

    _____

    _____

3. Even if you agree with the ACLU, what might have made their argument more convincing? _____

    _____

4. How much do your own attitudes and bias on the subject have to do with which argument you think is most convincing? _____

    _____

    _____

Application 1: Recognizing Attitude, Bias, and Inference in Other Materials

From a magazine, newspaper, or textbook, choose a selection and come up with your own questions about attitude, bias, and inference (at least one question about each). Bring the selection and questions to class and exchange with a classmate. Each of you should answer the other's questions. Discuss what you learned from each article by using critical reading skills.

D.   Putting It All Together

The word *critical* often connotes finding fault with something. But as you have seen in this unit, reading critically implies an attempt at objective judging so as to determine both merits and faults. Critical reading is thoughtful reading because it requires that the reader recognize not only what is being said at the literal level but also facts, opinions, attitudes, inferences, and bias. A reader who is not actively involved is not reading critically.

Knowingly or unknowingly, you make critical judgments all the time, from deciding on the type of toothpaste to buy to choosing a topic for an English theme. The trick is always to be aware of your critical judgments and to know the reasoning behind your decisions.

Making critical judgments is a two-way street. As a reader you must be aware of the judgments the author is making and you must also be aware of the judgments you make, based on evidence rather than bias. For instance, you may dislike the subject of history so much that you have a bias against anything you read before you even get started. Your mind is already partly closed to the author. On the other hand, you could be biased in favor of what you read and accept what is being said simply because you already agree with the author. True critical reading should leave you a little wiser, a little better informed, and less biased than before—about both the subject and yourself.

The following three reading selections can be used to practice increasing your reading speed of comprehension as well as developing your critical reading skills. You may want to look at your Student Record Chart to review your rate and comprehension scores from the last timed readings you did. You may want to just use these as reading comprehension practices and not time yourself. It's up to you and your instructor.

Each of the following reading practices contains comprehension and vocabulary checks that require using all the skills taught in this and the first unit of the book. Remember that you are competing against yourself. Try to learn from any mistakes you may make so that you can do better on each consecutive practice.

PRACTICE D-1: Timed Reading

Directions: Practice speed-reading strategies on the following 745-word selection. Start with a one-minute survey, making sure you look at the questions during the survey too. Push yourself to read faster than before.

Begin Timing: _____

SELF-ESTEEM IS EARNED, NOT LEARNED

MIKE SCHMOKER

1   The word *self-esteem* has become an educational incantation. Every educational discussion, every stated school district goal and mission takes a bow in its direction. Its influence on academic and behavioral standards in our schools cannot be overstated. There is even an official California Task Force to Promote Self-Esteem and Social Responsibility, and the University of California recently published a book linking low self-esteem to societal problems.

2   At first, the word seems innocent enough and something about which we should be concerned. But if the meaning of a word is its use, we must look to pop psychology, which gave us this word, in order to fully understand its importance. Before it reached education, it had already taken on the fatuous implication that what is precious can be gotten cheaply. Self-esteem, as it is now used, isn't something earned but given. It isn't wrought but spontaneously realized. Such thinking is inimical to what schools should be trying to accomplish.

3   What disturbs me is that self-esteem has been sentimentalized. The new self-esteem has less to do with forging a connection between it and achievement and more to do with simply creating good feelings.

4   This is an understandable reaction to a difficult problem. So many young people are burdened with negative, defeatist feelings. We want to help them, and the quicker the better. But as time has passed, it is mystifying that we have not seen this impulse for what it is. I've seen whole auditoriums full of students being told, indiscriminately, to feel good about themselves, being asked at random to stand up and give testimonials on how swell they are, and being reassured that by clinging to this confidence they will succeed mightily.

5   This is a flimsy notion, and no one believes it. Not for very long anyway. Like it or not, self-esteem is very much a function of such unyielding realities as what we can do, what we've done with what we have and what we've made of ourselves. And so the school—with every effort toward sensitivity, compassion and encouragement—should reinforce this, while cultivating ability, talent, decency and the capacity for sustained effort, the belief that you get what you pay for.

6   Shortcuts, such as routinely heaping inordinate praise on shoddy work, or lowering academic standards, do not work. Ask any teacher, in a moment of candor, if he or she can get average kids, the majority of students, to make a sufficient effort in school, make good use of class time or do fairly conscientious work on homework and assignments. An alarming number of teachers don't think so. Many complain of a malaise among students, adding that only about half of their students will even do homework. Despite this, there has never been more pressure for teachers to be enormously upbeat in dealing with students and student efforts. Promotion is nearly automatic, and grades are higher than ever.

7   What this tells students, at least tacitly, is that what they are doing is good enough and that our insistence on quality is a bluff.

8   It's ironic that the reason often cited for generous grading and reluctance to fail students centers on self-esteem. In the name of self-esteem, then, we are asked to give young people something they didn't earn in the mistaken hope that they can go on to master what is presumably harder than what they have already failed to learn.

9   What they do learn is to play the game, the essence of which is that standards are not based on what students should do, or are able to do, but on what they will do, no matter how low the common denominator. And that is, as we know, pretty low; among industrialized nations, we rank embarrassingly in every academic category.

10   But you'll seldom see these deficiencies reflected in American report cards. The plain, unpleasant truth is hidden behind the good grades, lost in the peculiarly positive climate that too often prevails in our schools. If you're not sure that's true, consider this: A recent international survey showed that South Korean students rank first in mathematics, American students near the bottom. When asked where they thought they ranked, the American students ranked themselves at the top and the Koreans at the bottom.

11   It is common knowledge that so much groundless praise can breed complacency. It can. And it has.

12   For our part, the best we can do is teach young people, in an atmosphere of compassion, that self-esteem is earned, often with considerable difficulty, and equip them to earn it.

Finish Timing: Record time here _____ and use the Timed Reading Conversion Chart in the Appendix to figure your rate: _____ wpm.

Comprehension Check

Directions: Answer the following questions without looking back.

1. The author's main idea or thesis is that

    a. self-esteem has been sentimentalized.

    b. self-esteem can be taught in the classroom.

    c. an official California Task Force to Promote Self-Esteem and Social Responsibility recently published a book linking low self-esteem to societal problems.

    d. we need to teach young people that self-respect is earned, often with difficulty.

2. What does the author mean when he says that "the word *self-esteem* has become an education incantation"? _____

    _____

    _____

    _____

3. The author states, "The new self-esteem has less to do with forging a connection between it and achievement and more to do with simply creating good feelings." Based on this, how do you think the author defines *self-esteem*? _____

    _____

    _____

    _____

4. T/F According to the author, self-esteem is a function of what we are capable of doing, what we've done with our ability, and what we've made of ourselves.

5. Explain why the author does not believe in automatic promotion. _____

_____

_____

_____

6. What does the author mean when he says that students "learn to play the game"?

_____

_____

_____

7. According to the author, where do American students rank academically among industrialized nations? To what does he attribute this? _____

_____

_____

8. According to a recent survey, where do American students academically rank themselves in mathematics in comparison to South Korean students? Where do they really rank? _____

_____

_____

_____

9. According to the author, too much groundless praise can breed or cause _____

_____

_____

10. Explain what the title means. _____

_____

_____

_____

Vocabulary Check

Part A

Directions: Define the following underlined words from the selection.

1. The word *self-esteem* has become an education <u>incantation</u>. _____

_____

2. We must look to <u>pop psychology</u>, which gave us this word ["self-esteem"]. _____

_____

3. So many young people are <u>burdened</u> with negative, defeatist feelings. _____

_____

4. They stand up and give <u>testimonials</u> on how swell they are. _____

_____

5. It is common knowledge that so much <u>groundless</u> praise can breed complacency.

_____

Part B

Directions: Write each word from the following list in the appropriate blank.

Candor   shoddy   conscientious   routinely   malaise

Shortcuts, such as **(6)** _____ heaping praise on **(7)** _____ work, or lowering academic standards, do not work. Ask any teacher, in a moment of **(8)** _____ if he or she can get average kids, the majority of students, to make a sufficient effort in school, make good use of class time or do fairly **(9)** _____ work on homework and assignments. An alarming number don't think so. Many complain of a **(10)** _____ among students. Despite this, there has never been more pressure for teachers to be enormously upbeat in dealing with students' efforts.

Record your rate and the results of the comprehension and vocabulary checks on the Student Record Chart in the Appendix. Each correct answer is worth 10 points, for a total of 100 points possible for comprehension and 100 points for vocabulary.

PRACTICE D-2: Timed Reading

Directions: Take about one minute to preview the following 465-word selection and questions. After your preview, time yourself on the reading.

Begin Timing: _____

PUSH FOR DE-EMPHASIS OF COLLEGE SPORTS

DAVID HOLAHAN*

1   How many exalted muck-a-mucks with advanced degrees to burn does it take to restate the obvious and then miss the whole point? Twenty-two in the case of the Knight Foundation Commission on Intercollegiate Athletics.

2   It took these wizards more than a year to determine that big-time college athletics are out of control, something high school equivalency degree holders have known for decades.

3   The Knight posse also recommended many wondrous things, including this startling caveat: Colleges should not admit athletes who are unlikely to graduate. Small wonder that news of this long-awaited report was buried on page 4 of my local sports section. Page 1 was devoted to pictures of "scholar-athletes" jumping about in short pants.

* David Holahan, a freelance writer, played football and baseball for Yale.

4   The principal advice of this pedantic treatise is that college presidents should take an active role in administering and overseeing their schools' athletic programs. Or, in plain language, let the big boss ride the tiger that big-time sports has become.

5   What a preposterous proposal. It presumes athletics are so important that the heads of universities should divert time and energy from overseeing education to monitoring the sideshow. The house is rotten to the core and the Knight panel recommends a fresh coat of paint.

6   What is wrong with big-time college sports is not who administers them or which department rakes in the booty or how many jocks can master majors like "family studies." What's wrong is the sports themselves, how perversely important they have become to the players, the coaches, the colleges, the alumni and the fans.

7   It would be tempting to say that money is the disease, the billions that TV networks pay schools to entertain us. But money is just the symptom. The root cause is that we simply value sports too highly. They have become the new opiate of the masses.

8   This is where the commission dropped the ball. Its 20 men and two women (men monitoring sports is a bit like foxes regulating chicken coops) should have insisted on de-emphasis. We are now in the midst of "March madness," CBS's term for the NCAA basketball tournament. Madness, indeed, with sanity nowhere in sight.

9   Even those athletes who do manage to pass their courses are doing so, by and large, so that they can continue their sporting careers. Education, if that is the right word for what these young men and women experience, is the means. Basketball, to cite the semi-pro sport du jour, is the end.

10   How sad that these teenagers head off to college thinking that being a star athlete is the most important, perhaps the only, goal to strive toward. Rarely does anything they encounter on sports-factory campuses disabuse them of this notion. They are there to run and jump and dribble. With a world of possibilities surrounding them, they limit themselves to the one thing they have already mastered. We all should be ashamed of ourselves.

Finish Timing: Record time here _____ and use the Timed Reading Conversion Chart in the Appendix to figure your rate: _____ wpm.

Comprehension Check

Directions: Answer the following questions without looking back.

1. The main idea or thesis of the article is that our society has placed too much value on college sports.

   a. True, because _____

   _____

   b. False, because _____

   _____

2. The intent of this article is to

   a. criticize the findings of the Knight Foundation Commission on Intercollegiate Athletics.

   b. advocate the findings of the Knight Foundation Commission.

   c. blame the overemphasis of the value of college sports on the presidents of the universities involved.

   d. show that many college athletes are more interested in sports than in getting
      an education.

3. The author's attitude toward his subject is

   a. playful.

   b. serious.

   c. angry with a touch of sarcasm.

   d. disinterest.

4. The author's question "How many exalted muck-a-mucks with advanced degrees
   to burn does it take to restate the obvious and then miss the whole point?" is an
   example of the way writers create tone.

   a. True, because _____

      _____

   b. False, because _____

      _____

5. We can infer from what the author says that he does not care for college sports.

   a. True, because _____

      _____

   b. False, because _____

      _____

6. Explain the statement that sports have "become the new opiate of the masses."

   _____

7. We can infer that the Knight Foundation Commission on Intercollegiate Athletics
   met for over a year to investigate college athletics.

   a. True, because _____

   b. False, because _____

8. What inference can we draw from paragraph 3 regarding the author's opinion of
   the Knight Foundation Commission? _____

   _____

9. What does the author mean when he says, "With a world of possibilities surrounding them, they [college athletes] limit themselves to the one thing they have
   already mastered"? _____

   _____

10. What inferences can we draw regarding *why* the author feels as he does about col-
    lege athletics? _____

    _____

Vocabulary Check

Directions: Define the following underlined words from the selection.

   1. many <u>exalted</u> muck-a-mucks with advanced degrees _____

      _____

2. recommended many wondrous things, including this startling <u>caveat</u> _____

_____

3. this pedantic <u>treatise</u> _____

_____

4. this <u>pedantic</u> treatise _____

_____

5. a <u>preposterous</u> proposal _____

_____

6. how <u>perversely</u> important _____

_____

7. to <u>cite</u> the semi-pro sport du jour _____

_____

8. to cite the semi-pro <u>sport du jour</u> _____

_____

9. <u>disabuse</u> them of this notion _____

_____

10. <u>intercollegiate</u> athletics _____

_____

Record your rate and the results of the comprehension and vocabulary checks on the Student Record Chart in the Appendix. Each correct answer is worth 10 points, for a total of 100 points possible for comprehension and 100 points for vocabulary. Discuss your results with your instructor.

PRACTICE D-3: Timed Reading

Directions: The author of the following essay, Macarena Hernández, is a writer for the *Dallas Morning News*. Time yourself as you read, looking for the author's arguments, opinions, biases and facts.

Begin Timing: _____

AMERICA, STAND UP FOR JUSTICE AND DECENCY

Macarena Hernández

1   On the last night of September, while they slept after a long day of work in the fields, six men were beaten to death with aluminum bats. One was shot in the head. Among the victims, a father and son killed in the same battered trailer.

2   The killers demanded money as they broke their bones.

Macarena Hernández, "America, Stand Up for Justice and Decency," *Dallas Morning News*, October 15, 2005. Reprinted with permission of the *Dallas Morning News*.

3   The victims were all Mexican farm workers living in rundown trailer parks spread across two counties in southern Georgia. They had earned the money the killers were after by sweating their days on cotton and peanut farms or building chicken coops—the kind of jobs you couldn't pay Americans enough to do.

4   In a few hours, the killers hit four trailers. In one, they raped a woman and shot her husband in the head, traumatizing their three small children, who were present. In others, they left at least a half-dozen men wounded. Some are still in the hospital with shattered bones, including broken wrists from trying to protect their faces from the bats.

5   The news of the killings in Georgia reverberated outside Tift and Colquitt counties, but it didn't cling to national headlines like you would expect with such a bloodbath. Two weeks later, residents are still afraid the attackers will come back, even though the Georgia Bureau of Investigation has arrested six suspects and charged them with the slayings.

6   Across the country, assaults on immigrants are common and happen at a much higher rate than reported. Two years ago in Grand Prairie, a pushcart ice cream vendor was shot to death and robbed. Seven months later, another one met the same fate in west Oak Cliff. In March, at a Far North Dallas apartment complex, two thieves raped and killed a 20-year-old woman. They slit her husband's throat.

7   In Dallas, attacks against immigrants are one reason individual robberies have gone up in the last five years. Authorities call undocumented immigrants "ready-made victims." Without proper documentation to open bank accounts, many resort to stashing their sweat-soaked earnings under mattresses, in kitchen cabinets, in their socks or boots. If they are robbed, many don't call police for fear of deportation or because, back home, cops aren't trusted, anyway.

8   Some solutions are simple and concrete, such as making it easier for immigrants to establish bank accounts. Wells Fargo and Bank of America are among the banks that require only a Mexican consulate-issued ID card to open an account; others require documentation many immigrants lack. If there was ever a reason for adopting the more lenient policy, this is it.

9   More globally, horrors like these demand that a nation descended from immigrants take a hard look at the ways we think and speak about these most recent arrivals.

10   When Paul Johnson, the mayor of Tifton, where three of the four attacks took place, responded by flying the Mexican flag at City Hall, some residents complained. "I did that as an expression of sorrow for the Hispanic community," he told reporters. "For those who were offended, I apologize, but I think it was the right thing to do."

11   Were the complainers angrier about the red, white and green Mexican flag fluttering in the Georgia air than they were about the horrific murders? Do they watch Fox's *The O'Reilly Factor*, where the anchor and the callers constantly point to the southern border as the birth of all America's ills? (Sample comment: "Each one of those people is a biological weapon.")

12   It is one thing to want to secure the borders and another to preach hate, to talk of human beings as ailments. Taken literally, such rhetoric gives criminals like those in southern Georgia license to kill; it gives others permission to look the other way. In this heightened anti-immigrant climate, what Mr. Johnson did was not only a welcome gesture, but a brave one, too.

13   There are those who will want to gloss over the deaths of these six men because they are "criminals" and "lawbreakers," in this country illegally. But regardless of where you stand on the immigration reform debate, you can't stand for the senseless death of the vulnerable.

14   We should all be outraged. We must demand justice. Or else the real criminals here will win.

Finish Timing: Record time here _____ and use the Timed Reading Conversion Chart in the Appendix to figure your rate: _____ wpm.

Comprehension Check

Directions: Answer the following questions without looking back.

1. Which of the following best states Hernández's thesis?

    a. Assaults on immigrants are common with little done about it.

    b. A nation descended from immigrants needs to take a hard look at the way we think and speak about recent arrivals.

    c. We need to establish more lenient policies to help provide documents many immigrants lack.

    d. We are living in a heightened anti-immigrant climate.

2. What events prompted Hernández to write this essay? _____

    _____

3. The author's attitude toward such banks as Wells Fargo and Bank of America is

    a. positive.

    b. negative.

    c. neutral.

    d. not able to tell.

4. Why did the mayor of Tifton, Georgia, fly the Mexican flag at City Hall?

    _____

5. Authorities call undocumented workers _____

    _____

6. What can we infer is Hernández's attitude toward *The O'Reilly Factor* television program and those who watch and agree with the anchors and commentators?

    a. favorable

    b. neutral

    c. delight

    d. disgust

7. What is the tone of Hernández's essay? _____

    _____

8. Is Hernández's essay based mostly on fact or opinion? _____

    _____

9. What inference can be drawn from Hernández's statement that the Georgia killings "didn't cling to national headlines like you would expect with such a bloodbath"? _____

    _____

    _____

10. Hernández says, "Regardless of where you stand on the immigration reform debate, you can't stand for the senseless death of the vulnerable." Explain whether or not this is a logical statement. _____

_____

_____

Vocabulary Check

Directions: Define the following underlined words from the selection.

1. <u>traumatizing</u> their three children

_____

2. <u>reverberated</u> outside Tift and Colquitt counties

_____

3. the more <u>lenient</u> policy

_____

4. for fear of <u>deportation</u>

_____

5. about the <u>horrific</u> murders

_____

6. human beings as <u>ailments</u>

_____

7. those who want to <u>gloss over</u>

_____

8. death of the <u>vulnerable</u>

_____

9. such <u>rhetoric</u> gives criminals permission

_____

10. where the <u>anchor</u> and the callers

_____

Record your rate and the results of the comprehension and vocabulary checks on the Student Record Chart in the Appendix. Each correct answer is worth 10 points, for a total of 100 points possible for comprehension and 100 points for vocabulary. Discuss your results with your instructor.

Questions for Group Discussion

1. As a group, pick any one of the reading selections in Practice C-4. After you agree on the author's thesis, take another side and disagree with the author. Support your views by showing errors in the author's support.

2. Pick any of the readings in this chapter and find examples of logical fallacies. Decide the effect of these fallacies on your understanding of the material.

3. As a group, discuss David Holahan's bias about college sports. Did he cause any of you to look at sports in a different light? Why do some of you agree or disagree with him? Are personal biases interfering with seeing his side? What arguments do you have for disagreeing with him?

4. As a group, concentrate on the immigration debate. Take pro and con sides and argue your positions.

5. As a group, see how many of you can use the following words in a sentence. Make certain you learn the ones you still may not be able to use or recognize by writing the definition in the blank space.

    a. preposterous _____

    b. lenient _____

    c. pedantic _____

    d. disabuse _____

    e. caveat _____

    f. treatise _____

    g. malaise _____

    h. shoddy _____

    i. candor _____

On Your Own

Pick ten new words you learned in this chapter, not necessarily those listed in question 5, and on a separate sheet of paper write a sentence for each word, using it correctly in context. Turn in the paper to your instructor.

If You Want

Go online and examine Web sites on one or more of the following subjects and share your findings in class:

    a. Virginity pledges

    b. Sex education

    c. Illegal immigration

    d. College sports: pro and con

A Final Check

At the beginning of this unit, you looked at a diagram that illustrated the three facets of comprehension. Now you have completed the unit that is represented by the left leg of the triangle.

For the diagram below, fill in the blank lines with information from this section. Working with a partner or small group is acceptable if your instructor sets up groups.

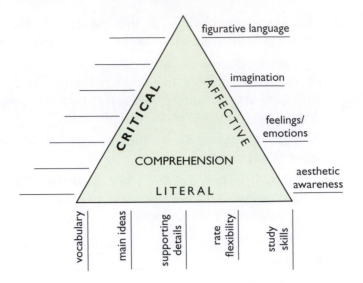

Hints: The first line has to do with information and judgments. The next four lines have to do with the author's worldview and how it influences our reading. The sixth line has to do with reading between the lines. The seventh line deals with what the reader does based on the information given.

When you have finished, check your answers with the triangle at the beginning of Unit Two, page 164.

CHAPTER SEVEN

Developing Computer Reading Skills

A.   Reading on the World Wide Web

In a relatively few years, the World Wide Web has become a major player in providing information on practically every subject. Daily, the number of homes and schools hooking up to the Internet grows. Many schools and colleges require students to buy computers and use the Internet as a matter of course, providing

Internet hookups in libraries and dormitories. Even hotels now provide rooms with Internet access. Many children in elementary schools are growing up learning how to read both print and electronic text. Some of us have to learn to read anew.

The fast-growing availability and use of computers and Web sites on the Internet have changed the way we read. As the sophistication of Web sites continues to grow, so must our skills in using them intelligently and correctly.

Right now you are reading traditional print, following along from the beginning of a passage to the end. You read in a single, familiar direction. Your eyes can glance over a whole page, noting titles, headings, and paragraph forms and lengths. You can quickly flip pages back and forth. You have been taught to read printed matter that conforms to an understood pattern.

Reading Web sites is different. You've probably already experienced reading on the Internet. If so, you know that data on many Web sites are not presented in a traditional way, varying widely in the way information is presented on the screen. The computer screen limits the amount of text you can see at one time, often surrounded by color, sounds, or animation. The information may not appear as a typical paragraph with topic sentence and supporting detail. Each sentence may itself be a topic needing further support provided on yet another screen page.

In most cases, reading on a computer screen is slower than reading printed text. Information is not presented in a linear fashion, but divided up into links. It becomes a matter of moving from link to link.

Web Site Links

Most Web sites lead you in many directions. You are offered choices, called links, which take you to other pages on the site. For instance, Figure 7.1 shows the home page (or first page) of a Web site for the University of California, Davis. Notice all the links above and below the photos, serving as a table of contents for the Web site. For information on any one of those topics, you click on it and wait while the site loads the page you want. How fast the page comes up depends on the computer's speed. Once you get to that page, you may have other link choices for more detailed information. Sometimes you will click on a subject link and discover it does not contain the information you want. You then have to go back to the home page and start over. Some Web sites, as in Figure 7.1, retain a list of the major links on one side of the screen so you can move from page to page.

An Example of Reading a Web Site

As an example of reading on the Internet, let's say you wanted to attend the University of California at Davis. You want to know their admissions requirements. On the home page in Figure 7.1, you click "Admissions." The page shown in Figure 7.2 loads on your screen. Notice the various links provided for admissions in Figure 7.2. As an undergraduate, you click "Undergraduate Admissions: All you need to know about UC Davis."

This brings up the UC Davis Undergraduate Admissions page shown in Figure 7.3. Now you have another batch of links to choose from. You want to learn when and how to apply to UC Davis and their requirements, so you click "Admissions" to get to the page shown in Figure 7.4. Once again, choices for various types of information in this section are provided. Notice more links are provided for selection depending on whether you're applying as a freshman, transfer student, or international student along with application basics.

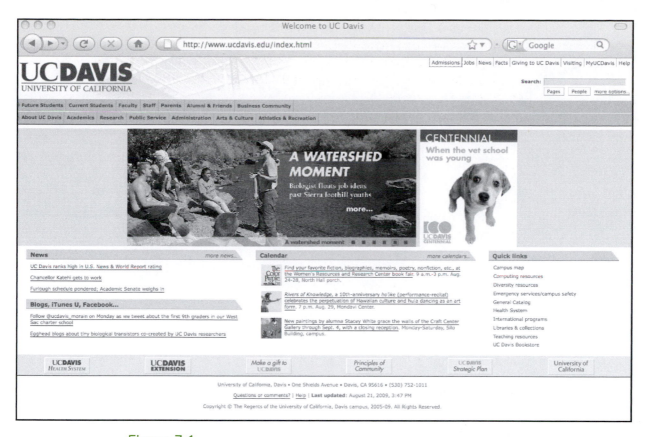

Figure 7.1

At this point you can see how different reading on the Web is compared with traditional printed text. While you may be clicking on one link, another user may be clicking on other links for different information. There is a skill in learning to follow multiple links or paths that contain what you want.

Many Web sites follow this UC Davis example: a home page with various links for you to follow. Clicking on the links provided serves as turning the pages in a book.

Web Reading Tips

Here are a few tips to help you get the most from reading on the Internet:

1. Be patient. Computers vary in speed, in screen size, and in the way they are linked to the Internet. Going from one link to another may take time, because the Web page may contain pictures, sound, or animation that can distract as well as aid. These all take time to load onto the computer screen. Sometimes a Web site may be "down" for some technical reason, and you may need to try loading the site later. It's also possible the site no longer exists. Many Web sites come and go.

2. Expect little of the information you are seeking on the first page of a Web site. Home pages are usually "grabbers." Sounds, movement, and flashing colors are often used to get your attention. Unlike when you read traditional print, you often must respond to these sights and sounds in order for any action to take place. Advertisements often pop up and intrude on your reading. This usually occurs only when a Web site has something to sell, but it's also a good way to question the legitimacy of the Web site.

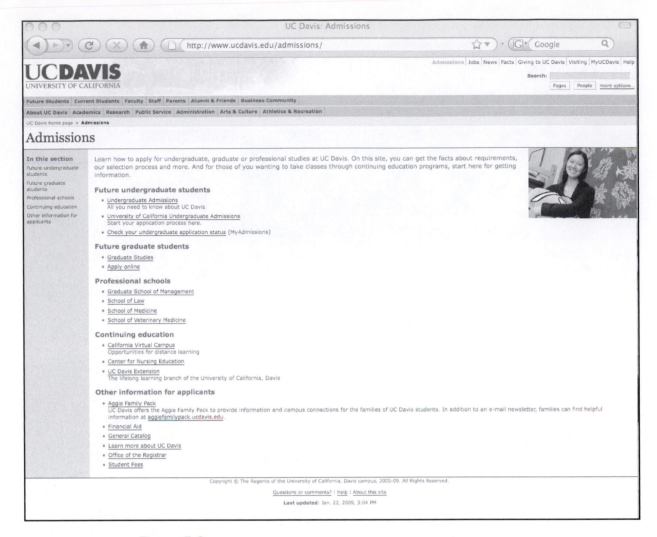

Figure 7.2

3. Read a Web site's home page carefully. Make certain the Web site contains the information you need. Notice the way the information is arranged on the screen. Look again at Figure 7.1. Notice that in the upper right-hand corner is a small box labeled "Search." This box may also be labeled "Find." If you don't see exactly what you want on the Web page itself, you can type in a keyword, such as "tuition costs," and click "Go." The Web site will bring up any pages with information it contains on tuition costs. Some Web sites, however, don't have this feature.

4. As you move from link to link, bookmark the beginning site's home page. At the top of your Internet browser, you'll see a function called Bookmarks or Favorites. You can save the Web site's location and open it up again later by clicking on the site's name.

5. Before you start clicking different links, determine which ones will lead you to what you want to know. You could spend a long time going from link to link without obtaining what you are looking for. The Web site may not be worth investigating, and you may need to select another Web site.

6. Print out any material you want to save to read later. It's advisable to take notes as you move from link to link, because some pages may not be printable, or you may need to return to that link at a later date.

Figure 7.3

Copyright (c) 2005–09, The Regents of the University of California. Used by permission.

7. Don't trust everything you read on the Internet. Anyone can create a Web site. Check to see who provided the information. Is it a trustworthy source? Is the information dated? What is the purpose of the Web site: to sell something or to provide knowledgeable information? Don't accept what is presented just because it is on the Internet.

Internet Language

The Internet contains millions of Web sites. A Web site address is known as the URL, or uniform resource locator. The Web address for the University of California, Davis, for instance, is: http://www.ucdavis.edu. The "http" stands for hypertext transport protocol, the language of the Web. The "www" refers to the World Wide Web. The last part of the address is called the domain name and ends with ".com" for commercial sites, ".edu" for educational sites, ".gov" for government

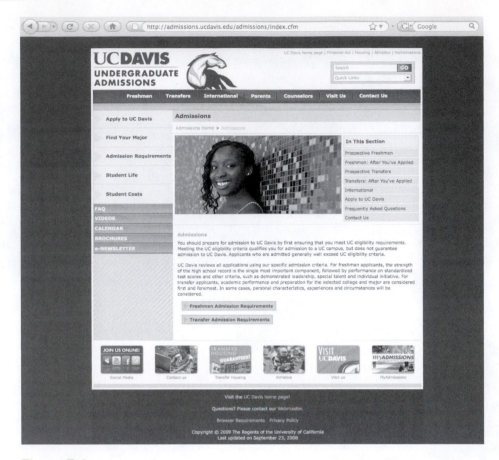

Figure 7.4

Copyright (c) 2005–09, The Regents of the University of California. Used by permission.

sites, and ".org" for nonprofit organizations. These can sometimes help in determining the legitimacy of some sites.

Search Engines

If you didn't already know the domain name of UC Davis, you could use one of many search engines on the Internet to find it. A search engine is like a directory for the Web. Some useful search engines are as follows:

Search Engine Name	URL
Google	http://www.google.com
Yahoo!	http://www.yahoo.com
AltaVista	http://www.altavista.com
WebCrawler	http://www.webcrawler.com
Go.com	http://www.go.com
Excite	http://www.excite.com

To reach a search engine, type a search engine address from the preceding list into your browser. When you visit one of these search engines, you will see a search box. Type in the keywords for a topic or person you want to research, and the search engine will list all the Internet sites it has indexed for that topic. Make certain your keywords aren't too broad or you will get thousands of useless listings. Narrow your keywords down to specific rather than broad areas.

Try different search engines. Some have better listings than others.

PRACTICE A-1: Reading on the World Wide Web

Directions: Place a *T* in the blank next to each of the following statements that is true.

_____   **1.** The Internet has become a major source for obtaining information on practically every subject.

_____   **2.** Reading on the Internet requires a different approach from the way we read printed text.

_____   **3.** A link is another term for the home page of a Web site.

_____   **4.** A Web site's address is known as a URL.

_____   **5.** A search engine can take you directly to the information you want on the Internet.

PRACTICE A-2: Understanding Web Sites

Directions: Answer the following questions in the spaces provided using the figures indicated.

Using Figure 7.1:

1. You are interested in finding out more about the students who attend UC Davis. What link would you click? _____

2. If you did not see a link for the information you wanted, what aids are provided to help your search? _____

3. How would you find the university's calendar of events? _____

_____

Using Figure 7.2:

4. How would you find information on financial aid? _____

_____

5. Is it possible to do off-campus coursework at the university? How do you know?

_____

Using Figure 7.3:

6. If you didn't find what you were looking for on this page, what link might you click on to find what you want? _____

_____

7. Where would you find information on the athletic programs at UC Davis?

_____

_____

Using Figure 7.4:

8. What would you click on if you wanted more information on transferring from another school to UC Davis? _____

_____

9. What would you click on if you wanted to know the dates of the Spring break?

_____

10. Where would you go to find information on when, where, and how to file an application for enrollment? _____

_____

PRACTICE A-3: The E-Mail and Blog Evolution

The Internet has brought with it another feature: e-mail. It, too, presents us with another way of reading. E-mail is often abbreviated, sometimes using symbols for words, such as the following:

:-)   used as a smile
;-)   used as a smile with a wink
:-(used to express sadness
8-)   used as a smile from a person with glasses

These symbols and others are known as *emoticons* or icons that express emotion. As the use of the Internet expands, so must our ability to read "Internet talk."

While e-mail has many personal and business advantages, disadvantages also exist. For instance, unscrupulous marketers flood e-mail inboxes with annoying *spam*, unwanted messages ranging from stupid to sick. As e-mail providers work to find filters to separate spam from legitimate messages, spammers work just as hard at finding new ways around the filters.

Be a careful reader of e-mail. Don't fall victim to some of the scams. Many people have fallen for cleverly worded and promising spam messages, from "Congratulations! You've just won the lottery," to "Our product guarantees you a happier sex life." If there is no way to find out the e-mail's legitimacy, delete it.

Current figures estimate that millions of blogs are on the Web. *Blogs* are Web texts written by one or more people and frequently updated, sometimes daily. Blogs might be called an online journal of someone's thinking on a particular subject. Often they invite others to join in the conversation. Students use them as a way to share writing or questions about a topic.

As a reader, remember that any information you obtain from blogs may or not be valid. Ask yourself, who is writing the blog? What are their credentials? Is what they are saying logical?

Blogs can be fun reading. Just be aware of the information source before accepting the content as valid.

Optional Exercise

Directions: Type in *blogs* in any search engine, such as Google or Yahoo, and explore some of the blog sites listed.

B.   Practices Using the Internet

The following practices require that you have access to a computer. If you do not have a personal computer, your school will have computer services available in the library or learning center that you can use.

PRACTICE B-1: Using Search Engines

Directions: Find the following Web sites by using one of the search engines mentioned on page 310 and write in the URL.

1. *The Washington Post* _____

2. The Biography Channel _____

3. OneLook Dictionary Search _____

4. Women in Sports _____

5. Infoplease almanacs _____

6. The Rock and Roll Hall of Fame and Museum, Cleveland

   _____

7. Museum of Modern Art, New York _____

8. The Internet Public Library _____

PRACTICE B-2: On Your Own: An Internet Training Guide

Directions: As a way to learn more about using the Internet, work through the Virtual Training Suite offered on Intute and written by lecturers and librarians from universities in England. While the site is geared toward British students, it can be a useful tool in learning how to use the Internet to help you with coursework, literature searching, teaching, and research. The site can be found at http://www.intute.ac.uk.

PRACTICE B-3: Visiting Sites on the Internet

Directions: Practice reading from the following Web sites to see how different Web pages are designed. Notice the various uses of color, sounds, text sizes, and fonts. Ask these three questions of the Web sites you visit:

1. Who or what organization created the Web site?

2. Is the information trustworthy?

3. What purpose does the Web site serve?
Web sites:

http://www.ed.gov
http://www.peacecorps.gov
http://promo.net/pg/history.html
http://www.bartleby.com/references
http://www.nytimes.com

http://www.house.gov
http://www.doaj.org
http://www.onion.com
http://www.innerbody.com

After you have found and evaluated some of the Web sites, pick one. Then, on another sheet of paper, write a summary of your experience of reading the Web site and turn it in to your instructor.

C.   Reading about the World Wide Web

PRACTICE C-1: Computer Use for Research and Information

Directions: As you read the following essay, apply what you learned in Chapter Two about reading for main ideas, supporting details, and identifying the author's thesis.

INTERNET RESEARCH AND INTERNET PLAGIARISM

from 123HelpMe.com

1   As wonderful as it is, the Internet is not the be-all and end-all of your research. A college-level term paper that uses only the Internet for information will probably not cover its subject adequately, and thus will not receive a high grade. There are several reasons for this. For one, the Internet tends to cover subjects more superficially than the printed literature, without the depth and context provided by a book. Most Internet sources also lack explicit citations to other sources for reference; such citation is an important part of articles found in professional journals and is one of the ways in which scholarly accountability is maintained.

2   Another important reason that the Internet should not be the primary information source for a term paper is the considerable variation in the quality of information available on the Internet. This variation is due to the Internet's lack of a standard for information quality. Printed, or "hardcopy," literature has a built-in safeguard to promote high quality information—peer-review. Peer-review means that the editor of the article or book has sent the manuscript to authorities in the subject matter (people like your professors). These reviewers evaluate the manuscript and reach a general consensus that the work meets the required standards. Reviewers cannot advise an editor to reject a manuscript simply because they might disagree with it. They can advise to reject it if there are flaws in the way in which the subject was investigated, if there are major internal inconsistencies, if the manuscript does not adequately deal with important counter arguments, or if the existing literature is not adequately referenced. Reviewers commonly offer suggestions to the writer for improving the manuscript before publication, and peer-reviewed publications are usually professionally edited as well. For example, this article has been peer-reviewed.

3   Another criticism of the Internet as a source of information for term papers is its ephemeral nature. The printed literature provides a permanent accessible record

123HelpMe.com, "Internet Research and Internet Plagiarism," 24 August 2009, http://www.123HelpMe.com/view.asp?id=22370.

stored in libraries. This is the knowledge base that scholars strive to improve and build upon, analogous to the foundation upon which a building is constructed. Information on the Internet, however, has no permanency, and is more like the shifting sands of a beach. What might be on a webpage today can easily be changed tomorrow. Information used to support an argument might not be there when someone tries to verify it later. In some cases, portions of the Internet are "archived" in order to preserve them for historical purposes; even so, this record probably has nothing like the permanence of published "hard-copy."

4   A final criticism of the Internet as a research tool concerns the sheer volume of randomly distributed material to be found there, and the difficulty of wading through it to locate specific information. This is like trying to find a needle in a haystack. Search engines help to solve this problem, but they have limitations. Search engines cannot, for example, help you choose an appropriate keyword for a search—a crucial skill when doing Internet research. Considerable thought must go into picking words or phrases that are fairly unique to your subject, or you will find that a search brings up lots of "bad hits," or inappropriate references.

5   Possible ways for quality control: check the web page where it resides: who put this information up? See below.

OPPORTUNITIES PROVIDED BY THE INTERNET

6   Despite its shortcomings, the Internet provides many research opportunities; as a starting point for finding an interesting subject, the Internet is unparalleled. It is analogous to an electronic encyclopedia with millions of entries and nearly as many authors. Since a few key words can locate many sources, you can readily determine the availability of Internet source materials for that topic. An Internet search can also alert you to controversial issues and differing points of view, which frequently make for good term paper topics.

7   For some types of information, the Internet is also unrivaled in its currency. In the area of climate research, government agencies and universities post some kinds of data to the Internet as it is collected. No printed reference can hope to achieve this degree of currency. However, this may not be all that useful for many term paper topics.

ASSESSING INTERNET SOURCES

8   It is important when using the Internet to evaluate your source. Several key traits should be used for evaluation purposes including currency, originality, accuracy, authority, purpose and objectivity (Kubly, 1997). These are discussed below. If you are skeptical about any of these traits after scrutinizing a source, the source should probably be discarded. As the old saying goes "if in doubt, leave it out."

9   Originality—Check the site for four essential elements: author's name, author's affiliation(s) or organization, page title, and page date. If one of these elements is missing you should probably assume that the author is not presenting original information, but rather is simply using information from another source. Most scholars want and deserve credit where credit is due. If you are still uncertain about the source of the information, check the document for citations and a reference list. Although not foolproof, the presence of references in an Internet source hints that the author understands and appreciates the need for verification of online information. This not only suggests a source with above average intellectual integrity, it also provides the opportunity to research the topic using the source's references. As a last resort, you might e-mail the page's author and ask about the source of the information.

10   Accuracy—Does the text contain any obvious grammatical, spelling, or punctuation errors? Do any statements or assertions in the document contradict other sources you have read? An individual or organization that does not concern itself with these types of errors cannot be trusted to provide reliable information.

11   Authority—Check the author's credentials if supplied. Does the author appear to be an authority on the subject. You might check a bibliographic database such as GeoRef to see if the author has published on the subject in peer-reviewed journals.

12   Purpose and objectivity—What is the intended purpose of the document; to inform, explain, or persuade? If informative or explanatory, are any significant conclusions drawn? If persuasive, does the author appear to have a bias? Does the author appear to provide only one side of a controversial issue? Does the author's affiliation lead you to question their objectivity? What is the intended audience for the document—the general public or the author's peers? In either case, are data supplied, and does the author indicate their source(s)? Is the methodology discussed so that the study can be replicated?

13   Ultimately, assessment of Internet sources requires critical thinking on the part of the reader. You must evaluate the quality of sources with respect to these criteria and decide for yourself whether or not to use a document.

WARNING AGAINST PLAGIARISM

14   One of the conveniences of the new Internet technologies is the cutting and pasting of text from one place to another. As a result, a sentence or paragraph from a webpage can be easily inserted into a term paper. This is wrong! The text of the term paper must be your own, and in your own words. To lift even a sentence—word for word or paraphrased—from another source constitutes plagiarism. Plagiarism is an intellectual dishonesty that in the scholarly world is the same as lying, cheating and stealing.

15   Some students believe that sentences or paragraphs can be lifted entirely provided that the source is cited. This is not correct. In the science world, sources for ideas or information are cited, but word for word text is hardly ever used except for historical purposes. Even if the source is cited, it is improper to paraphrase a sentence while retaining the original structure, because that implies the words are your own.

16   If you find a particularly elegant or useful phrase in the literature, it can be included in the term paper provided the phrase is within quotation marks and its source is cited. Larger textual passages should be indented, but this is very unusual in science articles (it is more common in the humanities and social sciences), and is generally discouraged in scientific writing.

17   Plagiarism can be avoided by reading the source material and taking notes and NEVER copying word for word. This must also apply to the Internet. Never cut and paste from a source into your term paper. As an added disincentive to cut and paste from the Internet, remember that, should your professor suspect that a phrase is not your own, the Internet could be easily searched for that phrase. Plagiarism from the Internet is very easy to catch!

Now answer the following questions.

1. Which of the following best states the author's thesis?

   a. There are several reasons the Internet can be a useful tool for term paper research, especially with the computer's ability to cut and paste material into a document.

    b. The Internet provides many opportunities for reliable research information on almost any subject.

    c. The use of Internet information in term papers requires critical evaluation of the accuracy and authority of the source and should never be used verbatim.

    d. Plagiarism is an intellectual dishonesty that in the scholarly world is the same as lying, cheating and stealing.

2. T /F The author believes that plagiarism can be avoided by reading the source material and by taking notes and never copying word for word.

3. T /F To check the authenticity of an Internet site, evaluate its timeliness, originality, accuracy, authority, purpose and objectivity.

4. Reread paragraph 2. What is the main idea? _____

_____

5. What advantage does print material (hardcopy) have over Internet information?

_____

Summary Review Practice

Directions: To keep in practice what you learned in Chapter Two, write a one-paragraph summary of the article "Internet Research and Internet Plagiarism" and turn it in to your instructor. Begin your paragraph with the words, "In the article "Internet Research and Internet Plagiarism" the author believes that . . ." and continue by supplying its thesis and what you think is the most important support.

PRACTICE **C-2**: Reading about Internet Literacy

Directions: The following selection is taken from the book *Literacy in the Cyberage: Composing Ourselves Online* by R. W. Burniske. The author feels there are three basic questions students should ask when they read any Web site. These three questions are referred to as a "rhetorical triangle of *ethos, logos,* and *pathos*":

    Ethos: Who or what organization created the Web document?
    Logos: Is the document's argument or position logical and coherent?
    Pathos: What emotional appeals are used (visual, sound, textual) to persuade the reader?

If you need to, feel free to return to these definitions for clarity as they appear in the selection.

CASE STUDY: THE STATE OF THE ONION

R. W. BURNISKE

1   Mr. Bellamy, the instructor of a rhetoric and composition seminar for undergraduates, had repeatedly admonished his charges to pay close attention to sources they selected from the Internet. All too often, he thought, students would browse the

Web looking for something "cool" to put into their essays without considering the source of the information they borrowed. To exacerbate matters, they often failed to provide proper documentation, revealing a scholarly approach that was as casual as it was careless. In the most celebrated instance, one student's citation for a Web site said nothing more than "Internet." Now, as his students prepared for their final essay of the semester, a proposal argument, Mr. Bellamy felt obliged to teach them a lesson in a most unusual manner.

2   He would pull an April Fools' Day prank.

3   If successful, it would teach his students the value of visual literacy and the dangers of virtual gullibility. More than anything, he wanted to teach them how to read a Web document with a more critical eye, examining information through the filters of ethos, logos, and pathos. By now, they knew enough about the rhetorical triangle to apply it to written words. They seemed quite capable of analyzing newspaper editorials and short essays that had served as the topic of class discussions. However, something happened when they turned to online sources featuring colorful graphics, animated icons, motion pictures, and sound. To practice what he preached as a composition teacher—"show, don't tell"—Mr. Bellamy wondered how he might demonstrate the consequences of weak visual and textual literacy skills. He wanted to present his students with a document that looked real, even sounded real, but came from an unreliable source or delivered misinformation.

4   So he went online and used a search engine to locate satirical Web sites. He didn't know where to begin, because he had never before looked for online, satirical publications. He was surprised to find so many but finally settled upon an article in *The Onion*, a weekly publication that specializes in satire (http://www.theonion.com). The article, "America Online to Build Three Million Home Pages for the Homeless," claimed that one of the largest Internet service providers in the United States had announced ambitious plans for a unique social service. Beneath its bold headline, the article featured America Online's (AOL) logo, a picture of Steve Case, the chief executive officer of AOL, and the image of a homeless man pushing a shopping cart full of belongings through snowy streets. Among other things, the article claimed that Mr. Case said "there is room enough for everyone in cyberspace," and that this new program was inspired by the belief that "no American should be without an address."

5   Mr. Bellamy liked this very much. It was just believable enough to fool gullible readers. The bold headlines, standard journalistic features, and details of the bogus social program established enough ethos to persuade some students that this was an authentic report; the photos of a smiling Steve Case and the man with his shopping cart would capture them through the emotional appeal of pathos; finally, the argument, though clearly flawed, was just persuasive enough to make less critical readers think it a sensible proposal. Would his students see right through this, or would they fall into this satirical web of deceit? Would the seductions of visual imagery overwhelm their ability to critique faulty logic ("Give a person a homepage, and you have given that person dignity")? Would they notice how this satire played with words, combining the ideas of a "home" and an "address" to create its humor? Mr. Bellamy honestly wasn't sure what would happen, but he decided to give this a try, typing up a brief prompt for an online discussion, one that would help "show" students what he had tried to "tell" them throughout the semester.

6   On April Fools' Day, Mr. Bellamy greeted his students as he would any other day, then announced that he wanted to hold a synchronous, online discussion to examine a "proposal argument" in preparation for the final essay assignment of the semester. The focus of the discussion would be a proposal he had discovered while reading an online article. He then divided the class of 21 students into three discussion groups, with students numbering off so that the members of the respective groups were not seated beside each other. Students were given five minutes to individually read and study the one-page article on the Internet. They were not allowed to discuss it with their classmates before joining their online groups, which would have approximately ten minutes for their synchronized discussion.

7   Much to his delight, the groups conducted an extremely animated debate over this proposal. In fact, it was one of the liveliest synchronous, online discussions Mr. Bellamy had ever witnessed. Despite a deliberate prompt, however, the students failed to consider all three points of the rhetorical triangle. To his amazement and alarm, he watched 21 of 22 students fall victim to the prank, engaging in a heated argument over this most foolish proposal. Not until Mr. Bellamy interrupted to ask a question about ethos did 1 student out of 22 pause to consider the source of the information.

STUDENT REFLECTIONS

8   What did the students learn from this exercise? Following the synchronous discussions and the revelation that this had been an April Fools' prank, Mr. Bellamy asked each student to read the transcript of the synchronous discussions, which he posted on the class Web site, and then type a brief reflection on what caused them to fall for this foolish prank. In the first of these, Jennifer B. offers one of the most common reactions, lamenting her failure to consider the source and pay attention to the ethos of the Web document.

> I fell for this April Fool's trick because I assumed it was from a legitimate source. Being in a classroom setting, I did not think that the exercise would be fake. I was concentrating more on the assignment than I was on the source. In reading the Interchange that took place after reading the article, I noticed only one person in the classroom said anything about The Onion as the source. Even after it was posted that the document was fake, no one responded. It was as if no one cared and that they were more concerned with the other aspects of the exercise. I fell into the same trap as the rest of the class. It has taught the class and myself to always begin with the legitimacy of the source.

9   Jennifer B.'s comments reveal a disturbing tendency, which one might describe as the "transferal of ethos" from one source to another. In this instance, Jennifer and her classmates transferred the teacher's ethos, and their expectations for the kind of article their teacher would choose, to the Web document they encountered. Based on informal surveys of students, this seems a common phenomenon. In the following reflection, Brent S. reinforces this notion. He explains his misreading as a consequence of blind faith in the professor and susceptibility to the pathos of the text and images he encountered, which resulted from a preoccupation with the article's appearance.

> Why did I fall for this article? Well, first of all, I guess I believed it because Mr. B. told us to read it. It was something he had found and gave to us. That gave it some credibility in my mind. I thought, "Well, Mr. B. gave it to us,

it's most likely not a joke." Why would he give us something to discuss if it weren't real? Now I know why he did it, but that is the main reason why I thought it was real. I also believed it because it looked real. It looked like any other article you would find in an on-line newspaper. It had pictures. It just looked authentic. This experience has hopefully taught me to be more critical of the things I read, especially when they are on the Internet.

10   There is also the matter of the message. Where the first two reactions stress ethos and pathos, Kara W.'s reflection touches the third point on the rhetorical triangle. She notes the way in which preoccupation with an item's logos—and the heated debates it inspires—can blunt one's attention to other points on the triangle.

> I bought into the article simply because I did not check out the source or author. In fact, it seems that the entire group focused on the logos of his argument, and a little on the pathos. But no one gave a single thought on his ethos. We all overlooked the fact that there was no author, no credentials, and no justification as to why this guy has any authority to write the article. Strange, seeing as how this class emphasizes all THREE parts of the rhetorical triangle, and we manage to totally ignore one. In the future, we must all be more wary of where the information is coming from.

11   Obviously, statements like these are cause for hope, suggesting that this student has learned a valuable lesson about the rhetorical analysis of Web sites. As this final reflection indicates, an exercise such as this helps students learn a good deal about visual literacy and their own skills. Kelly, the author of the following reflection, had already created her own Web pages and used the Internet extensively for research, yet she couldn't resist the seductions of this satirical presentation. Rather than attempt to explain or excuse her misreading of the document, she seizes this opportunity to look upon her own mistakes and learn from them. Much to her credit, she draws valuable lessons from the exercise, recognizing her own tendencies and realizing the actions she must take in order to prevent future misreadings.

> It is interesting to see the discussion others had about the subject. It seems I was not the only one who was duped into thinking AOL was actually going to implement this program. It just shows how people are incredibly vulnerable. It is a little bit scary to think that I can be tricked so easily. This was a harmless joke, but if I believe everything I read then I could be giving people false information and perhaps harming myself and others. In the future, I need to look at the source more carefully. If I would have just looked at the address I would have seen that this did not come from AOL. It is important to examine the address. Who is writing it? Why are they writing it? What audience are they writing to? And what message are they trying to portray? These are some of the questions I need to start asking myself instead of immediately divulging [sic] into the article.

SEEING IS BELIEVING (AND OTHER SATIRICAL LESSONS)

12   There are many lessons to be learned from this exercise, but perhaps one of the most important echoes John Berger's earlier observation: "The way we see things is affected by what we know or what we believe." These students, who in many ways are fairly typical undergraduates at a public university, fell for this prank because of

what their eyes told them they were seeing. Aesthetically, this item looked like something they might find in the online version of a newspaper or magazine. The bold font style, the color photos, and the AOL logo made them believe they were looking at an authentic document. However, the key to this exercise, and one that Mr. Bellamy understood intuitively, is the manner in which the item is presented. Had the teacher prefaced the exercise by saying, "I thought we'd have some fun on April Fools' Day by looking at some satirical Web sites," students would have brought that expectation—that "belief system"—to their reading of the document. However, since the teacher tied the exercise to the students' assignment—a proposal argument—they brought different expectations with them, expectations that influenced what they saw and how they interpreted it. This speaks volumes about the importance of teaching visual literacy skills. Although educators may not think in these terms yet, the exponential growth of the World Wide Web and Internet connectivity in schools compels them to find ways to teach visual literacy. Exercises like Mr. Bellamy's may help students resist the seductions of fancy graphics and overcome the visual cues that excite the passion of pathos and overwhelm judgment of the author's credibility and logos.

Comprehension Check

Directions: Answer the following questions without looking back. Try to answer using complete sentences.

1. What is the author's thesis or main idea? _____

_____

_____

2. Why did Mr. Bellamy, the instructor, conduct his April Fools' Day prank on his students? _____

_____

3. What Web site did Mr. Bellamy use in his experimental prank?

_____

4. What features did the Web site have that made Mr. Bellamy think it would be useful in his teaching? _____

5. What did the Web site claim that AOL was going to do? _____

_____

6. How much time were students given to read and study the Web page? _____

7. How many of the twenty-two students in his class fell victim to the prank?

_____

8. John Berger is quoted as saying, "The way we see things is affected by what we know or what we believe." Explain what this has to do with reading on the Internet.

_____

_____

9. Circle any of the following that are lessons for reading on the Internet that students learned from Mr. Bellamy's assignment.

    a.   Begin by checking the legitimacy of the Web source.

    b. Don't believe what's on a Web site just because it looks "real."

    c. Don't be taken in by the visuals on a page; examine them.

    d. Don't believe everything you read, even if it's assigned by an instructor.

  10. Do you think you would have been fooled by Mr. Bellamy's prank? Why or why not? _____

Vocabulary Check

Directions: Define the following underlined words from the selection.

1. He had repeatedly <u>admonished</u> his charges to pay close attention to sources they selected from the Internet. _____

2. To <u>exacerbate</u> matters, they often failed to provide proper documentation. _____

3. One student's <u>citation</u> for a Web site said nothing more than "Internet." _____

4. It would teach his students the value of visual literacy and the dangers of <u>gullibility</u>. _____

5. He went online and used a search engine to locate <u>satirical</u> Web sites. _____

6. There is room enough for everyone in <u>cyberspace</u>. _____

7. Would the <u>seductions</u> of visual imagery overwhelm their ability to critique faulty logic? _____

8. He wanted to hold a <u>synchronous</u>, online discussion to examine a "proposal argument." _____

9. She offers one of the most common reactions, <u>lamenting</u> her failure to consider the source. _____

10. <u>Aesthetically</u>, this item looked like something they might find in the online version of a newspaper or magazine. _____

Record the results of the comprehension and vocabulary checks on the Student Record Chart in the Appendix. Each correct answer is worth 10 points, for a total of 100 points possible for comprehension and 100 points for vocabulary.

Remember to make vocabulary cards for any words that gave you trouble.

Summary Review Practice

Directions: To keep in practice what you learned in Chapter Two, write a one-paragraph summary of the article "Case Study: The State of the Onion" and turn it in to your instructor. Identify the author and article title and summarize what Bellamy's students learned.

PRACTICE C-3: Vocabulary Review

Directions: The following words are from reading exercises you have read in this chapter. Write each word in the appropriate blank. Any words you discover you don't know, add to your vocabulary.

| scrutinizing | admonished | gullibility | infinite | permanency |
| lamenting | exacerbate | cyberspace | citation | ephemeral |

1. One criticism of the Internet as a source of information for term papers is its _____ nature.

2. He wanted to teach his students the value of visual literacy and the dangers of _____.

3. Information on the Internet has no _____ and is more like the shifting sands of a beach.

4. Using the Internet, students can tap into an _____ variety of endless subjects.

5. If you are skeptical about the accuracy of a site's information after _____ the source, the source should be discarded.

6. The student offered one of the most common reactions, _____ her failure to consider the source.

7. The instructor repeatedly _____ his students to check the validity of their sources.

8. There is room enough for everyone in _____.

9. To _____ matters, students often failed to provide proper documentation.

10. One student's _____ for a Web site said nothing more than "Internet."

D.   Putting It All Together

PRACTICE D-1: Timed Reading

Directions: The following selection can be used as a Timed Reading if so assigned. You may want to review the comments about timing your reading on pages 103–106 before you begin. Check your reading rate score from the last timed reading you did and try to read at least 50 wpm faster.

The article appeared in the *New York Times* in 1997. As you read for the author's thesis and main ideas, determine if the information is dated or if it still has value for today's Internet usage.

Begin Timing: _____

HOW STUDENTS GET LOST IN CYBERSPACE

STEVEN R. KNOWLTON

1   When Adam Pasick, a political science major at the University of Wisconsin at Madison, started working on his senior honors thesis this fall, he began where the nation's more than 14 million college students increasingly do: not at the campus library, but at his computer terminal.

2   As he roamed the World Wide Web, he found journal articles, abstracts, indexes, and other pieces of useful information. But it wasn't until he sought help from his professor, Charles H. Franklin, that he found the mother lode.

3   Dr. Franklin steered Mr. Pasick to thousands of pages of raw data of a long-term study of political attitudes, information crucial to Mr. Pasick's inquiry into how family structure affects political thinking.

4   The Web site containing all this data is no secret to political scientists, Dr. Franklin said, but can be hard for students to find.

5   "It is barely possible that if you did a Web search, you would show it up," he said. "Whether the average undergraduate could is another question." It would be even harder for the uninitiated to find their way around the site, he said. "One of the things you're missing on the Web is a reference librarian."

6   It is just such difficulties that worry many educators. They are concerned that the Internet makes readily available so much information, much of it unreliable, that students think research is far easier than it really is. As a result, educators say, students are producing superficial research papers, full of data—some of it suspect—and little thought. Many of the best sources on the Web are hard to find with conventional search engines or make their information available only at a steep price, which is usually borne by universities that pay annual fees for access to the data.

7   Mr. Pasick, 21, of Ann Arbor, Mich., whose conversation is filled with computer and Web search terms, admits that he would never have found the site, much less the data, on his own.

8   "All the search engines are so imprecise," Mr. Pasick said. "Whenever I have tried to find something precise that I was reasonably sure is out there, I have had trouble."

9   Dr. David B. Rothenberg, a philosophy professor at the New Jersey Institute of Technology, in Newark, said his students' papers had declined in quality since they began using the Web for research.

10   "There are these strange references that don't quite connect," he said. "There's not much sense of intelligence. We're indexing, but we're not thinking about things."

11   One way to improve the quality of students' research is to insist that students be more thorough, said Elliot King, a professor of mass communication at Loyola College of Maryland and author of "The Online Student," a textbook for on-line searching.

12   "Because information is so accessible, students stop far too quickly," he said. If a research paper should have 15 sources, he said, the professor should insist students find, say, 50 sources and use the best 15. When Dr. King assigns research papers in his own classes, he insists that students submit all the sources they did not use, along with those they finally selected.

13   The jumble in Web-based student papers mirrors the information jumble that is found on line, said Gerald M. Santoro, the lead research programmer at the Pennsylvania State University's Center for Academic Computing in State College, PA.

14   The Internet, he said, is commonly thought of as a library, although a poorly catalogued one, given the limitations of the search engines available. But he prefers another analogy.

15   "In fact, it is like a bookstore," Dr. Santoro said, explaining that Web sites exist because someone wants them there, not because any independent judge has determined them worthy of inclusion.

16   Dr. William Miller, dean of libraries at Florida Atlantic University in Boca Raton, and the immediate past president of the Association of College and Research Libraries, cautioned that free Web sites were often constructed "because somebody has an ax to grind or a company wants to crow about its own products." And he said that the creators of many sites neglect to keep them up to date, so much information on the Web may be obsolete.

17   "For the average person looking for what is the cheapest flight to Chicago this weekend, or what is the weather like in Brazil, the Web is good," Dr. Miller said. But much of its material, he added, is simply not useful to scholars.

18   Yet despite the Web's limitations, educators like Dr. King still see it as a way to "blast your way out of the limitations of your own library."

19   Some of the most valuable information comes from home pages set up by the government and universities. One example, said Dr. King, was research conducted by a student trying to find information on cuts in financing for the Corporation of Public Broadcasting. The relevant books in the college's library were few and outdated, he said, but, with his help, the student found full texts of Congressional hearings about public broadcasting's budget.

20   "Her essay no longer consisted of relying on books or magazines," he said, "but in getting raw data on which the books and magazines are based."

21   On the Web, students can also find electronic versions of the most popular academic journals, the mainstay of research for faculty and advanced students. Most university libraries now have electronic subscriptions to a few hundred journals. Dr. Miller warned, however, that while that may be a tenth of the journals in the library of a small liberal arts college, it is a tiny fraction of the journals subscribed to by a large research university, which may order more than 100,000. The trend is clearly toward electronic versions of academic journals, he added, but most are still not on line and the ones that are tend to be expensive. On-line subscriptions, for instance, can often run into thousands of dollars a year.

22   The time will surely come, Dr. Miller said, when most academic journals are on line, "but you'll need either a credit card number or a password" from an institution that has bought an electronic subscription. "And if you don't have one or the other, you won't get in," he said.

23   When Mr. Pasick turned to Dr. Franklin for help, the professor's expertise was only one of the necessary ingredients for success. The other was the University of Wisconsin's access to the Web site, as one of 450 research institutions that pay up to $10,000 a year for the privilege. (The site is operated by the Interuniversity Consortium for Political and Social Research, at http://www.icpsr.umich.edu.)

24   Even at an institution with the resources to take full advantage of cyberspace, there are some forms of assistance that the Web will never provide, some educators say.

25   Dr. Santoro describes academic research as a three-step process: finding the relevant information, assessing the quality of that information, and then using that information "either to try to conclude something, to uncover something, to prove something or to argue something." At its best, he explained, the Internet, like a library, provides only data.

26   In the research process, he said, "the Internet is only useful for that first part, and also a little bit for the second. It is not useful at all in the third."

Finish Timing: Record time here_____and use the Timed Reading Conversion Chart in the Appendix to figure your rate:_____wpm.

Comprehension Check

Directions: Answer the following questions without looking back. Try to answer using complete sentences.

1. What is the author's thesis or main idea? _____

    _____

2. Why do some students think that research using the Internet is easier than it is?

    _____

3. Why are many of the best sources on the Web hard to find or to obtain?

    _____

4. What does one professor suggest doing that would improve the quality of a student's research on the Web? _____

    _____

5. One person quoted in the article believes that the Internet should not be thought of as a library but as a bookstore. What does he mean? _____

    _____

    _____

6. Why, according to one source, are many free Web sites not reliable? _____

    _____

7. Who creates some of the most valuable home pages? _____

    _____

8. What is the mainstay of research on the Web for faculty and advanced students?

    _____

9. Dr. Santoro describes academic research as a three-step process. What are the three steps?

    1. _____

    2. _____

    3. _____

10. Why do you think the information in this article is or is not relevant today?

    _____

Vocabulary Check

Directions: Define the following underlined words from the selection.

1. . . . not at the campus library, but at his computer <u>terminal.</u>

    _____

2. As he roamed the World Wide Web, he found journal articles, <u>abstracts</u>, indexes, and other pieces of useful information. _____

3. Dr. Franklin steered Mr. Pasick to . . . information <u>crucial</u> to Mr. Pasick's inquiry.

_____

4. It would be even harder for the <u>uninitiated</u> to find their way around the site.

_____

5. Many of the best sources on the Web are hard to find with <u>conventional</u> search engines. _____

6. All the search engines are so <u>imprecise</u>.

_____

7. Because information is so <u>accessible</u>, students stop far too quickly.

_____

8. Web sites were often constructed because somebody has an <u>ax to grind</u>

_____

9. . . . or a company wants to <u>crow</u> about its own products.

_____

10. Creators of many sites neglect to keep them up to date, so much information on the Web may be <u>obsolete</u>.

_____

Record your rate and the results of the comprehension and vocabulary checks on the Student Record Chart in the Appendix. Each correct answer is worth 10 points for a total of 100 points possible for comprehension and 100 points for vocabulary.

PRACTICE D-2: Timed Reading

Directions: The following selection can be used as a Timed Reading if so assigned. You may want to review the comments about timing your reading on pages 000–000 before you begin. Check your reading rate score from the last timed reading you did and try to read at least 50 wpm faster.

Begin Timing: _____

YAHOO IN CHINA

WILLIAM H. SHAW AND VINCENT BARRY

1. Shi Tao is a thirty-seven-year-old Chinese journalist and democracy advocate. Arrested for leaking state secrets in 2005, he was sentenced to ten years in prison. His crime? Mr. Shi had disclosed that the Communist Party's propaganda department had ordered tight controls for handling the anniversary of the infamous June 4, 1989, crackdown on demonstrators in Beijing's Tiananmen Square. A sad story, for sure, but it's an all too familiar one, given China's notoriously poor record on human rights. What makes Mr. Shi's case stand out, however, is the fact that he was arrested and

convicted only because the American company Yahoo revealed his identity to Chinese authorities.[78]

2.   You see, Mr. Shi had posted his information anonymously on a Chinese-language website called Democracy Forum, which is based in New York. Chinese journalists say that Shi's information, which revealed only routine instructions on how officials were to dampen possible protests, was already widely circulated. Still, the Chinese government's elite State Security Bureau wanted to put its hands on the culprit behind the anonymous posting. And for that it needed Yahoo's help in tracking down the Internet address from which huoyanl989@yahoo.com.cn had accessed his e-mail. This turned out to be a computer in Mr. Shi's workplace, Contemporary Business News in Changsha, China.

3.   A few months after Shi's conviction, the watchdog group Reporters Without Borders revealed the story of Yahoo's involvement and embroiled the company in a squall of controversy. After initially declining to comment on the allegation, Yahoo eventually admitted that it had helped Chinese authorities catch Mr. Shi and that it had supplied information on other customers as well. But the company claimed that it had no choice, that the information, was provided as part of a "legal process," and that the company is obliged to obey the laws of any country in which it operates. Yahoo cofounder, Jerry Yang, said: "I do not like the outcome of what happens with these things . . . but we have to comply with the law. That's what you need to do in business."

4.   Some critics immediately spied a technical flaw in that argument: The information on Mr. Shi was provided by Yahoo's subsidiary, in Hong Kong, which has an independent judiciary and a legal process separate from that of mainland China. Hong Kong legislation does not spell out what e-mail service providers must do when presented with a court order by mainland authorities. Commentators pointed out, however, that even if Yahoo was legally obliged to reveal the information, there was a deeper question of principle involved. As the *Financial Times* put it in an editorial: "As a general principle, companies choosing to operate in a country should be prepared to obey its laws. When those laws are so reprehensible that conforming to them would be unethical, they should be ready to withdraw from that market." Congressional representative Christopher H. Smith, a New Jersey Republican and chair of a House subcommittee on human rights, was even blunter: "This is about accommodating a dictatorship. It's outrageous to be complicit in cracking down on dissenters." And in an open letter to Jerry Yang, the Chinese dissident Liu Xiabo, who has himself suffered censorship, imprisonment, and other indignities, wrote: "I must tell you that my indignation at and contempt for you and your company are not a bit less than my indignation and contempt for the Communist regime. . . . Profit makes you dull in morality. Did it ever occur to you that it is a shame for you to be considered a traitor to your customer Shi Tao?"

5.   Whether profit is dulling their morality is an issue that must be confronted not just by Yahoo but also by other Internet-related, companies doing business in China. Microsoft, for example, recently shut down the MSN Spaces website of a popular Beijing blogger whose postings had run afoul of censors. Google has agreed to apply the Chinese censors' blacklist to its new Chinese search engine. And a congressional investigative committee has accused Google, Yahoo, and Cisco of helping to maintain in China "the most sophisticated Internet control system in the world." In their defense, the companies ask what good it would do for them to pull out of the Chinese market. They contend that if they resist the Chinese government and their operations are closed down or if they choose to leave the country for moral reasons, they would only deny to ordinary Chinese whatever fresh air the Internet, even filtered and censored, can provide in a closed society. It's more important for them to stay there,

From William H. Shaw and Vincent Barry, *Moral Issues in Business*, 11th Edition, Wadsworth, 2010, pp. 248–249.

play ball with the government, and do what they can to push for Internet freedom. As Yahoo chairman Terry S. Semel puts it: "Part of our role in any form of media is to get whatever we can into those countries and to show and to enable people, slowly, to see the Western way and what our culture is like, and to learn." But critics wonder what these companies, when they are complicit in political repression, are teaching the Chinese about American values.

6.   Some tech companies are turning to the U.S. government for help. Bill Gates, for example, thinks that legislation making it illegal for American companies to assist in the violation of human rights overseas would help. A carefully crafted American anti-repression law would give Yahoo an answer the next time Chinese officials demand evidence against cyber-dissidents. We want to obey your laws, Yahoo officials could say, but our hands are tied; we can't break American law. The assumption is that China would have no choice but to accept this because it does not want to forgo the advantages of having U.S. tech companies operating there.

7.   Still, this doesn't answer the underlying moral questions. At a November 2007 congressional hearing, however, a number of lawmakers made their own moral views perfectly clear. They lambasted Yahoo, describing the company as "spineless and irresponsible" and "moral pygmies." In response, Jerry Yang apologized to the mother of Shi Tao, who attended the hearing. Still, Yahoo has its defenders. Robert Reich, for instance, argues that "Yahoo is not a moral entity" and "its executives have only one responsibility . . . to make money for their shareholders and, along the way, satisfy their consumers." And in this case, he thinks, the key "consumer" is the Chinese governments.

Finish Timing: Record time here —————— and use the Timed Reading Conversion Chart in the Appendix to figure your rate: —————— wpm.

Comprehension Check

Directions: Answer the following questions without looking back.

1. How did the Chinese government discover that Shi Tao, a journalist, had anonymously posted state secret information on a Chinese Web site? _____

    _____

2. The information Mr. Shi posted was

    a. highly sensitive information on how to deal with protests.

    b. about a crackdown on Tiananmen Square in 1989.

    c. information about China's elite State Security Bureau.

    d. already circulated routine instructions on how officials were to dampen possible protests.

3. T/F   Yahoo admitted that it had helped Chinese authorities catch Mr. Shi but refused to supply information on other Yahoo customers.

4. What excuse did Jerry Yang, cofounder of Yahoo, offer as a reason for revealing Mr. Shi's identity? _____

    _____

5. What flaws did some critics find in Yahoo's decision to inform on Mr. Shi?

   a. Yahoo's subsidiary is in Hong Kong and has a different legal process separate from mainland China.

   b. When a country's laws are so reprehensible that conforming to them would be unethical, a company should withdraw from that country's market.

   c. Doing so is accommodating a dictatorship.

   d. All of the above.

   e. None of the above.

6. Which of the following companies are also complying with the Chinese government's request for some censorship and control of the Internet?

   a. Microsoft

   b. Google

   c. Cisco

   d. All of the above

   e. None of the above.

7. Why do some companies believe it is better to cooperate with the Chinese Government's requests? _____

   _____   _____

8. T/F Some tech companies want the U.S. government to pass a law making it illegal for American companies to assist in the violation of human rights overseas.

9. T/F Jerry Yang apologized to the mother of Mr. Shi.

10. T/F Defenders of Yahoo claim that Yahoo is not a moral entity and that its only obligation and responsibility as a company is to its shareholders.

Vocabulary Check

Directions: Define the following underlined words from the selection.

1. . . . a Chinese journalist and democracy advocate. . .

   _____

2. . . .embroiled the company in a squall of controversy. . .

   _____

3. . . . .embroiled the company in a squall of controversy. . .

   _____

4. . . .declined to comment on the allegation. . .

   _____

5. . . .Yahoo's subsidiary in Hong Kong. . .

   _____

6. . . .to be complicit in cracking down on dissenters. . .

   _____

7. . . .the laws are so reprehensible. . .

   _____

8. . . .evidence against <u>cyber-dissidents</u>. . .

_____

9. . . .they do not want to <u>forgo</u> the advantages

_____

10. . . .not a moral <u>entity</u>. . .

_____

Record your rate and the results of the comprehension and vocabulary checks on the Student Record Chart in the Appendix. Each correct answer is worth 10 points for a total of 100 points possible for comprehension and 100 points for vocabulary.

Before you go on to the next chapter, make certain you understand any mistakes or problems you may have encountered in this chapter. It is important that you learn from mistakes, so don't despair when you make them. Accept mistakes as normal. Making mistakes is often the best way to discover what you do and don't know.

Remember to make vocabulary cards for any words that gave you trouble.

Questions for Group Discussion

1. As a group, discuss the moral issues raised in "Yahoo in China." Was the company a "traitor" to its customer, as Liu Xiabo believes? Was Yahoo right or wrong to assist the Chinese authorities? What would you have done if you were in charge of Yahoo?

2. Discuss what each of you has learned from reading this chapter. Each person should state something he or she didn't know about the Internet before reading this chapter. Who in your group has had the most experience on the Web and is willing to help those with less experience?

3. Referring back to "Case Study: The State of the Onion" (pp. 318–321), discuss the three fundamental questions referred to as *ethos*, *logos*, and *pathos*. How helpful will knowing these fundamental questions be as you read more Web sites?

4. Discuss how useful the Internet is or will be to each of you as students.

5. As a group, see how many of you can use the following words in a sentence. Make certain you learn the ones you still may not be able to use or recognize by writing the definition in the blank space.

a. admonish _____

b. exacerbate _____

c. cyberspace _____

d. synchronous _____

e. lament _____

f. abstracts _____

g. imprecise _____

h. terminal _____

i. obsolete _____

j. aesthetic _____

On Your Own

Pick ten new words you learned in this chapter, not necessarily those listed in question 5 for group discussion, and on a separate paper write a sentence for each word, using it correctly in context. Turn in the paper to your instructor

A Final Check

At the beginning of this unit, you looked at a diagram that illustrated the three facets of comprehension. Now you have completed the unit that is represented by the left leg of the triangle.

For the diagram below, fill in the blank lines in this section. Working with a partner or small group is acceptable if your instructor sets up groups.

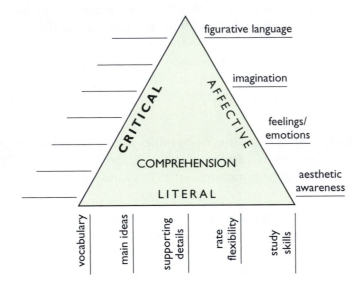

Hints: The first line has to do with information and judgments. The next four lines have to do with the author's worldview and how it influences our reading. The sixth line has to do with reading between the lines. The seventh line deals with what the reader does based on the information given.

When you have finished, check your answers with the triangle at the beginning of Unit Two.

UNIT THREE

AFFECTIVE COMPREHENSION

Jacky Chapman/Janine Wiedel Photolibrary/Alamy

What Is Affective Comprehension?

Knut Hamsun wrote, "One must know and recognize not merely the direct but the secret power of the word." This unit is about the "secret power of the word," or affective comprehension.

Affective comprehension, most simply put, is your reaction to what you read at the literal and critical levels of understanding. It is your intellectual and emotional response to what you read. Why, for instance, do some people prefer to read factual materials rather than fiction? Why do some people react favorably and others negatively to a novel such as *Moby Dick*? Why do some people read fiction merely for recreation, whereas others find it personally enlightening? These differences are based on people's affective reaction to the type of material that they read.

Why do people find pleasure in reading? Here are some affective reasons:

We read to free ourselves from the grind and the misery and big ticking time-bomb questions of life. We read for the same reason we walk alone in the woods or squeeze our ears between headphones. We all need contemplative time, time away, time in another world altogether. For me, that happens when I pick up a good book—or, for that matter, a good newspaper. (T. C. Boyle, author)

When it came my turn to read, I still remember the feeling of betrayal. "See Spot run. Run, Spot, run." Seriously? But then came E. B. White and Laura Ingalls Wilder, Mark Twain and Harper Lee, Kurt Vonnegut and J. R. R. Tolkien, and I got it. I understood, you're sitting right there, reading, and you're anywhere, everywhere. (Veronique de Turenne, journalist)

I read because it is one of the very few satisfying escapes from reality that isn't fattening and doesn't destroy brain cells. (Amy Koss, author)

Why do readers bother with books that challenge their intellects? For that matter, why do authors go to the trouble of writing them? Because they hunger for new experiences, new perspectives from which they can learn. They aren't afraid of the esoteric, the rebellious or the righteous. William Faulkner is one of the great figures in America literature, and he's also considered one of the most challenging.... But tackling a challenging author like Faulkner can do wonders for your critical-thinking skills. Some of his most effective works are accessible and even conventional; yet they illustrate his complex vision of the South—and humanity as a whole—with power, beauty and simplicity. (Jack Clemens, freelance writer)

We read to learn. We read to live another way. We read to quench some blind and shocking fire. We read to weigh the worth of what we have done or dare to do. We read to share our awful secrets with someone we know will not refuse us. We read our way into the presence of great wisdom, vast and safe suffering, or into the untidy corners of another kind of life we fear to lead. With the book we can sin at a safe distance. With Maugham's artists in *The Moon* and *Sixpence*, we can discommit ourselves of family responsibility and burn our substance and our talent in bright colors on a tropical isle. (Frank Jennings, from *This Is Reading*)

Unless we react at an affective level, a personal, meaningful level, reading becomes dull and uninteresting. It becomes nothing more than a series of isolated drills in which you read and answer questions to plot on a chart.

Once you have mastered basic reading skills, it is important to move into the world of facts and opinions, ideas, and feelings. As a good reader, you will become your own teacher, using the learned skills to rebuild and reorganize your thoughts and beliefs. That can happen only when you have affective reactions to what you read.

Affective comprehension also has to do with our tastes and appreciation of the skills involved in writing. For instance, many people prefer to read *Reader's*

Digest because it takes a collection of readings from a variety of sources and condenses them for easier and faster reading. What they end up reading is seldom the original work; in fact, the language is frequently changed or written at a lower level. This may be a convenient way to read from many sources, but some readers prefer reading the original works. It's a matter of preference and taste.

Our tastes in reading often change as we ourselves change. For example, as a college student you may be required to read a book that is considered a classic. At the time in your life that you are reading it, you may be bored by the work and wonder what all the praise is about. Years later, a rereading of that book may provide you with the answers to your own questions that you weren't ready for during college. Does your present lack of appreciation for, say, Herman Melville's *Moby Dick* mean you lack taste? Do you have poor affective comprehension? Will you "appreciate" it when you're eighty years old? Why do critics think it's such a great work? Answers to these questions are all part of developing affective comprehension.

Some people try to rely solely on their intellect as a way to see and respond to the world. While reason is important, it is just as important to stay in touch with our feelings; it's what makes us human. When we lose touch with our feelings, we lose a part of our humanity, the part of us that lets us know we're alive. Reacting affectively is to react openly, to share our feelings with others, and to know that others can, have, and will feel as we do.

What Does This Unit Cover?

Much of our affective reaction has to do with our feelings. Someone once said that our feelings are our sixth sense, the sense that interprets, analyzes, orders, and summarizes the other five senses. Whether we feel and appreciate the fear, joy, shock, or passion an author wants us to feel through words depends on our ability to feel them in real life. The inability to react to what we read with appropriate feelings is to miss a large part of what total comprehension is all about.

This unit contains two chapters. The first practices in Chapter Eight, through the use of pictures, advertisements, and expository writings, will help you understand your affective reaction to a variety of materials. The second set of practices develops your ability to see how figurative language is used to create images and analogies as used in poetry. You have already done some drills in figurative language in Unit Two; this chapter will explore your affective reactions to words at the literal, critical, and affective levels of comprehension.

Chapter Nine provides practices in reading short fiction. Reading fiction requires a different approach from expository writing. Just as painters deal with different colors and designs to give us an image of how they see things, so do writers paint pictures with words. They stimulate our senses—taste, touch, smell, sight, and sound—with word images. How well a writer can create impressions and emotional reactions for us often depends on his or her use of figurative language.

In this unit it is important to discuss some of the questions in class. Only through interacting with others, sharing your feelings, and listening to those of others, will you begin to develop your affective levels of comprehension. Good discussions are frequently frustrating because there often doesn't seem to be a "correct" answer. (It's especially frustrating to instructors who want all questions to have right or wrong answers in order to make grading your responses easier!) But sometimes there are no "right" answers; it's important to listen to others as their sixth sense (feelings) interprets their literal and critical thought processes.

What Should You Know after Completing This Unit?

As in previous units, you should strive to accomplish some objectives by the time you finish this unit. You should be able to:

1. Recognize how writers use figurative language to stimulate our senses.

2. Recognize images in both fictional and nonfictional writings.

3. Write a definition of *affective comprehension*.

4. See how closely tied together literal, critical, and affective levels of comprehension are.

5. Approach the various types of literature with an awareness of what is expected of you as a reader in each case.

6. Know all three facets of the comprehension triangle:

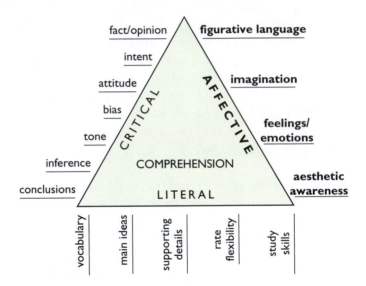

7. If you have personal objectives of your own, write them down on a separate sheet of paper and share them with your instructor.

CHAPTER EIGHT

Developing Affective Awareness

A.   Responding Affectively

One important element involved in developing reading comprehension is your affective or emotional involvement with what you read. Without an affective reaction to what you read, comprehension would be just matter-of-fact and rather dull. Some things, such as scientific and historical facts, can be presented and received with little or no affective reaction. But the whole range of human emotions is also communicated through the written word. The concern of this chapter is your affective reaction to what you read.

There are both negative and positive affective reactions. You may begin reading a poem, story, or essay with a positive attitude, only to discover that what you are reading isn't really interesting or moving or agreeable to you. This legitimate type of negative response comes about because of the literature itself, not because of a prereading judgment on your part. It is also possible to approach something you read with a preconceived bias, or to let your emotional reaction to what you read warp your critical judgment. Only when your affective reaction is based on critical evaluation and judgment is it a valid reaction.

Everyone reacts affectively. The idea is to develop your awareness of why your affective reaction is what it is, to investigate the reasons behind your emotional and intellectual responses. For instance, many readers lack interest in fiction and its literary effects and values. They just want the facts, the quick bottom line. They think that reading fictional literature is useless and unproductive, perhaps even slightly immoral. Many people think that reading literature is too pleasure oriented, too elite, or only for a select few oddballs. Some even feel that because literature is "made up," it is not related to real life; it's untrue, humorless, and boring. These are all affective reactions, but they all are based on an unaware, undeveloped sense of aesthetics and reflect poor affective understanding. If nothing else, literature *is* a reflection of life, and because of the affective involvement necessary for reading fiction, it often can teach us more about ourselves and others than can factual writings.

The point of this chapter is to help you open up to affective communication. Practices include reacting to pictures as well as to words in order to help you understand what affective comprehension is, give you more ways to develop your affective reactions, and expose you to a variety of affective experiences. As you do the exercises in this chapter, ask yourself why you are reacting as you do. When you have finished, you should be closer to reaching objectives 3, 4, and 5 for this unit: to be able to write a definition of *affective comprehension*; to understand the interrelationship among literal, critical, and affective comprehension; and to approach various types of imaginative literature with an awareness of what is expected of you as a reader.

Reading and Reacting to Advertisements

You are surrounded by advertisements—on television, in magazines and newspapers, and on the radio. These ads influence us in both subtle and not-so-subtle ways. If you see twenty ads a day that encourage you to value new cars as a path to a better life, you are prone to think you need a new or different car.

We often don't think of "reading" ads, yet this is certainly one of the most common reading tasks people do. Learning how to read ads is the subject of a full course, but this section will show you how two strategies help you become more effective and affective readers of advertisements.

One way advertisements and pictures work is by leading you to *evaluations*, or examinations and judgments. You evaluate when you decide one college class is better than another, when you choose one brand of pizza over another, or when you decide how to spend your free time. Evaluations are a part of your everyday life, but they can also be a problem when you make evaluations without thinking about, being aware of, or analyzing them. Advertisements may lead you to these unconscious evaluations by playing on your feelings. You may not think you're paying any attention to the advertisements or you may ignore the effect they have on you—but that doesn't lessen their impact on you. You can learn to examine ads for evaluations and then decide whether you agree with that evaluation. If the ad talks about being happy, for example, what sort of evaluation of happiness are you getting? What does the ad imply will make you happy?

A second way advertisements work is through their *use of language*. Ads tend to use few words, and each word usually has multiple *connotations*—meanings that are associated with or underlie the dictionary definitions or *denotations*. Words such as *pleasure* and *good times* carry many connotations for most of us. You probably get a feeling of positive emotions when these words appear. If you see a female in a picture and one person refers to her as a "girl" while the other person refers to her as a "lady," what are the different connotations you would get from these words? One has the connotation of youth or inexperience, and the other connotes an older woman of a certain refinement.

Practices A-1 and A-2 will help make you more aware of how ads function and how you "read" them. The other two practices (A-3 and A-4) help you develop affective reactions to an essay and a modern fable.

PRACTICE A-1: An Ad

Directions: Answer the following questions about the advertisement for the American Society of Travel Agents on page 340 that shows a man in a rowboat.

1. In ads, the pictures carry much of the message. Jot down a few words that express your first evaluation of the picture of the man and the boat in the ad. _____
   _____
   _____

2. What do you assume is the intended audience for this ad (gender, age, other)? Why do you make this assumption? _____
   _____

3. The text "This isn't what I thought they meant by 'singles cruise'" has double meanings and connotations. What are two of the meanings? _____
   _____
   _____

4. What is the intention of mentioning what "the brochure" said in the first line of the text? What did the consumer find out or not find out from the brochure?
   _____

5. What does the text say a travel agent will save you? Why are these three details listed in this particular order and manner? _____

This isn't what I thought they meant by 'singles cruise'.

Yes, but the brochure *did* mention the great workout facilities.
Next time, don't chance it. Use a professional travel agent.
They'll save you time, money...and maybe your vacation.
Call 1-800-965-ASTA or visit www.astanet.com.

Without a travel agent, you're on your own.

Reprinted by permission of American Society of Travel Agents.

6. Explain the relationship of the caption under the picture and the highlighted line at the end of the text: "Without a travel agent, you're on your own." _____

_____

7. What, besides travel agents, is the ad "selling"? _____

_____

8. After examining the entire ad more carefully, now what is your affective reaction to the ad? _____

_____

PRACTICE A-2: Another Ad

Directions: Look at the ad for boxLot on page 342. Then answer the following questions.

1. Jot down a few words that express your first reaction to the ad. _____

_____

_____

2. How do you evaluate the woman in the ad from the bicycle she has bought and the clothes she is wearing? _____

_____

3. Who is the ad directed to? Explain your evaluation of audience here. _____

_____

_____

4. The text "Now, my life is complete" equates a "complete life" with what? Explain.

_____

_____

5. What connotations do you associate with the first line of text: "What would it take to make you happy?" How would you answer the question of what would make you happy? _____

_____

_____

6. What is the intent of this ad? _____

_____

7. How does the text "Finders. Keepers." play on familiar refrains? What is the effect of the period between the two words? _____

_____

8. After examining the ad carefully, what is your reaction to the ad now? _____

_____

_____

Now, my life is complete.

What would it take to make you happy?
Whatever it is, try boxLot.com, or call 1-877-4boxLot.
The ultimate find in online auction and commerce.

boxLot™

Finders. Keepers.

Introducing Linda Ellerbee

In a nutshell, Linda Ellerbee is a well-respected journalist, a best-selling author, an award-winning television producer, a breast cancer survivor, a mother and grandmother, and one of the most sought-after speakers in America.

Her journalism career includes working at CBS, NBC, and ABC. Her *NBC News Overnight* program, which she wrote, won the duPont-Columbia award for "the best written and most intelligent news program ever." As an ABC News anchor, she won an Emmy for her work on *Our World*.

In 1987, Ellerbee started Lucky Duck Productions, producing *Nick News* for Nickelodeon, which has collected three Peabody Awards, another duPont-Columbia Award, and four Emmys for outstanding children's programming. *Nick News* is known for Ellerbee's respectful and direct way of speaking to children about important issues. In 2004, Ellerbee won an Emmy for her series *When I Was a Girl*, shown on WE: Women's Entertainment. Her production company continues to produce special programs for ABC, CBS, HBO, PBS, Lifetime, MTV, and many others.

Ellerbee's writing, even on serious subjects, often reflects a humorous touch:

I have always felt that laughter in the face of reality is probably the finest sound there is and will last until the day when the game is called on account of darkness. In this world, a good time to laugh is any time you can.

Her books include *Move On*, from which the following selection is taken; *And So It Goes*; and *Take Big Bites*. She has also written an eight-part fiction series titled *Get Real* for middle-school readers.

For more information on Linda Ellerbee, type her name in any search engine and explore some of the sites listed.

Practice A-3: An Essay

Directions: Read the following selection and answer the questions that follow, rereading any paragraphs as required.

WHEN TELEVISION ATE MY BEST FRIEND

LINDA ELLERBEE

1   I was eight years old when I lost my best friend. My *very first very* best friend. Lucy hardly ever whined, even when we kids played cowboys and she had to be Dale Evans. Nor did she cry, even when we played dodge ball and some big kid threw the ball so hard you could read *Spalding* backward on her legs. Lucy was worldclass.

2   Much of our time together was spent in my back yard on the perfect swing set: high, wide, built solid and grounded for life. But one June day long ago, something went wrong. I was swinging as high as I could, and still higher. The next time the swing started to come back down, I didn't. I just kept going up. And up.

3   Then I began to fall.

4   "Know what? Know what?" Lucy was yelling at me.

5   No, I didn't know *what*. All I knew was that my left arm hurt.

6   "Know what? For a minute there, you flew. You seemed to catch the wind and . . . soar! Right up until you must have done something wrong, because you fell."

7   Wearing a cast on my broken arm gave me time to work out the scientifics with Lucy. Our Theory was that if you swing just high enough and straight enough, and you jump out of the swing at just the right moment and in just the right position—*you just might fly*.

8   July was spent waiting for my arm to heal. We ran our hands across the wooden seat, feeling for the odd splinter that could ruin your perfect takeoff. We pulled on the chains, testing for weak links.

9   Finally came the day in August when my cast was off, and Lucy and I were ready. Today we would fly.

10   Early that morning, we began taking turns—one pushing, one pumping. All day we pushed and pumped, higher and higher, ever so close. It was almost dark when Lucy's mother hollered for her to come home right this minute and see what her daddy had brought them.

11   This was strictly against the rules. Nobody had to go home in August until it was altogether dark. Besides, Lucy's daddy wasn't a man to be struck with irresistible impulses like stopping at the horse store and thinking, *Golly, my little girl loves ponies! I better get her one!*

12   So we kept on swinging, and Lucy pretended not to hear her mother—until she dropped *Lucee* to *Lucille Louise*. Halfway through the fourth *Lucille Louise*, Lucy slowly raised her head as though straining to hear some woman calling from the next county.

13   "Were you calling me, Mother? Okay, okay, I'm coming. Yes, ma'am. *Right now*."

14   Lucy and I walked together to the end of my driveway. Once in her front yard, she slowed to something between a meander and a lollygag, choosing a path that took her straight through the sprinklers. Twice.

15   When at last Lucy sashayed to her front door, she turned back to me and, with a grin, gave me the thumbs-up sign used by pilots everywhere. *Awright*. So we'd fly tomorrow instead. We'd waited all summer. We could wait one more day. On her way in the house, she slammed the screen door.

16   *Bang!*

17   In my memory, I've listened to that screen door shut behind my best friend a thousand times. It was the last time I played with her.

18   I knocked on the door every day, but her mother always answered saying Lucy was busy and couldn't come out to play. I tried calling, but her mother always answered saying Lucy was busy and couldn't come to the phone. Lucy was busy? Too busy to play? Too busy to fly? She had to be dead. Nothing else made sense. What, short of death, could separate such best friends? We were going to fly. Her thumb had said so. I cried and cried.

19   I might never have known the truth of the matter, if some weeks later I hadn't overheard my mother say to my father how maybe I would calm down about Lucy if we got a television too.

20   A what? What on earth was a *television?* The word was new to me, but I was clever enough to figure out that Lucy's daddy had brought home a television that night. At last I knew what had happened to Lucy. The television ate her.

21   It must have been a terrible thing to see. Now my parents were thinking of getting one. I was scared. They didn't understand what television could do.

22   "Television eats people," I announced to my parents.

23   "Oh, Linda Jane," they said, laughing. "Television doesn't eat people. You'll love television just like Lucy. She's inside her house watching it right this minute."

24   Indeed, Lucy was totally bewitched by the flickering black and white shapes. Every afternoon following school, she'd sit in her living room and watch whatever there was to watch. Saturday mornings, she'd look at cartoons.

25   Autumn came. Around Thanksgiving, I played an ear of corn in the school pageant. Long division ruined most of December. After a while, I forgot about flying. But I did not forget about Lucy.

26   Christmas arrived, and Santa Claus brought us a television. "See?" my parents said. "Television doesn't eat people." Maybe not. But television changes people. It changed my family forever.

27   We stopped eating dinner at the dining-room table after my mother found out about TV trays. Dinner was served in time for one program and finished in time for another. During the meal we used to talk to one another. Now television talked to us. If you absolutely had to say something, you waited until the commercial, which is, I suspect, where I learned to speak in 30-second bursts.

28   Before television, I would lie in bed at night, listening to my parents in their room saying things I couldn't comprehend. Their voices alone rocked me to sleep. Now Daddy went to bed right after the weather, and Mama stayed up to see Jack Paar. I went to sleep listening to voices in my memory.

29   Daddy stopped buying Perry Mason books. Perry was on television now, and that was so much easier for him. But it had been Daddy and Perry who'd taught me how fine it can be to read something you like.

30   Mama and Daddy stopped going to movies. Most movies would one day show up on TV, he said.

31   After a while, Daddy and I didn't play baseball anymore. We didn't go to ball games either, but we watched more baseball than ever. That's how Daddy perfected The Art of Dozing to Baseball. He would sit in his big chair, turn on the game and fall asleep within minutes. At least he appeared to be asleep. His eyes were shut, and he snored. But if you shook him, he'd open his eyes and tell you what the score was, who was up and what the pitcher ought to throw next.

32   It seemed everybody liked to watch television more than I did. I had no interest in sitting still when I could be climbing trees or riding a bike or practicing my takeoffs just in case one day Lucy woke up and remembered we had a Theory. Maybe the TV hadn't actually eaten her, but once her parents pointed her in the direction of that box, she never looked back.

33   Lucy had no other interests when she could go home and turn on "My Friend Flicka." Maybe it was because that was as close as she would get to having her own pony. Maybe if her parents had allowed her a real world to stretch out in, she wouldn't have been satisfied with a 19-inch world.

34   All I know is I never had another first best friend. I never learned to fly either. What's more, I was right all along: television really does eat people.

1. The essay is basically an affective reaction, in words, to the author's
   a. loss of her best friend to television.
   b. loss of her normal family routine after they got a television.
   c. Both (a) and (b).
   d. None of the above.

2. Explain how well paragraphs 11–12 do or do not capture the feelings of young children being called home from play. _____ _____

3. Be eight years old again and put yourself in paragraph 18. Describe how you might feel at that moment. _____ _____ _____

4. What is the function of paragraph 25? _____ _____

5. What emotion(s) does paragraph 28 attempt to convey? _____ _____

6. How does the author feel about what she describes in paragraphs 29–31? _____

7. The concluding line, which states that "television really does eat people," is a metaphor. Explain what she means. _____ _____ _____

8. Does television "eat people" at your house? Explain. _____ _____ _____

PRACTICE A-4: A Modern Fable

Directions: Read the following fable and answer the questions that follow.

THE PRINCESS AND THE TIN BOX

JAMES THURBER

1   Once upon a time, in a far country, there lived a king whose daughter was the prettiest princess in the world. Her eyes were like the cornflower, her hair was sweeter than the hyacinth, and her throat made the swan look dusty.

2   From the time she was a year old, the princess had been showered with presents. Her nursery looked like Cartier's window. Her toys were all made of gold or platinum or diamonds or emeralds. She was not permitted to have wooden blocks or china dolls or rubber dogs or linen books, because such materials were considered cheap for the daughter of a king.

3   When she was seven, she was allowed to attend the wedding of her brother and throw real pearls at the bride instead of rice. Only the nightingale, with his lyre of gold, was permitted to sing for the princess. The common blackbird, with his boxwood flute, was kept out of the palace grounds. She walked in silver-and-samite slippers to a sapphire-and-topaz bathroom and slept in an ivory bed inlaid with rubies.

4   On the day the princess was eighteen, the king sent a royal ambassador to the courts of five neighboring kingdoms to announce that he would give his daughter's hand in marriage to the prince who brought her the gift she liked the most.

5   The first prince to arrive at the palace rode a swift white stallion and laid at the feet of the princess an enormous apple made of solid gold which he had taken from a dragon who had guarded it for a thousand years. It was placed on a long ebony table set up to hold the gifts of the princess's suitors. The second prince, who came on a gray charger, brought her a nightingale made of a thousand diamonds, and it was placed beside the golden apple. The third prince, riding on a black horse, carried a great jewel box made of platinum and sapphires, and it was placed next to the diamond nightingale. The fourth prince, astride a fiery yellow horse, gave the princess a gigantic heart made of rubies and pierced by an emerald arrow. It was placed next to the platinum-and-sapphire jewel box.

6   Now the fifth prince was the strongest and handsomest of all the five suitors, but he was the son of a poor king whose realm had been overrun by mice and locusts and wizards and mining engineers so that there was nothing much of value left in it. He came plodding up to the palace of the princess on a plow horse and he brought her a small tin box filled with mica and feldspar and hornblende which he had picked up on the way.

7   The other princes roared with disdainful laughter when they saw the tawdry gift the fifth prince had brought to the princess. But she examined it with great interest and squealed with delight, for all her life she had been glutted with precious stones and priceless metals, but she had never seen tin before or mica or feldspar or hornblende. The tin box was placed next to the ruby heart pierced with an emerald arrow.

8   "Now," the king said to his daughter, "you must select the gift you like best and marry the prince that brought it."

9   The princess smiled and walked up to the table and picked up the present she liked the most. It was the platinum-and-sapphire jewel box, the gift of the third prince.

10   "The way I figure it," she said, "is this. It is a very large and expensive box, and when I am married, I will meet many admirers who will give me precious gems with which to fill it to the top. Therefore, it is the most valuable of all the gifts my suitors have brought me and I like it the best."

11   The princess married the third prince that very day in the midst of great merriment and high revelry. More than a hundred thousand pearls were thrown at her and she loved it.

12   *Moral: All those who thought the princess was going to select the tin box filled with worthless stones instead of one of the other gifts will kindly stay after class and write one hundred times on the blackboard "I would rather have a hunk of aluminum silicate than a diamond necklace."*

1. Which prince did you think the princess would choose? _____ Why?

   _____

   _____

   _____

   _____

2. Why is it important to the story that the poorest prince be described last? _____

   _____

   _____

   _____

   _____

3. Much of the humor in this piece comes from the author's use of incongruity, things that don't fit or are illogical, such as the language the princess uses compared with the fairy-tale setting. What are some other incongruous aspects of the story, language or otherwise? _____

   _____

   _____

   _____

   _____

4. Satire is used to poke fun at things. Here the author pokes fun at our human frailties. Is he satirizing the princess, the reader, or both? Explain. _____

   _____

   _____

   _____

   _____

5. If you were the princess, which prince would you have selected and why? _____

   _____

   _____

   _____

   _____

6. What does the moral at the end of the tale imply? _____

   _____

   _____

   _____

Application 1: Responding Affectively to an Advertisement

Find an advertisement that you feel uses language or photographs to reach either your emotions or your desires. Bring it to class and share your advertisements with classmates.

B.   Recognizing Images and Analogies in Affective Language

Images and Analogies

In literature, **imagery** is a term used to refer to the use of words to compare ideas, things, or feelings with something else. A writer might say, "She looks very unhappy," or, "Her face looks like she learned she only has twenty-four hours to live." The first statement is a literal one; the second is an *analogy*. The second statement allows us to *imagine* (from which the term *imagery* comes) how the person feels rather than just telling us. Because we can imagine what it might feel like to learn we don't have long to live, the author taps our feelings through the analogy.

Imagery is important in fiction and nonfiction. Almost all good writing uses imaginative or figurative language, but it is especially important in writing poetry, short stories, and novels. It often requires that a writer carefully select words that provide strong connotative feelings in us. In the preceding example, "only twenty-four hours to live" connotes death within a day's time. In turn, that connotes a negative image, one we are supposed to feel.

To see more closely how this works, read the following short poem two or three times before answering the questions that follow.

The Death of the Ball Turret Gunner

Randall Jarrell

From my mother's sleep I fell into the State
And I hunched in its belly till my wet fur froze.
Six miles from earth, loosed from its dream of life,
I woke to black flak and the nightmare fighters.
When I died they washed me out of the turret with a hose.

Answer the following questions.

1. Write the denotative and connotative meanings of the words from the poem in the spaces provided.

	Denotation	**Connotation**
a. mother	_____	_____
b. sleep	_____	_____
c. State	_____	_____
d. fur	_____	_____

2. What is the analogy being drawn between "my mother's sleep" and waking to the "black flak and the nightmare fighters"?

    _____

    _____

3. What images are created in the following lines from the poem?

a. "From my mother's sleep I fell into the State" (Why is "State" capitalized?)

_____

_____

b. "I hunched in its belly"

_____

_____

c. "my wet fur froze"

_____

_____

d. "Six miles from earth"

_____

_____

e. "washed me out . . . with a hose"

_____

_____

4. What is the tone of the poem? _____

_____

5. What is the author's attitude toward his subject? _____

_____

6. Write a one-sentence literal statement that says what the poem implies. _____

_____

_____

_____

Let's look at question 6 first. While wording will be different for everyone, the basic idea behind this poem is that "War is hell," "In war, death is common and indiscriminate," or "Some lives are treated as expendable in war." But rather than say such things at a literal level, the author chooses to make us _feel_ the hell of war or the death of innocent people forced into a situation that is not their choosing. How do we know this?

The author knows that the word _mother_, literally the female parent, generally connotes feelings of love, security, warmth, and home life. _Sleep_ connotes quiet and peacefulness, especially when the author says "my mother's sleep." It's a pleasant image; but it's quickly lost when he falls "into the State." The capital on the word causes us to think about government, an institution that has sent him to war. But the word also can refer to his state of mind, the change from a pleasant, safe home environment to now being at war in the belly of an airplane. It's a rude awakening from "my mother's sleep." The author also draws a strong analogy between the safety of home and the "black flak and the nightmare fighters." He's gone from pleasant dreams to nightmares.

Likewise, fur is soft. We use it for warmth and decoration on our clothes. But the use of the word _fur_ could also remind us of the animal from which we get fur. Is the author implying through this image that humans become animal-like by going to war? There's irony in this image. The image of "my wet fur froze" implies or suggests that he may be sweating from fear. At the literal level, his perspiration freezes at six miles up in a bomber plane.

From the image "From my mother's sleep I fell into the State," we then feel for this young man who recently was safe at home suddenly finding himself at war in a bomber (*State* could also refer to the actual plane itself). The image "hunched in its belly" offers a cramped feeling, like an animal hiding; in this case, he is both a hunter, looking for the enemy, and the hunted, being chased by an enemy. The word *belly* literally refers to the ball turret under the bomber, where gunners used machine guns to shoot down fighter planes. But *belly* (perhaps his mother's womb) is made analogous to the airplane's "womb." One is safe and one isn't; thus more contrast is made between the safety of home and the dangers of war six miles high.

The image of the last line is ugly. We are left with him dead and the almost callousness of washing out his remains from the turret in order to make room for the next person. When we put all these things together, we can say that the tone of the poem is ghastly, grim, deadly. The attitude of the author toward war is obviously negative, but more than that he wants us to see and feel for the innocent victims of the folly of war. By using figurative language, the author creates images that are hard to forget and affect us at a level at which a plain, literal statement never could.

The following practices will help you see how authors use affective language in a variety of ways.

PRACTICE B-1: Lines from Poetry

Directions: Following are some quotations and short passages from poetry. In the blanks provided, write what you think is the *literal* meaning of the passage.

1. "The pen is mightier than the sword." (Edward Bulwer-Lytton) _____

   _____

   _____

   _____

2. "The Lord is my shepherd; I shall not want." (Psalm 23:1) _____

   _____

   _____

   _____

3. "Was this the face that launched a thousand ships,
   And burnt the topless towers of Ilium?" (Christopher Marlowe)

   _____

   _____

   _____

4. "There is no frigate like a book
   To take us lands away." (Emily Dickinson)

   _____

   _____

   _____

5. "God's in his heaven—
    All's right with the world!" (Robert Browning)

_____

_____

_____

6. "A little learning is a dangerous thing." (Alexander Pope) _____

_____

_____

_____

7. "But love is blind." (William Shakespeare) _____

_____

_____

_____

PRACTICE B-2: Images in a Poem

Directions: Mention the word _poem_ to some readers and they immediately think of a poem like
the one in this practice. It is made up of four stanzas (groups of lines), and the last
word in every other line rhymes. Many poems are not structured this way, however, as
you will see later. Read the following poem and answer the questions that follow. You
may refer back to the poem as often as necessary.

Oh, My Love Is Like a Red, Red Rose (about 1788)

Robert Burns (1759–1796)

Oh, my love is like a red, red rose
    That's newly sprung in June;
My love is like the melody
    That's sweetly played in tune.

So fair art thou, my bonny lass,   5
    So deep in love as I;
And I will love thee still, my dear,
    Till a' the seas gang dry.   _go_

Till a' the seas gang dry, my dear,   10
    And the rocks melt wi' the sun;
And I will love thee still, my dear,
    While the sands o' life shall run.

And fare thee weel, my only love!
    And fare thee weel awhile!   15
And I will come again, my love
    Though it were ten thousand mile.

1. What is your first reaction to this poem? What did it make you think about? _____

    _____

    _____

2. Which lines in each stanza end with words that rhyme? _____

    _____

3. What is the intent of the poem? _____

    _____

4. The title of the poem uses simile. What other simile is in the poem? _____

    _____

    _____

5. What is the author expressing through the following images?

    a. "Till a' the seas gang [go] dry"

    _____

    b. "And the rocks melt wi' the sun"

    _____

    c. "While the sands o' life shall run"

    _____

6. How do you think the person to whom this poem was intended would respond to such a declaration of love? Why? _____

    _____

    _____

PRACTICE B-3: Intent and Attitude in a Poem

Directions: Robert Burns's poem in the previous practice uses many similes. The poem by Sylvia Plath in this practice uses metaphors, and unlike Burns's poem it has no divided stanzas or rhyme scheme. Read the poem aloud. As you read, pay attention to the punctuation at the end of each line. It will help you see how the author wants the poem to be read. Look for the author's attitude and intent in the poem.

Metaphors (1960)

Sylvia Plath (1932–1963)

I'm a riddle in nine syllables,
An elephant, a ponderous house,
A melon strolling on two tendrils.
O red fruit, ivory, fine timbers!
This loaf's big with its yeasty rising.   5
Money's new-minted in this fat purse.
I'm a means, a stage, a cow in calf.
I've eaten a bag of green apples,
Boarded the train there's no getting off.

1. What is the poem about? _____

   _____

2. Each line in the poem is a _____

   _____

3. To whom or what do each of the lines refer? _____

   _____

4. What is the author's attitude toward the subject of the poem? _____

   _____

5. What is the author's intent in writing this poem? _____

   _____

6. What does the speaker in the poem have in common with a riddle? (line 1) _____

   _____

7. Why do you think "nine" syllables are used? Why not another number?

   _____

8. What is the significance, if any, in the number of lines in the poem?

   _____

9. What is your reaction to this poem? _____

   _____

PRACTICE B-4: Two Versions of the Lord's Prayer

Directions: Following are two published versions of Matthew 6:9–13, more commonly known as the Lord's Prayer. Read both of them and answer the questions that follow.

Version A

Our Father who art in heaven,
Hallowed be thy name.
Thy Kingdom come.
Thy will be done,
        On earth as it is in heaven.
Give us this day our daily bread;
And forgive us our debts,
        As we also have forgiven our debtors;
And lead us not into temptation,
        But deliver us from evil.

Version B

Our Father in heaven:
May your name be kept holy,
May your Kingdom come,
May your will be done on earth
        As it is in heaven.
Give us today the food we need;
Forgive us the wrongs that we have done,

And we forgive the wrongs that others have done us;
Do not bring us to hard testing, but
  Keep us safe from the Evil One.

1. Which version do you think is a more recent translation of the Bible? _____

    _____

2. Why? _____

    _____

    _____

3. Which version do you prefer? _____

    _____

4. Why? _____

    _____

5. Which version uses more figurative language than the other? _____

    _____

6. How do the two versions compare in meaning? _____

    _____

PRACTICE B-5: Quick Quiz

Directions: Answer the following questions as thoroughly as you can. The quiz has two parts.

Part A

Following are some quotations and short passages from poetry. In the blanks provided, write what you think is the *literal* meaning of the passage.

1. Ignorance is bliss." (Thomas Gray) _____

    _____

    _____

2. "Where liberty dwells, there is my country." (John Milton) _____

    _____

    _____

    _____

    _____

3. "Husbands are awkward things to deal with; even keeping them in hot water will
    not make them tender." (Mary Buckley) _____

    _____

    _____

    _____

    _____

    _____

_____

_____

4. "Early to bed, early to rise, makes a man healthy, wealthy, and wise." (Benjamin Franklin) _____

_____

_____

_____

_____

_____

5. "All the world's a stage." (William Shakespeare) _____

_____

_____

_____

_____

_____

Part B

Define the following terms.

1. imagery _____

_____

2. metaphor _____

_____

3. simile _____

_____

4. figurative language _____

_____

5. "the secret power of the word" _____

_____

6. affective comprehension _____

_____

Turn in the quiz to your instructor.

C.   Putting It All Together

The following practices will help you use the information from this chapter and all the previous ones. As you do them, apply all the reading skills you have learned so far.

PRACTICE C-1: An Essay

Directions: Quickly read the title and first paragraph of the following essay, then answer the questions here.

1.   What do you think the essay will discuss? _____

_____

_____

2.   Do you think you will enjoy reading the essay? _____

Why? _____

_____

Now read the essay, applying all the skills you have learned.

POETRY IS DEAD: DOES ANYBODY REALLY CARE?

BRUCE WEXLER

1   It is difficult to imagine a world without movies, plays, novels and music, but a world without poems doesn't have to be imagined. I find it disturbing that no one I know has cracked open a book of poetry in decades and that I, who once spent countless hours reading contemporary poets like Lowell and Berryman, can no longer even name a living poet.

2   All this started to bother me when heiress Ruth Lilly made an unprecedented donation of $100 million to Poetry Magazine in November. An article published on the Poetry International Web site said critics and poets agreed that the gift "could change the face of American poetry."

3   Don't these critics and poets realize that their art form is dead? Perhaps not. They probably also don't realize that people like me helped kill it.

4   In high school, I, like most of my classmates, hated the poetry unit in English class that surfaced annually with the same grim regularity as the gymnastics unit in physical education. Just as I was a good athlete who detested the parallel bars, I was an avid reader who despised rhymed and rhythmic writing. Plowing through tangled symbol and allusion, I wondered why the damn poets couldn't just say what they meant.

5   Then I went to college and at some point, I got it. Maybe it was when I was infatuated with some girl and read "I Knew a Woman" by Theodore Roethke: "I knew a woman, lovely in her bones/When small birds sighed, she would sigh back at them." Or maybe it happened when I read Keats's odes or Eliot's "Prufrock" or that haunting line in Frost: "I have been one acquainted with the night." For the next 10 years or so, I was hooked. I read poetry, wrote it and recited verse to impress dates.

6   And then my interest waned. On the surface, I suppose it was because I had other interests that demanded my time and attention: I got married, had children, pursued my career, bought a house. With apologies to Frost, I began to find more relevance in articles about interest rates than essays on the sprung rhythm of Hopkins.

7   Society, too, was changing in a way that did not favor the reading of poetry. From the Me Generation of the '70s to the get-rich-quick '80s, our culture became intensely prosaic. Ambiguity, complexity and paradox fell out of favor. We embraced easily defined goals and crystal-clear communication (Ronald Reagan was president, presiding over the literalization of America). Fewer politicians seemed to quote contemporary poets in speeches, and the relatively small number of name-brand, living American poets died or faded from view.

8   By the '90s, it was all over. If you doubt this statement, consider that poetry is the only art form where the number of people creating it is far greater than the number of people appreciating it. Anyone can write a bad poem. To appreciate a good one, though, takes knowledge and commitment. As a society, we lack this knowledge and commitment. People don't possess the patience to read a poem 20 times before the sound and sense of it takes hold. They aren't willing to let the words wash over them like a wave, demanding instead for the meaning to flow clearly and quickly. They want narrative-driven forms, stand-alone art that doesn't require an understanding of the larger context.

9   I, too, want these things. I am part of a world that apotheosizes the trendy, and poetry is just about as untrendy as it gets. I want to read books with buzz—in part because I make my living as a ghostwriter of and collaborator on books—and I can't remember the last book of poetry that created even a dying mosquito's worth of hum. I am also lazy, and poetry takes work.

10   In my worst moments, I blame the usual suspects for my own failings: the mainstream media, the Internet, the fast-food mentality. If it weren't for the pernicious influence of blah, blah, blah . . . Ultimately, though, there's no one to blame. Poetry is designed for an era when people valued the written word and had the time and inclination to possess it in its highest form.

11   I really do believe that poetry is the highest form of writing. Read Yeats's "The Wild Swans at Coole," Whitman's "When Lilacs Last in the Dooryard Bloom'd," Thomas's "Fern Hill," and you'll experience the true power of art. They touch the heart and the head in ways that movie-makers (our current artistic high priests) can only dream of.

12   April was National Poetry Month, a fact I know only because it was noted in my younger daughter's school newsletter. I celebrated by finding out the name of our poet laureate (Billy Collins) and reading one of his poems. This may not seem like much, but I have television shows to watch, best sellers to read and Web sites to visit before I sleep.

Comprehension Check

Directions: Answer the following questions.

1. Which of the following best states the thesis of this essay?
   a. Poetry is no longer read by most people.
   b. Poetry is the only art form where the number of people creating it is far greater than the number who appreciate it.

    c. Like the author, people see little value in poetry as it requires too much time to understand poems.

    d. The author believes poetry is the highest form of writing that can touch the heart and the head in ways no other art forms can.

2. The tone of the essay is mostly

    a. humorous.   **b.** serious.

    c. sarcastic.   **d.** nasty.

3. The author's intent is to _____

_____

4. T/F We can infer from the essay that the author is upset with himself for no longer reading poetry.

5. What does the author mean when he says of poetry that "people like me helped kill it"? _____

_____

_____

6. T/F We can infer that the author has read and is familiar with many poets.

7. T/F By sharing his guilt in no longer taking time to read poetry, the author manages not to offend or blame his readers who also don't read and appreciate poetry.

8. What prompted the author to write this essay? _____

_____

_____

9. T/F Wexler believes poetry has fallen out of favor because society, rather than dealing with ambiguity, complexity and paradox, has embraced easily defined goals and crystal-clear communication.

10. As a reader, why is it important not to take what Wexler says too literally? _____

_____

_____

_____

Vocabulary Check

Directions: Define the following underlined words from the selection.

    1. an <u>unprecedented</u> donation _____

_____

    2. I was <u>infatuated</u> with _____

_____

3. I read Keat's <u>odes</u> _____

_____

4. that <u>haunting</u> line in Frost _____

_____

5. my interest <u>waned</u> _____

_____

6. became intensely <u>prosaic</u> _____

_____

7. when <u>paradox</u> fell out of favor _____

_____

8. <u>presiding</u> over the literalization of America _____

_____

9. a world that <u>apotheosizes</u> the trendy _____

_____

10. <u>a dying mosquito's worth of hum</u> _____

_____

Record the results of the comprehension and vocabulary checks on the Student Record Chart in the Appendix. Each correct answer is worth 10 points, for a total of 100 points possible for comprehension and 100 points for vocabulary. Make certain you understand any errors before going on to the next practice.

PRACTICE C-2: Reactions to "Poetry Is Dead. Does Anybody Really Care?"

Directions: Following are partial "Letters to the Editor" from *Newsweek* where the Bruce Wexler article in Practice C-1 appeared. In the space following each partial letter, explain why you think the letter writer is or is not correct.

A. Probably the goofiest thing Wexler says is this: "I really do believe that poetry is the highest form of writing." What a sad commentary on his own apathy! If I boil his article down to two sentences, I get this: "I truly believe poetry is the highest form of writing, but I'm too apathetic and/or too lazy to read it. But I need to make a quick buck, so I'll write an article about the death of poetry for Newsweek, the extent of my research being I find the name of our current poet laureate and read (drum roll please!) one of his poems." Actually, the goofiest thing about Wexler's article is that you printed it. (Michael R. Burch)

_____ _____

_____ _____ _____

B. I'm not sure which is more disturbing: The fact that a virtually anonymous middle-aged white guy has lost touch with American poetry is evidently grounds for coverage in a national news magazine, or that Wexler never seems to consider that his disinterest in poetry may well be a failing in himself, rather than in the art form. (Victor Infante)

_____

_____

_____

C. By Bruce Wexler's own jaded and begrudging admission, poetry is not only very much alive, but impossible to kill off. As he suggests with unintended irony, it's the culture that refuses to do the work to read poetry which is in fact dead from the neck up. If your idea of art is a bouquet of bourgeois sentiments, then stick to the sensationalism of contemporary movies and music that are purged of all genius, emotion and thought. But if you want to break open the frozen sea within you, as Kafka put it, then immerse yourself in a poem. (Patrick Pritchett)

_____

_____

PRACTICE C-3: A Poem

Directions: The following poem was written by Billy Collins, poet laureate for the United States in 2002–2003, and mentioned in Practice C-1. Read the poem aloud two or three times. Look for the author's intent and attitude concerning the subject of the poem and your own reactions to what he has to say. Then answer the questions that follow.

Introduction to Poetry
Billy Collins
I ask them to take a poem
and hold it up to the light
like a color slide

or press an ear against its hive.

I say drop a mouse into a poem
and watch him probe his way out,

or walk inside the poem's room
and feel the walls for a light switch.

I want them to waterski
across the surface of a poem
waving at the author's name on the shore.

But all they want to do
is tie the poem to a chair with rope
and torture a confession out of it.

They begin beating it with a hose
to find out what it really means.

From *The Apple That Astonished Paris* by Billy Collins, University of Arkansas Press, 1988. Copyright © 1988 by Billy Collins. Reprinted with permission of The University of Arkansas Press.

1. What is the speaker's attitude toward reading a poem? _____

    _____

    _____

2. What is the author's primary intent in this poem? _____

    _____

    _____

3. What senses does the author believe are necessary for understanding a poem? (Look again at the first four stanzas.) _____

    _____

4. Who is the "they" in the last two stanzas? _____

    _____

5. What do you think the author means when he says he wants "them to waterski across the surface of a poem"? _____

    _____

    _____

    _____

6. What effect is created by the use of the phrases "tie the poem to a chair," "torture a confession," and "beating it with a hose"? _____

    _____

    _____

7. What image from the poem stands out the most for you? _____

    _____

8. What is your reaction to the poem? _____

    _____

Discuss these answers in class. There are no right or wrong answers to these, although some may be more thoughtful than others. It's important to see how others responded to these questions. (To tell the truth, we feel that questions such as the preceding one are more important than trying to answer questions such as "What does the poem mean?")

   Now, meet the author of the next selection by reading the following introduction to Langston Hughes. Another way to find current information on, quotations by, or pictures of this author is to use the World Wide Web. Type the author's name in any search engine and explore some of the sites listed.

Introducing Langston Hughes

Some critics have called Langston Hughes the most representative of black American writers. Over a forty-five-year period, Hughes wrote in every major literary genre. He was a poet, a dramatist, a short-story writer, a journalist, an editor, and a translator. His earliest works were poems published in his high school magazine. His published works include fourteen books of poetry, two

novels, a number of short-story collections, and several plays, including texts for stage musicals.

In 1922, Hughes dropped out of Columbia University after a year and took odd jobs. Four years later, he enrolled in Lincoln University in Pennsylvania; he graduated in 1929. By then, he had published two books of poems and had become one of the leading writers of the "Harlem Renaissance," a productive period of African-American creativity in the arts during the 1920s.

In 1931, Hughes received an award for his novel *Not without Laughter*. The award helped Hughes decide to become a writer:

> I'd finally and definitely made up my mind to continue being a writer—and to become a professional writer, making my living from writing. So far that had not happened. Until I went to Lincoln I had always worked at other things: teaching English in Mexico, truck gardening on Staten Island, a seaman, a doorman, a cook, a waiter in Paris night clubs or in hotels or restaurants. . . .
>
> Then I had a scholarship, a few literary awards, a patron. But those things were ended now. I would have to make my own living again—so I determined to make it writing. I did. Shortly, poetry became bread; prose, shelter and raiment. Words turned into songs, plays, scenarios, articles, and stories.
>
> Literature is a big sea full of many fish. I let down the nets and pulled.
> (From Langston Hughes, *The Big Sea*, Knopf, 1940, p. 335)

When the Great Depression occurred, Hughes's political views were strongly to the left. But with the advent of World War II, Hughes's radicalism began to decline. He wrote radio scripts and songs supporting the war effort. In 1942, he became a columnist with the African-American weekly *Chicago Defender*. With the 1947 Broadway success of his musical play *Street Scene*, Hughes's main professional interest was the theater. But he continued to turn out several books of poems as well as fiction and nonfiction until his death in 1967.

The following practice is taken from Hughes's *The Big Sea*, the first volume of his autobiography. Your instructor or Learning Center may have a DVD of a film version of *Salvation*; if so, you may want to view it and compare it with what you are about to read.

PRACTICE C-4: Narration

Directions: Quickly survey the following selection, reading the title, the first paragraph and last paragraph, and the questions. Then time yourself as you read the selection.

Begin Timing: _____

SALVATION

LANGSTON HUGHES

1   I was saved from sin when I was going on thirteen. But not really saved. It happened like this. There was a big revival at my Auntie Reed's church. Every night for weeks there had been much preaching, singing, praying, and shouting, and some very hardened sinners had been brought to Christ, and the membership of the church had grown by leaps and bounds. Then just before the revival ended, they held a special meeting for children, "to bring the young lambs to the fold." My aunt spoke of it for days ahead. That night I was escorted to the front row and placed on the mourners' bench with all the other young sinners, who had not yet been brought to Jesus.

2   My aunt told me that when you were saved you saw a light, and something happened to you inside! And Jesus came into your life! And God was with you from then on! She said you could see and hear and feel Jesus in your soul. I believed her. I had heard a great many old people say the same thing and it seemed to me they ought to know. So I sat there calmly in the hot, crowded church, waiting for Jesus to come to me.

3   The preacher preached a wonderful rhythmical sermon, all moans and shouts and lonely cries and dire pictures of hell, and then he sang a song about the ninety and nine safe and in the fold, but one little lamb was left out in the cold. Then he said: "Won't you come? Won't you come to Jesus? Young lambs, won't you come?" And he held out his arms to all us young sinners there on the mourner's bench. And the little girls cried. And some of them jumped up and went to Jesus right away. But most of us just sat there.

4   A great many old people came and knelt around us and prayed, old women with jet-black faces and braided hair, old men with work-gnarled hands. And the church sang a song about the lower lights are burning, some poor sinners to be saved. And the whole building rocked with prayer and song.

5   Still I kept waiting to see Jesus.

6   Finally all the young people had gone to the altar and were saved, but one boy and me. He was a rounder's son named Westley. Westley and I were surrounded by sisters and deacons praying. It was very hot in the church, and getting late now. Finally Westley said to me in a whisper: "God damn! I'm tired o' sitting here. Let's get up and be saved." So he got up and was saved.

7   Then I was left all alone on the mourners' bench. My aunt came and knelt at my knees and cried, while prayers and songs swirled all round me in the little church. The whole congregation prayed for me alone, in a mighty wail of moans and voices. And I kept waiting serenely for Jesus, waiting, waiting—but he didn't come. I wanted to see him, but nothing happened to me. Nothing! I wanted something to happen to me, but nothing happened.

8   I heard the songs and the minister saying: "Why don't you come? My dear child, why don't you come to Jesus? Jesus is waiting for you. He wants you. Why don't you come? Sister Reed, what is this child's name?"

9   "Langston," my aunt sobbed.

10   "Langston, why don't you come? Why don't you come and be saved? Oh, Lamb of God! Why don't you come?"

11   Now it was really getting late. I began to be ashamed of myself, holding every-thing up so long. I began to wonder what God thought about Westley, who certainly hadn't seen Jesus either, but who was now sitting proudly on the platform, swinging his knickerbockered legs and grinning down at me, surrounded by deacons and old women on their knees praying. God had not struck Westley dead for taking his name in vain or for lying in the temple. So I decided that maybe to save further trouble, I'd better lie, too, and say that Jesus had come, and get up and be saved.

12   So I got up.

13   Suddenly the whole room broke into a sea of shouting, as they saw me rise. Waves of rejoicing swept the place. Women leaped in the air. My aunt threw her arms around me. The minister took me by the hand and led me to the platform.

14   When things quieted down, in a hushed silence, punctuated by a few ecstatic "Amens," all the new young lambs were blessed in the name of God. Then joyous sing-ing filled the room.

15   That night for the last time in my life but one—for I was a big boy twelve years old—I cried. I cried, in bed alone, and couldn't stop. I buried my head under the quilts, but my aunt heard me. She woke up and told my uncle I was crying because the Holy Ghost had come into my life, and because I had seen Jesus. But I was really crying because I couldn't bear to tell her that I had lied, that I had deceived everybody in the church, and I hadn't seen Jesus, and that now I didn't believe there was a Jesus any more, since he didn't come to help me.

Finish Timing: Record time here_____ and use the Timed Reading Conversion Chart in the Appen-dix to figure your rate: _____ wpm.

Comprehension Check

Directions: Answer the following questions, applying a mixture of literal, critical, and affective comprehension.

1. What is the name of the main character in the story? _____

_____

2. He is _____ years old.

   a. ten   b. eleven

   c. twelve   d. thirteen

3. Where does most of the story take place? _____

_____

4. Place a check mark in front of each statement that you believe is an example of figurative language:

   _____ **a.** "bring the young lambs to the fold"

   _____ **b.** "sat there calmly in the hot, crowded church"

_____ **c.** "old men with work-gnarled hands"

_____ **d.** "the whole building rocked with prayer and song"

5. T/F "The whole room broke into a sea of shouting" is an example of a simile.

6. T/F "The membership of the church had grown by leaps and bounds" is an example of a metaphor.

7. The attitude of the author toward himself as a young boy is one of

   a. embarrassment.   **b.** slight amusement.

   c. sarcasm.   **d.** hatred.

8. Why does the boy wait so long to "get saved"? _____

   _____

9. Why did the boy cry that night? _____

   _____

10. What is the point of the story? _____

   _____

   _____

   _____

Vocabulary Check

Directions: Define the following underlined words from the selection.

1. a big <u>revival</u> at my aunt's church _____

   _____

2. bring the young lambs to the <u>fold</u>   _____

   _____

3. <u>dire</u> pictures of hell _____

   _____

4. he was a <u>rounder's</u> son _____

   _____

5. waiting <u>serenely</u> for Jesus _____

   _____

6. swinging his <u>knickerbockered</u> legs _____

   _____

7. surrounded by <u>deacons</u> _____

   _____

8. <u>punctuated</u> by a few ecstatic "Amens" _____

   _____

9. <u>ecstatic</u> "Amens" _____

_____

10. on the <u>mourners' bench</u> _____

_____

Record your rate and the results of the comprehension and vocabulary checks on the Student Record Chart in the Appendix. Each correct answer is worth 10 points, for a total of 100 points possible for comprehension and 100 points for vocabulary. If you are in doubt as to why any of your answers are wrong, check with your instructor.

> ### Application 2: Recognizing Images in Affective Language
>
> Go to http://www.poems.com. Select another Billy Collins poem and read it, looking for unusual images created through figurative language. If you can, print out the poem and bring it to class to share with your classmates.

Questions for Group Discussion

1. In the selections in this chapter, a variety of word images through metaphors and similes are presented. Which images are most memorable—and why?

2. Who in your group reads poetry, short stories, and novels? Share the titles and names of authors you enjoy reading. What enjoyment do you get from reading fiction?

3. Which of the selections brought out the strongest emotional reactions? As a group, discuss reasons for these affective reactions.

4. If you have viewed the Heinle Film Series DVD of Langston Hughes's *Salvation*, do you feel that the author's tone and intent in the reading selection come through in the film as well? Why or why not?

5. As a group, see how many of you can use the following words in a sentence. Make certain you learn the ones you still may not be able to use or recognize by writing the definition in the blank space.

a. ecstatic _____

b. waned _____

c. paradox _____

_____

d. prosaic _____

e. dire _____

f. serenely _____

g. unprecedented _____

h. revival _____

i. aesthetic _____

j. metaphor _____

On Your Own

Pick ten new words you learned in this chapter, not necessarily those listed in question 5 for group discussion, and on a separate sheet of paper write a sentence for each word, using it correctly in context. Turn in the paper to your instructor.

CHAPTER NINE

Reading Affectively Effectively

A.   Reading Short Stories Affectively

When you go to a football game or some other sports event, you go knowing that you will encounter traffic problems and parking problems, you will be surrounded by thousands of people, you will have to put up with all types of people and noises, and you will probably sit far from the action. Yet you accept all that in order to become a part of the event itself. When you watch television, you know that you are going to have programs interrupted by commercials; yet in spite of these breaks, you are willing and able to get back into the program after several minutes. When you go to a movie, you are willing to sit in the dark surrounded by three walls and a big screen as light filters through moving film. In each case, you are willing to go along with what is expected of you so that for a time you can get involved in what you are seeing and feeling.

To read imaginative literature (novels, short stories, and poems), you need to be willing to go along with what is expected of you, too. In this case, you are expected to enter the world of the author, who may want you to go back in the past, or forward to the future, or to share the present as the writer sees it. You must be willing to enter the imagination of the writer and attempt to see how he or she sees and feels life. In order to do this, you must understand how to read the form the writer chooses to use. Just as you have learned to identify a thesis in an essay, to identify paragraph forms and structure, to separate fact from opinion, and to recognize how language creates tone and reveals attitude and intent, so, too, you need to understand how to approach the reading of imaginative literature.

The last chapter introduced you to affective language used in short stories and poetry. You saw how important it is to read beyond the words and to relate to the "secret power" of language. Here's part of a novel by Jay McInerney, *Story of My Life*. Read it, then answer the questions that follow. Feel free to reread the passage if needed in order to answer the questions.

STORY OF MY LIFE

JAY MCINERNEY

1   The party goes on for three days. Some of the people go to sleep eventually, but not me. On the fourth day they call my father and a doctor comes over to the apartment, and now I'm in a place in Minnesota under sedation dreaming the white dreams about snow falling endlessly in the North Country, making the landscape disappear, dreaming about long white rails of cocaine that disappear over the horizon like railroad tracks to the stars. Like when I used to ride and was anorectic and I would starve myself and all I would ever dream about was food. There are horses at the far end of the pasture outside my window. I watch them through the bars.

2   Toward the end of the endless party that landed me here I am telling somebody the story of Dick Diver. I had eight horses at one point, but Dick Diver was the best. I traveled all over the country jumping and showing, and when I first saw Dick, I knew he was like no other horse. He was like a human being—so spirited and nasty he'd jump twenty feet in the air to avoid the bamboo of the trainer, then stop dead or hang a leg up on a jump he could easily make, just for spite. He had perfect conformation, like a statue of a horse dreamed by Michelangelo. My father bought him for me; he cost a fortune. Back then my father bought anything for me. I was his sweet thing.

3   I loved that horse. No one else could get near him, he'd try to kill them, but I used to sleep in his stall, spend hours with him every day. When he was poisoned, I went into shock. They kept me on tranquilizers for a week. There was an investigation, but nothing came of it. The insurance company paid off in full, but I quit riding. A few months later, Dad came into my bedroom one night. I was like, uh oh, not this again. He buried his face in my shoulder. His cheek was wet, and he smelled of booze. I'm sorry about Dick Diver, he said. Tell me you forgive me. He goes, the business was in trouble. Then he passed out on top of me, and I had to go and get Mom.

4   After a week in the hatch they let me use the phone. I call my Dad. How are you? he says.

5   I don't know why, it's probably bullshit, but I've been trapped in this place with a bunch of shrink types for a week. So just for the hell of it I go, Dad, sometimes I think it would have been cheaper if you'd let me keep that horse.

6   He goes, I don't know what you're talking about.

7   I go, Dick Diver, you remember that night you told me.

8   He goes, I didn't tell you anything.

9   So, okay, maybe I dreamed it. I was in bed after all, and he woke me up. Not for the first time. But just now, with these tranqs they've got me on, I feel like I'm sleepwalking anyway, and I can almost believe it never actually happened. Maybe I dreamed a lot of stuff. Stuff that I thought happened in my life. Stuff I thought I did. Stuff that was done to me. Wouldn't that be great. I'd love to think that 90 percent of it was just dreaming.

1. Besides "a place in Minnesota," there are clues that let us know where the narrator is. Where do you think the person is? _____

2. Is the narrator male or female? What makes you think so? _____

3. Describe the narrator. _____

4. Who killed Dick Diver and why? _____

5. What kind of life do you think the narrator has led? _____

Considering that the narrator is "under sedation" and is looking out at horses through a window with bars on it, we can infer that the narrator is in a hospital, perhaps the psychiatric ward or a rest home for drug addicts. Again, we assume the storyteller has taken a drug overdose because of the reference to a three-day party, the "long white rails of cocaine," and the need for a doctor on the fourth day.

It's not immediately apparent that the narrator is female, but it becomes more probable as we read. The references to starving herself, being anorectic, and riding horses certainly don't mean she is a female, but by the time we've read more, especially her reference to being her father's "sweet thing," it's a good assumption. We hear of more young women being anorectic than young men.

The narrator is probably in her late teens or early twenties, based on her language: "He goes...," "I go...," "He goes..." is the vernacular of a younger person. Her father is apparently still responsible for her, because he is the one she calls, and he is the one who called the doctor and had her institutionalized. We can assume that she comes from a wealthy family, because she had eight horses at one time and "traveled all over the country jumping and showing." Happy when she had her horses, she certainly is unhappy now, wishing she had "maybe dreamed a lot of stuff" that happened in her life, "stuff that was done to me." Her father drinks too much, and we gather that, because his business was failing at one point, he killed her favorite horse for the insurance money. We see her as a child who had plenty of material things, but not the kind of love and attention she wanted or needed. She hints she was spoiled: "Back then my father bought anything for me." The death of her horse was probably a turning point in her life, especially after learning her father's role in it. She has turned to drugs and is now in some type of hospital on tranquilizers—not a happy person.

Rather than tell us all these things literally, the author has asked us to enter the world of the girl/woman telling the story. If we are alert to the clues the author provides, we read beyond the words and begin to understand things that perhaps even the character telling the story doesn't understand or say directly. We enter the life of a fictional character, but we see reality as we know it must be for some—and sometimes for ourselves.

Now let's say that you have been assigned a short story to read in an English class. You start reading it, but you don't know exactly what you are expected to look for. You feel a bit uncomfortable because you are not used to reading imaginative literature. Here is a set of guide questions you can use with any story or novel to help you get a little more from your reading.

Literal Questions

1. Who is the main character? What is she or he like?
2. Who are other important people in the story? What is their relationship to the main character?
3. What is happening?
4. Where and when is everything happening?

Critical Questions

5. What seems to be the point of the story (called *theme*)? If the author were writing an essay instead of a story, what would the thesis be?
6. How does the title relate to the theme?
7. What events, scenes, and/or characters are used to develop the theme?

Affective Questions

8. Explain your feelings for the characters in the story.
9. What passages seem particularly well written or effective?

10. Why do you like or dislike the story?

11. What aspects of yourself or others do you see in the story?

These questions are certainly not the only ones, nor necessarily the best ones. But they give you a starting place, a direction toward understanding what it takes to enter into imaginative literature and get something from it.

The following practices will give you a chance to become more familiar with reading and understanding imaginative literature.

PRACTICE A-1: Reacting to Fictional Passages

Directions: Following are some short fictional passages containing figurative language. Read each one and answer the questions that follow.

1. "…inside we ate in the steady coolness of air by Westinghouse." (From Philip Roth, *Goodbye Columbus*)

    a. This quote is an example of figurative language. Restate the quote in literal terms. _____

    _____

    b. What can you infer from the quote about the weather outside? _____

    _____

2. "… women, with their Cuban heels and boned-up breasts, their knuckle-sized rings, their straw hats, which resembled immense wicker pizza plates." (From Philip Roth, *Goodbye Columbus*)

    a. Would you call this a flattering description? _____

    _____

    b. What figurative phrases support your answer to question 2a? _____

    _____

    _____

3. "When my parents have somebody over they get lemonade and if it's a real racy affair, Schlitz in tall glasses with 'They'll Do It Every Time' cartoons stencilled on." (From John Updike, "A & P")

    a. Literally state what the narrator is telling about his parents. _____

    _____

    _____

    b. What is the narrator's tone? Sarcastic? Friendly? Embarrassed? _____

    _____

    _____

4. "The flames, as though they were a kind of wild life, crept as a jaguar creeps on its belly toward a line of birch-like saplings that fledged an outcrop of the pink rock. They flapped at the first of the trees, and the branches grew a brief foliage of fire. The heart of flame leapt nimbly across the gap between the trees and then went swinging and flaring along the whole row of them." (From William Golding, *Lord of the Flies*)

a. Why is the fire like a wild animal? _____
_____
_____

b. List four descriptive words or phrases the author uses to give the fire life. _____
_____
_____

5. "She slides through the door with a gust of cold and locks the door behind her and I see her fingers trail across the polished steel—tip of each finger the same color as her lips. Funny orange. Like the tip of a soldering iron. Color so hot or so cold if she touches you with it you can't tell which." (From Ken Kesey, *One Flew over the Cuckoo's Nest*)

a. From this description, can you infer whether the narrator likes or dislikes the woman? _____

b. What feelings do you get from the description of the woman? _____
_____
_____

c. List at least three phrases that cause you to feel the way you do. _____
_____
_____

6. "Lying in this third-story cupola bedroom, he felt the tall power it gave him, riding high in the June wind, the grandest tower in town. At night, when the trees washed together, he flashed his gaze like a beacon from this lighthouse in all directions over swarming seas of elm and oak and maple." (From Ray Bradbury, *Dandelion Wine*)

a. Is the overall mood of this passage pleasing or frightening? _____
_____

b. Why? _____
_____
_____

c. What is meant by "the trees washed together"? _____
_____

d. The bedroom is being compared to what? _____

e. How can you tell? _____
_____

7. "The fresh-plowed earth heaved, the wild plum buds puffed and broke. Springs and streams leapt up singing. He could hear the distant roar of the river swelling in the gorge. The clear blue skies stretched out above him like the skin of a puffed fiesta balloon. The whole earth strained and stretched with new life." (From Frank Waters, *The Man Who Killed the Deer*)

a. Is the overall mood of this passage pleasing or frightening? _____
_____

b. Why? _____

c. What time of year would you infer is being described? _____
_____

    d. Why? _____

_____

_____

8 "It unrolled slowly, forced to show its colors, curling and snapping back whenever one of us turned loose. The whole land was very tense until we put our four steins on its corners and laid the river out to run for us through the mountains 150 miles north. Lewis' hand took a pencil and marked out a small strong X in a place where some of the green bled away and the paper changed with high ground, and began to work downstream, northeast to southwest through the printed woods." (From James Dickey, *Deliverance*)

    a. What is the "it" that "unrolled slowly"? _____

    b. How do you know? _____

_____

_____

    c. What clue does the author give as to how many people the "us" and "we" refer to?

_____

_____

    d. What can you infer from the passage is going on? _____

_____

_____

_____

_____

PRACTICE A-2: Images in Fiction

Directions: Figurative language, as you remember from Chapter Five, is used in an imaginative rather than a literal sense. Forms of figurative language include metaphor, simile, cliché, and hyperbole. Go back to Chapter Five, Section B, page 216 if you need to refresh your memory about any of these concepts before you do the next two exercises.

      Read each of the following fictional selections. On the first line that follows each selection, write the word *figurative* if you think the selection is mostly figurative or *literal* if you think it is mostly literal. On the second line, write the numbers of all the sentences in the selection that you feel contain figurative language.

1.   (1) Dr. Rankin was a large and rawboned man on whom the newest suit at once appeared outdated, like a suit in a photograph of twenty years ago. (2) This was due to the squareness and flatness of his torso, which might have been put together by a manufacturer of packing cases. (3) His face also had a wooden and a roughly constructed look; his hair was wiglike and resentful of the comb. (4) He had those huge and clumsy hands which can be an asset to a doctor in a small upstate town where people still retain a rural relish for paradox, thinking that the more ape-like the paw, the more precise it can be in the delicate business of a tonsillectomy. (From John Collier, "De Mortuis")

_____

_____

2.   (1) The morning of June 27th was clear and sunny, with the fresh warmth of a full-summer day; the flowers were blossoming profusely and the grass was richly green.

(2) The people of the village began to gather in the square, between the post office and the bank, around ten o'clock; in some towns there were so many people that the lottery took two days and had to be started on June 26th, but in this village, where there were only about three hundred people, the whole lottery took less than two hours, so it could begin at ten o'clock in the morning and still be through in time to allow the villagers to get home for noon dinner. (From Shirley Jackson, "The Lottery")

_____

_____

3.   (1) She was going the inland route because she had been twice on the coast route. (2) She asked three times at the automobile club how far it was through the Tehachapi Mountains, and she had the route marked on the map in red pencil. (3) The car was running like a T, the garage man told her. (4) All her dresses were back from the cleaners, and there remained only the lace collar to sew on her black crepe so that they would be all ready when she got to San Francisco. (5) She had read up on the history of the mountains and listed all the Indian tribes and marked the route of the Friars from the Sacramento Valley. (6) She was glad now that Clara Robbins, the "Math" teacher, was not going with her. (7) She liked to be alone, to have everything just the way she wanted it, exactly. (From Meridel Le Sueur, "The Girl")

_____

_____

4.   (1) Braggioni catches her glance solidly as if he had been waiting for it, leans forward, balancing his paunch between his spread knees, and sings with tremendous emphasis, weighing his words. (2) He has, the song relates, no father and no mother, nor even a friend to console him; lonely as a wave of the sea he comes and goes, lonely as a wave. (3) His mouth opens round and yearns sideways, his balloon cheeks grow oily with the labor of song. (4) He bulges marvelously in his expensive garments. (5) Over his lavender collar, crushed upon a purple necktie, held by a diamond hoop: over his ammunition belt of tooled leather worked in silver, buckled cruelly around his gasping middle: over the tops of his glossy yellow shoes Braggioni swells with ominous ripeness, his mauve silk hose stretched taut, his ankles bound with the stout leather thongs of his shoes. (From Katherine Anne Porter, "Flowering Judas")

_____

_____

5.   (1) The midafternoon winter sun burned through the high California haze. (2) Charles Dudley, working with a mattock in a thicket of overgrowth, felt as steamy and as moldy as the black adobe earth in which his feet kept slipping. (3) Rain had fallen for five days with no glimmer of sunshine, and now it seemed as if the earth, with fetid animation, like heavy breath, were giving all that moisture back to the air. (4) The soil, or the broom which he was struggling to uproot, had a disgusting, acrid odor, as if he were tussling with some obscene animal instead of with a lot of neglected vegetation, and suddenly an overload of irritations—the smell, the stinging sweat in his eyes, his itching skin, his blistering palms—made him throw the mattock down and come diving out of the thicket into the cleaning he had already achieved. (From Mark Schorer, "What We Don't Know Hurts Us")

_____

_____

_____

PRACTICE A-3: Reading a Short Story

Directions: As a way to direct your thinking as you read the following short story, answer the questions that appear at various points. Some questions require predicting or guessing what you think will happen. Write your answers on a separate sheet of paper to be turned in to your instructor.

1. Read the title of the next story. What do you think this story will be about? What will happen? Why?

THE STORY OF AN HOUR

KATE CHOPIN

1   Knowing that Mrs. Mallard was afflicted with a heart trouble, great care was taken to break to her as gently as possible the news of her husband's death.

2   It was her sister Josephine who told her, in broken sentences; veiled hints that revealed in half concealing. Her husband's friend Richards was there, too, near her. It was he who had been in the newspaper office when intelligence of the railroad disaster was received, with Brently Mallard's name leading the list of "killed." He had only taken the time to assure himself of its truth by a second telegram, and had hastened to forestall any less careful, less tender friend in bearing the sad message.

3   She did not hear the story as many women have heard the same, with a paralyzed inability to accept its significance. She wept at once, with sudden, wild abandonment, in her sister's arms. When the storm of grief had spent itself she went away to her room alone. She would have no one follow her.

2. **Which of your ideas in answer to question 1 can still be correct?**

3. **Now what do you think will take place? Why?**

4   There stood, facing the open window, a comfortable, roomy armchair. Into this she sank, pressed down by a physical exhaustion that haunted her body and seemed to reach into her soul.

5   She could see in the open square before her house the tops of trees that were all aquiver with the new spring life. The delicious breath of rain was in the air. In the street below a peddler was crying his wares. The notes of a distant song which someone was singing reached her faintly, and countless sparrows were twittering in the eaves.

6   There were patches of blue sky showing here and there through the clouds that had met and piled one above the other in the west facing her window.

7   She sat with her head thrown back upon the cushion of the chair, quite motionless, except when a sob came up into her throat and shook her, as a child who has cried itself to sleep continues to sob in its dreams.

8   She was young, with a fair, calm face, whose lines bespoke repression and even a certain strength. But now there was a dull stare in her eyes, whose gaze was fixed away off yonder on one of those patches of blue sky. It was not a glance of reflection, but rather indicated a suspension of intelligent thought.

Kate Chopin, "The Story of an Hour," from *The Bedford Anthology of World Literature: The Nineteenth Century, 1800–1900*, Bedford/St. Martins, 2003, pp. 931–932.

9   There was something coming to her and she was waiting for it, fearfully. What was it? She did not know; it was too subtle and elusive to name. But she felt it, creeping out of the sky, reaching toward her through the sounds, the scents, the color that filled the air.

10   Now her bosom rose and fell tumultuously. She was beginning to recognize this thing that was approaching to possess her, and she was striving to beat it back with her will—as powerless as her two white slender hands would have been.

4. Which of your ideas about what will happen are still possible?

5. What new ideas do you have about what will happen now?

11   When she abandoned herself a little whispered word escaped her slightly parted lips. She said it over and over under her breath: "free, free, free!" The vacant stare and the look of terror that had followed it went from her eyes. They stayed keen and bright. Her pulses beat fast, and the coursing blood warmed and relaxed every inch of her body.

12   She did not stop to ask if it were or were not a monstrous joy that held her. A clear and exalted perception enabled her to dismiss the suggestion as trivial.

13   She knew that she would weep again when she saw the kind, tender hands folded in death; the face that had never looked save with love upon her, fixed and gray and dead. But she saw beyond that bitter moment a long procession of years to come that would belong to her absolutely. And she opened and spread her arms out to them in welcome.

14   There would be no one to live for her during those coming years; she would live for herself. There would be no powerful will bending hers in that blind persistence with which men and women believe they have a right to impose a private will upon a fellow-creature. A kind intention or a cruel intention made the act seem no less a crime as she looked upon it in that brief moment of illumination.

15   And yet she had loved him—sometimes. Often she had not. What did it matter! What could love, the unsolved mystery, count for in face of this possession of self-assertion which she suddenly recognized as the strongest impulse of her being!

16   "Free! Body and soul free!" she kept whispering.

6. Were you right? How did you know?

7. Now what will happen?

17   Josephine was kneeling before the closed door with her lips to the keyhole, imploring for admission. "Louise, open the door! I beg; open the door—you will make yourself ill. What are you doing, Louise? For heaven's sake open the door."

18   "Go away. I am not making myself ill." No; she was drinking in a very elixir of life through that open window.

19   Her fancy was running riot along those days ahead of her. Spring days, and summer days, and all sorts of days that would be her own. She breathed a quick prayer that life might be long. It was only yesterday she had thought with a shudder that life might be long.

20   She rose at length and opened the door to her sister's importunities. There was a feverish triumph in her eyes, and she carried herself unwittingly like a goddess of Victory. She clasped her sister's waist, and together they descended the stairs. Richards stood waiting for them at the bottom.

8. How close were your ideas to what happened?

9. What will happen now and why do you think so?

21   Some one was opening the front door with a latchkey. It was Brently Mallard who entered, a little travel-stained, composedly carrying his gripsack and umbrella.

He had been far from the scene of the accident, and did not even know there had been one. He stood amazed at Josephine's piercing cry; at Richards' quick motion to screen him from the view of his wife.

22   But Richards was too late.

23   When the doctors came they said she had died of heart disease—of joy that kills.

10. Irony is defined as an inconsistency between what might be expected and what actually occurs. Discuss any irony you see in this story.

Turn in your answers to your instructor. Answers are all subjective.

Practice A-4: Another Short Story

Directions: Read the title of the following story. Based on the title, predict what the story will be about. As you know, reading fiction is different from reading expository writing. Learning to form your own questions and predictions as you read will help both your concentration and comprehension.

OUTPATIENT

ROSALIND WARREN

1   The waiting room is crowded. Mothers watch fidgety children, couples sit together on drab sofas, adult children talk in soothing voices to elderly parents. Everyone in the waiting room has someone with them. Luisa has come alone.

2   "New patient?" the receptionist asks. Luisa nods.

3   The receptionist hands her a clipboard that holds a form. "You'll have to fill this out," she says. When Luisa returns it a few moments later, the receptionist looks it over. "You haven't filled in your occupation," she says.

4   "Hypnotist," says Luisa.

5   "Oh?" The receptionist meets Luisa's eyes. They're unusual eyes. Clear blue, almost violet. They often remind people of deep bodies of water.

6   "It's the family business," says Luisa. "Both my parents were hypnotists. As were two of my grandparents."

7   "How lovely," says the receptionist.

8   "The doctor will see me right away," says Luisa, still looking into the receptionist's eyes. She enunciates each word slowly and carefully.

9   "But we call people in the order they arrive."

10   "I arrived first," says Luisa.

11   "You arrived first," agrees the receptionist.

12   Luisa has barely glanced at Life magazine's special Winter Olympics issue when a nurse calls her name. She follows the nurse down a corridor to a small examining room. The nurse hands her the usual skimpy garment, telling Luisa to remove her clothes and put it on. When the nurse leaves, Luisa strips, puts the thing on, and sits down on the edge of the examination table. It's cool. Almost immediately she has goose bumps.

13   Luisa doesn't look great in the drab shapeless garment, but she looks better than most. She is of an indeterminate age. Certainly past forty. She would probably be

described as "well preserved." She is tall and strong-looking and has longish red hair. Not beautiful but striking. The nurse comes back in and smiles when she notices that Luisa's fingernails and toenails are painted cherry blossom pink.

14   "Stand on the scale," she instructs. Luisa gets on the scale, and the nurse adjusts the indicator back and forth, minutely, until it finally rests on 130.

15   "One hundred thirty," she says.

16   Luisa turns to look at her. "What about my eyes?" she asks.

17   "Hmmm?" the nurse says, writing. She looks up and meets Luisa's eyes. "Oh!" she says. She gazes at Luisa for a moment. "They're such a nice color," she says.

18   "Really?" asks Luisa. "Tell the truth."

19   "They're a little weird."

20   "Scary?" asks Luisa.

21   "Nope." The nurse smiles. "I like them."

22   Luisa smiles. I weigh one fifty-seven," she says. The nurse glances down at her clipboard and frowns. She erases the 130 and writes 157.

23   "But I carry it well," says Luisa. "Don't I?"

24   "You certainly do," says the nurse. "Now I have to take your blood pressure. She straps the arm band on, pumps it up, and looks at it. "One hundred ten over sixty," she says.

25   "One twenty over seventy," Luisa says. The nurse gazes at her blankly. "I'm sorry," says Luisa. "But these silly games are quite harmless, and they're crucial if I'm to stay in practice. I'll stop if it disturbs you."

26   The nurse smiles. "It doesn't disturb me." She writes 120 over 70 on Luisa's chart. "I think it's interesting."

27   "What happens now?" Luisa asks.

28   "You wait for Dr. Heller."

29   "I probably don't even need Dr. Heller," says Luisa. "I'm ninety percent sure I've got bronchitis. Everyone in my family has bronchitis. Everyone on my *block* has bronchitis. But I can't just write myself out a prescription for antibiotics, can I?"

30   "No," says the nurse. "You can't."

31   "What's Dr. Heller like?" Luisa asks.

32   "He's very nice."

33   "Tell the truth."

34   "He's a complete jerk," says the nurse. Then she looks startled, and they both burst out laughing.

35   "But he's a very competent doctor," the nurse says. "He can diagnose your bronchitis as well as the next doc."

36   "Thanks for putting up with me," says Luisa. "You will feel happy for the rest of the day. You will walk around thinking life is a piece of cake."

37   "I certainly look forward to that," says the nurse.

38   Luisa snaps her fingers. The nurse blinks, then moves quickly to the door. "Dr. Heller will be right with you," she says as she leaves. She has left the clipboard with Luisa's chart on the table, and Luisa quickly changes her weight and blood pressure to the correct numbers.

39   Time passes. Ten minutes. Twenty minutes. Nothing happens. The nurse had left her with the impression that the doctor would be right in. Clearly, he won't be. There is nothing to distract her. She should have brought her magazine with her. She imagines parading out into the waiting room dressed as she is to retrieve her copy of Life. She decides against it.

40   She looks around the room. It's a generic examination room. No windows. No pictures or photos. Nothing interesting or unusual to hold her attention. Luisa hasn't much interest in things, anyway. Things rarely hold surprises; people do.

41   Another twenty minutes pass. Luisa is beginning to think they've forgotten all about her. She's starting to feel woozy. It angers her. Sitting here half dressed is the last thing she needs. She knows that in examining rooms up and down this hallway sick people sit in skimpy hospital garments waiting for the doctor. It's more convenient for him this way. She tries to calm herself. This treatment isn't life-threatening, she tells herself. It may be dehumanizing and demoralizing, but it won't kill you. They only do it this way because they can get away with it.

42   Finally the door opens and a big man in a white coat breezes in. He's in his mid-thirties, large and bearded. He looks like a lumberjack. His blue eyes are intelligent but not particularly kind. He moves in a rush.

43   "Well, Luisa," he says loudly, glancing down at the clipboard, "I'm Dr. Heller. What's the trouble?"

44   "Sorry to keep you waiting," says Luisa.

45   "Hmmm?" he says, scanning her chart.

46   "I said I was sorry to keep you waiting."

47   He looks up at her. "Symptoms?" he asks.

48   "Fever," she says. "Sore throat. Bad cough. I think I have bronchitis."

49   "I'm the doctor," he says, making notations on her chart. He places his stethoscope on her back. "Cough!" he barks.

50   Luisa coughs as he moves his stethoscope about on her back and then her chest. His movements are all precise and quick, and his touch is firm and cold. He looks into the distance, concentrating. He doesn't look at her.

51   "It began two weeks ago," Luisa says. "I woke up with a bad sore throat. Three days later I began running a slight fever." She stops. He isn't listening.

52   "How much pain have you caused your patients by not listening to them?" she asks quietly.

53   "Hmmm?" He takes a thermometer from a drawer. "Open," he says, angling the thermometer toward her mouth. Luisa pushes it away.

54   "Listen to me!" she says.

55   He stops and looks at her, his eyes dark and angry. Their eyes meet. It's a struggle. But Luisa is angry.

56   "You will slow down and give me a good, thorough examination," she says finally. "You will take your time, pay attention, and explain the reason for each procedure. You will listen to me when I speak. Not only am I older than you and deserving of your respect for no other reason, but I live in this body. I may know something about it that can help you."

57   The doctor gazes at her, unblinking.

58   "I'm not just a body with an illness," says Luisa. "I'm a person. You care about my feelings."

59   "I care about your feelings," he says. He sounds doubtful.

60   But he continues the examination at a much slower, kinder pace, and Luisa is surprised at how good he is. His cold hands even seem to warm up slightly. But it's clear that he's fighting the impulse to race through the exam and get on to the next patient.

61   "Why are you in such a hurry?" she asks.

62   "I have so many patients. I hate to keep them waiting."

63   "You don't care about that. Tell the truth."

64   "You've got a fabulous body," he says. "I love older women with big breasts."

65   "Not about that," she laughs. "Why are you in such a hurry?"

66   "This way I stay in control."

67   "What if you aren't in control?"

68   "I have to be in control."

69   "Why?"

70   "I'm the doctor."

71   "And you're the doctor because you have to stay in control," says Luisa. "Right?"

72   "Yes," he says. "I do like your eyes. They're . .

73   "What?"

74   "Calming."

75   He finishes the examination. "You have bronchitis," he says. "I'm writing you a prescription for 500 mg of ampicillin."

76   "What would make you listen to your patients?" she asks. "What would make you care?"

77   "Nothing," he says. He is writing the prescription. "Take this four times daily with plenty of water." He hands it to her and turns toward the door.

78   "Wait," she says.

79   He stops. "Take your clothes off," she says. He turns around and stares into her eyes. He begins to unbutton his shirt.

80   As he removes his clothing, Luisa puts hers back on. By the time he's naked, she's fully clothed. He stands there looking very pale. He has goose bumps. She hands him the hospital garment. He puts it on.

81   "You will sit here and wait," she says, "until the nurse comes looking for you. You'll see what it's like."

82   He sits down on the edge of the examination table and sighs.

83   She pauses at the door. "When the nurse comes, you'll forget about me."

84   "I'll forget about you." He sounds happy about that.

85   "But you'll never forget the next half hour."

86   As Luisa leaves the room, she sees the nurse heading toward her with a clipboard. "Dr. Heller is in the examining room," she tells the nurse. "He asked not to be disturbed for at least a half hour. But he wanted you to explain to the patients who are waiting that there'll be a delay. And to apologize."

87   "That's new," says the nurse.

88   "That's right," says Luisa. She meets the nurse's eyes. "Have an interesting day," she says.

Comprehension Check

Directions: Answer the following questions. You may look back if you need to do so.

Literal Questions

1. Who is the main character in the story? _____

    _____

2. Where and when is everything happening? _____

    _____

3. Summarize the story in one sentence. _____

    _____

    _____

Critical Questions

4. What is the theme of the story? In other words, if the author were writing an essay instead of a story, what would the thesis be? _____

_____

5. How does the title relate to the theme? _____

_____

_____

6. What events, scenes, or characters are used to develop the theme? _____

_____

_____

Affective Questions

7. What affective reactions did you have as you read the story? _____

_____

_____

8. Explain your feelings for the main character in the story. Have you ever experienced a visit to a doctor's or other professional's office similar to the one described in the story? _____

_____

_____

9. What aspects of yourself or others do you see in the story? _____

_____

_____

10. Why do you like or dislike the story? _____

_____

_____

Questions for Group Discussion

1. Discuss your affective reactions to the story "Outpatient"—that is, why you did or did not like the story. What purpose does a story such as this serve?

2. Discuss a time when you wished you had Luisa's hypnotic powers.

3. What do you think can be learned from reading literature? Has the reading of any fictional literature taught you anything about yourself or others?

The next selection is by Gary Soto. Start by reading about the author. Another way to find current information on, quotations by, or pictures of this author is to use the World Wide Web. Type in the author's name in any search engine and explore some of the sites listed. Soto's Web site is http://www.garysoto.com.

Introducing Gary Soto

A respected poet, an innovator of the short essay form, and a professor of English and Chicano Studies at the University of California, Berkeley, Gary Soto has written numerous volumes of poetry and several collections of short stories and essays. Among Soto's many awards are the 1985 American Book Award and the 1985 Before Columbus Foundation American Book Award. In 1990, his *Who Will Know Us?* was nominated as an American Library Association Notable Book. He is also the recipient of a Guggenheim Fellowship and an Award for Merit from the Fresno (California) Area Council of English Teachers for inspiring the young people of San Joaquin Valley through his writing.

Soto's work not only reveals vivid moments and experiences growing up Chicano but also taps into childhood and adult experiences that we all share. He often writes of small events and experiences that affect us and remain important all our lives.

In his introduction to *New and Selected Poems* (1995), Soto tells us how he started writing.

Having come from a family with no books,...I didn't know the continuity of ancient literature, the mechanics of writing, or the mesmerizing effect poetry can have on its readers.... By early 1973, I was devouring contemporary American poetry and Latin American poetry, a literary border crossing that I couldn't fathom. Reading Pablo Neruda, I was fascinated by his energy and the lush, occasionally surrealistic landscapes. I was bewildered by what must have been the godly permission this poet received to write so strangely. I wanted such permission, too....

A timid writer, I gazed over my meager poems in fear of grammatical glitches.... But by summer 1973, after my fear of writing poorly had disappeared, I knew my pulse was timed to the heart of this [San Joaquin] valley.

I began writing my first poems in 1973, and soon fell in with the poets of Fresno—Leonard Adame, Omar Salinas, Ernesto Trejo, and Jon Veinberg. We were all wrestling with words and arguing over silly and large matters.... Except for Jon, we were all Chicanos and, determined to realize our talents, we settled in for the long haul. We trusted our instincts and wrote poems that first appeared in college magazines. Then, as young poets will do, we got gutsy. We licked stamps and sent out poems because we wanted to be published, just as our teachers were published, in literary magazines. We were on our way on this gray and rusty tanker called Poetry. (From Gary Soto, *New and Selected Poems*, Chronicle Books, 1995, pp. 1–3)

Practice A-5 is a short story by Gary Soto taken from his narrative collection *Living up the Street*. Notice how he takes a unique childhood experience and turns it into a universal story for us all.

PRACTICE A-5

Directions: Read the following selection, putting together all the literal, critical, and affective skills you have learned.

1, 2, 3

GARY SOTO

1   When I was seven years old I spent most of the summer at Romain playground, a brown stick among other brown kids. The playground was less than a block from where we lived, on a street of retired couples, Okie families, and two or three Mexican families. Just before leaving for work our mother told us—my brother Rick, sister Debra, and me—not to leave the house until after one in the afternoon, at which time I skipped off to the playground, barefoot and smiling, my teeth that were uneven and without direction. By that hour the day was yellow with one-hundred-degree heat, the sun blaring high over the houses. I walked the asphalt street with little or no pain toward a mirage of water that disappeared as I approached it.

2   At the playground I asked for checkers at the game room, unfolded the board under the elm that was cut with initials and, if he was there, I played with Ronnie, an Okie kid who was so poor that he had nothing to wear but a bathing suit. All summer he showed up in his trunks, brown as the rest of us Mexicans, and seemed to enjoy himself playing checkers, Candyland, and Sorry. Once, when I brought him an unwrapped jelly sandwich in my hand, the shapes of my fingers pressed into the bread, he took it and didn't look into my eyes. He ate very slowly, deliberating over each move. When he beat me and had polished off his sandwich, he turned away without a word and ran off to play with someone else.

3   If Ronnie was not there and no one else challenged me, I just sat under the tree stacking checkers until they toppled over and I started again to raise that crooked spine of checkers a foot high.

4   If there were only little kids—four or five-year-olds who could count to ten—I played Candyland, a simple game of gum drops and sugar canes down a road to an ice cream sandwich. I remember playing with Rosie, a five-year-old whose brother Raymond got his leg broken when he was hit by a car. I was not around that day, but I recall racing a friend to where it had happened to look at the dried blood on the curb. My friend and I touched the stain. I scratched at it so that a few flakes got under my nails, and no matter how I picked and sucked at them, they wouldn't come out. We both ran home very frightened.

5   Rosie sat across the picnic-like table from me, her stringy hair spiked with a few flowers, and called me "Blackie" when it was my turn to spin the wheel and move down the candyland road. I didn't hit her because she had six brothers, five of them bigger than me. To smack her would have meant terror that would last for years. But the truth was that she liked me, for she offered me sunflower seeds from her sweaty palms and let me spit the shells at her.

6   "Spin the wheel Blackie," she said with a mouthful of her seeds and sniffling from a perennial cold, a bubble of snot coming and going.

7   "OK, tether-ball-head," I countered. Both of us laughed at each other's cleverness while we traded off spitting shells at one another, a few pasting themselves to our foreheads.

8   One Saturday morning a well-dressed man let his daughter try the slide. Rosie ran over to join the little girl, who was wearing a dress, her hair tied into a neat pony tail. Her shoes were glossy black and she wore socks with red trim. Rosie squealed at the little girl and the girl squealed back, and they both ran off to play while the father sat with his newspaper on the bench.

9   I went and sat on the same bench, shyly picking at the brittle, green paint but not looking up at the man at first. When my eyes did lift, slowly like balloons let go, I took it all in: His polished shoes, creased pants, the shirt, and his watch that glinted as he turned the page of his newspaper. I had seen fathers like him before on the *Donna Reed Show* or *Father Knows Best*, and I was pleased that he was here at *our* playground because I felt that we were being trusted, that nearby, just beyond our block, the rich people lived and were welcoming.

10   He looked up from the newspaper at me and forced a quick smile that relaxed back into a line as he returned to his paper. Happily I jumped from the bench and rushed to play with Rosie and the little girl, hoping to catch the man's eye as I swung twice as high as the girls and parachuted with great abandon to land like a frog. He looked up to smile, but dropped his eyes back to the newspaper as he recrossed his legs.

11   But then it happened. The little girl fell from the swing while Rosie was pushing her. Startled by her sudden crying, the man's eyes locked on the scene of Rosie hovering over his daughter crying on the ground. He jumped up yelling, "You filthy Mexican." He picked up his daughter who had stopped crying, and then, turning to Rosie who was saying that she hadn't done anything, he shoved her hard against the chain link fence so that her sunflower seeds flew in every direction. She got up bent over, her breath knocked out, mouth open wide as a cup and a string of saliva lengthening to the ground.

12   Three of her brothers were playing Chinese checkers under the tree, and when they saw what had happened they ran to fight the man with handfuls of redwood chips that they had scooped up from the play area. Like the rest of us, the brothers, who ranged from eight to fourteen, wore T-shirts and cut-offs but with no shoes— sons of the very poor. But unlike the rest of us, they were fierce brawlers who would go at it even with older kids as they flew up like chickens against those who got them mad.

13   Yelling, "You nigger people," his raised arm blocking the puffs of redwood chips, the man was backed into the merry-go-round while his daughter, some distance away, clung to the chain link fence. He charged one brother and pushed him to the ground only to feel a handful of redwood chips against his face. Coughing, he grabbed another brother and threw him to the ground while still another threw a softball at his back. In pain, the man turned around and chased the brother, but was stopped by the coach who had come running from the baseball game on the other side of the playground.

14   "Don't touch him," the coach warned the man, who was shouting whatever wild insults came to his mind. The coach tried to coax him to calm down, but the man, whose eyes were glassy, raved rabidly as his arms flailed about.

15   I had been watching from upside-down on the bars, but got down to help Rosie gather her seeds. She was on her knees, face streaked and nose running. I pinched up three seeds from the ground before I turned to stand by the brothers who were still taunting the man with Coke bottles they had pulled from the garbage. Suddenly the

man broke down and as loudly as he had screamed names, he screamed that he was sorry, that he didn't know what he was doing. He gathered his daughter in his arms, repeating again and again that he was sorry. The coach ushered him to the gate while the brothers, two of them crying, yelled that they were going to get him.

16   "You are no one, mister. You think you can do this to us because we're little," one said with his Coke bottle still cocked and ready.

17   I wanted to run for them as they left for their car, to explain that it was a mistake; that we also fell from the swings and the bars and slide and got hurt. I wanted to show the man my chin that broke open on the merry-go-round, the half-moon of pink scar. But they hurried away, sweaty from the morning sun, the man's pants and shirt stained with dirt and the little girl's limp dress smudged from her fall, and in some ways looking like us.

18   I returned to Rosie who was still collecting her seeds, and feeling bad but not knowing what to do, I got to my knees and asked if she wanted to play. I touched her hair, then her small shoulders, and called her name. She looked up at me, her face still wet from crying, and said, "Go away, Blackie."

Comprehension Check

Directions: Answer the following questions.

Literal Questions

1. Who is the main character?
   a. Dirty young girl named Rosie
   b. Seven-year-old boy called "Blackie"
   c. Ronnie, a poor "Okie" boy
   d. Blackie's sister Debra
   e. The man with the newspaper

2. T/F   The story takes place in summer at a playground.

3. Who are the two characters around which the conflict takes place? _____

   _____

4. The conflict in the story first occurs when
   a. Ronnie runs off after beating Blackie at checkers.
   b. Blackie spits sunflower seeds at Rosie.
   c. Rosie's brothers threaten the well-dressed man on the bench.
   d. the well-dressed girl falls off the swing.
   e. the well-dressed man yells at Rosie's brothers.

Critical Questions

5. T/F   One of the themes in the story seems to show that prejudice creates both anger and insecurity.

6. How would the story be different if it were told through the eyes of the man with the newspaper instead of the young boy? _____

_____

_____

7. What does the narrator mean when the well-dressed girl hurries away "in some ways looking like us"? _____

_____

_____

8. What point is Soto making by having the narrator make that statement?_____

_____

_____

Affective Questions

9. Find a metaphor or a simile used in the story and explain the effect it has on your reaction to the story. _____

_____

10. What aspect of yourself or others do you see in the story? _____

_____

Discuss your answers in class. Then record the result of the comprehension checks on the Student Record Chart in the Appendix. Each correct answer is worth 10 points, for a total of 100 points possible for comprehension.

Questions for Group Discussion

1. In many ways, Gary Soto's book is a novel about growing up. How does the narrator see himself at the beginning of the story, and how does he change after the incident with the well-dressed man and his daughter?

2. The first paragraph tells us a lot about the setting and the character. Explain what the author sets up in this introduction.

3. Explain the significance of games in this story.

4. What details does the narrator use to show poverty?

5. What do the well-dressed man and his daughter represent to the narrator?

6. Rosie's brothers are "fierce brawlers." What do you think the narrator feels about their fighting?

7. If you could talk to Rosie and the narrator at the end of the story, what would you want to say or do?

B.   Reading Exposition Affectively

It is just as important to read exposition with affective awareness as it is with fiction. The practices in this section are expository, using narration and description.

PRACTICE B-1

Directions: Read the following essay once. Then read it again, this time noticing in particular the way the author uses figurative language to develop her tone and attitude. Then answer the questions that follow the essay.

I HATE MY IPHONE

VIRGINIA HEFFERNAN

1   The iPhone was charging. Refined, introverted, mysteriously chilled, my new $200 tile of technology lay supine on a side table, gulping power from the wall.

2   Actually, the iPhone probably sips, like a lipsticky girl with a vodka drink. It usually does things in a cute way. Whatever. At 4 in the morning, I was in bed, fighting rage. I couldn't stop thinking about that device's tarty little face and those yapping "apps" you can download for it. The whole iPhone enterprise seemed to require so much attention, organization, explanation, praise, electricity. I know—I know: in the morning, Apple's latest miracle machine would fill my palm with meaning and magic. So why couldn't I contain my annoyance? I had no new-thing excitement. It dawned on me: I hated my iPhone.

3   I was late to get one—and maybe that's the problem. Maybe my hopes for the iPhone curdled in the time it took for my perfectly good T-Mobile plan to expire so I could switch to balky AT&T and purchase one. But I had bided my time. And, really, my enthusiasm survived right up to the moment at the AT&T counter, post-sale, when a saleswoman transferred my address book from my battered BlackBerry to the sweetie-pie iPhone.

4   "Can you set up my e-mail too?" I asked. She handed me the phone and told me what to type. Pressing her good nature, I asked if she'd do that part too, since I wasn't yet handy with the iPhone's character-entry system—the 2D screen-based simulation of the qwerty keyboard.

5   She gave me a hard look. Truly, as if she was supposed to be on the lookout for people like me. "It's your phone," she replied briskly. "It's time you started typing on it."

6   It's time. She was like a nurse for newborns, urging me—a new mother—to step up and change a diaper or something. And I felt just like a sullen new mom, not ready for her role. "Can you just do it this one time?" I said weakly. She poked in the necessary codes. She didn't trust me, but she let me take the iPhone home anyway.

7   I didn't trust myself, either. There were warning signs. I didn't rush to explore the phone or load it up with apps. I didn't fantasize about its features, as I did with the feedable Baby Alive doll when I was 6 or with my first Macintosh, when I was 19. Instead, the iPhone stayed in my bag. A hard weight with glossy surfaces, it kept aloof from the animal warmth of my leather wallet. I didn't even face the iPhone again until it rang, or chimed—or produced some audio confection that seemed cloyingly churchy.

8   You can see I wasn't thinking clearly. To answer the phone, I had to touch the screen. Years of not touching screens—so as not to smudge or scar—made me wary. But I brushed the "answer call" and up came fragments of my mother's cheerful voice.

AT&T no doubt works like a charm in other areas, but as I'd been warned, it wasn't so hot on holding calls where I live. I let it drop my mom. I hunted for a keypad to call her back, but it was gone.

9   The morning after my sleepless night of charging the phone, a text message arrived from a colleague, about breakfast. It came up in a little dialogue bubble, as if we were characters in a comic book.

10   Now I had to reply. My throat tightened. "Running late," I decided on. "See you in 15 min."

11   What came out was this: "Runninlate. See you in 15 Mon."

12   Why? Why, because of course that's what I typed! What did I know of this wacko kind of typing? I spent my adolescence touch-typing, convinced my life would be passed secretarially, my left pinkie building novelty muscle manning the *A.* Then the technology changed, and I improvised an inelegant three-finger style for computer keyboards.

13   Then years ago, when I bought a BlackBerry, I adapted again. My two hands met as if in prayer, as the thick thumbs took center stage. I liked it. Thinking with my thumbs made sense in a way that thinking with nails and feebler fingers never would or did. And the transformation of thumb-twiddling into typing! Nervous motion was turned productive, as it is in knitting or whittling. Ingenious.

14   Oh, God. I really was losing it. As I composed my running-late text, the iPhone's iciness deepened my revulsion. Did this device, which was built never to be cradled, ever warm up? I was also mortified by my illiteracy. My right index finger—the only digit precise enough to hit the close-set virtual iPhone keys—seemed an anemic, cerebral thing, designed for making paltry points in debating club. I repeatedly stabbed to the right of my target letter. It was like being 4 again—or being 90. I couldn't see, it seemed; I couldn't point; I couldn't connect.

15   And so the iPhone made suggestions. Did I want to say Ride? Ripe? Ruin? No. I wanted to say Running. You know, the way a human might. But with its know-it-all suggestions, the iPhone seemed to want to be more human, more helpful, jollier than I was! The vaunted Apple user-friendliness was exposed, before my eyes, as bossiness and insincerity.

16   I refused to fight further with the smug phone. Off sailed my text—the work of a blithering idiot.

17   At breakfast, my colleague said she loved her iPhone. She insisted my typing would improve, but she clearly has more native index-finger skills than I do. I asked her if she thought the iPhone was "coy" or "cold," and she looked at me blankly. As I spoke I felt like a chippy freak—one of those people too intransigently cranky even to like Barack Obama, or recycling, or the Internet. I thought of how clearly the iPhone suits the moment: Apple once again getting ahead of the game, offering something cuter and funner and more Appley than anyone else.

18   The failure to appreciate the iPhone was all mine. But I decided not to dwell on that. "I thought you might be back," the AT&T saleswoman said as I walked in the door. "So?" I said. "You were right." With some satisfaction, she took the iPhone, and I walked away with a new BlackBerry and money to spare.

Now answer the following questions.

1. In the blanks, write what you think is the literal meaning of the following images from the selection:

   a. lay supine on a side table, gulping power from the wall.

b. the iPhone probably sips, like a lipsticky girl with a vodka drink.

_____

c. She was like a nurse for newborns

_____

d. produced some audio confection that seemed cloyingly churchy.

_____

e. it wasn't so hot on holding calls where I lived

_____

f. the iPhone's iciness deepened my revulsion

_____

2. The author tells us in her title that she hates her iPhone. What are some of her reasons?

_____

_____

3. Explain how the author's use of descriptive figurative language helps develop her tone.

_____

Practice B-2

Directions: This is a timed-reading practice. Before you start, look at your Student Record Chart in the Appendix and note your last timed-reading rate and comprehension scores. Try to better your rate without any loss of comprehension.

Now briefly survey the article, then begin timing, applying all the reading skills you have learned.

Begin Timing: _____

HIGH ANXIETY

RANDYE HODER

1   I noticed the small, dark-skinned man with the ill-fitting blue suit as soon as he walked into the area where I was sitting at New York's John F. Kennedy International Airport. I was reading a newspaper, waiting to board a flight to Los Angeles, when he caught my eye. Rumpled and holding his boarding pass tightly, he had no coffee, no carry-on luggage, no book or magazine.

2   He seemed nervous. He was jumpy. He stared a lot—first at me, then at a young woman a few seats to my left, then at an even younger woman across from us. For a moment the man just stood there, shifting his eyes from one to the other. He then fixed his gaze on a well-dressed businessman who was so engrossed in his novel that

Randye Hoder, "High Anxiety," *Los Angeles Times* Magazine, November 14, 2004. Reprinted with permission from Randye Hoder.

he didn't seem to notice. The dark-skinned man abruptly sat down next to the businessman, nudged him with his elbow, showed him his boarding pass and spoke to him in a language that I did not recognize.

3   The startled businessman jerked upright, squeezed an inch or two away from the stranger and shrugged his shoulders as if to say, "I don't know, ask them." He pointed in the direction of the airline's gate attendants. As soon as the man got up and walked toward the gate, the four of us, without uttering a word, exchanged a look that said: That was weird. Really weird.

4   The others went back to what they had been doing—reading, chatting on a cell-phone, eating a bite of lunch—before the man in the blue suit appeared. But by then, he had my full attention. I watched him approach the gate attendants, both of whom were helping other passengers. Again, the man seemed oblivious to the concept of personal space. He walked past the line of travelers waiting to be helped, stepped up to the counter and stood shoulder to shoulder with the passenger at the head of the line. It was as if he hadn't noticed her there.

5   He shoved his boarding pass into the hand of a gate attendant. She took it from him and nodded her head, pointing first to the gate entrance and then at her watch. She held up 10 fingers as if to indicate that it would be 10 minutes before the flight began boarding. The man turned around and walked back toward me and the others. He sat down next to the businessman, giving him a tad more space this time, and proceeded to fidget and stare at us anew.

6   I hoped that the strange man had aroused the gate attendant's suspicion, as he had mine. I was disappointed when he did not. I wanted someone, preferably someone in authority, to take action. I already was grappling with whether I should say something myself—indeed, whether in our post-Sept. 11 world, I had a responsibility. After all, aren't we supposed to be vigilant, to report any suspicious behavior? Haven't we been told that doing anything less is forsaking our obligation as good citizens? Wouldn't only a fool bite her tongue these days?

7   Still, maybe I was overreacting. Perhaps he was a nervous flyer. Maybe he was just a weary traveler, a foreigner in a country whose language he didn't speak and whose ways he didn't fully understand. Maybe he was mentally disturbed—a man who should elicit our compassion, not our distrust.

8   But what if he was something else: a fanatic with a box-cutter hidden in his suit? A radical in the mold of Richard Reid, the would-be shoe bomber, who at one point had been detained for suspicious behavior? El Al airlines, among others, closely studies passengers' demeanor as a way to thwart terrorists, noting that people about to do bad things often act stressed.

9   Then again, what if I was letting my fears—and, even worse, my prejudices—get the best of me? Would I have felt the same way if he were blond?

10   When the attendant called for first-class passengers to board, the businessman stood up, grabbed his carry-on bag and took his place in line. The man in the blue suit followed him like a shadow. The businessman later told me that he got so close, it felt like "he was trying to pick my pocket."

11   I was still waiting to board, along with the two young women. We exchanged another glance. "Did that guy creep you out, or what?" one of the women asked. We all agreed that he was definitely creepy.

12   "Should I say something?" I asked them.

13   They both shrugged their shoulders, unwilling to make a fuss—but perfectly happy for me to do so.

14   We boarded the flight and I looked to see where the man was seated. Suddenly—I'm still not sure why—I decided to take the plunge. I found the purser and told

her that a man on our flight had been acting oddly. I recounted the behaviors that I found disconcerting and told her that several other passengers also seemed alarmed. A flight attendant agreed, telling the purser that when the man boarded, she too thought something about him was off.

15   I pointed out the man to the purser and took my seat. Minutes later, he was escorted off the plane, leaving me with a strange mix of emotions: simultaneously relieved yet filled with guilt. I asked the purser what would happen to him now. She said the airline would find someone who spoke the language of his native Pakistan and review his itinerary.

16   After telling the purser about my conflicted feelings, she told me that the decision to remove the passenger was not hers. She had consulted the pilot, and he made the call. She told me that she too had felt torn, and that she had cried when the man was removed from the flight. The other flight attendant was more stoic. "Better safe than sorry," she said. "If he turns out to be OK, the worse thing that happened to him was [that he was] delayed."

17   Perhaps. But assuming he was innocent, he suffered a terrible humiliation. What's more, he must have been very, very afraid. And fear, I can tell you, is a dreadful thing.

Finish Timing. Record time here _____ and use the Timed Reading Conversion Chart in the Appendix to figure your rate: _____ wpm.

Comprehension Check

Directions: Answer the following questions without looking back at the essay.

1. What is the subject of this essay? _____

    _____

2. What is the thesis or main idea of this essay? _____

    _____

3. Explain the meaning of the title. How does it relate to the point the author is making?

    _____

    _____

    _____

4. Where did the events described in the essay take place? _____

    _____

5. Which of the following describes the man who made the author nervous?

    a. Small, dark-skinned

    b. Wore a rumpled, blue suit

    c. Stared at people

    d. Had no coffee or carry-on luggage

    e. All of the above

6. We can infer that the businessman was more irritated with the Pakistani's behavior toward him than his concern that he might be a terrorist.

    a. True because _____

    b. False because _____

7. The author struggled with her conscience before deciding to alert her fears to the flight crew.

    a. True because _____

    b. False because _____

8. The author felt guilty after telling the purser about the Pakistani's behavior.

    a. True because _____

    b. False because _____

9. Who made the decision to remove the man from the plane?

    a. The purser

    b. The flight attendant

    c. The gate attendants

    d. The pilot

10. The author ends her essay by saying, "What's more, he must have been very, very afraid. And fear, I can tell you, is a dreadful thing." Explain what she means.

_____

_____

Vocabulary Check

Directions: Define the following underlined words from the selection.

1. <u>Rumpled</u> and holding his boarding pass

_____

2. <u>engrossed</u> in his novel

_____

3. <u>oblivious</u> to the concept of personal space

_____

4. <u>bite her tongue</u> (figure of speech)

_____

5. should <u>elicit</u> our compassion

_____

6. a man who studies passengers' <u>demeanor</u>

_____

7. a way to <u>thwart</u> terrorists

_____

8. the phrase <u>"followed him like a shadow"</u> is called a

_____

9. I found <u>disconcerting</u>

_____

10. review his <u>itinerary</u>

_____

Record the results of the comprehension and vocabulary checks on the Student Record Chart in the Appendix. Each correct answer is worth 10 points, for a total of 100 points possible for comprehension and 100 points for vocabulary. Discuss your scores with your instructor.

Questions for Group Discussion

1. How many ethnic backgrounds are represented in your group? Discuss some of the differences in attitudes held toward religion, family, education, occupation, and fashions. How do these differences affect who you are and the lifestyle you live?

2. Discuss the fear and prejudice found in the essay "High Anxiety." Has anything she says in her essay affected you? How would you react to someone acting in a manner you thought strange or possibly dangerous?

PRACTICE B-3

Directions: Answer the following questions. Then read the essay that follows. You or your instructor may want to time your reading.

1. What is a *barrio?* _____

_____

2. Briefly describe your neighborhood. _____

_____

Now survey the 1,350-word article to see what rate you can apply to the reading of the selection while still obtaining good comprehension. Apply all the skills you have learned.

Begin Timing: _____

THE BARRIO

ROBERT RAMIREZ

1   The train, its metal wheels squealing as they spin along the silvery tracks, rolls slower now. Through the gaps between the cars blink a streetlamp, and this pulsing light on a barrio streetcorner beats slower, like a weary heartbeat, until the train shudders to a halt, the light goes out, and the barrio is deep asleep.

2   Throughout Aztlán (the Nahuatl term meaning "land to the north"), trains grumble along the edges of a sleeping people. From Lower California, through the blistering Southwest, down the Rio Grande to the muddy Gulf, the darkness and mystery of dreams engulf communities fenced off by railroads, canals, and expressways. Paradoxical communities, isolated from the rest of the town by concrete columned monuments of progress, and yet stranded in the past. They are surrounded by change. It eludes their reach, in their own backyards, and the people, unable and unwilling to see the future, or even touch the present, perpetuate the past.

3   Leaving from the expressway or jolting across the tracks, one enters a different physical world permeated by a different attitude. The physical dimensions are impressive. It is a large section of town which extends for fifteen blocks north and south along the tracks, and then advances eastward, thinning into nothingness beyond the city limits. Within the invisible (yet sensible) walls of the barrio, are many, many people living in too few houses. The homes, however, are much more numerous than on the outside.

4   Members of the barrio describe the entire area as their home. It is a home, but it is more than this. The barrio is a refuge from the harshness and the coldness of the Anglo world. It is a forced refuge. The leprous people are isolated from the rest of the community and contained in their section of town. The stoical pariahs of the barrio accept their fate, and from the angry seeds of rejection grow the flowers of closeness between outcasts, not the thorns of bitterness and the mad desire to flee. There is no want to escape, for the feeling of the barrio is known only to its inhabitants, and the material needs of life can also be found here.

5   The *tortillería* fires up its machinery three times a day, producing steaming, round, flat slices of barrio bread. In the winter, the warmth of the tortilla factory is a wool *sarape* in the chilly morning hours, but in the summer, it unbearably toasts every noontime customer.

6   The *panadería* sends its sweet messenger aroma down the dimly lit street, announcing the arrival of fresh, hot sugary *pan dulce*.

7   The small corner grocery serves the meal-to-meal needs of customers, and the owner, a part of the neighborhood, willingly gives credit to people unable to pay cash for foodstuffs.

8   The barbershop is a living room with hydraulic chairs, radio, and television, where old friends meet and speak of life as their salted hair falls aimlessly about them.

9   The pool hall is a junior level country club where *chucos*, strangers in their own land, get together to shoot pool and rap, while veterans, unaware of the cracking, popping balls on the green felt, complacently play dominoes beneath rudely hung *Playboy* foldouts.

10   The *cantina* is the night spot of the barrio. It is the country club and the den where the rites of puberty are enacted. Here the young become men. It is in the taverns that a young dude shows his *machismo* through the quantity of beer he can hold, the scores of *rucas* he has had, and his willingness and ability to defend his image against hardened and scarred old lions.

11   No, there is no frantic wish to flee. It would be absurd to leave the familiar and nervously step into the strange and cold Anglo community when the needs of the Chicano can be met in the barrio.

12   The barrio is closeness. From the family living unit, familial relationships stretch out to immediate neighbors, down the block, around the corner, and to all parts of the barrio. The feeling of family, a rare and treasurable sentiment, pervades and accounts for the inability of the people to leave. The barrio is this attitude manifested on the

countenances of the people, on the faces of their homes, and in the gaiety of their gardens.

13   The color-splashed homes arrest your eyes, arouse your curiosity, and make you wonder what life scenes are being played out in them. The flimsy, brightly colored, wood-frame houses ignore no neon-brilliant color. Houses trimmed in orange, char- treuse, lime-green, yellow, and mixtures of these and other hues beckon the beholder to reflect on the peculiarity of each home. Passing through this land is refreshing like Brubeck, not narcotizing like revolting rows of similar houses, which neither offend nor please.

14   In the evenings, the porches and front yards are occupied with men calmly talk- ing over the noise of children playing baseball in the unpaved extension of the living room, while the women cook supper or gossip with female neighbors as they water the *jardines*. The gardens mutely echo the expressive verses of the colorful houses. The denseness of multicolored plants and trees give the house the appearance of an oasis or a tropical island hideaway, sheltered from the rest of the world.

15   Fences are common in the barrio, but they are fences and not the walls of the Anglo community. On the western side of town, the high wooden fences between houses are thick, impenetrable walls, built to keep the neighbors at bay. In the barrio, the fences may be rusty, wire contraptions or thick green shrubs. In either case you can see through them and feel no sense of intrusion when you cross them.

16   Many lower-income families of the barrio manage to maintain a comfortable standard of living through the communal action of family members who contribute their wages to the head of the family. Economic need creates interdependence and closeness. Small barefooted boys sell papers on cool, dark Sunday mornings, deny themselves pleasantries, and give their earnings to *mamá*. The older the child, the greater the responsibility to help the head of the household provide for the rest of the family.

17   There are those, too, who for a number of reasons have not achieved a relative sense of financial security. Perhaps it results from too many children too soon, but it is the homes of these people and their situation that numbs rather than charms. Their houses, aged and bent, oozing children, are fissures in the horn of plenty. Their wooden homes may have brick-pattern asbestos tile on the outer walls, but the tile is not convincing.

18   Unable to pay city taxes or incapable of influencing the city to live up to its duty to serve all the citizens, the poorer barrio families remain trapped in the nineteenth century and survive as best they can. The backyards have well-worn paths to the out- houses, which sit near the alley. Running water is considered a luxury in some parts of the barrio. Decent drainage is usually unknown, and when it rains, the water stands for days, an incubator of health hazards and an avoidable nuisance. Streets, costly to pave, remain rough, rocky trails. Tires do not last long, and the constant rattling and shak- ing grind away a car's life and spread dust through screen windows.

19   The houses and their *jardines*, the jollity of the people in an adverse world, the brightly feathered alarm clock pecking away at supper and cautiously eyeing the chil- dren playing nearby produce a mystifying sensation at finding the noble savage alive in the twentieth century. It is easy to look at the positive qualities of life in the barrio, and look at them with a distantly envious feeling. One wishes to experience the feel- ings of the barrio and not the hardships. Remembering the illness, the hunger, and feeling of time running out on you, the walls, both real and imagined, reflecting on living in the past, one finds his envy becoming more elusive, until it has vanished alto- gether.

20   Back now beyond the tracks, the train creaks and groans, the cars jostle each other down the track, and as the light begins its pulsing, the barrio, with all its meanings, greets a new dawn with yawns and restless stretchings.

Finish Timing: Record time here _____ and use the Timed Reading Conversion Chart in the Appendix to figure your rate: _____ wpm.

Comprehension Check

Directions: Answer the following questions.

1. What is the thesis or main idea of this article? _____
   _____
   _____
   _____

2. What is a barrio? _____
   _____
   _____

3. What is the author's attitude toward the barrio he describes? _____
   _____
   _____

4. The phrase "from the angry seeds of rejection grow the flowers of closeness between outcasts, not the thorns of bitterness" is an example of a simile.
   a. True, because _____
   b. False, because _____

5. "…this pulsing light on a barrio streetcorner beats slower, like a weary heartbeat" is an example of a metaphor.
   a. True, because _____
   b. False, because _____

6. Explain Ramirez's use of walls and fences to help develop his theme of cultural isolation. _____
   _____
   _____
   _____

7. How does the author's use of words such as *closeness, home, family, refuge,* and *neighborhood* help us understand how those who live in the barrio feel about it?
   _____
   _____

8. What is Ramirez describing when he says, "the brightly feathered alarm clock pecking away at supper and cautiously eyeing the children"? _____

9. Ramirez states, "One wishes to experience the feelings of the barrio and not the hardships." What are some of those feelings and what are some of the hardships?

Feelings	Hardships
_____	_____
_____	_____
_____	_____

10. Does Ramirez give any evidence to indicate that the people in the barrio want to leave? _____ Explain. _____

_____

_____

Vocabulary Check

Directions: Define the following underlined words from the selection.

1. paradoxical communities, isolated from the town _____

_____

2. it eludes their reach _____

_____

3. to touch the present, to perpetuate the past _____

_____

4. a world permeated by a different attitude _____

_____

5. the leprous people are isolated from the rest _____

_____

6. The stoical pariahs…accept their fate _____

_____

7. The stoical pariahs of the barrio _____

_____

8. complacently play dominoes _____

_____

9. thick, impenetrable walls _____

_____

10. an incubator of health hazards _____

_____

Record your rate and the results of the comprehension and vocabulary checks on the Student Record Chart in the Appendix. Each correct answer is worth 10 points, for a total of 100 points possible for comprehension and 100 points for vocabulary. Discuss your scores with your instructor.

Application: Practicing Aesthetic Awareness

Aesthetics (pronounced es-the-tiks) has to do with appreciation of beauty or what is pleasing to the senses. As a good reader, you want to become aware of the aesthetics involved in good writing. It is one thing to understand what you read, but even better to appreciate the way something was written. In her book, *Ruined by Reading*, Lynne Sharon Schwartz says:

> We may read for facts alone: the eye skims along, alert for key words, and when they appear, like red lights on a highway, it slides deftly to a halt. That kind of reading propelled me out of graduate school. However useful, it does not feel like true reading but more like shopping, riffling through racks for the precise shade of blue. I would have made a poor and ludicrous scholar, like a diva singing ditties in TV commercials, or a pastry chef condemned to macrobiotic menus…. Like the bodies of dancers or athletes, the minds of readers are genuinely happy and self-possessed only when cavorting around doing their stretches and leaps and jumps to the tune of words.

It may take a second or third reading of her paragraph for you to understand what she is saying about "true reading." And that's her point. Your affective comprehension is enhanced when you respond not only to the literal and critical levels of a written work, but also to its aesthetic or artistic creation.

Find a poem, short story, or essay that you appreciate for its aesthetic as well as its entertaining value and share it with your classmates or instructor.

C.   Putting It All Together

By now, you ought to have a deeper understanding of the meaning of, and the need for, developing reading versatility. Approaches to reading are as varied as the types of reading materials that exist and the reasons for reading them. This chapter has shown you some approaches to reading imaginative literature. It brings

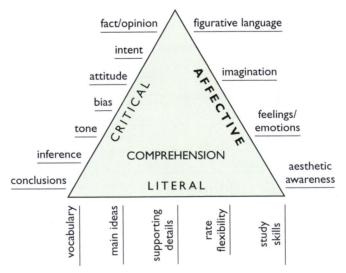

together the general content of all three units in the book. As the Unit Three introduction told you, total comprehension is a combination of the literal, critical, and affective levels of understanding. Good comprehension brings everything you've learned separately into play. The diagram on page 400 shows the many facets of comprehension.

You should be aware, from doing previous practices, that a short poem may take longer to read and understand than a chapter in a textbook. You can read some materials quickly, even skim and scan them, whereas others require rereading. Good imaginative literature seldom communicates on a literal level only. It is necessary to use your imagination, to interpret symbols, and to breathe life into characters, settings, and situations.

Developing reading versatility requires more than reading this book. It requires a lifetime of reading and reacting, at all levels of comprehension.

Introducing Barbara Kingsolver

Barbara Kingsolver grew up in eastern Kentucky, but never intended to stay there. Options were limited, she says: "Grow up to be a farmer or a farmer's wife." After graduating in 1977 from DePauw University in Indiana with a major in biology, Kingsolver continued her graduate studies at the University of Arizona in Tuc-

son, receiving a master of science degree. To support herself, she worked as an archaeologist, copy editor, X-ray technician, housecleaner, biological researcher, and translator of medical documents.

Before becoming a well-known, bestselling author, she worked as a science writer for the University of Arizona and published numerous articles in such places as *The Nation*, the *New York Times*, and *Smithsonian*. In 1986, she won an Arizona Press Club award for outstanding feature writing. When some of her earlier articles appeared later in her collection of essays, *High Tide in Tucson: Essays from Now or Never*, she was awarded an honorary doctorate of letters from DePauw University.

During the time between 1985 and 1987, Kingsolver worked as a freelance journalist. But at night, she wrote fiction. Married in 1985 and pregnant a year later, she suffered from insomnia. Her doctor recommended that she scrub the bathroom tiles with a toothbrush. Instead, she sat in a closet and began to write her first novel, *The Bean Trees*. Published in 1988, *The Bean Trees* was well received not only by critics but also by the general reading public. In an interview with *Publishers Weekly*, Kingsolver says, "A novel can educate to some extent. But first a novel has to entertain— that's the contract with a reader.... I want an English professor to understand the symbolism while at the same time I want people I grew up with—who may not often read anything but the Sears catalogue—to read my books."

Following *The Bean Trees*, Kingsolver wrote *Homeland and Other Stories* (1989), the novels *Animal Dreams* (1990) and *Pigs in Heaven* (1993), *The Poisonwood Bible* (1998), *Prodigal Summer* (2000), and another collection of essays, *Small Wonder* (2002). Kingsolver claims she never writes about herself, even though people who know her assume that some of her work is autobiographical.

"I don't even write about real people. That would be stealing, first of all. And second of all, art is supposed to be better than that. If you want a slice of life, look out the window. An artist has to look out that window, isolate one or two suggestive things, and embroider them together with poetry and fabrication, to create a revelation. If we can't, as artists, improve on real life, we should put down our pencils and go bake bread." (From http://www.harpercollins. com/catalog/author_xml.asp?authorID=5311)

For more information on Barbara Kingsolver, type in the author's name in any search engine and explore some of the sites listed. Kingsolver's personal Web page is http://www.kingsolver.com.

PRACTICE C-1

Directions: Barbara Kingsolver's novel *Pigs in Heaven* has been delighting readers for several years. This selection is from the first chapter of that book and introduces us to the main character.

Begin Timing: _____

QUEEN OF NOTHING

BARBARA KINGSOLVER

1   Women on their own run in Alice's family. This dawns on her with the unkindness of a heart attack and she sits up in bed to get a closer look at her thoughts, which have collected above her in the dark.

2   It's early morning, April, windless, unreasonably hot even at this sun-forsaken hour. Alice is sixty-one. Her husband, Harland, is sleeping like a brick and snoring. To all appearances they're a satisfied couple sliding home free into their golden years, but Alice knows that's not how it's going to go. She married him two years ago for love, or so she thought, and he's a good enough man but a devotee of household silence. His idea of marriage is to spray WD-40 on anything that squeaks. Even on the nights when he turns over and holds her, Harland has no words for Alice—nothing to contradict all the years she lay alone, feeling the cold seep through her like cave air, turning her breasts to limestone from the inside out. This marriage has failed to warm her. The quiet only subsides when Harland sleeps and his tonsils make up for lost time. She can't stand the sight of him there on his back, driving his hogs to market. She's about to let herself out the door.

3   She leaves the bed quietly and switches on the lamp in the living room, where his Naugahyde recliner confronts her, snug as a catcher's mitt, with a long, deep impression of Harland running down its center. On weekends he watches cable TV with perfect vigilance, as if he's afraid he'll miss the end of the world—though he doesn't bother with CNN, which, if the world did end, is where the taped footage would run.

From *Pigs in Heaven* © Barbara Kingsolver 1993. Reprinted by kind permission of the author.

Harland prefers the Home Shopping Channel because he can follow it with the sound turned off.

4   She has an edgy sense of being watched because of his collection of antique headlights, which stare from the china cabinet. Harland runs El-Jay's Paint and Body and his junk is taking over her house. She hardly has the energy to claim it back. Old people might marry gracefully once in a while, but their houses rarely do. She snaps on the light in the kitchen and shades her eyes against the bright light and all those ready appliances.

5   Her impulse is to call Taylor, her daughter. Taylor is taller than Alice now and pretty and living far away, in Tucson. Alice wants to warn her that a defect runs in the family, like flat feet or diabetes: they're all in danger of ending up alone by their own stubborn choice. The ugly kitchen clock says four-fifteen. No time-zone differences could make that into a reasonable hour in Tucson; Taylor would answer with her heart pounding, wanting to know who'd dropped dead. Alice rubs the back of her head, where her cropped gray hair lies flat in several wrong directions, prickly with sweat and sleeplessness. The cluttered kitchen irritates her. The Formica countertop is patterned with pink and black loops like rubber bands lying against each other, getting on her nerves, all cocked and ready to spring like hail across the kitchen. Alice wonders if other women in the middle of the night have begun to resent their Formica. She stares hard at the telephone on the counter, wishing it would ring. She needs some proof that she isn't the last woman left on earth, the surviving queen of nothing. The clock gulps softly, eating seconds whole while she waits; she receives no proof.

6   She stands on a chair and rummages in the cupboard over the refrigerator for a bottle of Jim Beam that's been in the house since before she married Harland. There are Mason jars up there she ought to get rid of. In her time Alice has canned tomatoes enough for a hundred bomb shelters, but now she couldn't care less, nobody does. If they drop the bomb now, the world will end without the benefit of tomato aspic. She climbs down and pours half an inch of Jim Beam into a Bengals mug that came free with a tank of gas. Alice would just as soon get her teeth cleaned as watch the Bengals. That's the price of staying around when your heart's not in it, she thinks. You get to be cheerleader for a sport you never chose. She unlatches the screen door and steps barefoot onto the porch.

7   The sky is a perfect black. A leftover smile of moon hides in the bottom branches of the sugar maple, teasing her to smile back. The air isn't any cooler outside the house, but being outdoors in her sheer nightgown arouses Alice with the possibility of freedom. She could walk away from this house carrying nothing. How those glass eyeballs in the china cabinet would blink, to see her go. She leans back in the porch swing, missing the squeak of its chains that once sang her baby to sleep, but which have been oppressed into silence now by Harland's WD-40. Putting her nose deep into the mug of bourbon, she draws in sweet, caustic fumes, just as she used to inhale tobacco smoke until Taylor made her quit.

Finish Timing: Record time here _____ and use the Timed Reading Conversion Chart in the Appendix to figure your rate: _____ wpm.

Comprehension Check

Directions: Answer the following questions.

1. Describe the main character, both from details given in the story and what you infer about her. _____

   _____

   _____

2. Another character is the husband, whom we see only through Alice's eyes. Give three details about him that help explain his character. _____

   _____

   _____

3. When is the story taking place, and how does that time affect the story? _____

   _____

   _____

4. Kingsolver is a master of figurative language. Find at least three examples of figurative language in the selection. _____

   _____

5. In the second paragraph, the main character summarizes her marriage by saying, "His idea of marriage is to spray WD-40 on anything that squeaks." Explain this statement. _____

   _____

6. Near the end of paragraph 5 is the explanation of the title of this selection, "Queen of Nothing." Explain what the term means. _____

   _____

7. What do you infer about Alice's relationship with her daughter Taylor? _____

   _____

   _____

8. What is your reaction to the main character (Alice) in this selection? _____

   _____

9. What seems to be the point of the story (or theme) from this selection? _____

   _____

10. What passages or sentences seem especially well written or effective to you?

    _____

Vocabulary Check

Directions: Explain in your own words each of the following underlined figurative expressions.

1. This dawns on her with <u>the unkindness of a heart attack.</u> _____

   _____

   _____

2. to get a closer look at her thoughts, which have <u>collected above her in the dark</u>

_____

_____

3. Harland is sleeping like a brick _____

_____

_____

4. feeling the cold seep through her <u>like cave air</u> _____

_____

_____

5. the Naugahyde recliner,... <u>snug as a catcher's mitt</u> _____

_____

_____

6. The Formica countertop is patterned with <u>pink and black loops like rubber bands</u> <u>lying against each other</u> _____

_____

7. Like rubber bands... <u>all cocked and ready to spring like hail</u> across the kitchen

_____

_____

8. the clock <u>gulps softly, eating seconds</u>... while she waits _____

_____

9. Alice would <u>just as soon get her teeth cleaned as watch the Bengals</u> _____

_____

_____

10. A leftover smile of moon hides in the bottom branches of the sugar maple _____

_____

_____

Record your rate and the results of the comprehension vocabulary checks on the Student Record Chart in the Appendix. Each correct answer is worth 10 points, for a total of 100 points possible for comprehension and 100 points for vocabulary.

PRACTICE C-2

Directions: The following textbook selection discusses the power of cultural myths and how they can affect our critical thinking ability. Before you read it, answer the following questions.

1. What do you think is meant by *cultural myth*? _____

_____

2. Define *the American dream.* _____

_____

3. Define *critical thinking.* _____

_____

4. What is your idea of success? _____

_____

Now apply everything you have learned about reading with versatility. Then answer the questions that follow.

CULTURAL MYTHS AS OBSTACLES TO CRITICAL THINKING

GARY COLUMBO, ROBERT CULLEN, AND BONNIE LISLE

1   Culture shapes the way we think; it tells us what "makes sense." It holds people together by providing us with a shared set of customs, values, ideas, and beliefs, as well as a common language. We live enmeshed in this cultural web: it influences the way we relate to others, the way we look, our tastes, our habits; it enters our dreams and desires. But as culture binds us together it also selectively blinds us. As we grow up, we accept ways of looking at the world, ways of thinking and being that might best be characterized as cultural frames of reference or cultural myths. These myths help us understand our place in the world—our place as prescribed by our culture. They define our relationships to friends and lovers, to the past and future, to nature, to power, and to nation. Becoming a critical thinker means learning how to look beyond these cultural myths and the assumptions embedded in them.

2   You may associate the word "myth" primarily with the myths of the ancient Greeks. The legends of gods and heroes like Athena, Zeus, and Oedipus embodied the central ideals and values of Greek civilization—notions like civic responsibility, the primacy of male authority, and humility before the gods. The stories were "true" not in a literal sense but as reflections of important cultural beliefs. These myths assured the Greeks of the nobility of their origins; they provided models for the roles that Greeks would play in their public and private lives; they justified inequities in Greek society; they helped the Greeks understand human life and destiny in terms that "made sense" within the framework of that culture.

3   Our cultural myths do much the same. Take, for example, the American dream of success. Since the first European colonists came to the "New World" some four centuries ago, America has been synonymous with the idea of individual opportunity. For generations, immigrants have been lured across the ocean to make their fortunes in a land where the streets were said to be paved with gold. Of course, we don't always agree on what success means or how it should be measured. Some calculate the meaning of success in terms of multi-digit salaries or the acreage of their country estates. Others discover success in the attainment of a dream—whether it's graduating from college, achieving excellence on the playing field, or winning new rights and opportunities for less-fortunate fellow citizens. For some Americans, the dream of success is the very foundation of everything that's right about life in the United States. For others, the American dream is

From *Rereading America: Cultural Contexts for Critical Thinking and Writing*, 6th edition. Bedford/ St. Martin's, 2004.

a cultural mirage that keeps workers happy in low-paying jobs while their bosses pocket the profits of an unfair system. But whether you embrace or reject the dream of success, you can't escape its influence. As Americans, we are steeped in a culture that prizes individual achievement; growing up in the United States, we are told again and again by parents, teachers, advertisers, Hollywood writers, politicians, and opinion makers that we, too, can achieve our dream—that we, too, can "Just Do It" if we try. You might aspire to become an Internet tycoon, or you might rebel and opt for a simple life, but you can't ignore the impact of the myth. We each define success in our own way, but, ultimately, the myth of success defines who we are and what we think, feel, and believe.

4   Cultural myths gain such enormous power over us by insinuating themselves into our thinking before we're aware of them. Most are learned at a deep, even unconscious level. Gender roles are a good example. As children we get gender role models from our families, our schools, our churches, and other important institutions. We see them acted out in the relationships between family members or portrayed on television, in the movies, or in song lyrics. Before long, the culturally determined roles we see for women and men appear to us as "self-evident": it seems "natural" for a man to be strong, responsible, competitive, and heterosexual, just as it may seem "unnatural" for a man to shun competitive activity or to take a romantic interest in other men. Our most dominant cultural myths shape the way we perceive the world and blind us to alternative ways of seeing and being. When something violates the expectations that such myths create, it may even be called unnatural, immoral, or perverse.

CULTURAL MYTHS AS OBSTACLES TO CRITICAL THINKING

5   Cultural myths can have more subtle effects as well. In academic work they can reduce the complexity of our reading and thinking. A few years ago, for example, a professor at Los Angeles City College noted that he and his students couldn't agree in their interpretations of the following poem by Theodore Roethke:

My Papa's Waltz

The whiskey on your breath
Could make a small boy dizzy;
But I hung on like death:
Such waltzing was not easy.

We romped until the pans
Slid from the kitchen shelf;
My mother's countenance
Could not unfrown itself.

The hand that held my wrist
Was battered on one knuckle;
At every step you missed
My right ear scraped a buckle.

You beat time on my head
With a palm caked hard by dirt,
Then waltzed me off to bed
Still clinging to your shirt.

6   The instructor read this poem as a clear expression of a child's love for his blue-collar father, a rough-and-tumble man who had worked hard all his life ("a palm caked hard by dirt"), who was not above taking a drink of whiskey to ease his mind, but who also found the time to "waltz" his son off to bed. The students didn't see this at all. They saw the poem as a story about an abusive father and heavy drinker. They seemed unwilling to look beyond the father's roughness and the whiskey on his breath, equating these with drunken violence. Although the poem does suggest an element of fear mingled with the boy's excitement ("I hung on like death"), the class ignored its complexity—the mixture of fear, love, and boisterous fun that colors the son's memory of his father. It's possible that some students might overlook the positive traits in the father in this poem because they have suffered child abuse themselves. But this couldn't be true for all the students in the class. The difference between these interpretations lies, instead, in the influence of cultural myths. After all, in a culture now dominated by images of the family that emphasize "positive" parenting, middle-class values, and sensitive fathers, it's no wonder that students refused to see this father sympathetically. Our culture simply doesn't associate good, loving families with drinking or with even the suggestion of physical roughness.

7   Years of acculturation—the process of internalizing cultural values—leave us with a set of rigid categories for "good" and "bad" parents, narrow conceptions of how parents should look, talk, and behave toward their children. These cultural categories work like mental pigeonholes: they help us sort out and evaluate our experiences rapidly, almost before we're consciously aware of them. They give us a helpful shorthand for interpreting the world; after all, we can't stop to ponder every new situation we meet as if it were a puzzle or a philosophical problem. But while cultural categories help us make practical decisions in everyday life, they also impose their inherent rigidity on our thinking and thus limit our ability to understand the complexity of our experience. They reduce the world to dichotomies—simplified either/or choices: either women or men, either heterosexuals or homosexuals, either nature or culture, either animal or human, either "alien" or American, either them or us.

8   Rigid cultural beliefs can present serious obstacles to success for first-year college students. In a psychology class, for example, students' cultural myths may so color their thinking that they find it nearly impossible to comprehend Freud's ideas about infant sexuality. Ingrained assumptions about childhood innocence and sexual guilt may make it impossible for them to see children as sexual beings—a concept absolutely basic to an understanding of the history of psychoanalytic theory. Yet college-level critical inquiry thrives on exactly this kind of revision of common sense: academics prize the unusual, the subtle, the ambiguous, the complex—and expect students to appreciate them as well. Good critical thinkers in all academic disciplines welcome the opportunity to challenge conventional ways of seeing the world; they seem to take delight in questioning everything that appears clear and self-evident.

QUESTIONING: THE BASIS OF CRITICAL THINKING

9   By questioning the myths that dominate our culture, we can begin to resist the limits they impose on our vision. In fact, they invite such questioning. Often our personal experience fails to fit the images the myths project: a young woman's ambition to be a test pilot may clash with the ideal of femininity our culture promotes; a Cambodian immigrant who has suffered from racism in the United States may question our professed commitment to equality; a student in the vocational track may not see education as the road to success that we assume it is; and few of our families these days fit the mythic model of husband, wife, two kids, a dog, and a house in the suburbs.

10   Moreover, because cultural myths serve such large and varied needs, they're not always coherent or consistent. Powerful contradictory myths coexist in our society and our own minds. For example, while the myth of "the melting pot" celebrates equality, the myth of individual success pushes us to strive for inequality—to "get ahead" of everyone else. Likewise, our attitudes toward education are deeply paradoxical: on one level Americans tend to see schooling as a valuable experience that unites us in a common culture and helps us bring out the best in ourselves; yet at the same time we suspect that formal classroom instruction stifles creativity and chokes off natural intelligence and enthusiasm. These contradictions infuse our history, literature, and popular culture; they're so much a part of our thinking that we tend to take them for granted, unaware of their inconsistencies.

11   Learning to recognize contradictions lies at the very heart of critical thinking, for intellectual conflict inevitably generates questions. Can both (or all) perspectives be true? What evidence do I have for the validity of each? Is there some way to reconcile them? Are there still other alternatives? Questions like these represent the beginning of serious academic analysis. They stimulate the reflection, discussion, and research that are the essence of good scholarship. Thus, whether we find contradictions between myth and lived experience, or between opposing myths, the wealth of powerful, conflicting material generated by our cultural mythology offers a particularly rich context for critical inquiry.

Comprehension Check

Directions: Answer the following questions.

1. Which of the following are examples of how culture binds us as a group?
    a. It provides us with a shared set of customs.
    b. It provides us with values, ideas, and beliefs.
    c. It binds us through a shared language.
    d. All of the above

2. T/F According to the authors, just as culture binds us together, it also selectively blinds us.

3. T/F Greek myths, though not true in the literal sense, assured the Greeks of the nobility of their origins, provided role models for public and private lives, and justified inequities in their society.

4. T/F The American dream of success is an example of a cultural myth.

5. While cultural values help us make practical decisions in everyday life, they also impose rigidity in our thinking and limit our ability to understand the complexity of our experience. Give an example of how this might be true.

    _____

    _____

6. How do the authors define good critical thinking in academic disciplines?

    _____

    _____

7. How can we begin to resist the limits that cultural myths impose on our thinking?

   _____

   _____

8. T/F   The myth of "the melting pot" and the myth of individual success are what the authors call contradictory myths.

9. Provide an example of a cultural myth you have grown up with.

   _____

   _____

10. Reread the Roethke poem "My Papa's Waltz," applying the skills you learned in Chapter Seven. Explain your interpretation of the poem.

   _____

   _____

Vocabulary Check

Directions: Define the following underlined words from the selection.

1. as prescribed by our culture _____

2. the primacy of male authority _____

   _____

3. a cultural mirage _____

   _____

4. years of acculturation _____

   _____

5. they reduce the world to dichotomies _____

   _____

6. Ingrained assumptions _____

   _____

7. academics prize the unusual, the subtle, the ambiguous _____

   _____

8. our professed commitment _____

   _____

9. our attitudes are deeply paradoxical _____

   _____

10. some way to reconcile them _____

   _____

Record the results of the comprehension and vocabulary checks on the Student Record Chart in the Appendix. Each correct answer is worth 10 points, for a total of 100 points possible for comprehension and 100 points for vocabulary.

Questions for Group Discussion

1. Discuss some of the cultural myths that people in your group have grown up with. How do they affect critical thinking?

2. This chapter and the previous chapter deal with fiction and poetry as one kind of valuable reading. Should the study of such literature be a requirement in college? Why or why not?

3. Discuss what "High Anxiety" and "Culture Myths as Obstacles to Critical Thinking" have in common. What messages do they contain that can be helpful to you?

4. As a group, see how many of you can use the following words in a sentence. Make certain you learn the ones you still may not be able to use or recognize by writing the definition in the blank space.

   a. affective _____

   b. primacy _____

   c. embedded _____

   d. countenance _____

   e. heterosexual _____

   f. dichotomies _____

   g. stoic _____

   h. pariahs _____

   i. penetrable _____

   j. ambiguous _____

On Your Own

Pick ten new words you learned in this chapter, not necessarily those listed in question 4, and on a separate sheet of paper write a sentence for each word, using it correctly in context. Turn in the paper to your instructor.

A Final Check

Now you should have a good understanding of how all three facets of comprehension work together in the diagram. The final area is now ready for your review. Fill in the blanks in this section on the diagram on the next page. Working with a partner or small group is acceptable if your instructor sets up groups. *Hints*: The first line corresponds to the kind of language that fosters affective awareness. The second line deals with a key element of your mind that is needed for understanding fiction and poetry. The third line has to do with what part of you is needed for full comprehension of literature. The final line is a term that refers to your sensitivity to literature.

   When you have finished, check your answers with the triangle at the beginning of Unit Three.

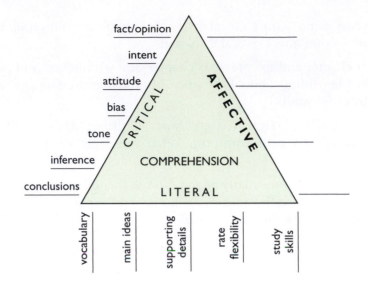

APPENDIX

STUDENT READING CONVERSION CHART

STUDENT RECORD CHART

STUDENT READING CONVERSION CHART

Directions: Your reading rate (words per minute or wpm) can be found in the following chart. In the first column, find the number of minutes and seconds it took you to read an article. Locate the column for the article you read and reference the wpm across from your time. For example, if you read "In Praise of the F Word" in 3 minutes and 45 seconds, your rate would be 261 wpm.

Time	"In Praise of the F Word" WPM	"Putting Reading in Its Proper Place" WPM	"Tilting the Level Playing Field" WPM	"America: The Multi-National Society" WPM	"Bring Back the Draft" WPM
1:00	980	460	872	1650	980
1:15	784	368	727	1320	784
1:30	653	307	623	1100	653
1:45	560	262	545	943	560
2:00	490	230	484	825	490
2:15	436	204	436	733	436
2:30	392	184	396	660	392
2:45	356	167	363	600	356
3:00	327	153	335	550	327
3:15	302	141	311	508	302
3:30	280	131	291	471	280
3:45	261	123	273	440	261
4:00	245	115	256	413	245
4:15	231	108	242	388	231
4:30	218	102	229	367	218
4:45	206	97	218	347	206
5:00	196	92	208	330	196
5:15	187		198	314	187
5:30	178		190	300	178
5:45	170		182	287	170
6:00	163		174	275	163
6:15	157		168	264	157
6:30	151		161	254	151
6:45	145		156	244	145
7:00	140		150	236	140
7:15	135		145	228	135
7:30	131		141	220	131
7:45	126		136	213	126
8:00	123		132	206	123
8:15	119		128	200	119
8:30	115		125	194	115
8:45	112		121	189	112
9:00	109		118	183	109
9:15	106		115	178	106
9:30	103		112	174	103
9:45	101		109	169	101
10:00				165	

STUDENT READING CONVERSION CHART—CONTINUED

Time	"All the News That's Fit to Post" WPM	"Vox Humana" WPM	"Talk, Not Torture, Gets the Information" WPM	"What's on TV Tonight?" WPM	"Self-Esteem Is Earned, Not Learned" WPM
1:00	1,100	980	1,100	784	745
1:15	890	784	890	653	596
1:30	741	653	741	560	497
1:45	635	560	635	490	426
2:00	556	490	556	436	373
2:15	494	436	494	392	331
2:30	445	392	445	356	298
2:45	405	356	405	327	271
3:00	371	327	371	302	248
3:15	342	302	342	280	229
3:30	318	280	318	261	213
3:45	297	261	297	245	199
4:00	278	245	278	231	186
4:15	262	231	262	218	175
4:30	247	218	247	206	166
4:45	234	206	234	196	157
5:00	222	196	222	187	149
5:15	212	187	212	178	142
5:30	202	178	202	170	135
5:45	193	170	193	163	130
6:00	185	163	185	157	124
6:15	178	157	178	151	119
6:30	171	151	171	145	115
6:45	165	145	165	140	110
7:00	159	140	159	135	106
7:15	153	135	153	131	103
7:30	148	131	148	126	99
7:45	143	126	143	123	96
8:00	139	123	139	119	
8:15	135	119	135	115	
8:30	131	115	131	112	
8:45	127	112	127	109	
9:00	124	109	124	106	
9:15	120	106	120	103	
9:30	117	103	117	101	
9:45	114	101	114		
10:00	110		110		

STUDENT READING CONVERSION CHART—CONTINUED

Time	"Push for De-Emphasis of College Sports" WPM	"America, Stand Up for Justice and Decency" WPM	"How Students Get Lost in Cyberspace" WPM	"Yahoo in China" WPM	"Salvation" WPM
1:00	465	700	1,100	875	913
1:15	372	560	890	700	730
1:30	310	467	741	583	609
1:45	266	400	635	500	522
2:00	233	350	556	437	457
2:15	207	311	494	389	406
2:30	186	280	445	350	362
2:45	169	255	405	318	332
3:00	155	233	371	292	304
3:15	143	215	342	269	281
3:30	133	200	318	250	261
3:45	124	187	297	233	244
4:00	116	175	278	219	228
4:15	109	165	262	206	215
4:30	103	156	247	194	203
4:45	98	147	234	184	192
5:00	93	140	222	175	183
5:15	89	133	212	167	174
5:30	85	127	202	159	166
5:45		122	193	152	159
6:00		117	185	146	152
6:15			178	140	146
6:30			171	135	144
6:45			165	130	141
7:00			159	125	140
7:15			153	121	138
7:30			148	117	135
7:45			143	113	130
8:00			139	109	125
8:15			135	106	119
8:30			131	103	115
8:45			127	100	110
9:00			124	97	

STUDENT READING CONVERSION CHART—CONTINUED

Time	"High Anxiety" WPM	"The Barrio" WPM	"Queen of Nothing" WPM
1:00	1,100	1,350	670
1:15	890	1,086	536
1:30	741	905	447
1:45	635	779	383
2:00	556	675	335
2:15	494	600	298
2:30	445	535	268
2:45	405	485	244
3:00	371	449	223
3:15	342	415	206
3:30	318	379	191
3:45	297	359	179
4:00	278	339	168
4:15	262	319	158
4:30	247	299	149
4:45	234	280	141
5:00	222	270	134
5:15	212	255	128
5:30	202	240	122
5:45	193	230	117
6:00	185	220	112
6:15	178	210	107
6:30	171	200	103
6:45	165	197	99
7:00	159	190	96
7:15	153	181	
7:30	148	178	
7:45	143	170	
8:00	139	168	
8:15	135	160	
8:30	131	153	
8:45	127	150	
9:00	124	144	
9:15	120	138	
9:30	117		
9:45	114		
10:00	112		

STUDENT RECORD CHART

Directions: Record your reading rate, comprehension, and/or vocabulary check scores for the reading practices on this chart. Calculate your reading rate for the timed readings from the Student Reading Conversion Chart in this Appendix. Calculate your comprehension and vocabulary check scores as follows: Each correct response is worth 10 points, for a total of 100 points possible for each check.

Unit One: Literal Comprehension

Selection Title	Reading Rate (wpm)	Comprehension Check	Vocabulary Check
Chapter One			
"What You Should Look for in a Dictionary"			
"Is *Ain't* a Word?"			
"In Praise of the F Word"			
Chapter Two			
"Superman and Me"			
"Thinking: A Neglected Art"			
"Putting Reading in Its Proper Place"			
"Tilting the Level Playing Field? It's Nothing New"			
Chapter Three			
"Ethics"			

Unit Two: Critical Comprehension

Selection Title	Reading Rate (wpm)	Comprehension Check	Vocabulary Check
Chapter Four			
"How Good Are Your Opinions?"			
"America: The Multinational Society"			
"Bring Back the Draft"			
Chapter Five			
"Thirst for a Hero Can Get Us in Hot Water"			
"Do Away with Public Schools"			
"Teach, Don't Preach, the Bible"			
"Gods Are Created in Our Own Image"			
"All the News That's Fit to Post"			
"Vox Humana"			
"Talk, Not Torture, Gets the Information"			
"What's on TV Tonight? Humiliation to the Point of Suicide"			
Chapter Six			
"Self-Esteem Is Earned, Not Learned"			
"Push for De-Emphasis of College Sports"			
"America, Stand Up for Justice and Decency"			
Chapter Seven			
"Case Study: The State of the Onion"			
"How Students Get Lost in Cyberspace"			
"Yahoo in China"			

Unit Three: Affective Comprehension

Selection Title	Reading Rate (wpm)	Comprehension Check	Vocabulary Check
Chapter Eight			
"Poetry Is Dead: Does Anybody Really Care?"			
"Salvation"			
Chapter Nine			
"1, 2, 3"			
"High Anxiety"			
"The Barrio"			
"Queen of Nothing"			
"Cultural Myths as Obstacles to Critical Thinking"			

INDEX